Developing Teachers and Teaching Practice

'An important contribution in the field. One of its major strengths is that it represents a truly international research perspective. The editors are to be congratulated for their ability to select fifteen well-researched papers spanning ten countries.'

Professor Maureen Pope, University of Reading.

Pressure is increasing on all those involved in education, from teachers to policy makers, to transform schools as organizations, while continuing to implement effective new approaches to teaching and learning. The demand is not only to reach attainment targets, but also to be accountable for teaching methods.

Developing Teachers and Teaching Practice brings together a selection of the papers given at the ninth conference of the International Study Association of Teachers and Teaching (ISATT). The collection takes as a central theme the issue of education as a key concern within the international rhetoric of globalization.

Developing Teachers and Teaching Practice covers three major areas:

- Changing Understandings offers insights about the nature of teaching and learning, including the key new research area of emotions;
- Sites and Sources explores the nature of teacher learning;
- Reform and Renewal looks at the impact of major policy initiatives on the work of teachers internationally.

Developing Teachers and Teaching Practice contains contributions from some of the best-known academics in this field, and will be of great interest to teacher educators and educational researchers internationally.

Ciaran Sugrue is a member of the Education Faculty at St. Patrick's College, Dublin City University. **Christopher Day** is Professor of Education and Co-ordinating Director of the Centre for Research on Teacher and School Development at the School of Education, University of Nottingham.

Developing Teachers and Teaching Practice

International research perspectives

Edited by
Ciaran Sugrue and Christopher Day

RoutledgeFalmer
Taylor & Francis Group
London and New York

First published 2002
by RoutledgeFalmer
11 New Fetter Lane, London EC4P 4EE

Simultaneously published in the USA and Canada
by RoutledgeFalmer
29 West 35th Street, New York, NY 10001

RoutledgeFalmer is an imprint of the Taylor & Francis Group

Typeset in Times New Roman and Gill Sans by Exe Valley Dataset, Exeter

Printed and bound in Great Britain by
The Cromwell Press, Trowbridge, Wiltshire

British Library Cataloguing in Publication Data
A catalogue record for this book is available from the British Library

Library of Congress Cataloguing in Publication Data
Developing teachers and teaching practice: international research perspectives / Ciaran Sugrue and Christopher Day (editors)
p. cm.
"This volume presents a selection of two hundred papers given at the ninth biennial conference of the International Study Association of Teachers and Teaching (ISATT) that was hosted by St. Patrick's College, Drumcondra, Dublin in July 1999" – Introd.
Includes bibliographical references and index.
1. Comparative education–Congresses. 2. Teaching–Cross-cultural studies–Congresses. 3. Teachers–Cross-cultural studies–Congresses. 4. Learning–Cross-cultural studies–Congresses. I. Sugrue, Ciaran. II. Day, Christopher, ACP.

LB43.D48 2001
371.1–dc21 2001031772

ISBN 0-415-26254-2

Contents

Tables and figures

Tables

Figures

Contributors

Jane Ashdown is a Clinical Associate Professor in the Department of Teaching and Learning at New York University's School of Education where she is also responsible for the co-ordination of services for the continuing professional education of teachers. She has been director of the Department's Reading Recovery Project for the past four years and is currently working on a cost-effectiveness study of this program.

Beatrice Avalos, currently co-ordinator of the project for Improving Initial Teacher Education, Ministry of Education Chile, was Professor of Education at the University of Papua New Guinea (1988–94) and before that Senior Lecturer in Education at the University of Wales, Cardiff (1974–88). She has extensive experience in research and innovation in the field of teacher education and education in developing countries. Publications include: *Teaching Children of the Poor* (IDRC, 1986), *Initial Teacher Training. Approaches to Teacher Preparation* (Commonwealth Secretariat, 1991), *Teaching in Papua New Guinea: A Perspective for the Nineties* (University of Papua New Guinea, 1991), *Issues in Science Teacher Education* (IIEP, 1995), *La Formación de Profesores. Perspectiva y Experiencias* (Santillana, 1999).

Douwe Beijaard is Associate Professor at ICLON Graduate School of Education at Leiden University, The Netherlands. His major research interests are teachers' professional identity, learning and professional development of teachers, and teacher evaluation.

Cheryl J. Craig was formerly a Social Sciences and Humanities Research Council of Canada doctoral and post-doctoral fellow, and is currently an Associate Professor in the Department of Curriculum and Instruction, College of Education, University of Houston. Her research interests are teachers' knowledge as expressed in school contexts and narrative research methodologies.

Christopher Day is Professor of Education and Co-ordinating Director of the Centre for Research on Teacher and School Development at the School of Education, University of Nottingham. He has worked as a schoolteacher, teacher educator and local authority adviser. He is editor of *Teachers and Teaching:*

Theory and Practice, co-editor of *Educational Action Research* and *Journal of In-Service Education*. Professor Day is secretary of ISATT (International Study Association on Teachers and Teaching). In addition to *Leading Schools in Times of Change* (Open University Press, 2000), recent publications include *The Life and Work of Teachers: International Perspectives in Changing Times,* (co-editor and contributor) (Falmer Press, 2000), *Developing Teachers: Challenges of Lifelong Learning (*Falmer Press, 1999), *Educational Research in Europe: Yearbook 2000* (co-editor)*, (*Leuven-Apeldoorn, Garant, 2000), and *Developing Leadership in Primary Schools,* (co-author) (Paul Chapman Ltd, 1998).

Ruth Ethell is director of Teacher Education at the University of Otago, Dunedin, New Zealand. Her research interests include teacher thinking processes, reflective practice, beginning teacher development and self-study of teacher education.

Andy Hargreaves is Professor of Education in the department of Theory and Policy Studies, and co-director of the International Centre for Educational Change, at the Ontario Institute for Studies in Education of the University of Toronto. He is Editor-in-Chief of the *Journal of Educational Change* and the author and editor of many books in the field of educational change including *Learning to Change* (with Lorna Earl), (2001); *Changing Teachers, Changing Times*, (1994) and *What's Worth Fighting For Out There*? (with Michael Fullan), (1998).

Fernando Hernández Doctor in Psychology (University of Barcelona). is a senior lecturer on Art Education and Visual Culture in the Fine Arts Faculty at the University of Barcelona and Vice-president of the Humanities Division. He is co-director of the book series *Repensar la educación* (Rethinking education), published by Octaedro, which was widely distributed in Spain and Latin America, and a member of the Quality Research Group: Professional Development, Innovation and New Technologies. He is working on the approach of Art Education as a Cultural Visual Knowledge, where the development processes of understanding play an essential role. He is also exploring the use of Telecommunication to improve the quality of student teachers' professional competencies. He is the co-ordinator of the Doctoral program on Art Education for Understanding Visual Culture, where several research projects are carried out on how primary and secondary students understand Visual Cultures issues and notions.

Jyrki Huusko puts his ideas in practice as a principal of a junior school in Joensuu, Finland. He completed his doctoral studies at the University of Joensuu and continues his work there as a docent.

Jukka Husu is a researcher at the Department of Teacher Education, University of Helsinki. His special interests are research on teachers' practical knowledge and the issues of virtual classroom. He has published several articles in international journals and is a co-writer of the book *Teachers' Pedagogical Thinking: Theoretical Landscapes, Practical Challenges* (Peter Lang).

Cees Klaassen, is Associate Professor of Educational Sciences, Department of Educational Sciences, University of Nijmegen. Nijmegen, The Netherlands. He publishes in the field of curriculum and educational theory, socialization theory and research, sociology of education and teacher education and training. His present research interests include teacher professionalism; the moral assignment of the school and citizenship education.

Michael Kompf is an Associate Professor in the Department of Graduate Studies, and Director of The Centre for Adult Studies and Distance Learning in the Faculty of Education at Brock University in St. Catharines, Ontario. He has a variety of theoretical and practical interests that find focus in the study and practice of adult development, learning and teaching. His most recent book *The Craft of Teaching Adults*, 3rd Edition (2001) is co-edited with Thelma Barer Stein. Recent writing and presentations have included exploring Native issues, individual and organizational Eldership, retirement and personal development, and the social implications of distance learning. Michael is a member of several professional associations and current Chair of the 28-country membership International Study Association on Teachers and Teaching (ISATT).

Tapio Kosunen works in Helsinki, Finland as Special Adviser to the Minister of Education. He completed his doctoral studies at the University of Joensuu and continues his work there as a docent.

Han A. Leeferink is junior researcher in the Department of Educational Sciences at the University of Nijmegen. He is doing research in the field of orientations of school leaders, teachers, parents and students towards moral education, and the moral school community. He is working on his PhD.

John Loughran was a high school science teacher before moving to the Faculty of Education at Monash University. He has been actively involved in teacher education for the past decade through his teaching in Science and Teaching and Learning in Pre-service Teacher Education. His research interests include teacher-as-researcher, reflective practice, science education and teaching and learning. Recent publications include *Developing Reflective Practice*, *Researching Teaching*, *Opening the Classroom Door* (Loughran and Northfield), and *Teaching about Teaching* (Loughran and Russell) (all published by Falmer Press).

Milbrey W. McLaughlin is the David Jacks Professor of Education and Public Policy at Stanford University (USA). She is Co-Director of the Center for Research on the Contexts of Teaching and Director of the John Gardner Center for Youth and their Communities.

Marilyn McMeniman is Dean, Faculty of Education, Griffith University, Queensland, Australia. Her specializations include language acquisition and learning, teaching and learning processes (strategic learning), and motivation to learn.

Jorunn Møller is an Associate Professor in the Department of Teacher Education and School Development, University of Oslo, Norway. Her major research interests and writings are in the areas of educational administration, action research and supervision. She is responsible for a Head Teacher Program at the University of Oslo, and has for three years been a Project Leader of a national program for School Leadership. She was elected Chair of Nordic Educational Research Association in 1999. Before entering her job at the university, she worked as a teacher in a lower secondary school, and as a consultant at regional level.

Paulien Meijer is Assistant Professor and teacher educator at ICLON Graduate School of Education at Leiden University, The Netherlands. Her main research interests are teacher cognition, teacher learning, and research methodology.

Jonathan Neufeld was the translator (for Michael Huberman) of 'La vie des enseignants' (The lives of teachers, 1995). He currently writes and teaches as a curriculum theorist at Brock University, St. Catherines, Canada. Jonathan specializes in the philosophy of learning and has a particular interest in the developing education of the adult learner.

Juana M. Sancho. Doctor in Psychology (University of Barcelona) is a senior lecturer at the department of Teaching Methods and Educational Management (University of Barcelona). She is co-director of the book series Repensar la Educación (Rethinking education), published by Octaedro, which was widely distributed in Spain and Latin America, co-ordinator of the Quality Research Group: Professional Development, Innovation and New Technologies, and a board member of several national and international educational journals. The research carried out in the last ten years has oriented her latest work to explore the need to design, develop, implement and evaluate "new learning environments" to respond to the educational challenges of the emerging societies. She has participated as partner and co-ordinator in several European projects.

Ciaran Sugrue was an elementary school teacher and school inspector before becoming a member of the Education Faculty at St. Patrick's College, Dublin City University, where he teaches courses on teaching and curriculum to undergraduate student teachers and courses in educational leadership, continuing professional development and qualitative research methods to postgraduate students. His research interests include educational change, schools reform and educational leadership, continuing professional development for teachers and qualitative research methods, and he has published widely in all of these areas. He is currently engaged in research on the life history of school principals as part of an international comparative study, and on the quality of continuing professional development for Irish teachers. He is general editor of *Irish Educational Studies*. He published *Complexities of Teaching: Child-centred Perspectives* with Falmer Press in 1997.

Nico Verloop is Professor of Education and Dean of ICLON Graduate School of Education at Leiden University, The Netherlands. His main research interests are teacher cognition and teacher evaluation.

Peter Woods is a Research Professor in Education at The University of Plymouth, and also at The Open University, where formerly he was Director of the Centre for Sociology and Social Research. He has been researching 'creative teaching in primary schools' since the 1980s. His latest books, *Teachable Moments* (1996, with Bob Jeffrey) (both Open University Press), and (with Mari Boyle and Nick Hubbard) *Multicultural Children in the Early Years* (Multilingual Matters, 1999) are products of this research. He has also published work on qualitative methodology, the most recent being *Researching the Art of Teaching*, (Routledge, 1996), and *Successful Writing for Qualitative Researchers* (Routledge, 1999).

Acknowledgements

When compiling an international text such as this, the co-operation of many individuals is vital. Consequently, we are indebted to several people whom we cannot acknowledge individually but whose input and co-operation were both valued and valuable.

Our gratitude to all those who submitted papers for possible inclusion in the text and who waited patiently for a response while the final selection was in process. We are grateful also to the authors who are included for their prompt responses to queries of detail relating to their contributions.

We are most grateful to Anna Clarkson of RoutledgeFalmer who made valuable comments on the original book proposal and for her facilitation of the publication process. In Dublin, Clíona Uí Thuama and Siobhán Nolan played a key role as custodians of the materials and were relentless in their pursuit of authors when e-mail messages remained unanswered. Without their attention to detail it would not have been possible to complete the text. In Nottingham also, at various points along the way, Wendy James was an important conduit between the publishers and the editors, her computer skills were used to good effect and her e-mails too became another 'front' in our pursuit of authors as deadlines approached. Richard Willis (of Swales & Willis Publishing Consultants) completed the copy-editing process with super efficiency and was extremely easy to work with.

Finally, we wholeheartedly acknowledge the generosity of *Teachers College Record* for its imprimatur to publish the first chapter of this text by Andy Hargreaves; it draws on some similar material as a paper by the same author that is to appear in TCR in the near future.

Introduction

The international rhetorics of globalization and market forces impact on national and local educational agendas in a variety of ways. There is a growing consensus in these post-modern times that education is a key if not the key concern, and teachers are the 'frontline' troops in creating a bridgehead to a more positive, secure and successful life for today's young citizens. There is consistent and increasing pressure on teachers, school leaders, administrators, policy-makers and researchers to construct new understandings, insights and practices to bring about transformations in schools as organizations, while simultaneously inventing more appropriate, efficient and effective approaches to teaching and learning that are consonant with individual needs as well as national aspirations and economic competitiveness. While the walls of privatism may continue to be a dominant cultural characteristic of many schools and school systems, as the boundaries between school and community become more permeable, there is increasing pressure on teachers to be accountable not only for the attainment and achievement of their students but also for the ways in which they teach. Debates about which pedagogies are the most effective for which students and for which purposes are as passionate now as they were twenty years ago, and there is a growing industry for measuring pupil output in relation to teaching standards. In such circumstances, the classroom citadel is no longer a 'private' space in which to interact with students. Rather, there is demand for the walls of privacy to be transparent. The central message internationally, therefore, is that business as usual for schools and teachers is no longer an adequate response to a rapidly changing educational landscape.

This volume presents a selection of the two hundred papers given at the ninth biennial conference of the International Study Association on Teachers and Teaching (ISATT) that was hosted by St Patrick's College, Drumcondra, Dublin in July 1999. The theme of that conference was *Teachers and teaching: revisioning policy and practice for the twenty-first century.*

Our introduction is intended as a guide and summary to each of the three sections and the fifteen individual contributions which provide a variety of macro and micro research perspectives suggest tentative steps towards constructing that future by focusing on developing teachers and teaching. It also contains a critical overview of the field, situating the various macro and micro contributions within international flux and flows in relation to teacher development, school reform and educational change.

Section One, *Changing understandings*, accumulates a series of insights about the nature of teaching, learning, and schooling that have potential to influence policy and become levers for professional growth and renewal.

Chapter 1, *Teaching in a box: emotional geographies of teaching*, opens a Pandora's box on the emotions of teaching. Hargreaves argues that, in more stable and predictable times, it was possible for teachers to suppress emotions thus retaining a focus on the cognitive, but with many negative consequences both for teachers and their students. Drawing on an extensive data set of interviews with elementary and secondary teachers in Ontario, which focused upon parent–teacher relationships, Hargreaves, as part of his initial mapping of the emotional geographies of teaching, identifies five ways of seeing these emotions played out: socio-cultural, moral, professional, political and physical. His analysis is testament to the persistent subterranean presence and pervasiveness of emotions despite the various means deployed to marginalize emotions, that circumscribe, in the words of a contemporary song 'every move we make, every step we take'. He draws attention to the manner in which the press of the post-modern, characterized by precariousness, fragmentation and uncertainty, frequently works against teachers developing 'connectedness' with students, their parents and the worlds they inhabit. Instead, distance may be used by teachers as a device to construct perceptions of parents and their offspring as disinterested in learning, and disrespectful to teachers. His concluding exhortation for increased emotional understanding is a central tenet of his analysis that, in a climate of league tables, as well as market-place competitiveness, teaching is becoming for some, an emotional labour which is beyond their capacity to deliver effectively. More optimistically, dealing with this emergent emotional intensity may become a generative principle in redefining teaching in appropriate ways for the first decade of the twenty-first century, while also becoming the fulcrum for an emergent professionalism that embraces rather than circumscribes, controls or marginalizes the emotional geographies of teaching.

Chapter 2, *An Investigation into the pedagogical identity of the teacher*, provides practical embodiment of some of the realities that Hargreaves opens up for discussion in the first chapter. Here, Leeferink and Klaassen investigate teachers' perceptions of their responsibilities both for their own teaching and for the parents of their students in relation to child-rearing practices. They argue that this 'divison of labour' has become much more blurred and confused in recent years. Their study reveals a lack of adequate and frequent communication between teachers and parents in The Netherlands. Consequently, misunderstandings abound and rebound to the detriment of pupils. However, they also point out that recent emphasis on school effectiveness and a consequent narrowing of what constitutes effective schooling and success militates against teachers developing the expertise essential for more sustained dialogue with parents or finding adequate time to build the trust and openness necessary for a genuine sharing of responsibilities. The constant demands and disconnected reforms increase the emotional burden on teachers, and generate frustration rather than coherence. Although building communities of dialogue is essential, the time and opportunity to engage, and to re-establish priorities is, therefore, limited.

Chapter 3, *Educational research and teacher development: from ivory tower to tower of Babel,* represents a sustained and coherent critique of the dominant mode of inquiry within the academy particularly as it relates to teacher development. Rooted in Aristotelian rationality, systematically cultivated, revised and revitalized through dominant Western philosophical tracts, rationality with its constraints on what constitutes knowledge, how it is constructed and valued, continues to be played out today in academic texts and journals. The Canadian authors' generous reading of Nietzsche proposes a more radical approach to knowledge generation and teacher development that is rooted in biography and sustained questioning of habits of mind and enquiry into which we have been socialized. They argue against a reductionist approach implicit in a transcendental cognitive orientation while advocating the aphoristic and fragmented approach espoused and practiced by Nietzsche. They suggest that because his writing was conducted away from the constraining logics of the academy, he was able to undertake a more honest, disinterested exploration of received habits of thought. Given the false consciousness implicit in much that is written on teacher education, the authors' exhortations for a broader church in terms of what counts as legitimate and academically sanctioned knowledge is worthy of consideration: a challenge that awaits the academy's attention. A greater cacophony of voices rather than the inherent reductionist agenda that privileges coherence may ultimately be more rewarding – a tower of Babel rather than an ivory tower. However, from a practitioner perspective, some coherence may also be necessary if bad faith between the academy and schools is to be replaced by more trusting and open relations with potential to sustain learning communities rather than increase the burden on teachers, which is how professional development is perceived by many (over) burdened practitioners.

Chapter 4, *Navigating through pedagogical practice: teachers' epistemological stance towards pupils,* reminds the reader of the nature of practical knowing and contrasts its uncertainty with the certainty frequently attributed to propositional knowledge. Husu's incisive philosophical framework of analysis begins with the Aristotelian notion of phronesis indicating that the nature of practical knowledge as such is, of necessity, rough hewn. Yet, Husu reveals the underlying rules and principles of practice inherent and embedded in teachers' knowing that are at once sophisticated while remaining open-ended. His analysis reveals the importance of an individual teacher stance, a way of being in the world that is moral and suffused with beliefs and values that blur the boundaries between the personal and the professional. When new managerialist rhetorics seek to reduce teaching to a more technical set of routine behaviours, Husu's analysis developed in the Finnish context is a timely reminder of the inseparability of these essential elements in teachers' 'non-scholastic stance'. He goes on to indicate the importance of social self, its embeddedness in wider socio-cultural forces and the importance of optimism and hope to the work of teachers. Both what teachers know and the manner in which it is known reveal at once the tenacity of teachers' routines and their robustness, while indicating also how difficult it is to alter them. Husu's is a timely reminder that without sustained professional dialogue and continuous support, the nonscholastic and organizational embeddedness of teachers' practical knowing makes it much more difficult to change. Policy elites which mandate changes, frequently without consultation with teachers, underestimate the complexity of practice and do little to ensure transformation of dominant routines of teaching and learning.

Chapter 5, *Teaching and learning in the new millennium*, begins from the perspective that child-centred teaching, much maligned in recent years, has much to contribute to teaching and learning in the new millennium. Woods is powerfully positioned to make this argument for he has spent much of the past three decades documenting in detail aspects of creative and imaginative teaching in English primary schools while in recent years this work has indicated the need to build teachers' capacity to create space, time and opportunity to fire pupil's enthusiasm despite the constraints of nationally prescribed curricula and the straitjacket imposed by the process of inspection in England. However, Woods' argument has much wider ramifications than revitalization of the primary school sector. He argues persuasively that learners' involvement in their own learning is more vital than ever in an economic context where the rhetoric of lifelong learning is pervasive, but the learning continues to be prescriptive, thus alienating learners rather than winning them to the cause of 'life-wide' as well as lifelong learning. His instructive use of the metaphor of 'banger' racing on the skills and expertise of those who race such cars, indicates that much learning happens indirectly, vicariously, by observation, conversation and action, rather than by direct instruction, a point that is increasingly lost in environments where only quantifiable test scores are considered acceptable indicators of progress, attainment (rather than achievement) and effective teaching. He concludes that there is much about current schooling that needs to be unlearned if learning is to be appropriately facilitated in ways more attuned to the twenty-first rather than the nineteenth century.

Section Two, *Sites and sources*, shifts the focus from insights and new understandings that have the potential to be generative principles in relation to teacher development, to the nature of teacher learning, its possible sites and sources.

Chapter 6, *Sites and sources of teacher learning*, is the lead paper in this section where McLaughlin draws on an Aladdin's cave of research data provided by the Bay Area Schools Reform Collaborative (BASRC) in California to illustrate and illuminate the complex nature of teacher learning. She indicates that teachers need all forms of knowledge – that which is usually termed foundational as well as practical – and these can be brought together in powerful ways by systematic enquiry undertaken by teachers themselves and supported by various means so that their practice becomes more overtly evidence based. Framed in this manner, the BASRC initiatives sought to cultivate teacher learning while simultaneously identifying its sites and sources. Her evidence indicates that teachers' capacity to learn is constrained to a significant degree by their prior learning as well as the manner in which that learning has taken place. Additionally, the paper demonstrates the complex nature of teacher learning, its cyclical, social and uneven character, but in an uneven manner that frequently pushes teachers to revisit recent assumptions. The research also revealed that teacher learning may be dependent initially on external sources and in a top-down, somewhat coercive manner that later may empower learners to take more responsibility for their own learning. The research suggests, however, that teacher learning is time-consuming and challenging and there are no guarantees of success, even with significant expertise available and additional resources. Nevertheless, McLaughlin concludes on a note of optimism, that by systematically building learning communities, the potential exists for teachers to sustain their learning and their capacity for learning even in difficult circumstances. The concomitant of this message, particularly for policy-makers, is that teacher learning is never easy, and in constant need of systematic and sustained support if it is to have a reasonable chance of being sustained over time, thus ensuring the continuing development necessary in times of change.

Chapter 7, *Professional development as 'interference'? Insights from the Reading Recovery in-service course,* moves from large-scale school-wide reform initiatives to the impact of externally initiated classroom-focused innovation on individual's lives and work in the micro-cauldron of the reading recovery classroom in New York. Ashdown begins from the perspective that recognition of conflict by researchers and policy-makers as an integral and inevitable element of school reform processes is often of little consolation to classroom teachers who are called upon to implement them and that it fails to take account of its toll on teachers who must change aspects of their practice in order to conform. Such teacher learning may, she suggests, be a form of interference that generates tensions and feelings of self-doubt while generating lack of congruence between teachers' beliefs, as well as feelings of isolation from colleagues rather than increasing competence. Ashdown's research demonstrates that selecting individual teachers as a vehicle for change in isolation from school colleagues is fraught with difficulties; and that, while a whole school approach may have more potential to transform teaching and learning, such approaches too have potential for generating conflict. There may be a case, therefore, for increasing teachers' capacities to deal with conflict, tolerance for ambiguity and uncertainty if reform aimed at better quality teaching and learning for all are to succeed.

Chapter 8, *School portfolio development: a way to access teacher knowledge,* investigates teacher portfolio development in America as another potential site and source of teacher development. Craig's contribution is rooted in the emergent tradition of teachers' personal practical knowledge and narrative ways of knowing and she connects this perspective with reform agendas through portfolio writing at five school sites in Houston. While privileging teacher narrative as an embodied means of knowing, Craig seeks to build school portfolios that enable teachers to reflect critically on their own learning and to establish their priorities within a wider context of mandated educational reforms. Here, too, it becomes obvious that tensions and conflicts abound as issues such as whose voice and what concerns are afforded prominence within the emerging portfolios are addressed. Once again, it is apparent that, regardless of the perspective from which reforms emanate – external mandates or teachers' immediate concerns – learning is context bound, difficult and challenging. There is no professional 'crock of gold' at the end of such inquiries. Rather, the further horizon consistently reveals another mountain to climb in the pursuit of development for improvement.

Chapter 9, *Understanding and articulating teacher knowledge,* documents teachers' ongoing analysis of their approach to facilitating learning among their pupils as another fruitful source of teachers' learning. Loughran interviews three distinct but related groups of teachers who, for various periods of time, have been engaged in systematic inquiry into their teaching. These teachers begin from a perspective that puts students' learning at the centre of the act of teaching and constantly emphasizes, 'teaching for understanding'. Such inquiry over time provides a number of important insights in relation to teacher professional development that appear to be well tested in praxis, both in the author's Australian context, and also in other contexts where professional support groups and learning communities have been encouraged. Enabling students, even very young elementary school pupils, to reflect on their own learning style, and the styles of others that compliment their own learning, has a positive influence that enables learners to take much greater responsibility for their own learning almost from the very beginning of schooling. Teachers, in such circumstances, become critically self-aware of classroom dynamics from the learners' perspective in contrast to the more 'tunnelled' or blinkered way of seeing teaching that continues to put teachers at the centre of classroom activities. As part of the process of critical inquiry into their practice, with support from the academy, teachers become aware of the need to invent a language of practice, to excavate and analyse it and to communicate it to others. Loughran discovers, not surprisingly, that it takes considerable time and effort to invent a shared language of practice. His insights begin to explain, also, why taking teachers from classrooms and making them professional development facilitators, frequently does not work; and that teachers benefit from working in interdisciplinary teams when some research suggests that a subject-matter focus is vital for professional support groups. Finally, Loughran indicates that real-time learning for teachers requires sustained and systematic inquiry, where their tacit knowledge can be made explicit, changed and revitalized through the conduit of a language of practice that has to be invented as integral to processes of inquiry which are owned and sustained by teachers themselves.

Chapter 10, *Examining teachers' interactive cognitions using insights from research on teachers' practical knowledge,* the final chapter in this section, seeks to locate another source of teachers' practical knowledge, in this instance, within their interactive cognitions. In this highly structured psychological approach, Meijer and her colleagues from The Netherlands utilize stimulated recall interviews as a means of documenting and probing teachers' embedded pedagogical content and contextual knowledge that influence their moment-by-moment decisions during the act of teaching. Their careful and detailed analysis of twenty lessons indicates a kind of unity and coherence in teachers' theories of practice. In doing so, however, the research also implicitly indicates the resilience of routines of practice and the difficulty of altering them. When attempts are made to alter elements of practice it appears that the integrative function of existing theories of practice tends to reject the 'new' intrusion. Readers with a particular interest in this kind of research will find the authors' elucidation on particular aspects of stimulated recall interviews of interest from a methodological perspective, while the substantive import of their work reinforces the findings of a plethora of other research that teachers are unlikely to succeed in developing new pedagogical routines unless they are scaffolded appropriately and supported until adequate mastery is achieved. Only in this way is it likely that new routines will be 'integrated' into existing repertoires rather than 'rejected' as disruptions to embedded aspects of teachers' well-established theories of practice.

Section 3, *Reform and renewal*, links major policy initiatives that seek structural and curricular reforms with their impact on the lives and work of teachers in different national contexts.

Chapter 11, *How do we do it? global rhetoric and the realities of teaching and learning in the developing world*, the overarching paper in this section, comes from a developing country context. Beatrice Avalos from Chile foregrounds the impact of global rhetorics on teachers' lives and work in a number of developing countries. Because reform rhetorics travel much faster in the post-modern world, it is frequently the case that reform initiatives, which are prescriptive with their solutions derived from Western contexts, are advocated by financial institutions and these become major burdens on teachers in poorly developed regions of the world. From their perspective, lack of infrastructure, basic pay, sanitary conditions, and overcrowding are daily realities, and implementation of western solutions in such circumstances can often, with good reason, be vigorously resisted. However, it would be a mistake to presume that lessons from such contexts do not speak to issues of restructuring, reform and teacher learning in more favourable economic and social circumstances. Avalos distils five 'lessons' from the detritus and data of struggling initiatives that appear instructive in a global context.

First, when teachers feel excluded, alienated from, and put upon by policy-makers, they frequently resort to scapegoating students, their parents and communities for lack of school success; they look to conditions and constraints rather than to the quality of their teaching as primary causes of 'failure'. For teachers to focus on their teaching, conditions must be favourable. Second, it is necessary to create a 'zone of tolerance' to enable teachers to scrutinize critically their own work. Third, the policy context of reform needs to pay adequate attention to implementation strategies and support mechanisms. Without such supports, all but the most committed and heroic teachers will perceive the chances of success as unattainable and resist mandates rather than transform them into meaningful routines of practice. Fourth, not everything can be changed at once. Consequently, teachers must be given the opportunity, at school and district level, to distil priorities from the growing litany of reforms that adorn most education systems: it is necessary to find a balance between continuity and change and in less developed contexts, where teachers' content and pedagogical knowledge base is relatively weak, there is greater need for enabling and supportive frameworks to build capacity. However, given the complexity of teaching, the need for such support and continuity in every school context should not be under estimated. Fifth, support for teacher development comes in many forms and needs to be facilitated. Avalos too indicates that learning is essentially social. Supports that recognize the informal and incidental nature of teacher learning, in the long term, may be more vital than more traditionally conceived forms of teacher support where they are obliged to 'bring back' new knowledge to put into practice in schools. Finally, teacher salaries are emerging as a major consideration in both developed and developing contexts. Nations are being asked to put a value on the contribution of teachers' work and the quality of teaching is inextricably bound up with monetary reward and emerging forms of professionalism appropriate for the twenty-first century.

Chapter 12, *Between professional autonomy and bureaucratic accountability: the self-managing school within a norwegian context*, provides a fine grained analysis of the impact of structural reforms, a policy of self-managing schools, as they are played out within two senior secondary schools in Norway and within their local administrative context. Møller's paper draws attention to the fact that all reform is local as it impacts on the lives and work of principals, teachers, administrators, students, their parents and local representatives. The reader is also reminded of the impact of established cultures and traditions within schools, and the personal biographies and career trajectories of the teachers who work in these organizations. In such circumstances, the policy interaction up close can be perceived as one of continuous adaptation, where struggles for power and autonomy are buffeted by wider forces that seek to make teachers more accountable and where the rhetoric of decentralization has potential to increase managerialism and bureaucratization to the extent that teachers become defensive and distracted from their primary focus on the quality of teaching and learning in their classrooms. Møller's evidence and analysis indicates clearly that new alliances and allegiances are being forged in the power struggles that ensue when such structural reforms are attempted. It cannot be taken for granted that teachers can continue to determine their pedagogical priorities in an international climate where management and attendant attempts to insist on greater accountability, frequently in rather narrow simplistic ways, may need to be resisted in the interest of a more appropriate and more broadly constructed professionalism. She concludes that the jury is out, at least in terms of the success of reform efforts in Norwegian schools.

Chapter 13, *A critical first step in learning to teach: confronting the power and tenacity of student teachers' beliefs and preconceptions*, reports research that puts the initiation of student teachers into the teaching profession in New Zealand under the microscope. It is generally accepted that student teachers' lay theories of teaching, although informally developed over the period of their apprenticeship of observation that they serve throughout their schooling, are particularly resilient; and without moving beyond tacit acceptance of their existence, rather resistant to change or replacement by more elaborate and research-based notions of teaching and learning. Ethell demonstrates very successfully just how robust such theories are by working intensively with nine pre-service teachers for a number of weeks. Her work confirms other studies that indicate that student teachers' lay theories place a premium on personality characteristics such as caring and being available. Thus, the significance of content and/ or pedagogical content knowledge are underplayed and perceived as less significant for 'good' teaching than having the 'right' personal traits. Ethell appears to have been able to develop the critical and reflective capacities of the small group of students with whom she worked intensively. However, such circumstances are a long way from mainstream teacher education programmes and the intensity of the work required to challenge and interrogate the beliefs and preconceptions that underpin such lay theories. The intensity of her work with these students focuses attention on the demands such engagement with student teachers necessitates, thus making its implementation much more problematic. Yet further research into this aspect of teacher development is vital if critical reflective dialogue is to become a generative principle in teachers' continuing professional development more generally throughout their teaching careers.

Chapter 14, *Shared and subjective in curriculum making: lessons from Finnish teachers,* reports on national curricular reforms mandated centrally by the Finnish Government while putting the responsibility for implementation on teachers and school communities. Not surprisingly, the evidence provided by Kosunen and Huusko indicates patchy and uneven results. The studies that these authors conducted reinforce a number of emerging concerns that resonate with the findings of studies conducted in other countries. The global rhetoric of devolution of decision-making to the level of the school has quite different trajectories within national borders, usually shaped by national history. School principals increasingly find themselves being more accountable for the quality of teaching and learning but frequently also without the authority to be able to call others, particularly those who dictate policy from outside the school, to account. The Finnish experience demonstrates very clearly that professional development cannot be mandated from the centre and that it cannot occur without sustained support and outside expertise. The isolation of teachers and their sense of individualism are particularly robust and are considerable barriers to a more collegial approach to curricular and pedagogical reform. In the Finnish experience particularly, conflict avoidance, self-censorship, circumscribed professional dialogue to the extent that there was little meaningful engagement, and the kind of trust and openness that are characteristic of professional support groups and learning communities, appeared only in small groups (cliques) of teachers. Such cliques may be a necessary stage in the process of building professional communities, but they may also be indicative of an arrested cultural reform, where individualism or small-scale collectivism becomes the dominant characteristic. Here too, the Finnish experience indicates that business as usual, in a 'stop-go', in-service mindset is no longer an adequate response to a rapidly changing educational landscape. Strategies need to be identified, supported and adequately resourced to sustain real-time learning of teachers throughout their careers if they are to continue to provide the best quality learning opportunities for students.

Chapter 15, *A case study on the relationship between the innovative process of a secondary school and the reform of the Spanish national curriculum*, provides evidence from Spain of the political nature of educational restructuring and curricular innovation. Sancho and Hernández document a school's experience of becoming comprehensive from a previous situation where pupils were segregated at age fourteen. The experience they describe finds many resonances internationally also. Teachers' initial enthusiasm generated commitment and liberal amounts of personal time were spent in meetings and discussions.

However, teachers lacked the skills and expertise to document their reform journey, and conflicts soon emerged between teachers themselves, teachers and parents, teachers and administrators. In such circumstances, it becomes increasingly difficult to sustain an innovation's momentum so that new attitudes and pedagogical routines become embedded in a different emerging school culture which is more appropriate to the new order. More than anything else, this Catalonian example indicates the ways in which the political nature of school reform impacts upon the effectiveness of education at school level when a change of government reversed the decision for comprehensivisation of secondary schooling. It may be that whereas teachers are initially politically naive about school reform, one of the unintended consequences of multiple reform efforts at national level within many systems, will be the emergence of a new active professionalism among educators characterized by more insistence on being part of policy-making, as critical consumers of policy rather than mere implementers of mandates designed by policy elites.

As we have written this introduction and reflected upon the rich quality of the work of colleagues from a range of educational, cultural and research contexts, we have been amazed by the similarities of the research findings. Throughout, we read of the ways in which successive centralist reforms, for all their good intentions, seem to ignore the need to take into account the complexities of school culture, teacher identity and successful implementation in schools and classrooms. Repeatedly, in these and other researches which the authors of the chapters cite, we are told of the core emotional components central to good teaching, of teachers' resistance to change which is imposed without due regard to their own sense of personal and professional self, of the need for active participation and ownership as experts in practical knowledge of students, and the dilemmas of classroom life; of the need for recognition of the complexity of teaching and learning which requires teachers to engage in continuing critical reflection upon themselves, their work and the contexts in which they teach and students learn if they are to provide the best possible opportunities for learning and achievement. From a different perspective, also, it seems that those in universities do have something to offer which might make a difference to understanding and practices in policy, school and classroom contexts. The continuing job of those in academe is to 'connect' through research and development which is of perceived relevance to these communities of practice, which is accessible and which generates knowledge, at times by working closely alongside and in collaborative sustained relationships, at times by working apart. We believe that this modest volume and the ongoing work of the members of the International Study Association of Teachers and Teaching represents one such contribution to developing teachers and teaching.

Ciaran Sugrue
St. Patrick's College
Dublin City University

Christopher W. Day
School of Education
Nottingham University

Section 1

Changing understandings

Chapter 1

Teaching in a box

Emotional geographies of teaching[1]

Andy Hargreaves

Introduction

If you want to improve learning, improve teaching! The injunction contained within this deceptively simple equation has driven numerous research and reform efforts over the years to define and improve the quality of teaching. Training teachers in the skills and strategies of 'effective' pedagogy, setting and applying professional standards of what teachers should know and be able to do, even testing teachers periodically on their basic, subject-matter knowledge – these are the sorts of methods that reformers have employed to try and raise standards in teaching. These prevalent reform strategies and the research agendas that feed them – on teacher thinking, teacher planning, teacher behaviour and professional knowledge – address some of what is important in teaching. Setting standards of what teachers should know and be able to do can certainly help insure the profession against truly awful teaching, against ignorance and incompetence in our classrooms. Moreover, professional standards can spur teachers and their systems on towards learning and acquiring more sophisticated and effective skills and strategies over time. But somehow, measures such as this miss a lot of what matters most in developing really good teaching. They do not quite get to the heart of it.

When people recall the truly great or dreadful teachers they have encountered in their lifetime, it is not usually this knowledge, skill, thinking or planning (or their absence) that stand out most to them. We remember our best teachers not just or even mainly for being knowledgeable, well organized or even for acting like consummate 'reflective practitioners.' Our best teachers, rather, stand out because they were inspiring, enthusiastic, caring, forgiving, supportive, indeed 'thoughtful' in the widest sense of the word (Clark, 1995).

My best teacher, Miss Hindle, was the only teacher in elementary school who let us stay in at recess, who allowed and encouraged us to produce a student newspaper in class-time throughout the year, who admonished us but quickly forgave us for our indiscretions, and who exuded a constant, irrepressible enthusiasm about teaching and learning. When I visited her ten years later, just before I became a teacher, and she was in late career, the emotional infection of her enthusiasm still suffused her classroom. Just two years ago, I discovered that she was still alive and I sent her one of my books, explaining how her example as a teacher had influenced my own writing (and perhaps, therefore, the views of some of those who read it). That she wrote back appreciatively, and movingly was pleasing but not especially surprising. More surprising and also satisfying was that at the age of 85, she still spontaneously recalled my passion as a student for and my adeptness at Spanish dancing (in revealing this, I am trusting that my colleagues will not insist on any encore performances).

Our worst teachers stand out as much as, sometimes more than, our best ones. They still haunt us not because of their ignorance or incompetence but because of the cruelty, sarcasm, thoughtlessness or sheer stultifying boredom they inflicted on our classroom existence. When I was 12 years old and attending an academic English grammar school, my father died suddenly. No teacher at my school ever discussed this with me. Academic learning was paramount. I never knew whether they knew about my dad's death. About that time, and for several years afterwards, I had a French teacher, who seemed to rule his classrooms with a reign of terror. He would, for example, shake misbehaving students, and drag ones he found talking at the back of the class to the front, scattering desks across the room in his wake. As is usual in emotional memory work (Crawford *et al.*, 1992), my recollections of this man came back to me in deeply embodied ways – in images of his stunted, Napoleonic stature; his yellow, nicotine-stained teeth; the spit he sprayed through the gaps in them; the foul odour of his breath as he thrust his face at you if you dared to disobey him or give him the wrong answer. One of his most common teaching strategies was to ask questions in French of individual students, in strict rotation around the class. 'What is your sister called?', 'Where did you go on vacation this year?', 'What is your father's job?'. For three years, I approached every French lesson in fear that he would ask me this last question, and I would be unable to answer it. Time and again, I rehearsed my defiant retort of 'Mon pére est mort, Monsieur.' He never did ask me the question. But my daily fear that he might created within me a block in second language learning, that persists to this day.

Strong or weak, good or bad, emotion is integral to all teaching, not just the best and worst of it. As I have argued elsewhere, policy strategies designed to improve or raise standards in teaching and learning rarely acknowledge this vital emotional dimension. Often, emotions are excluded from professional standards' frameworks, teacher evaluation schemes, student learning targets and even from the basic idea of 'reflective practice' in teaching. Where emotions are officially acknowledged as being relevant to teaching and learning issues, this recognition is usually conditional or restricted. For example, emotions are recognized in the school effectiveness literature as providing a context for learning – in terms of there needing to be a safe and orderly climate in which learning takes place (Mortimore *et al.*, 1988). Similarly, the guidance and counselling literature points to the necessity for systems of care and support to deal with students' emotional or 'personal' problems that might otherwise interfere with their learning (Hargreaves, forthcoming). Alternatively, emotions are sometimes viewed as a form of learning – in terms of developing self-esteem or acquiring emotional competence (see, for example, Goleman, 1995). Rarely, though, do policymakers acknowledge that emotions are integral to and foundational for all teaching and learning.

A baseline proposition underpinning this paper is that teaching and learning are always emotional practices. This does not mean that teaching and learning are solely emotional practices. In reality, emotion and cognition, feeling and thinking, combine together in all social practices in highly complex ways (Damasio, 1994; Oatley, 1991). But teaching and learning are irretrievably emotional practices. There is always an emotional dimension to them. In his classic text, *On Understanding Emotion*, Norman Denzin (1984: 89) argues that an emotional practice is

> An embedded practice that produces for the person, an expected or unexpected emotional alteration in the inner and outer streams of experience. . . . Emotional practices make people problematic objects to themselves. The emotional practice radiates through the person's body and streams of experience, giving emotional culmination to thoughts, feelings and actions.

As an emotional practice, teaching activates, colours and expresses teachers' own feelings and actions as well as the feelings and actions of others with whom teachers interact. Teachers are engaged in an emotional practice when they enthuse their students or bore them, when they are approachable to parents or stand-offish with them, when they trust their colleagues or are suspicious of them. All teaching is therefore inextricably emotional either by design, or default.

In recent years, an expanding body of literature has sought to remedy the neglect of emotion in the fields of teaching and teacher development, by providing theoretical and empirical grounds that honour the place of emotion in teaching. We are, for example, seeing increasing number of papers and books that expound and expand upon the virtues of caring teachers (Noddings, 1992; Acker, 1992; Elbaz, 1993), passionate teaching (Fried, 1995), thoughtful teaching (Clark, 1995), and tactful teaching (van Manen, 1995). The literature also points to the importance of cultivating greater hope (Fullan, 1997), attentiveness (Elbaz, 1993) and emotional intelligence (Goleman, 1995; Fullan, 1999; Day, 1998) among teachers, and to the significance of emotionality in particular areas of the curriculum such as arts education (e.g. Eisner, 1986).

This important literature provides a counter discourse to the more technical and cognitive conceptions of teaching and teacher development that dominate the language of educational policy and administration. At the same time, writers in these traditions tend to advance a view of teachers' emotions and emotionality that is broadly personal and psychological – indeed, sometimes Pollyanna-like. Becoming a tactful, caring or passionate teacher is treated as largely a matter of personal disposition, moral commitment or private virtue. What is missing or underemphasized in this literature is how the emotions and emotionality of learning, teaching and teacher development take particular forms according to how the work of teaching is configured and organized in particular times and contexts.

In this respect, it is also important to understand some of the more unsettling and even darker emotions of teaching such as guilt, shame, anger, jealousy, envy and fear. The literature of teaching and teacher development would benefit from understanding and explaining these profane emotional realities of people's worklives, as well as celebrating the more 'sacred' ones of care, tact, affection and so on (e.g. Fineman, 1993). A small collection of studies does already suggest how the emotional lives of teachers are being adversely affected and sometimes seriously damaged by high-stakes inspection processes (Jeffrey and Woods, 1996), stress-inducing reform strategies (Woods *et al.*, 1997; Nias, 1999), the risks of collaborative teacher research (Dadds, 1993), authoritarian leadership styles among principals (Blase and Anderson, 1995) and the general speeding-up, intensification and extensification (spreading out) of teachers' work (Hargreaves, 1994). But, across the range of what teachers do, we do not yet have a systematic or interconnected understanding of how emotions are embedded in and shaped by the changing conditions of teachers' work; nor of how these emotions manifest themselves in and affect teachers' interactions with students, parents, administrators and each other. This chapter takes the first steps in developing such an understanding by setting out a preliminary conceptual framework of teachers' emotions as they are embedded in the conditions and interactions of their work. I characterize this framework in terms of what I call emotional geographies of teaching.

The emotions of teaching and educational change

The data on which the chapter is based are drawn from a study of the emotions of teaching and educational change which comprised interviews with 53 teachers in a range of elementary and secondary schools in the province of Ontario in Canada. The sample was distributed across fifteen varied schools of different levels, sizes and serving different kinds of communities (i.e. urban, rural, suburban). In each school, we asked principals to identify a sample of up to four teachers that included the oldest and youngest teachers in the school, was gender mixed, contained teachers with different orientations to change, represented a range of subject specializations (within secondary schools), and (where possible) included at least one teacher from an ethnocultural minority.

The interviews lasted for 1–1½ hours and concentrated on eliciting teachers' reports of their emotional relationships to their work, their professional development and educational change. A substantial part of the interview drew on methodological procedures used by Hochschild (1983) in her key text on the sociology of emotion, *The Managed Heart: The Commercialization of Human Feeling*. It asked teachers to describe particular episodes of positive and negative emotion with students, colleagues, administrators and parents. This chapter is mainly based on teachers' reports about episodes involving their emotional relationships with parents and students. While one-time interviews have limitations as ways of getting others to access and disclose their emotions (and we are therefore now complementing our methodology with long-term discussion groups), they bring to the surface new topics and themes in previously unexplored areas, and they enable us to identify patterns and variations in teachers' emotions across different school contexts, and different kinds of teachers. Also, the particular nature of our database (that of critical episodes) highlights what is emotionally significant and compelling to teachers, not how frequently or infrequently the episodes that teachers describe occur in general.

The interviews were analysed inductively with the assistance of the computer program *Folio Views*. Data were extracted electronically, then marked, coded and grouped into increasingly larger themes, ensuring that all identified pieces of data were accounted for and included in the framework.

Conceptual framework

The approach taken by *The emotions of teaching and educational change* project is broadly social constructionist. Our immediate interest is not in the brain circuitry and psychology that stimulates and organizes emotion. Nor is it in Darwinian understandings of the biological dynamics of basic emotions such as fear that we share in common with other animals. Neither, is the project concerned with long-standing philosophical debates about whether the passions disturb rational thought or enhance it, and about whether thought organizes feeling, or feeling organizes thought (e.g. James, 1917). In taking a social constructionist view, rather, the project is concerned with how teachers' emotions are experienced and represented in various contexts and in patterns of interaction with others who are part of teachers' working lives.

The theoretical framework for this social constructionist understanding of teachers' emotions is grounded in two basic concepts: emotional understanding and emotional geographies. According to Denzin, emotional understanding

> is an intersubjective process requiring that one person enter into the field of experience of another and experience for herself the same or similar experiences experienced by another. The subjective interpretation of another's emotional experience from one's own standpoint is central to emotional understanding. Shared and shareable emotionality lie at the core of what it means to understand and meaningfully enter into the emotional experiences of another.
>
> (Denzin 1984, p. 137)

Teaching, learning and leading all involve emotional understanding as people reach into the past store of their own emotional experience to interpret and unravel, instantaneously, at-a-glance, the emotional experiences and responses of others. Emotional understanding can be established through a number of means. Denzin describes emotional 'infection' (spreading our own optimistic or pessimistic moods to others), and vicarious emotional understanding (where we empathize with characters' lives or predicaments through theatre or literature, for example), as two such means. One of the key ways in which emotional understanding develops, however, is through long-standing, close relationships with others. Without such relationships, teachers (indeed anyone) will experience emotional misunderstanding where they 'mistake their feelings for the feelings of the other' (Denzin, 1984: 134). In schools where such close relationships do not exist, where teachers do not know students well (Sizer, 1992), they will frequently misconstrue student exuberance for hostility, or parent respect for agreement, for example. Emotional misunderstanding strikes at the foundations of teaching and learning – lowering standards and depressing quality. If we misunderstand how students are responding, we misunderstand how they learn. Successful teaching and learning therefore depend on strong emotional understanding, on establishing close bonds with students (and to a lesser extent, with colleagues and parents as well) and on creating the conditions in teaching that make this understanding possible.

Emotional understanding is achieved not just by acts of personal will, sensitivity or virtue. It is not simply a result of emotional competence or of exercising one's emotional intelligence. Similarly, emotional misunderstanding occurs not just because of personal flaws or deficiencies in empathy or other emotional competences. Rather, Denzin argues that emotional misunderstanding is a pervasive and chronic feature of everyday interactions and relationships where those human engagements are not ones of shared experience, or where they have not developed to a level of close and common understanding.

School-teaching is full of spurious emotion. Schools are places where boredom is often misinterpreted as studious commitment, or frustration is viewed as hyperactivity, for example. Willard Waller more than touched on the sources of such misunderstandings as long ago as 1932, in his discussion of what he called 'the teacher stereotype'.

> The teacher stereotype is a thin but impenetrable veil that comes between the teacher and all other human beings. The teacher can never know what others are really like because they are not like that when the teacher is watching them.
>
> (Waller 1932, p. 49)

The classroom, like the community, argued Waller, is a place where teachers are necessarily distanced from those who are immediately around them.

> Social distance is characteristic of the personal entanglements of teachers and students. It is a necessity where the subordination of one person to another is required, for distance makes possible that recession of feeling without which the authority of another is not tolerable.
>
> Between adult and child is an ineradicable social distance that seems at times an impassable gulf (which) . . . arises from the fact that. . . the adult has found his place in the world and the child has not.
>
> To the natural distance between adult and child is added a greater distance when the adult is a teacher and the child is a student, and this distance arises mainly from the fact that the teacher must give orders to the child. They cannot know each other, for we can never know a person at whom we only peer through institutional bars.
>
> (Waller 1932, pp. 279–80)

Waller's insights about the role of social distance in teachers' work, although expressed with a characteristic excess of cynicism by today's standards, nonetheless point to how emotional understanding or misunderstanding in teaching is created and organized by what I term emotional geographies of schooling. I define the concept of emotional geographies as referring to the spatial and experiential patterns of closeness and/or distance in human interactions and relationships that help create, configure and colour the feelings and emotions we experience about ourselves, our world and each other.

Emotional geographies help us identify the threats to the basic emotional bonds and understandings of schooling that are posed by excessive distance or closeness in people's interactions or relationships. Analysis of data from the emotions project points to several forms of emotional distance (and closeness) that can threaten emotional understanding among teachers, students, colleagues and parents. These are sociocultural distance, moral distance, professional distance, political distance and physical distance.[2] This paper draws somewhat selectively on the data set concerning teachers' reports of their interactions with parents to illustrate what particular emotional geographies of teaching look like in practice. More detailed and systematic presentations of the project's empirical findings are available elsewhere.

Before detailing the specific emotional geographies of teaching that surfaced in our project, it is important to establish two caveats. First, there are no 'natural' or 'universal' rules of emotional geography in teaching or in other areas of human interaction. There is no ideal or optimal closeness or distance between teachers and others that transcends all cultures and work contexts. The emotional geographies of teacher–parent relations are typically characterized by greater professional distance in Hong Kong (Lee, 1998), for example, than in many parts of South America (Bernhard, 1999). These differences reflect important cross-cultural variations in how people experience and express different aspects of emotionality in their lives (Kitayama and Marcus, 1994). Emotional geographies are, in this sense, culture-bound, not context-free.

Second, the emotional geographies of human interaction are more than

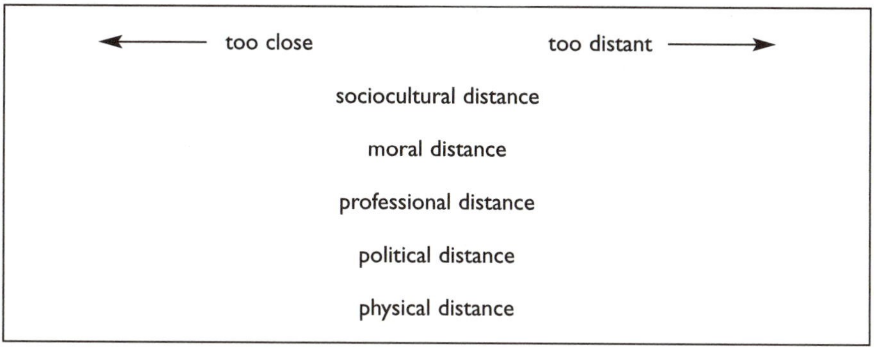

Figure 1.1 Emotional geographies of teacher–parent relationships.

strictly physical phenomena. We can feel distant from people who are right next to us; close to loved ones who are miles away. Emotions therefore have what Shields (1991) calls imaginary geographies of psychological closeness or distance as well as physical ones. The emotional geographies of teaching are therefore subjective as well as objective in nature (Figure 1.1).

Emotional geographies

Socio-cultural distance

In today's rapidly changing post-modern world, more and more children belong to cultures that are different from and unfamiliar to those of their teachers. Coming predominantly from lower middle- and upper working-class backgrounds (Lindblad and Prieto, 1992), in a profession of limited ethnocultural diversity, teachers are socioculturally distanced from many of their students' families. They often find themselves teaching 'other people's children' (Delpit, 1993). Students' families are also changing in their structure and form (Elkind, 1997), and now increasingly comprise single-parent families, blended families, families with parents who spend much of their lives apart, families without parents at all and busy families entrapped in what Hochschild (1997) calls the 'time bind' where the demands of work place emotional pressures on commitments at home.

What this all means for many teachers whose mean age is well into the forties in most Western countries (OECD, 1998) is that their students today are, in Bigum and Green's (1993) words, 'aliens in the classroom'. Likewise, to teachers, these students' parents are 'aliens in the community'. All too often, teachers look at students and parents with growing incomprehension. They are physically, socially and culturally removed from the communities in which they teach and do not know where parents and students are coming from.

The socio-cultural distance between teachers, on the one hand, and students and parents on the other, often leads teachers to stereotype and be stereotyped by the communities they serve. There is more to this stereotyping than Waller's traditional teacher authority. Popkewitz (1998), for example, shows how teachers in poor urban and rural schools use 'populational reasoning' to ascribe (usually negative) characteristics in a blanket way to the students and communities they serve. Yet, culturally different parents often have much to offer that teachers do not appreciate or cannot engage with. Bernhard (1999), for example, describes how Latino parents (including ones who have held highly qualified positions in South America) find that their children's 'Canadian' early childhood education teachers employ unfamiliar and misleading specialized language (for example, by designating their child as 'special'), use bland and uncommunicative report cards, and seem generally cool and distant towards children and their parents (even though, in their own sociocultural terms, the 'Canadian' teachers perceive themselves as being very caring indeed).

The differences and changes in parents and communities that teachers see are not in their imaginations, but many educators see them as largely changes for the worse. As our data confirm, teachers often have assumptions and expectations about parental interest and support that are socio-culturally biased, misconstruing problems of poverty as problems of single-motherhood or poor parenting generally (Levin and Riffel, 1997).

> (A mother's) child was just a joy . . . lovely girl. She was the oldest of five kids. She was in grade four. She was given so many responsibilities at home that she seldom had a chance to do her homework. And I keep on at mom – 'she's got to get her homework done, she's in grade 4, she's going to get more and more'. . . . Don't you understand that?' 'I'm a working mom. When I was her age I had to look after the kids' (so the teacher arranged for her to stay in at recess). . . . Anyway at the very end of the year, the mom took me to the office . . . and she said, 'Jenny's never had such a bad teacher. . . . You say that she's below level in language and that's a lie. I know she can do it – she's just lazy'. . . . She's verbally abusing her daughter who's a lovely kid. . . . Jenny was there and there were a couple of kids cleaning up in the classroom, and I felt embarrassed for Jenny. . . . I couldn't understand where this mom was coming from. . . . (I felt) just so incredulous . . . I understand that she must be busy – five kids, she's busy . . . and yet the child . . . has to have an education. And why isn't the mom understanding this?. . . . I was hurt because the mom didn't realize all that I was doing; but angry and upset at the fact that the mom didn't realize what a gem she had in this child'.

Teachers may also regard parents' failure to attend meetings or other officially organized events as their failure to support their children or the school (Burgess *et al.*, 1991). In a secondary school that had changed from being in a small village to a highly diverse expanding community, within a short period of time, one teacher in our study said, 'parents are busy people too, so when we offer a parent's night, we don't get a big population of parents coming. They're busy'. Another remarked, 'we're trying to reach out and to bring parents in and to involve them move in the life of the school but at the same time, parents are really stressed and I think parents are sort of abdicating the responsibility of educating the kids to an institution'.

Other teachers, especially at the elementary level are inclined to measure parenting or 'sensitive mothering' of young children against a yardstick of practice that is culturally skewed towards middle-class norms (Vincent and Warren, 1998). Some teachers in our study complained, for example, about parents who lied to cover up their children's absences, bought their children expensive presents when they were still suspended from school, let their teenagers drive irresponsibly, failed to prevent their young adolescents from smoking and drinking, or did not view swearing in class as a problem. In a number of cases, teachers were concerned, indeed deeply upset that parents did not seem to care for their children at all.

> I find the most frustrating experience is when you phone home and you can tell by the tone of the parent that they don't care. They too have given up.

> If the parent has given up on their own child, it's going to be very difficult for a teacher to get across to a student as well. . . . We deal with that on a daily basis.
>
> One child in grade six . . . is a very nice kid but I really think mom is nuts. . . . She had ended up locking him out. She had taken money from him and then he had taken it back to pay for the camping trip. She found out and accused him of stealing and so he wasn't allowed to go on the camping trip. I felt really bad for the kid. I worry about him, I guess. I see him in four or five years down the road running away or decking her . . . (I feel) disgust towards his mother.

Teachers' perceptions that parents did not care for their children provoked feelings of incredulity, hopelessness and even disgust among them. There was a difference, an otherness about these parents that teachers found hard to understand or penetrate. Notwithstanding all the pressures and demands that some parents demonstrably had to endure, how could they fail to love their children, not care for them properly, or be unprepared to support their education? Teachers were at a loss to know where these parents were coming from. The socio-cultural distance between them seemed just too great.

In the most extreme cases, the 'otherness' of parents and their attitudes toward their own children, is not just mystifying to parents; it is a source of danger and personal threat. All but one of these cases were reported by elementary teachers whose characteristically more frequent and intense interactions with difficult or argumentative parents were experienced as more imminently disturbing to them. Here, parents were not just socio-culturally distanced from the teacher, but also physically too close! Teachers' comments communicated a sense of intrusion into, even pollution of their world that the 'otherness' of some parents threatened. In all these cases, teachers made negative judgements and psychologized about 'problem' parents and families, viewed the differences as deficiencies, and stigmatized parents as 'mad,' 'crazy' or 'screamers' – thereby undermining the rationality and legitimacy of their opposition and criticism. Negative attributions to parents and families by teachers included:

- a Caribbean father from a 'split family – father doesn't talk to mother, mother doesn't talk to father' who, when offered a separate interview, 'started to ask me ridiculous questions and grill me over the phone about things that were completely unreasonable and wouldn't take no for an answer . . . and it was just crazy. They're just venting on you. And that happens fairly frequently unfortunately.'
- a teacher who described how 'what we find with kids who have severe behavioural problems is that very often you'll see these kids come out of single-parent households and sometimes you'll find that the relationship between the child and let's say, the mother, is an extraordinary close one, to the point where the child has . . . almost a kind of a special role and . . . the mother inadvertently makes a career of advocating for the child', of her child's 'dysfunction' giving 'her an opportunity to organize her life

> around that'. . . . 'This particular child is very bonded to his mother, and it's a black family' (in this instance, the mother had felt that this teacher's refusal to grant hall passes to her son was 'a racist issue').

In these cases, parents were not only different, they were irrationally and incomprehensibly dangerous. They were 'screamers' who 'blurted' into the teacher's face, 'grilled' them about their judgements or 'vented' on them.

None of this is meant to deny that some parents, as a cross-section of society, are indeed difficult and even dangerous. Many parents, like people generally, are far from perfect. But too often, teachers see only obstacles in the changing lives and cultures of their students, families and communities, rarely opportunities. Without stronger efforts to bridge the socio-cultural gap between teachers and many parents and students, and to create better emotional understanding among them, then parental deficiencies are likely to be exaggerated in teachers' eyes, deficiencies will sometimes be imputed inaccurately and unfairly, and teachers will have less access to the knowledge and emotional understanding that would help them deal more effectively with the conflicts that are provoked by the most troublesome parents.

Moral distance

Emotions are moral phenomena. They are intimately and inextricably bound up with our purposes. Purposes, the things that are important to us, often drive or trigger our emotions. At the same time, emotions help us choose among a wide variety of options in a highly complex world by narrowing down our choices (Brody and Hall, 1995). Oatley and Jenkins (1996) argue that

> In real life, a purely logical search through all the possibilities is not possible. . . . Nevertheless we must act . . . despite our limitations, we must take responsibility for our actions and suffer their effects. This is why emotions or something like them are necessary to bridge across the unexpected and the unknown to guide reason, and to give priorities among multiple goals.

People experience happiness when they are achieving their goals or suspended from them (as in holidays or listening to music) (Oatley, 1991). Achievement and success bring satisfaction and pleasure. With parents, teachers in the emotions project experienced positive emotion when they received gratitude, appreciation, agreement and support from them. As one teacher said, 'the more comments that I hear back then I know I am still, after 25 years, on the right track and still somehow getting to the students and still relating to the students in a positive way.' Another remarked on how 'this morning, I was totally spoiled with parents who were saying that I taught their kids a lot.' Such appreciation for teachers' dedication and success was 'energizing – it makes you want to go out and try new things. It opens up creativity and makes you want to risk;' 'it picks you up – makes you feel good. It erodes some of the stress that's come along with all the other changes that have happened in education,' 'you're encouraged to try harder and do more in your program.' As one teacher puts it, 'if people keep throwing you little pieces of food, you will keep coming back.'

Clear indication of moral agreement and support as well as appreciation created a kind of closeness between teachers and parents. Now, as Marcus and Kitayama (1994) argue, this need for positive feedback about personal success may be greater in Western and especially American culture where individual achievement is prized highly, and the expectation to feel something good all the time is culturally widespread. Indeed, these observations may explain why, despite a widespread equality ethic in teaching where teachers are reluctant to acknowledge that any colleague is better than any other (Campbell, 1996), teachers in our study welcomed being singled out publicly by parents as special, different from or even better than their colleagues – in school council meetings, letters to the principal, or donations to the school, for example. Despite these caveats, the widespread reality in Western schooling is that moral closeness with and support from students and parents, as well as from colleagues and administrators, reinforces teachers' sense of purpose and is a source of positive and energizing emotion for them.

By contrast, negative emotion can occur when there is a great moral distance between teachers and others, when teachers feel that purposes are being threatened or have been lost. Nias (1991), for example, has described how the English National Curriculum created senses of grief, loss, bereavement and (literally) demoralization among those who first had to implement it. Similarly, when teachers' purposes are at odds with those around them, anxiety, frustration, anger and guilt affect everyone who is involved. Such emotion can be educationally damaging, leading teachers and others to focus inwards, and lose energy and enthusiasm for their work (Goleman, 1995: 10).

The effects of moral distance and conflicting purposes are especially apparent in teachers' interactions with parents, for example, in cases where

- a parent who did not understand current teaching approaches and why their child may not be achieving, demanded to see curriculum documents and insisted that the teacher should be teaching differently.
- a parent volunteer in elementary school who was seen as ambitious for her child, went behind the teacher's back to solicit additional, more difficult work from the teacher of the next grade. 'She went to the next grade up hoping that if he knew all of this material then the next year he would just breeze through it. She has sort of lost the purpose of having a program that is current.'
- a parent volunteer followed a teacher's class to the computer laboratory and argued that the program being pursued there was insufficiently rigorous (whereas the teacher's contrary purpose was to get students feeling comfortable with computers).

In cases like these, teachers were questioned about their competence, expertise, program decisions and assessment practices – at heart, their very purposes. Teachers were angry, outraged and upset when their purposes, judgement, expertise and basic professionalism were criticized by parents. Having these academic purposes and expertise questioned was, in fact, the strongest source of negative emotion among teachers in our study.

Moral difference and distance is not, of itself, a problem in schooling or teaching. Indeed, as Maurer (1996) argues, we often learn more from people who are different from us than ones who are the same. The point in organizations is not to hope that people already share the same goals. In a complex, post-modern world of shifting values and great cultural diversity, this aspiration is increasingly impractical (Hargreaves, 1994). More than this, taking refuge in small self-affirming communities of tightly shared values, as for example in schools of choice, runs the risk of developing organizations and cultures that are balkanized, inward and exclusionary in nature. Successful organizations, rather, are ones that establish the means and the motivation for people to work together towards common purposes. Indeed, it is this very act of narrowing distance and working through difference that can make organizations emotionally vital (Goleman, 1998).

As Goleman (1998: 220) argues, achieving the optimum level of openness in working through difference within organizations 'can be a delicate, emotionally loaded matter. Too easy a consensus risks a low-quality decision, while too much contention results in a lack of unity and resolve.' In teaching, our data suggest that in their interactions with parents, it is the lack of means to work through moral differences that is often the source of difficulty. This problem is rooted in the geography of professional distance, which I discuss next.

Professional distance

The social distance between teacher and child, or teacher and parent of which Waller (1932) spoke earlier is not only a result of adult–child authority relations, or even the institutionalized office of teaching. It is also a matter of professional distance, and this, as Grumet (1988) points out, is a gendered issue:

> Female teachers complied with the rationalization and bureaucratization that pervaded the common schools as the industrial culture saturated the urban areas. Rather than emulate the continuous and extended relation of a mother and her maturing child, they acquiesed to the graded schools – to working with one age group for one year at a time. Rather than demand the extended relation that would bind them over time to individual children, they agreed to large group instruction where the power of the peer collective was at least as powerful as the mother/child bond.
>
> (Grumet 1988, p. 55)

Schoolteaching has become in many ways, an occupation with a feminine caring ethic trapped within a rationalized and bureaucratized structure. The ambivalent and uncertain status of teaching has also pushed teachers to clamour for greater pay and recognition – to pursue what Ivor Goodson and I have called 'classical professionalism' (Hargreaves and Goodson, 1996).

Yet, while many of the core activities of teaching and learning require close emotional understanding between teachers, parents and students, the 'classical' idea of professionalism has been modelled on the traditionally male preserves of medicine and law, which require professionals to avoid emotional entanglements with their clients' problems and maintain professional distance from them (Grumet, 1988). The dilemma for teachers is that while they are supposed to care for their students, they are expected to do so in a somewhat clinical and detached way – to mask their emotions with parents and control them when they are around students.

Autonomy and independence help make the job of masking, of maintaining some emotional distance, easier. Larson (1977) identifies the criterion of autonomy as a crucial one that helps distinguish professional from non-professional work. Johnson (1972) takes many of these and other classical criteria of professionalism to represent ideologies of self-promotion rather than realities of practice where professionals' self-interests are often privileged over those of their clients. Moreover, Friedson (1994) argues that common-sense discourses of professionalism and behaving like a professional have been captured by managerialism as a way to control white-collar workers.

One consequence of adopting the classical masculine model of professional autonomy is that it distances teachers from those around them. Speaking of and about women educators especially, Grumet (1988: 58) reflects that 'when we attempt to rectify our humiliating situation by emulating the protectionism and elitism of the other "professions", we subscribe to patriarchy's contempt for the familiar, for the personal . . . for us'.

In our study, when teachers experienced negative emotion in their interactions with parents, it was questioning of their expertise, of their instructional knowledge, of the judgements for which they felt uniquely qualified, that disturbed them most. Reflecting on the significance of the episodes that they described, teacher after teacher was irate or incredulous about parents' failure to understand teachers' practices. A secondary teacher who had previously worked in industry portrayed the inviolable and almost sacrosanct nature of his expertise in the following way.

> Parents think that they're the experts in education and it amazes me. I sent a note home saying that (the father) wasn't qualified (to critize the teacher's assessment practices) and this got him a little annoyed. And we had conversations. And I said, 'what would you think if I presumed to walk into your office and tell you how to do your job after you've been there for however long you've been at your job. And yet you think you can comment on my job? You're not even qualified. Good, you're concerned about your kid. But don't think you're going to intimidate me into giving him more marks, because you're not . . .' (Parents) have such naive expectations. And yet they have no problems commenting on what's going on in the classroom. And I think that's a sad reflection on the public's perception of teaching and what's going on in teaching. They don't trust teachers. They think that we're lazy and that we're largely responsible for a lot of the problems with their kids, and they're wrong.

An elementary teacher who complained about a parent criticizing her curriculum programming in computer-based education 'was disturbed in the fact that she was questioning what I was doing as a teacher. I'm the one with the expertise! I'm the one with the education! I'm the one with the degree! She is to be there to help.'

When teachers reported their expertise being questioned, they rarely seemed to entertain doubts about whether their own judgements might have been flawed or incorrect. They made remarks such as 'I was so sure that I was not wrong,' 'they still felt that they were right and I still felt I was right' and 'the only thing that has really changed has been my attitude towards her (the mother)'.

Teachers who preserve their professional autonomy by keeping parents at a distance might protect themselves from parental criticism, but they also insulate themselves from praise and support. Teachers in our study welcomed positive feedback from parents. It was the most frequently cited source of positive emotion for them. Yet a number of teachers felt that much as they welcomed positive feedback from parents, it was all too rare. Teachers, they said, do not hear enough positive comments from parents; parents do not see them often enough. It was 'too easy to shut your door' in teaching. Positive parental feedback is, in this sense, embedded in a scarce emotional economy of parent–teacher interactions. Ongoing feedback was especially rare at the secondary level, where the norm of professional distance severely constrained the opportunities for more authentic interaction. Here especially, the problems of professional distance were further compounded by difficulties of physical distance in teacher-parent interactions.

Physical distance

The most self-evident emotional geography of teaching is a physical one. Emotional understanding and the establishment of emotional bonds with teachers and parents requires proximity and some measure of intensity or frequency in interaction. We cannot know or understand people we rarely meet; nor can we be understood by them in return. Our data suggest that secondary school teaching is a place where the difficulties of physical distance are especially acute.

In secondary schools, reported communications with parents were overwhelmingly episodic and infrequent, and either took place in staged meetings or through non-face-to-face mechanisms of written notes and telephone calls. Over half of the incidents of positive emotion reported by teachers took place at parents' nights when they received praise and thanks for their efforts. A British study of parents' nights shows that in the eight minutes or so they have to talk together, secondary school teachers tend to set the agenda, dominate the talk and show little responsiveness to parents' knowledge about their own children. By contrast, only two citations of positive emotion among elementary teachers in our study referred to parents' nights – both of these involving teachers of older, middle-school age children. Of the remaining nine incidents of positive emotion cited by secondary teachers, four took place through the indirect means of the telephone or written communication (compared with one at the elementary level). Only one positive communication cited by secondary teachers took place in an informal setting – this involving a teacher in our only rural secondary school site who described positive encounters with a parent in the community. In elementary schools, by contrast, half of the instances of positive emotion (the largest category) involved informal discussions with parents and parent volunteers in and around the school.

Similar patterns occurred in teachers' reports of negative emotional incidents with parents. Among secondary teachers, the vast majority of reported negative emotional episodes took place on the telephone (eleven out of sixteen cases). These largely concerned problems of attendance and behaviour. Three more took place in writing, and just one occurred on parent's night (whose stage-managed nature helps insulate teachers against the possibility of negative emotional outbursts). Only one reported episode of negative emotion at the secondary level occurred in a more informal setting. Conversely, elementary teachers reported that negative emotional episodes were more spread out – with four instances occurring informally with parent volunteers, two taking place when parents came into the school, three happenning on the telephone and one being in writing.

Just as secondary teachers seem to have less emotionally intense relationships with students compared with their elementary colleagues (Hargreaves, 1999), they have less emotionally intense relationships with those students' parents as well. These interactions are infrequent and intermittent, and they take place primarily through indirect communication or at staged events. To the socio-cultural distance that cultural diversity and changing families often place between teachers and parents, secondary schools add a professional distance of relatively formal and stage-managed interactions, as well as a physical distance of infrequent and non-face-to-face communication that can make emotional understanding and strong partnerships between teachers and parents even more difficult to establish. Together, these three emotional geographies of secondary teaching pose significant threats to the possibilities for better emotional understanding between teachers and the changing parents that they serve.

Political distance

Emotions are not just a personal matter. They are bound up with people's experiences of power and powerlessness. Teaching, in this sense, is rife with emotional politics. Blase and Anderson (1995), for example, describe how teachers experience anger, resignation, depression, anxiety or (among favoured insiders) satisfaction when they work for authoritarian principals.

In the case of parents, while teachers may sometimes endeavour to put them professionally at a distance, the problem is that sometimes parents get physically too close. This occurred among the elementary teachers described earlier who would recall parents grilling them, venting on them or 'blurting' things into their face. Interestingly, much of our vocabulary for emotion and for power is also a spatial, geographical one. People are central or peripheral, 'up' or 'down' on the inside track, or 'out of things' (Stallybrass and White, 1986). As Kemper (1995) argues, 'a very large number of human emotions can be understood as responses to the power and/or status meanings and implications of situations'. Kemper's work shows that when we experience increases in our own power, we feel more secure because we are protected. When our status increases, we feel happiness, satisfaction and contentment along with pride if we are responsible for the increased status, and gratitude if someone else is. Conversely, and equally importantly, when our power is reduced, we experience feelings of fear and anxiety that result from compulsion; and when we undergo loss of status, we feel anger at those who are responsible, shame if we hold ourselves responsible, and depression if the situation seems irredeemable to us.

Power relationships with parents are unclear and uncertain. While teachers can fend off parental criticism about their judgement and expertise, in the area of behaviour and attendance, they must sometimes rely on active parental support to achieve their goals. Where parents and teachers are morally distanced from each other, parents' failure to support or 'back-up' teachers in relation to their children's attendance or behaviour problems provoked negative emotion in teachers – the second most common source of it, in fact.

In the face of this missing support, teachers felt exasperated and powerless. If parents refused to co-operate, teachers felt they could not coerce them legally into doing so – 'the law ties our hands on it. If the parent allows the kid to stay home, there's nothing I can do about that.' Or they might be afraid of parents – 'I don't have the nerve to . . . confront the parents about lying.' Or they would feel powerless to combat the extensive socialization effects of the home:

> I thought I had their support in how to deal with this situation. When he is getting these sorts of rewards at home for negative behaviour there is very little that I can do here. . . . I felt a sense of hopelessness in working with this child to help him solve some of his problems.

In the emotional geography of schooling, teachers prefer to be politically superior to parents, securing their active support, rather than parents having power over them, even if it is only the power of default or veto.

When teachers were asked to describe an incident when they had had to mask their emotions to fit the situation, by far the largest number of cases concerned interactions with parents. Teachers who had to mask or manage their emotions in their encounters with parents recounted their experiences in the following ways:

> I am not good at having people yell at me . . . whenever something happens like that, that gets really icky, I get tingles up the back of my spine and get butterflies in my stomach. It is like when I go on stage. I get nervous as soon as I end the situation, a feeling of calm comes over me. I am really good at dissipating that kind of thing. . . . I try to calm it down. I felt lots of fear. I wondered what he was going to do. Is he going to go to the vice principal? Is he going to hit me? (younger female, secondary).

> Sometimes, when a parent calls and they're sort of being very pointed in their criticism over the phone, you get very defensive and you feel like 'Hey, wait a minute, you know, I've done this, this, this and this.' And, you know, 'don't tell me how to do my job. And you know there's those kinds of feelings that come out. You feel annoyed that there is this person who keeps phoning and saying you're not doing your job and you just sort of wish he'd go away. But you also feel this sort of sense of responsibility because you can step back from him and say, 'well, maybe he's not handling this the best way he could' (male, secondary teacher).

> I am very explosive by nature and I usually will (blow up) but in some situations and I think I have the foresight in this one, I just back right away, and I say, 'I am way too angry to discuss this with you right now. I will discuss it later'. And then you collect your thoughts and you kind of huff and puff and then you come at it again, which is a recent addition to my coping strategies (secondary, younger female).

> There's been the odd time where they come in and have been very aggressive. And I've got to remain calm and stick to the issue of how we can help this student without getting involved in the emotional part of it. And I find it, personally, very difficult to try and defuse a person who's upset, so I have to pretend that I'm calm and focussing when inside I'm all upset. I find that difficult dealing with upset parents (elementary, older female).

> You can't help but get angry and upset by it. . . . You have to remain and not get defensive and just do the best you can to defuse the situation and meet and hopefully make the parent more aware (male, elementary teacher).

> She was completely misinformed by her son that everybody is 'necking' out in the yard. That is absolutely not true. I was angry. I could feel the adrenaline starting to flow at all these accusations that were completely unfounded – adrenaline and anger. . . . As a result we discussed it. I tried to stay calm which I managed to do. She went away, she was happy and realized that . . . the situation as she saw it wasn't correct (elementary, older female).

Interactions with parents can provoke fear, anger, anxiety and other disturbing emotions when power plays are at work. It is not surprising, therefore, that teachers sometimes want to avoid, minimize or stage-manage such interactions. Teachers do not welcome their purposes being obstructed or challenged, nor do they like the power of their professional expertise to be undermined.

Goleman (1995) describes this masking as emotional competence. He sees it as integral to achieving success in the workplace. Hochschild, meanwhile, describes the act as one of emotional labour; in which the masking is somehow sacrificial, exploitative, inauthentic. In her classic text on the subject, Hochschild writes:

> This labour requires one to induce or suppress feelings in order to sustain the outward countenance that produces the proper state of mind in others. . . . This kind of labour calls for a coordination of mind and feeling, and it sometimes draws on a source of self that we honour as deep and integral to our personality.
>
> (Hochschild 1993, p. 7)

For Hochschild, emotional labour is a largely negative phenomenon. It involves trading-in part of the self for the security and reward that people get from their employers, or for the profitable rewards that accrue from commercial encounters. Critics, however, argue that this view underplays the pleasures of acting, interplay and playfulness that emotional labour also involves (e.g. Fineman, 1993). In her Marxian inspired analysis, Hochschild perhaps overestimates the exchange value of emotional labour (as in the profit value of a salesperson's smile), at the expense of the use value of such labour (what that labour creates and recreates in oneself and in others) as an authentic act of sincere emotional giving.

Reseachers of other occupations argue that whether masking emotion is a mark of competence or exploitation depends on the power relationships and purposes at stake in any setting. Competence or fulfilment is likely to be the effect when people can act in accordance with their own values and can identify with the expectation of the role. Emotion management and masking is likely to be more laborious, however, when values and identification are somehow sacrificed.

An especially insightful and helpful work here for understanding the emotional politics and emotional labour of the kinds of 'laborious' teacher–parent interactions described earlier is Stenross AND Kleinmann's study of emotional labour among detectives.[3] Stenross and Kleinmann (1989) found that only the emotional labour that detectives performed with victims was troublesome to them whereas they enjoyed the challenges of it when working with criminals. Criminals were the 'real stuff' of detective work that detectives looked forward to the most. Emotional displays by criminals were judged inauthentic by detectives and therefore discarded as not requiring any attention.

Victims' emotions, however, did not help the detectives solve their cases, yet they were judged to be authentic and in need of attention. Victims tried to give detectives instructions and tell them what leads to follow, yet were also often unsupportive or unappreciative of their efforts. Victims nonetheless had to be treated respectfully since they might complain to the detectives' supervisors and accuse them of being unsupportive. In the face of possible reprimand and pressure from above, detectives regarded victims as emotional burdens to be endured as they carried out their work.

While parents and students are not, of course, victims and criminals, the comparison between teachers and detectives does transfer in the sense that like detectives, teachers work with two groups – one of which is seen as core to their work (and in a position of lesser power to them), and the other of which is less core, but still influential (indeed necessary), as well as being in a more ambivalent relation of power.

The political geographies or emotional politics of teacher–parent relations are therefore quite complex – given teachers' desire to place a physical and professional distance between themselves and parents at the secondary level, along with the threat and anxiety which arises where teachers' and parents' purposes are dissonant, cultures are different, and relationships seem physically too close.

Conclusions

Emotions, I have argued, are integral to teaching. One way we can move beyond simply advocating less rationalization and more passion in teaching is by understanding why teachers' emotions are configured in particular ways in the organizational life of schools. The conceptual framework of emotional geographies, I have argued, begins to provide a way for us to make sense of the forms of excessive distance and closeness that threaten the emotional understanding which is foundational to high-quality teaching and learning. Paying attention to the socio-cultural, moral, professional, physical and political geographies of teaching may help us understand better how to create stronger emotional understanding in teaching and learning relationships, and how to avert or alleviate the threats to that understanding.

Mere contact and physical as well as professional closeness are not themselves sufficient to develop strong emotional understanding, however. There must also be efforts to acknowledge, empathize with, discuss and reconcile the different purposes that parents and teachers have for children's education, and that otherwise put a damaging moral distance between them. As our elementary teacher data show, where great moral distances exist between teachers and parents, and their purposes are at odds with each other, physically close and frequent interactions will only magnify conflict and frustration between them. 'Parent power' in this sense, is likely to exacerbate teachers' anxieties and increase the extent of masking in their interactions, rather than relieve these things.

Political distance is also a threat to people whose interactions are physically close. Where teacher-parent relations are characterized by power-plays rather than partnerships, negative emotion is always somewhere near the surface. Our data suggest that physically closer, more frequent interactions between teachers and parents will therefore exacerbate rather than alleviate negative emotions between them unless educators also make serious efforts to be less professionally distant with parents, unless teachers and parents are politically open and respectful of each other, and unless both parties show more readiness to listen to and engage with each other's purposes for their children's education.

In a culturally diverse, increasingly unequal and rapidly changing world, building strong, reciprocal partnerships with others to develop the depth of emotional understanding on which successful learning among and caring for all students depends has never been more necessary. But in a world where parents are more demanding, teaching is changing, the cultural differences are widening, and teachers are unbearably overloaded, teachers' understandable inclination is to close their classroom doors, contain the demand, and manage the interaction as best as they can. Ironically, however, building better emotional understanding with students and their parents really requires teachers to 'move towards the danger' (Maurer, 1995) in working with those of whom they have been most anxious and afraid, to form better, more productive alliances (Hargreaves and Fullan, 1998). In short, it requires teachers to redefine the emotional geography of teacher–parent relationships.

Better emotional understanding and the quality of education that comes from it also requires a reversal in many educational policies. Instead of putting teachers back in their classroom boxes by overloading the curriculum, increasing the content focus, reducing teachers' time out and class to interact with others, and standardizing their interactions with those around them – these policies need to give teachers the discretion, the conditions and the opportunities to develop and exercise their emotional competence of caring for, connecting with and developing emotional understanding among all those whose lives and actions affect the children that they teach.

Notes

1 This paper is drawn from a project on The Emotions of Teaching and Educational Change funded by the Social Science and Humanities Research Council of Canada.
2 While dimensions of emotional geography are the most prominent in the data, other dimensions are also plausible and there remains considerable room for further development of the theory of emotional geographies.
3 I am especially grateful to my graduate assistant, Sue Winton, for drawing this work and her own insightful interpretation of it to my attention.

References

Acker, S. (1992) 'Creating careers: women teachers at work'. *Curriculum Inquiry* 22(2): 141–63.

Bigum, C. and Green, B. (1993) 'Aliens in the classroom', *Australian Journal of Education* 37(2): 119–41.

Blase, J. and Anderson, G. (1995) *The Micropolitics of Educational Leadership*, London: Cassell and New York: Teachers' College Press.

Brody, L. and Hall, J. (1995) 'Gender and emotions', in M. Lewis and J. Haviland (eds) *Handbook of Emotions* New York and London: Guilford Press.

Burgess, R., Herphes, C. and Moxan, S. (1991) 'Parents are welcome: headteachers and mothers' perspectives on parental participation in the early years', *Qualitative Studies in Education* 4(2): 95–107.

Campbell, E. (1996) 'Ethical implications of collegial loyalty as one view of teacher professionalism', *Teachers and Teaching: Theory and Practice* 2(2): 191–208.

Clark, C. (1995) *Thoughtful Teaching*. London: Cassell.

Crawford, J., Kippax, S., Onyx, J., Gault, U. and Benton, P. (1992) *Emotion and Gender*. London: Sage.

Dadds, M. (1993) 'The feeling of thinking in professional self-study', *Educational Action Research* 1(2): 287–303.

Damasio, A. (1994) *Descartes Error: Emotion, Reason, and the Human Brain*, New York: Putnam.

Day, C. (1998) *Developing Teachers: The Challenges of Lifelong Learning?*, London: Falmer Press.

Delpit, L. (1993) *Other People's Children: Cultural Conflict in the Classroom*, New York: The New Press.
Denzin, N. (1984) *On Understanding Emotion*, San Francisco: Jossey-Bass.
Eisner, E. (1986) 'The primary experience and the politics of method', *Educational Researcher* 17(5): 15–20.
Elbaz, F. (1993) 'Attentiveness, and caring for difference: the moral voice in teaching', *Teaching and Teacher Education*, 8(5–6): 421–32.
Elkind, D. (1997) 'Schooling in the postmodern world', in A. Hargreaves (ed.), *Rethinking educational change with heart and mind*, 1997 ASCD Yearbook. Alexandria, VA: Association for Supervision and Curriculum Development.
Fineman, S. (ed.) (1993) 'Organizations as emotional arenas', in *Emotions in Organizations*, London: Sage Publishing.
Fried, R. (1995) *The Passionate Teacher*, Boston: Bacon Press.
Friedson, E. (1994) *Professionalism Reborn*. Chicago: University of Chicago Press.
Fullan, M. (1997) *What's Worth Fighting For in the Principalship*? Toronto: Elementary Teachers Federation of Ontario.
—— (1999) *Change Forces: The Sequel*, London and Philadelphia: Falmer Press.
Goleman, D. (1995) *Emotional Intelligence*, New York: Bantam Books.
—— (1998) *Working with Emotional Intelligence*, New York: Bantam Books.
Grumet, M. (1988) *Bitter Milk: Women and Teaching*, Amherst: University of Massachusetts.
Hargreaves, A. (1994) *Changing Teachers, Changing Times: Teachers' Work Culture in the Postmodern Age*, London: Cassells and New York: Teachers' College Press.
—— (1999) 'The psychic rewards (and annoyances) of classroom teaching', in M. Hammersley (ed.) *Researching School Experience: Ethnographic Studies of Teaching and Learning*, London and New York: Falmer Press.
Hargreaves, A. and Fullan, M. (1998) *What's Worth Fighting For Out There*? Toronto: Elementary Teachers' Federation of Ontario and New York: Teachers' College Press.
Hargreaves, A. and Goodson, I. (1996) 'Teachers' professional lives: aspirations and actualities', in I. Goodson and A. Hargreaves (eds) *Teachers' Professional Lives*. New York: Falmer Press.
Hochschild, A. R. (1983) *The Managed Heart: The Commercialization of Human Feeling*, Berkeley: University of California Press.
Hochschild, A. R. (1997) *The Time Bind*, New York: Metropolitan Books.
James, W. (1917). *Selected Papers in Philosophy*, London: J. M. Dent and Sons.
Jeffrey, B. and Woods, P. (1996) 'Feeling deprofessionalized: the social construction of emotions during an OFSTED inspection', *Cambridge Journal of Education* 126(3): 235–343.
Johnson, T. (1972) *Professions and Power*, London: Macmillan.
Kemper, T. K. (1995) 'Sociological models in the explanation of emotions', in M. Lewis and J. Haviland (eds.) *Handbook of Emotions*, London and New York: Guilford Press.
Kitayama, S. and Marcus, H. R. (1994) 'The cultural construction of self and emotions: implications for social behaviour', in S. Kitayama and H. R. Marcus (eds.) *Emotion and Culture: Empirical Studies of Mutual Influence*, Portland, OR: Book News, Inc.
Larson, M. S. (1977) *The Rise of Professionalism*, Berkeley: University of California Press.
Lee, W. O. (1996) 'The cultural context for Chinese learners: conceptions of learning in the Confucian tradition', in D. A. Watkins and J. B. Biggs (eds.) *The Chinese Learner: Cultural, Psychological and Contextual Influences*, Melbourne: Comparative Education Research Centre, Hong Kong Faculty of Education, Hong Kong and Australian Council for Educational Research.

Levin, B. and Riffel, A. J. (1997) *Schools and the Changing World*, London: Falmer Press.
Lindblad, S. and Prieto, H. (1992) 'Schools experiences and teacher socialization: a longitudinal study of pupils who grew up to be teachers', *Teaching and Teacher Education* 8(5/6): 465–70.
Maurer, R. (1996) *Beyond the Wall of Resistance*, Austin, TX: Bard Books.
Mortimore, P., Sammons, P., Stoll, L. *et al.* (1988) *School Matters: The Junior Years*, Somerset: Open Books.
Nias, J. (1991) 'Changing times, changing identities: grieving for a lost self', in R. G. Burgess (ed.) *Educational Research and Evaluation: For Policy and Practice*, London: Falmer Press.
—— (1999) 'Teachers' moral purposes: stress, vulnerability, and strength', in Roland Vandenberghe and A. Michael Huberman (eds.) *Understanding and Preventing Teacher Burnout A Sourcebook of International Research and Practice*, New York: Cambridge University Press.
Noddings, N. (1992) *The Challenge to Care in Schools*, New York: Teachers' College Press.
Oatley, K. (1991) *Best Laid Schemes: The Psychology of Emotions*, Cambridge: Cambridge University Press.
Oatley, K. and Jenkins, J. (1996) *Understanding Emotions*, Cambridge, MA: Blackwell.
Organization for Economic Cooperation and Development (1998) *Education at a Glance*, Paris, France.
Popkewitz, T. S. (1998) *Struggling for the Soul: The Politics of Schooling and the Construction of the Teacher*, New York: Teachers' College Press.
Shields, R. (1991) *Places on the Margin: Alternative Geographies of Modernity*, London: Routledge.
Sizer, T. (1992) *Horace's School: Redesigning the American High School*, Boston: Houghlin Mifflin Co.
Stallybrass, P. and White, A. (1986) *The Poetics and Politics of Transgression*, London: Methuen.
Stenross, B. and Kleinman, S. (1989) 'The highs and lows of emotional labour: detectives' encounters with criminals and victims', *Journal of Contemporary Ethnography* 17(4): 435–52.
van Manen, M. (1995). *The Tact of Teaching: The Meaning of Pedagogical Thoughtfulness*, London, Ontario: Althouse Press.
Vincent, C. and Warren, S. (1998) 'Becoming a "better" parent? Motherhood, education and transition', *British Journal of Sociology of Education*, 19(2): 177–93.
Waller, W. (1932) *The Sociology of Teaching*, New York: Russell and Russell Press.
Woods, P., Jeffrey, B., Troman, G. and Boyle, M. (1997) *Restructuring Schools, Reconstructing Teachers*, Buckingham: Open University Press.

Chapter 2

An investigation into the pedagogical identity of the teacher

Han A. Leeferink and Cees A. Klaassen

Introduction

The instillation of values and norms and the fostering of citizenship have been the topics at the top of the political and social agendas of many countries in the last years. In addition to the formative task of the family, it is also expected that schools contribute to the development of norms, values, and citizenship (Bottery, 1990; Goodlad *et al.*, 1990; Klaassen 1996a).

Values and norms form a complex field of personal existentialism, of principles that give people's life and community significance (values), and rules which regulate interaction between people (norms). In the past, public debate about the task of education in this matter has regularly cropped up in times of moral crises and disappeared again for a certain time.

The importance of the pedagogical task of the school appears to be increasing as a result of the processes of modernization (Tom, 1984; Van Maanen, 1991; Klaassen, 1996b,c). Many people have loosened themselves from social class, family, marriage, employment, politics, the church, and the neighbourhood (Beck, 1992). In addition, it is frequently pointed out that, as a result of various social developments (e.g., combined motherhood–employment, an increasing number of single-parent families), parents are spending less time on child rearing than before and children are spending increasingly more time outside the family.

In his book, *Building Community in Schools*, Sergiovanni (1994) suggests how teachers, parents, and school administrators can contribute to the development of a 'community of mind' with shared values and opinions on the school. The school community should, in the opinion of Sergiovanni, be rebuilt into a community in which moral obligations, trust, and communal behaviour replace the business, contractual, and formal organizational approach that currently predominates. Schools must take on more of the characteristics of a true community (Lickona, 1988; Merz and Furman, 1997). Safe schools where children feel secure and at home are also advocated (Lewis *et al.*, 1996). 'Community formation' is said to be critical for the achievement, personal functioning (i.e., greater well-being), and social participation (i.e., less absenteeism, greater social skills) of students (Bryk and Driscoll, 1988; Mortimore *et al.*, 1988). Moreover, the relation of the school and the social surroundings should be strengthened (Clarke-Fowler and Klebs-Corley, 1996). A case is indeed increasingly being made for a 'community school' with anchors in the local community (Adler and Gardner, 1994). Parents and school must work together to raise moral children (Berreth and Berman, 1997).

In the discussion of the pedagogical task of the school, considerable importance is attached to the specific role of the teacher (Tom, 1984; van Maanen, 1991). In relation to the question of the significance for the teacher for the development of students' norms and values, it is important to determine teachers' perceptions of their pedagogical professionality and the goals of child rearing. It is important to consider how teachers think about the distribution of tasks between the school and family. Consideration of the pedagogical co-operation between the parents and the school is also important to consider.

The objectives of child rearing

The objectives of child rearing can be taken to be the general background criteria used by teachers to make choices and guide their behaviour. In the literature, a few hypotheses have been put forth with regard to the problematic relation between parents and teachers when it comes to joint child-rearing responsibility. From research by Cullingford (1984), it appears that parents expect the school primarily to prepare their child for employment and concentrate on the acquisition of good manners. In contrast, teachers tend to attach more importance to the development of individual autonomy and social objectives. Teachers are of the opinion that the teaching of good manners is a task for parents. Goodlad (1984) had also concluded that, in contrast to teachers, parents place more emphasis on the professional as opposed to personal development of children. According to Kohn (1969), a distinction can be made between two fundamental and mutually exclusive value orientations with regard to child rearing: self-determination versus conformity. This deeper distinction underlies apparently very different value orientations. In addition to the two value orientations of self-determination and conformity, attention will also be paid to opinions on social sensitivity.

In discussions pertaining to the pedagogical task of the school, considerable attention has been paid to the social aspects of child rearing. It is thus interesting in this connection to examine the extent to which an orientation towards self-determination is accompanied by an orientation towards more social goals. Independent students need not be socially sensitive students. To overcome a more egoistic form of self-determination in the present study, it was decided to include the category of social sensitivity. A fourth category of child-rearing objectives pertains to skills or the competence to think and communicate about values and norms. In various methods of value discourse, attention to such skills is assumed to be important (Oser, 1994; Power *et al.*, 1989; Paul, 1992). A final category of child-rearing objectives examined in the present research is the acquisition of such virtues as those propagated by proponents of 'character' education (Rusnak, 1998; DeRoche and Williams, 1998). This approach is concerned with developing virtue. The proponents of character education think that education should not engage students in complex moral dilemma's such as in Kohlberg's moral reasoning approach, but try to further the cause of virtue by positioning the teacher as moral authority (Lockwood, 1997).

Pedagogical attunement

Yet another basic concept utilized in the present research is pedagogical attunement (i.e., the relation between the school and parents). The importance of this relation lies in the assumption that the attunement of ideas with regard to child rearing requires regular contact between parents and teachers on the issue (Epstein *et al.*, 1997). In research concerned with the relation between parents and school, attention is particularly paid to the activities that schools expect of parents and much less to the attempts on the part of the schools to improve the parent–school relation. The degree of participation by parents in school activities is frequently employed to categorize parents as involved or not involved (Vandegrift and Greene, 1992). Research into the minimal participation of parents from lower social classes in school activities indicates a variety of reasons that underlie the phenomenon. Important causes of the observed discrepancy are the gap between the expectations of the school and the possibilities on the part of the parents to meet these expectations, the educational experiences of the parents themselves, status differences between the parents and the teachers, limited motivation for involvement, lack of time, and so forth (Harrold, 1993). Research on the involvement of parents typically pertains to a wide variety of activities in which the parents can participate: hands-on assistance, administrative–technical help, directly educational activities, and educational steering activities. This sequence is also often adopted as the starting point to motivate parents via lower forms of participation (hands-on assistance) to higher forms of participation (educational steering activities). The problem is that all kinds of activities are expected of parents without mutual attunement. It is necessary, therefore, to examine the activities that schools develop to involve parents in the school and, in particular, meetings and thinking with regard to child rearing (i.e. educational steering activities). In this light, it is also important to examine the explanations offered by the teachers themselves for the lack of participation of parents in school activities and how the teachers interact with parents who are rarely or completely not involved in the school.

Framed against the above perspectives, the research reported in this chapter raises two central questions:

1 What are teachers' perceptions of the aims of child rearing and the distribution of tasks between the school and family?
2 What are teachers' expectations with regard to pedagogical attunement?

Quantitative and qualitative research methods

Respondents

A total of fifty-three teachers of children between 7 and 11 years of age participated in the present study. The research provides a broad picture of the various opinions of teachers with regard to the content (objectives) and attunement problems (family–school relations). With this aim in mind, it was deliberately decided to select a small number of schools (six) for study.

Design and variables

A combination of quantitative and qualitative research methods were utilized. First, the opinions of teachers with regard to the objectives of child rearing and pedagogical attunement were measured via the administration of a questionnaire in six schools. Second, the results of the questionnaire were explored in greater detail by undertaking group interviews with a select sample of teachers in all of the six schools.

The questionnaire

The questionnaire solicited the opinions of the teachers with regard to the objectives of child rearing and pedagogical attunement. The variables concerned with the aims of child rearing were operationalized as follows: *self-determination*: building self-confidence; taking responsibility; entertaining one's own opinion; perseverance; a desire to understand things, curiosity; independence; autonomy; *conformity*: obedience, listening to adults; sensitivity to order and discipline; adapting to rules and other views; respect for others; good manners; *social sensitivity*: helpfulness; respect for those who think differently; concern for the happiness and pain of others; consideration for others; non-discrimination of others; tolerance; solidarity with others; *skills*: be open to the opinions of others; think critically; promote one's opinions; deal with critique; *virtues*: honesty; justice; self-discipline; reliability; a sense of duty. The teachers were asked about the extent to which they considered these objectives important for child rearing at school or in the family. The items were measured with the aid of a five-point scale (not important, a little important, neither important/unimportant, quite important, very important). With regard to the operationalizing of the concept of pedagogical attunement, it was decided to formulate the items with respect to content aspects (objectives, measures), communicate aspects (providing information, listening) and pedagogical aspects (behaviour, values). A number of different statements were than presented to the respondents. The items were also measured with the aid of a five-point scale (disagree completely, disagree somewhat, do not agree/disagree, agree somewhat, agree completely). The response of the teachers was quite satisfactory. More than 75 per cent of the teachers (i.e., fifty-three teachers) participated in the questionnaire research. Of the participating teachers, 69.5 per cent were female and 30.2 per cent were male.

The group interviews

Group interviews were undertaken with teachers in all of the schools to gain greater insight into the results of the questionnaire. Considerable attention was paid to clarifying the manner in which the teachers interpreted the notions employed within the questionnaire. In all of the schools, interviews were undertaken with a group of six teachers in the autumn of 1997. A prerequisite for participation in the group interview was completion of the questionnaire.

Analysis

The questionnaire data were examined using factor and descriptive analysis. For the analysis of the group interviews, the audio recordings were fully transcribed. The answers to all of the questions posed as part of the protocol were then categorized into the relevant rubric. For purposes of reliability, all of the transcribed texts were analyzed by two researchers and agreement sought where discrepancies occurred.

Quantitative research results

The objectives of child rearing

In the questionnaire, the opinions of the teachers regarding the objectives of child rearing were measured by way of three rubrics: (1) the importance generally attached by teachers to a specific child-rearing objective; (2) the attention to be paid to a specific child-rearing objective at home; and (3) the attention to be paid to a specific child-rearing objective at school. Factor analyses revealed two factors for each rubric.[1] The factors explained 40.2, 43.5, and 43.9 per cent of the variance from the general, home and school rubrics, respectively. The interpretation of the factor solutions appeared to be the same for the different rubrics. (The results for only the general rubric are therefore presented in Table 2.1.) The first factor consistently reflects a pattern of opinion concerned with self-determination and social sensitivity. The second factor consistently refers to aspects of obedience and conformity.

Pedagogical attunement

Factor analyses produced two factors, which together explained 49.3 per cent of the variance. Given that the factors highly correlated (0.65) after oblimin rotation, the factor matrix following such rotation was utilized in further analyses. The factors can be described as follows. The first factor pertains to the accessibility of the school and the teachers for parents and the general information provided by the school and teachers (Table 2.2). This factor is therefore referred to as service institution. The second factor specifically concerns the contact that the school has and maintains with the parents with regard to values, norms, and other child-rearing matters. This factor is therefore referred to as communication on child rearing.

To determine the internal consistency of the questionnaire scales, reliability analyses were undertaken. For each scale, a scale score was calculated in the form of an average item score. In Table 2.3, the reliability estimates (Cronbach's Alpha) for the scales related to the rubrics of general, home, school and pedagogical attunement are reported. All of the scales appear to be reliable.

Table 2.1. Varimax-rotated factor matrix, communality (h2), and percentage variance explained for the General Child-Rearing rubric.

Child-rearing objective	*f1*	*f2*	h2
General			
Justice	0.52	0.16	0.30
Respect for those who think differently	0.67	0.15	0.47
Taking others into consideration	0.57	0.26	0.40
Non-discrimination	0.61	0.16	0.40
Tolerance	0.62	0.27	0.46
Solidarity with others	0.54	0.31	0.39
Openness to the opinions of others	0.61	0.11	0.38
Critical thinking	0.61	−0.07	0.38
Capacity to justify one's own opinion	0.64	−0.03	0.41
Able to handle critique	0.57	0.24	0.39
Carrying responsibility	0.52	0.17	0.30
Have one's own opinion	0.53	0.15	0.30
Desire to know why certain things occur, inquisitiveness	0.50	0.16	0.28
Independent thinking and behaviour	0.54	0.07	0.30
Obedient, listens to adults	0.04	0.72	0.52
Feeling for discipline and order	0.16	0.65	0.45
Adapt to applicable rules and opinions	0.14	0.73	0.56
Respect for your elders	0.15	0.74	0.57
Having good manners	0.21	0.59	0.39
% Explained variance	30.3	9.8	40.2

Descriptive statistics

In Table 2.4, the descriptive statistics for each of the scales are presented. Most striking is that the teachers consider all of the child-rearing objectives to be important. At home and school, attention should be paid to the development of independence, social sensitivity and more conformity-directed objectives. The respondents appear to be satisfied with the school as a service institution (score: 4.59). With regard to communication on child rearing, however, teachers are less satisfied (score: 3.92).

Qualitative research results

Group interviews

As already mentioned, a protocol for the group interviews with the teachers was developed on the basis of the questionnaire results. The following questions were posed: Why do you think attention to self-determination and social sensitivity are important? What do the notions of self-determination

Table 2.2 Factor matrix following oblimin rotation (pattern matrix); communality (h2) and percentages explained variance for the rubric pedagogical attunement.

Pedagogical attunement	*f1*	*f2*	*h2*
Parents are adequately informed with regard to practical matters	0.43	0.13	0.27
The teacher is prepared to listen to parents	0 .92	−0.17	0.68
If problems occur at school, consultation is possible	0.52	0.21	0.46
Parents are not taken seriously by the school	−0.47	0.10	0.29
The school provides parents with little information on the work attitude of their child	−0.34	0.15	0.20
The school administration is accessible	0.68	0.07	0.52
The school administration is prepared to listen to parents	0.69	0.13	0.62
I'm very accessible	0 .91	−0.14	0.69
Parents can participate in discussions of value and norm questions	0.04	0.72	0.57
I always contact parents in cases of a problem in time	0.22	0.56	0.52
Parents can influence the child-rearing ideas of the school	−0.01	0.65	0.41
Parents are adequately informed with regard to content matters (objectives, manner of working)	0.13	0.64	0.54
Parents are adequately informed about the values and norms that the school considers important	−0.08	0.84	0.64
% Explained variance	41.9	7.4	49.3

Table 2.3 Reliability estimates (Cronbach's Alpha) for scales representing the opinions of teachers with regard to the objectives of child rearing and pedagogical attunement (N=328).

Category	*Number of items*	*Cronbach's Alpha*
Child-rearing objectives		
Self-determination/social sensitivity	14	0.8864
Conformity	5	0.8293
Child-rearing objectives Home		
Self-determination/social sensitivity	16	0.9185
Conformity	5	0.8289
Child-rearing objectives School		
Self-determination/social sensitivity	14	0.9066
Conformity	5	0.8246
Pedagogical attunement		
Service institution	8	0.8603
Communication with regard to child rearing	5	0.8484

and social sensitivity mean? Do you think it is logical for self-determination and social sensitivity to go together? What is the importance and meaning of the notion of conformity? What is the distribution of tasks between parents and school in the domain of child rearing? Are you satisfied with this distribution of tasks? Why are you less satisfied with communication on child rearing? Are parents sufficiently informed about the child-rearing ideas of the school? How could communication on child rearing be improved?

Objectives of child rearing and distribution of tasks

Teachers consider attention to the development of independence and social sensitivity both at home and at school to be very important. Educational and professional demands make the realization of these objectives a necessity in the eyes of teachers. A society that is continually getting harder and thereby demands that you stand up for yourself is also continually mentioned: 'You have to take a stand . . . certainly in this society. Things are getting so hard if you look around you. A kid has to stand up for himself 'cause if he doesn't he ends up in the middle of nowhere.' In addition, the realization of the aforementioned child-rearing objectives is considered important for the functioning of children at school, allowing all kinds of group activities to run effectively and for the personal development of the child.

When asked about the meaning of the notion self-determination, teachers think of making one's own decisions, solving problems, performing tasks independently, expressing one's opinion, and thinking critically. When asked about the meaning of the notion of social sensitivity, consideration for others and helping one another are mentioned in particular. Another qualification involves the embedding of the notion of self-determination within a particular

Table 2.4 Descriptive statistics for opinions on the objectives of child rearing and pedagogical attunement for teachers.

	Teacher n=47	
Source	*mean*	*sd*
Objectives		
Self-determination/social-sensitivity (G)	4.63	0.32
Conformity (G)	4.18	0.73
Self-determination/social-sensitivity (H)	4.57	0.37
Conformity (H)	4.28	0.72
Self-determination/social-sensitivity (S)	4.52	0.39
Conformity (S)	4.03	0.74
Pedagogical attunement		
Service institution	4.59	0.34
Child-rearing communication	3.92	0.45

social context. According to many teachers, self-determination is primarily aimed at the development of the personality of the child in current times with some room for social sensitivity while the notion had a much more individualistic reading in the sixties.

Teachers are also of the opinion that such notions as self-determination and social sensitivity cannot be considered independent of each other. They agree that the development of independence without some social sensitivity can lead to an egoistic form of individualism: 'Independence alone threatens to become something egoistic. You can be independent but you have to have a certain social feeling because you simply have to do things together at times.' Conversely, it is argued that the development of social sensitivity without attention to independence can lead to submissive behaviour and the neglect of one's own interests. 'When only social sensitivity is aspired to, you get people who completely ignore their own self-worth.' The meaning of the notion of social sensitivity should not, in the opinion of teachers, be construed as being blindly oriented towards the group.

In addition to these objectives, teachers emphasized the importance of attention at both home and school to more conformist objectives. The motives behind this lie in the battle against the indifference and survival mentality that prevail in the current chaotic and complex society. Most teachers consider conformity a 'condition' for functioning in society in general and in the school and family in particular. Rules, agreements, and good manners are needed to live together. Conformity is similarly seen as a prerequisite for the personal development and social behavior of students: 'You cannot have respect for another or express such respect without good manners. You are also more quickly pushed aside in a group, I think, when you behave rudely or without manners. In other words, it is good to have good manners.' The notion of conformity is interpreted as the provision of structure and creation of a peaceful and secure environment in which the formulation of rules, making of concrete agreements with children and consistent behaviour on the part of teachers are taken to be of great importance.

Of particular importance for pedagogical attunement are the opinions of the teachers with regard to the distribution of tasks in the area of child rearing, values, and norms. According to many teachers, a strict division does not exist between the two. The child-rearing role of the school is generally viewed as an extension of the child-rearing role of the parents or caregivers. The child-rearing tasks overlap and should, according to teachers, be attuned as much as possible to each other. The school and the parents should also supplement each other whenever and wherever necessary. Teachers are, nevertheless, of the opinion that the primary responsibility for child rearing lies with the parents.

The interviews with the teachers showed them to be quite critical of the manner in which parents raise their children. Teachers are of the opinion that parents provide their children with too little structure and impose insufficient demands on their children: 'A general experience for me is that children from families where real rules dominate and life is very secure, very structured and very pleasant but five o'-clock is five o'-clock tend to get along better and easier with other children than children who are left to decide for themselves. The latter miss the security needed as a base for functioning.' Teachers thus plead for greater peace in the family (i.e. children are saddled with too many social obligations according to teachers) and more consistent behaviour on the part of the parents when rules are broken or agreements are not met. A consequence of such child-rearing behaviour is, according to teachers, a shift of responsibility from the family to the school. According to teachers, parents brush their child-rearing responsibilities aside too easily and currently invest insufficient time in the rearing of their own children. The school is thus forced to invest extra time in child-rearing tasks to compensate for various shortcomings. 'I think we are more and more busy with child-rearing objectives that are obviously part of our task but not to the degree that we are now sometimes saddled with. I consider learning to listen and being motivated while you work to be child-rearing objectives as well. We have to fight much harder now to get children to a certain point. They don't get this from home. Some of them do, of course, but many of them don't.'

Pedagogical attunement

Parents are informed of school activities and expectations through information booklets, newsletters and information evenings as well as through parent evenings, some of which are organized around specific topics. The results of the group interviews show teachers to be generally happy with this aspect of the pedagogical attunement. A complaint shared by teachers concerns a particular group of parents.

The questionnaire showed teachers to be less satisfied with the relationship between parents and school when it comes to communication on child-rearing tasks. According to many teachers, child rearing is only an issue when a concrete problem presents itself (e.g., disagreements, bullying); parents are generally not aware of the child-rearing ideas of the school itself. 'I think that parents don't know how we work. I sometimes notice this in conversations. They are suddenly much more enthusiastic when they know how we are working with the children, although this depends on the individual parrents.' Most schools also lack a useful child-rearing policy. Two reasons for the lack of communication were presented in the group interviews. First, the emotionally charged nature of the topic, which gives a discussion on the topic a threatening character. 'Child rearing has certainly become a subject of discussion over the last years but as a failure in the eyes of some if one was to be honest: yeah, I have a problem with my child and wonder what I should do.' In addition to this, an (unconscious) presupposition exists on the part of teachers that the communication of information sufficiently meets the needs of parents. This appears to be a misconception in most cases. There is generally too little consultation. Teachers know virtually nothing about what the parents think of the child rearing at school. Teachers also make very little effort to understand the real reasons why parents are not more involved in the activities and policies of the school.

Conclusions

Teachers consider all of the child-rearing objectives to be important. At home and school, attention should be paid to- the development of independence, critical thinking, social sensitivity and more conformity-directed objectives. The interviews strongly suggest that the objectives of self-determination and social sensitivity are not independent of each other. Self-determination without social sensitivity can lead to an egoistic form of individualism. In the child-rearing expectation of teachers, the citizenship ideal of autonomy appears to be attached by definition to the carrying of social responsibility. The interviews indicate that teachers consider attention to conformist objectives particularly important to combat currently prevailing indifference in our complex society. The notion of conformity is not associated with (authoritarian) behaviour aimed at the creation of submissive behaviour. Rather, it appears that teachers consider the child-rearing objective of conformity to be a prerequisite for functioning in society, the family, and the school. Attention to conformity is also considered a prerequisite for the personal development and social functioning of the child.

Teachers believe that parents neglect attention to conformist ideas while this is partly a consquence of inadequate communication between parents and schools when it comes to child-rearing issues. Parents generally know too little about the child-rearing ideas of the school; teachers know virtually nothing about the child-rearing ideas of the parents. Child rearing is only an issue when a concrete problem presents itself. As a consequence, teachers form images of parents that are far removed from actual child-rearing practice. It is obvious that such images do not contribute to adequate pedagogical attunement between school and family.

How should the results now be evaluated? It is clear that no single procedure exists to realize adequate pedagogical attunement between school and family. Teaching and child rearing are much too complicated for this. Various studies have shown that involvement on the part of parents positively influences the general well-being and school achievement of students.

However, in a climate where there are increasing and often conflicting demands on teachers, to the point of overload, time for better and more frequent communication between home and school is not propitious. This situation is exacerbated by present-day discussions with regard to school effectiveness that, in turn, influences parents in their choice of school. In research concerned with the effective school, the cognitive achievements of students stand central. The educational learning process is thereby reduced to the pursuit of objectively measurable and comparable knowledge goals. Such a vision of education is particularly welcome, moreover, in these times with an emphasis on productivity, efficiency, and return. In the discussion of school selection motives, consideration of parents as consumers on the educational market is also increasingly the case. Parents are continually confronted with the question of which criteria should be used to select a school for their children. To lend parents a helping hand, the different research directions are often now connected to each other in social science and public discussions. The achievement performances of schools are presented in guidebooks to enable parents to make a responsible choice on the basis of objectively determined information. Once again, the information pertains to cognitive achievements only of students in different schools. The evaluation of schools on the basis of these criteria only constitutes a very limited approach to the problem (Rose, 1995; Bryk, 1988; Tesconi, 1995; Slee *et al.*, 1998; Riley and Nutall, 1994). In such an approach, the social, moral, aesthetic, and affective aims of education are continually marginalized. One possible consequence is that schools direct themselves at the cognitive aspects of the educational process because they are evaluated in these terms. In other words; if attention to the non-cognitive aims of education is not appreciated, then teachers will not invest much time or energy in the establishment of a child-rearing dialogue with parents.

Another dimension of this issue concerns the specific knowledge, skills, and attitudes that teachers require to conduct a well-structured dialogue with parents on the issue of child rearing. Research has shown traditional forms of participation (information evenings, report consultations, parent nights) to be generally characterized by a one-sided transfer of information from the school in the direction of the parents. For the establishment and maintenance of a dialogue between the school and parents on the topic of child rearing, it is more important to place the accent on the mutual exchange of information and experiences. To realize this, traditional forms of participation should be critically examined and alternative possibilities carefully considered. Of central importance, of course, is the creation of a climate in which both parents and teachers feel free to talk about their visions on child rearing. Research shows communication on child rearing to be experienced by many teachers as emotionally charged and therefore silent. Familiar relations must be created for a dialogue on the topic of child rearing to be successful. Many teachers may experience feelings of impotence because they are insufficiently qualified for the realization of such initiatives. In addition to this, many teachers may experience a discussion with regard to pedagogical attunement as a clear threat to their pedagogical autonomy. Nevertheless, successful pedagogical attunement between school and family means that teachers must account for their pedagogical practices much more than before. Schools are not very interested in critiques of their policies (Fine, 1993). Communication on such a sensitive topic as child rearing is possible only when all of the parties concerned consider that their perspectives and concerns are being taken seriously.

To get values' education at school and the pedagogical attunement between schools and families sufficiently off the ground, research will have to concentrated on school activities intended to stimulate the pursuit of the social, emotional, affective, and esthetic objectives of education. It will also be interesting to consider the extent to which attention to the non-cognitive aims of education affect the well-being and non-cognitive development of students. The possible connections between the non-cognitive and cognitive achievements of students should also be examined in future research. Such research should also address the different organizational and professional facets of school practice that may hinder communication within the school with regard to child-rearing issues. Finally, there is need to investigate how teachers can increase their competence and confidence to establish and maintain a dialogue with the external school environment.

Notes

1 To examine the underlying dimensions and reliability of the questionnaire *Child rearing at home and at school*, factor analyses were undertaken with the correlation matrices as the starting point with pairwise deletion. Given that different theoretical models could be distinguished for each rubric, use was made of iterative factor analysis. For which factor a clear dip in the eigenvalues if encountered is repeatedly examined. To guarantee the explanatory power of the factors, the following rule of thumb was followed: the factors should have an eigenvalue from the reduced correlation matrix of approximately 1.0. Deviation from this is only allowed if the interpretability of the factors is at issue. The interpretations of the factor loadings are based on the factor matrix after orthogonal rotation (Varimax) unless the factors highly correlate (higher than 0.50). In that case, use is made of the factor matrix follow oblique rotation. As soon as a factor intercorrelation was very high, it was useful to re-examine the factor solution. In addition in the determination of the best factor solution, attention was paid to the percentage of the variance explained. To assign the items to a particular factor, a loading of at least 0.40 on the relevant factor was required along with considerable discriminant validity. Items loading less than 0.40 but with considerable discriminant validity could, nevertheless, be assigned to the relevant factor. With respect to the communality values for the items: items loading lower than 0.15 were removed in principle. In cases of doubt, the item was kept and the extent to which it contributed to the reliability of the scale to be constructed was examined.

2 The research is part of a broader research-project in which parents participated also. The observed factor structure was based on the total group with both parents and teachers represented. For every rubric, the extent to which the factor structure held for the group of parents and the group of teachers independently was also examined. This consistently appeared to be the case. The different tables show the factor structures after removal of those items with an overly low discriminant and/or convergent validity.

References

Adler, L. and Gardner, S. (eds) (1994) *The Politics of Linking Schools and Social Services*, Bristol: Falmer Press.

Beck, U. (1992) *Risk Society. Towards a New Modernity*, London: Sage.

Berreth, D. and Berman, S. (1997) 'The moral dimensions of schools', *Educational Leadership* 54(8): 24–7.

Bottery, M. (1990) *The Morality of the School*, London: Cassell.

Bryk, A. (1988) 'Musings on the moral life of schools', *American Journal of Education* 96: 256–90.

Bryk, A. and Driscoll, M. (1988) *The School as Community: Theoretical Foundations, Contextual Influences, and Consequences for Students and Teachers*, Madison, WI: National Center on Effective Secondary Schools.

Clarke-Fowler, R. and Klebs-Corley, K. (1996) 'Linking families, building community', *Educational Leadership* 53(7): 24–6.

Cullingford, C. (1984) 'The battle for the schools: attitudes of parents and teachers towards education', *Educational Studies* 10(2): 113–9.

DeRoche, E. and Williams, M. (1998) *Educating Hearts and Minds. A Comprehensive Character Education Framework*, Thousand Oaks, CA: Corwin Press.

Eccles, J. S. and Harold, R. D. (1993) 'Parent-school involvement during the early adolescent years', *Teachers College Record* 94: 568–87.

Epstein, J., Coates, L., Salinas, K. C., Sanders, M. and Simon B. (1997) *School, Family and Community Partnerships*, Thousand Oaks, CA: Corwin Press.

Fine, M. (1993) '(Ap)parent involvement: reflections on parents, power, and urban public schools', *Teacher College Record* 94: 682–710.

Goodlad, J. I. (1984) *A Place Called School: Perspectives for the Future*, New York: McGraw-Hill.

Goodlad, J., Soder, R. and Sirotnik, K. (eds.) (1990) *The Moral Dimensions of Teaching*, San Francisco: Jossey-Bass.

Klaassen, C. (1996a) 'Socialization for moral democracy', in R. Farnen, H. Dekker, D. German and R. Meyenberg (eds) *Democracy, Socialization, and Conflicting Loyalties in East and West*, New York: Macmillan, pp. 163–172.

—— (1996b) 'Explicit and Implicit Values Education and the Crisis in Postmodern Society', in M. Valente (ed.) *Teacher Training and Values Education*, Lisboa: Universidade de Lisboa, pp. 153–164.

—— (1996c) 'Education and Citizenship in a Post-Welfare State', *Curriculum* 17(2): 62–74.

Kohn, M. (1969) *Class and Conformity, A Study in Values,* Homewood IL:, Dorsey Press.

Lewis, C., Schaps, E. and Watson, M. (1996) 'The caring classroom's academic edge', *Educational Leadership* 54(1): 16–21.

Lickona, Th. (1988) 'How parents and schools can work together to raise moral children', *Educational Leadership* 45(8): 36–8.

Merz, C. and Furman, G. (1997) *Community and Schools. Promise and Paradox*, New York: Teachers College Press.

Mortimore, P., Sammons, P. Stoll, L. Lewis. D. and Ecob, R. (1988) *School Matters: The Junior Years*, Somerset: Open Books.

Oser, F. K. (1994) 'Moral perspectives on teaching', *Review of research in Education* 20: 57–129.

Paul, R. W. (1992) *Critical Thinking: What Every Person Needs to Survive in a Rapidly Changing World*, Santa Rosa, CA: Foundation for Critical Thinking.

Power, F., Higgens, A. and Kohlberg, L. (1989) *Lawrence Kohlberg's Approach to Moral Education*, New York: Columbia University Press.

Riley, K and Nuttall, D. (eds.) (1994) *Measuring Quality: Education Indicators–United Kingdom and International Perspectives*, London: Falmer Press.

Rose, M. (1995) *Possible Lives – The Promise of Public Education in America*, New York: Penguin Books.

Rusnak, T. (ed.) (1998) *An Integrated Approach to Character Education*, Thousand Oaks, CA: Corwin Press.

Riley, K. and Nuttall, D. (eds) (1994) *Measuring Quality: Education Indicators–United Kingdom and International Perspectives*, London: Falmer Press.

Sergiovanni, Th. (1994) *Building Community in Schools*, San Francisco: Jossey-Bass.

Slee, R., Weiner, G. and Tomlinson, S. (eds.) (1998) *School Effectiveness for Whom?,* New York: Falmer Press.

Tesconi, Ch. (1995) 'Good schools', in *The Policy Environment Perspective*, Cresskill, NJ, Hampton Press.

Tom, A. R. (1984) *Teaching as a Moral Craft*, New York: Longmans.

Vandegrift, J. and Greene, A. (1992) 'Rethinking parent involvement', *Educational Leadership* 50(1): 57–9.

van Maanen, M. (1991) *The Tact of Teaching: The Meaning of Pedagogical Thoughtfulness*, Albany, NY: Suny Press.

Chapter 3

Educational research and teacher development

From ivory tower to tower of Babel

Jonathan Neufeld and Michael Kompf

> In any field of study not yet reduced (or elevated) to the status of a genuine science, thought remains the captive of the linguistic mode in which it seeks to grasp the outline of objects inhabiting its field of perception.
>
> White, 1973, p. xi

Introduction

In this chapter, we identify and critique a linguistic mode that is found in educational research pertaining to teacher education. We identify it as 'Aristotelian', and argue that its principles and methods captivate researchers. This linguistic mode has become very seductive, as it promotes the unification of teachers' consciousness with the objective world of their practical actions. The attraction to this mode is inspired by a drive to reduce the status of teachers' development to the level of a rational science. Important aspects of this academic project include the privileging of certain theories of language. Through a brief historical sketch, we show how figurative speech has been suppressed in favour of clear, rational explanation. This historical quest for rational, logical clarity is maintained in analyses of teacher education. We explain by outlining a theoretical argument on metaphor and dialectical reasoning before concluding with an alternative perspective rooted in Nietzsche. His perspective may offer the possibility of theorizing practice without relying upon theoretical mediation either of metaphor or of the confining path of dialectical reasoning.

The figurative language of the ivory tower

In his pioneering work, Elliott (1984) observed how several metaphors for education (i.e. preparation, initiation, liberation, and guidance) originate in common cultural discourse. Education may be construed as: (1) preparation (for life, work, war, etc.); (2) initiation (e.g. into a community; see also Peters, 1965; Oakeshott, 1975); (3) liberation (from alienation or cultural domination; see also Freire, 1971); and/or (4) guidance (see also Schimmel, 1975). Each of these four metaphors for education involves proceeding towards some culturally sanctioned end. Preparation points towards outcomes that will benefit the learner, enabling her/him to meet expectations. Initiation assumes the existence of theoretical and practical knowledge, along with worthwhile public practices (see Peters, 1965, p. 43 for a reference to the 'citadel of civilization'), and it moves towards getting the educated person to understand and love knowledge. Liberation moves towards freedom (e.g. participatory democracy or the dictatorship of the proletariat), and it involves 'empowering' the oppressed through enabling them to understand their alienated condition. Finally, guidance moves towards 'perfection' through imitation (usually of an individual who embodies a particular ideal). In all of these cases, metaphor fulfils a hortative and didactic function. For this reason, figurative language maintains significant status as a topic for educational research, especially as this research relates to teacher education.

The use of metaphor in curricula reaches back to ancient Greece. 'Metaphor' is rooted in the ancient Greek *metapherein*, which may be translated as 'transference'; and it shows up in the modern Greek *metaphora*, which may be translated as 'a vehicle of transport.' Thus metaphor may be seen as a vehicle that enables transference between experience and the language of thought. The transference between experience and thought has been the subject of many debates within the philosophical tradition rooted in Aristotle. Although Christian and positivist perspectives on language have complicated this debate, Aristotle's influence has been profound and exists to this day.

Johnson (1980) wrote that the late twentieth century interpretation of metaphor is directly connected to Aristotle's first extended treatment of the subject (384–22 BC). Aristotle defined metaphor as a poetic art by which the poet provided knowledge through reflective intuition (from Latin, *intueri*, to look upon). In his *Poetics*, Aristotle (1941, 1447b) wrote: 'Metaphor consists in giving the thing a name that belongs to something else'; the transference being either from generic to specific, or from specific to the more general, or from one specific category to another. This definition separated metaphor from a more literal truth, and this has complicated its value for the last 2,300 years (Johnson, 1980). Since Aristotle, the drive for precise articulation has led to the dichotomy of accurate versus inaccurate knowledge (as mediated through metaphor).

Like Aristotle, Cicero saw metaphor as a misuse of words and as a flight from precise meaning. Latin rhetoricians valued metaphor chiefly as a linguistic ornamentation of argumentative proofs (Johnson, 1980). Johnson added that medieval rhetoricians furthered this derisive interpretation of metaphor by referring to it as a stylistic device devoid of serious philosophical argument. They arrived at this opinion while attempting to establish the authority of biblical scriptures. Their attack was reinforced by a rising monastic tradition that emphasized the authentic outward expression of what were coming to be understood as intuitive truths of the mind. The scriptural basis for this orientation was to be found in biblical commandments against bearing false witness (Exodus 20: 16; Deuteronomy 5: 20; Matthew 19: 18).

The belief that figurative expressions amounted to a deviation from orthodox meaning remained in the philosophical tradition of Europe and North America until the present century (Johnson, 1980). It was reinforced during the seventeenth century when the foundations for ontological certainty began to shift from a belief in the unified sacred power of a monotheistic god to the belief in a unified secular power born of human consciousness. Rationalism and empiricism fueled the latter belief. Hence, while Descartes esteemed eloquence and loved poetry, he felt that both were underrated gifts of nature rather than fruits of study. Those who reason most cogently, and who polish their thoughts to make them clear and intelligible, are always most persuasive, even if they speak only a provincial dialect and have never studied rhetoric (Descartes, cited in Sallis, 1989, p. 28).

Toulmin (1990) noted that, between 1600 and 1700, philosophy began to pursue universally valid answers by developing a distinct separation between rationality/logic and rhetoric/emotions. According to this distinction, a 'good reason' for correct practice had to be universally justified through the use of rationally logical syllogisms, which was dependent upon a linear form of reasoning. According to Toulmin, from the seventeenth century onwards, this type of reasoning ensured that philosophical validity was dependent upon the internal relations of logical arguments. The rhetoric of figurative language was disdained, as it was considered imprecise, misleading, and therefore not a source of dependable knowledge. This philosophical context fed an early Anglo-American enthusiasm for logical positivism, which only enhanced hostility towards figurative language. Logical positivism assigned 'meaning' to propositions that could be given a truth value that corresponded to 'reality' (i.e. a body of verifiable propositions; see Sallis, 1989). In its quest for truth, positivism insisted that figures of speech were misleading and hindered clarity of meaning.

It was for Rousseau and the later German Romantics to revive an interpretation of metaphor that sought to address the relationship between emotionality and philosophical argument. According to Rousseau, truth may be a function of reason, but 'tropes' (i.e. the 'turning of phrases' from the ancient Greek *tropos*, 'a turning') are primordial because they are linked to the passions. It was Rousseau's recommendation, however, that such passions were to be sublimated into reason through proper education. While expressions inspired by passion were primordial, instruction was to lead learners to the world of self-conscious reason. Figurative language was the first language, but it had no truth value. Proper meaning could only be discovered with the assistance of reasoning (Rousseau, cited in Sallis, 1989, p. 29). The relationship that Rousseau established between metaphorical language and reason was transmitted to nineteenth century German philosophy. In Hegel's view, a trope referred to a strategy for structuring explanations. It served, therefore, a structural function and required the presence of: (1) a judging subject, (2) a subject to be judged, and (3) a relationship between subject and its judged (Hegel 1983, pp. 347–8). The interaction between subjective and objective realms, mediated through metaphor, creates a new meaning – one that is distinguishable from the original idea as subjectively perceived. Hegel's methodology for a science of consciousness provides a foundation for popular contemporary theories of metaphor – theories that are part of a long heritage bent on uniting the intuitive subject with the 'objective' world. These theories are transcendentally spiritual, as they address processes of thought that can only be mediated through metaphor. For example, as a theoretical 'vehicle of transport', metaphor can re-signify experience figuratively in a way that makes an original name 'turn' into another idea categorically. The actual practices of teaching and learning, as Elliott mentioned, can be conceptualized ideally as any one of preparation, initiation, liberation, or guidance. A 'species' of educational practice, to use Aristotle's term, can be differentiatially categorized according to any one of such 'species' of mediated practices. All, however, fall under the general 'genus' of 'education'.

One of the most influential of contemporary perspectives on metaphor is that proposed by Lakoff and Johnson (1980). They argue that metaphor is essential for interaction among conceptual systems. Lakoff and Johnson call these systems 'gestalts' but we understand these to be very similar to Aristotle's categorical distinctions of genus and species. In the case of educational research, traditional practices originating in the conceptual system of travel or biological growth would be understood to interact with the practical 'gestalt' of learning to teach in a school. Lakoff (1992b, p. 8) specializes in the study of conceptual systems – the largely unconscious systems of thought that determine how we think. Metaphor, in this analysis, enables correspondence across conceptual domains, typically from concrete spatial domains to a more abstract domain (p. 22). The study of metaphor, according to Lakoff, can yield a sort of dictionary of the unconscious. Lakoff assumes that there is an unconscious metaphorical language that functions separately from the body and its passions (Lakoff, 1992a). Since there is no way to get conscious control over the unconscious, he suggests that we be aware of the components of our metaphorical systems and of what they entail. Adopting this advice, Sfard (1998) recommends examining the guiding metaphors of acquisition and participation (which are used to represent the abstract realm of learning), and she cautions against depending on one to the exclusion of the other.

Aristotle's drive for precise articulation was motivated by a need to provide adequate and consistent grounds for scientific inquiry. Universally valid answers demanded tools of reasoning which were sound and these required equally valid correspondence theories to unite object-as-perceived and idea-as-imagined. Metaphor, conceptualized as a hermeneutic vehicle of transport is intended to act as the intermediary between the conceptual domains that determine how we think. It would behove researchers, consequently, to examine the performance of these vehicles since they guide correspondence between the objectively experienced world and subjective, intuitive deduction.

Figurative language and teacher development

One decade following Elliott's pioneering work, Bullough and Stokes (1994) identified several angles of research, most of which converge with regard to the preparation of teachers and all of which are concerned with how the latter identify themselves as pedagogues. These angles are 'images of self,' 'self-narratives,' and 'personal metaphors.' Bullough and Stokes begin by saying that metaphors can be used to represent and to reconstruct problems, and this assumes an implicit knowledge that needs to be made explicit. According to Bullough and Stokes, one of the most abstract of these implicit subconscious images is the preservice candidate's conception of him/herself as a teacher. The concrete experience of learning to teach requires a coherent self-image, and this develops through being socialized into the profession. Based on Lakoff and Johnson (1980), Bullough and Stokes argue that metaphors are the vehicles that unify these diverse realms. They insist that a large part of self-understanding is the search for appropriate metaphors that make sense of our lives. In short, conscious practice is based on a correct understanding of subconscious images.

One aspect of research on metaphor and teacher development is particularly concerned with the role metaphor plays in teacher socialization (see Carter, 1993, Connelly and Clandinin, 1988). Self-narratives invoke the metaphorical vehicles that allow teachers to articulate images of themselves in a purposeful and coherent fashion. Metaphors shift the emphasis from internal 'vision' to external 'voice,' thus enabling teachers to see a reflection of themselves through language and to create 'a self' in that image (Collins and Green, 1990). Beyond enabling teachers to create personal identities, metaphors also enable them to construct images of their students and colleagues (Bullough and Stokes, 1994). Metaphor unifies their experience, therefore, and assigns a narrative coherence to teachers' lives, leading them to communal practices by enabling them to identify with colleagues. In short, metaphor is a rhetorical vehicle for the transcendental unification of teachers' experience and cognitive images of self.

Clearly, the theory of metaphor most useful to teacher education research is the one that treats metaphor as a vehicle for unifying conceptual realms (e.g. the conscious with the subconscious, the internal vision with the external voice, etc.). To be developed (prepared, initiated, liberated), therefore, is to be rationally guided by a methodology that navigates among these realms. Metaphor enables teachers to forge a link between external stimulus and internal synthesis. As Sfard (1998) recommends, the onus fall on researchers to locate, analyse, and sharpen this link by deciding which metaphors are most effective.

Aristotle's influence extends beyond a concern for accuracy of meaning as mediated through metaphor. We will argue, further, that researchers may be captivated by habits of practice that may marginalize alternative perspectives on learning to teach. These habits are maintained and defended in order to claim the status of 'genuine science' for teacher education pedagogy.

Categorical knowledge endemic to the ivory tower

Aristotle is concerned with knowledge as *episteme* (the etymological root of the term 'epistemology'). An episteme is a body of knowledge about a subject (for our purposes, about the documentation of knowledge as it pertains to teacher education), and it is organized into a system of proofs, or demonstrations. These proofs constitute a body of research, or 'science.' To 'know something' about a subject is to know why it is what it is, rather than something else. This conception of knowledge can rely upon the authority of a community of researchers, which, in turn, appeals to a common methodology for obtaining reliable knowledge. The science of learning to teach is, by implication, demonstrative, endlessly debating competing definitions of teaching and learning, all of which are based upon elaborate systems of classifying teachers' knowledge. Aristotle provides the rules for such a categorical debate in *Topics* (1947).

Aristotle's 'categories' are, perhaps, his most heavily discussed notion, and their popularity is evident in research on teacher development. Most recently, Aristotle's perspective has been adapted by Orton (1997; to analyse how teachers think); by Bell (1993; to analyze literacy); by Schwab (1962) and, subsequently, by Connelly and Clandinin, (1988; to analyse the aims, method, and content of curriculum planning) and by Enns (1982, to analyze crisis intervention). Categories arise due to the human propensity to reflect on general questions concerning a given state. In our case, these questions concern the state of knowledge development as it relates to teachers (e.g., *what is* knowledge; *how much* knowledge is enough; what kind of knowledge is appropriate; where is knowledge procured; how is knowledge obtained; when is knowledge obtained; Smith, 1995, p. 57). Aristotle's categories may be referred to as 'predicables' as each category provides one possible relationship between subject and predicate. This fits well with the meaning of 'category,' which is the ancient Greek word for predication (*kategoria*).

Think of primary categories of knowledge (i.e., of ontological predicates) in simple grammatical terms. Where a human being is a neutral 'subject', its verbal predicates may be any number of qualities that attribute to it an essential nature. The human subject can be categorically objectified in diverse forms. It can, for example, be (1) genus: the product of a divine creator, or differentiated into (2) species: a conscious agent of rational choice. The most dominant quality in contemporary literature on learning to teach assigns the teacher with the potential to be a conscious agent of rational choice. Assumed categories are usually hidden underneath everyday descriptions – descriptions upon which we rely in order to interact and write about teachers in practical ways. It is not necessary to refer to these fundamental biases in order to engage in everyday ethical and practical discourse, none the less, they remain as grounds for theories of knowledge and they locate teachers in a cosmological order of things. In other words, researchers assume that fundamental categories of knowledge support their theoretical decisions as much as their practical prescriptions.

Ontological categories determine conceptions of the nature and appropriateness of knowledge. For example, if we believe (1) that a divine masculine Creator determines human subjectivity, then we might ultimately consider how we should follow His commandments when seeking knowledge. If we believe (2) that subjectivity is a consciousness possessing rational agency, then we might consider 'reasonable' approaches to logically defined problems. If we believe (3) that we are children of a goddess, then we might perceive the earth as a natural living organism. As we have already indicated, option (2) is the dominant choice of much of the literature dealing with knowledge as it relates to teaching and learning.

Although one's fundamental ontology may remain implicit when one analyses knowledge and its development, one's interpretation of selfhood (what it is good to be), of ethics (what it is right to do), and of epistemology (what constitutes reliable knowledge) does not. It is from 'objective standpoints' that researchers make sense of teacher development and, we would argue, of their own. Without objective representations, discussions of what it would mean to 'develop' as a teacher would be senseless to both teachers and researchers alike. Archetypal predicates can, therefore, as cultural landmarks, come to represent the ethically sanctioned goals of an educational curriculum, and it is important to emphasize that privileged attributes define the tacit epistemological stance of any given culture. In other words, it is what is understood to be our essential nature and our practical, moral predicament that will provide the basis for an implicit doctrine of knowledge in an explicit research literature. For example, if we believe that we are the products of a divine masculine Creator, then we may tacitly deal with each other as archetypal saints or sinners – the idea being to educate and socialize as many saints and as few sinners as possible. If, on the other hand, we believe that we are self-conscious agents confronting a problem-presenting world, then we might try to get our educators to refine autonomous problem-solving skills. Researchers who focus on teachers, and who assume ontology of self-conscious agency, may construct teachers as reflexive or active. One of the most useful of these constructions was theorized and then elaborated upon in the 1980s by Donald Schon (1983; 1987).

Clearly, researchers who write about teacher education as it relates to knowledge do so in the shadow of foundational goals and frameworks, the latter determining the correct procedures for attaining the former. Our foundational goals proclaim what it means to be a 'good' teacher, and these goals are framed by explicit epistemological prescriptions. All participants in the culture of the university will mutually accept the terms of reference, and they will provide codes of conduct within the 'ivory tower'. Conforming to these codes may be rewarded, while transgressing them may be met with penalty (often in the most subtle and insidious ways). Categories of knowledge function as guides for conducting research. According to these categories, researchers orient choices, decisions, and patterns of selection and analysis. (As in gendering, for example, a good illustration of how the neutral human being is burdened with all kinds of cultural baggage based solely on genitalia.)

The Aristotelian perspective on categorical knowledge and its development is driven by dialectical argument, and it is this type of argument that drives contemporary research questions concerning teachers' education. The term 'dialectical' comes from the ancient Greek verb *dialegesthai* (modern Greek: *dialektike*), which refers to a kind of exchange between opponents (Smith, 1995, p. 58). In contemporary terms, such an exchange characterizes the university defence, wherein the doctoral candidate must 'defend' her/his dissertation against the questioning of his/her committee. Aristotle was Plato's student for 20 years, and the dialectic method refers to the way in which Plato's Socrates engaged in the search for knowledge: he drew responses to questions by engaging people in competitive dialogue. In the *Republic*, Plato refers to this method of practicing philosophy as 'dialectic,' and he proposes that the leaders of his ideal political state be trained in it. Aristotle's *Topics* presupposes a context of argumentation that involves rules and judges, with the respondent defending a thesis against those who attempt to refute it. The polemics of such an encounter were intended to be a method of learning within which participants were to be trained in the art of critical thinking. Smith (1995, p. 59) observes that this form of practice serves the same purposes as do the exchanges that take place in scholarly journals and at academic conferences. Knowledge, as obtained through dialectical argumentation, serves as a means of socialization for, according to Aristotle, the premises of such argumentation must be accepted as orthodoxy. He defines orthodoxy as' accepted things [things that] seem so to everyone, or to most people, or to the wise – either to all of those, or to most of them, or to the most famous and celebrated' (*Topics* I, 1, 100b21–23). This definition characterizes the contemporary practice of scholarly 'peer review'.

The dialectical method enables one to deduce logical conclusions from premises conceded through argument (Smith 1995, p. 61). This works if (1) the desired conclusion follows from the given premises and (2) the respondent concedes those premises. Therefore, determining what various classes of researchers believe (especially what most believe and, most especially, what those considered 'most wise' believe) may enable us to predict which premises will be acceptable. It is necessary, therefore, to determine which class one's colleagues fall into and then to determine the scholarly argument most relevant to them. The dialectic, as standardized practice, consists in determining what is credible to various types of researchers. This being the case, it is necessary to find premises from which a desired conclusion will follow. In *Topics* II to VII, Aristotle provides a collection of argumentative rules, which he calls 'commonplaces' (*topoi*) – a term that originates in ancient systems for memorizing lists of items by associating each item with a standard set of imaginary places. Smith (p. 61) elaborates:

> They rest on a classification of conclusions according to form: each gives premise-forms from which a given form of conclusion can be deduced . . . the dialectical method of the *Topics* requires the joint application of 'locations' and the inventories of opinions. To find an argument, I first look up a location appropriate to my desired conclusion and use it to discover premises that would be useful; then I consult the relevant inventory of opinions to see if those premises are found there. If they are, I have my argument; all that remains is to case it into the form of questions and present them to my opponent. Assuming that my inventories of opinions are properly constructed and that I have correctly estimated what type of person my opponent is, I can reasonably count on my premises being accepted.

Dialectical argumentation is, therefore, a competitive research activity involving strategy, tactics, and triumph. The fundamental characteristic of the dialectical game, however, is that arguments based on premises that lead to specific conclusions must be valid; that is, they must be acceptable to all players, so that the conclusions are a necessary consequence of the premises. With regard to dialectical inquiry, the existence of commonly held opinions is important. As Aristotle states (1962, VII.I, II45b2–7) 'a sufficient measure of correctness of an account is that it solve all the puzzles in the commonly held opinions about a subject and nevertheless retain as many of those opinions as possible'.

To conclude this section, let us examine one significant account of how dialectical principles play themselves out in curriculum inquiry. Connelly and Clandinin (1988, pp. 81–97) attempt to recover the meaning of curriculum in Aristotelian terms and to embark on a discussion of the tools that are useful for such a recovery. As they write: 'when there appears to be a babble of voices about something that we all agree is significant, then what we need to help sort things out is a set of topics that help define the subject as experienced, while ruling no one's views out of order. We call these topics "commonplaces of curriculum" ' (p. 83).

They identify these commonplaces as:

- Knowledge of subject matter (including methods)
- Knowledge of milieu
- Knowledge of learner
- Knowledge of teacher (or of self)

A quick scan of the literature reveals how teachers' education can be organized conveniently into these four categorical domains. For example, knowledge of subject matter and methods has been explored in depth by such authors as Shulman (1987) and Ayers (1988). Over the years, the milieu of teaching has been the subject of writings by Ben-Peretz (1991), Calgren and Lindblad (1991), and Giroux (1989, 1992), among others. Doyle (1985), for example, as well as Martin and Kompf (1996) discuss knowledge of learners and their 'needs.' And, as I have shown throughout this chapter, Connelly and Clandinin (1988), Carter (1990), and Bullough and Stokes (1994) have researched knowledge of self (among others).

Connelly and Clandinin (1988, p. 85) argue that, while there may be different foci within each category, and while arguments concerning curriculum may focus on a single category, categories are inescapable analytical tools when it comes to examining trends and conflicts pertaining to curriculum inquiry. Using categories for the sake of inquiry, they add, may involve mixing them so that theory may be demonstrated through practice (see their reading of Dewey (1938). The recovery of meaning involves integrating theory and practice, which, in turn, reconstructs new, more productive relationships between theoretician and practitioner. Connelly and Clandinin explicitly propose a dialectic relationship for such a reconstruction (p. 87). They argue that theoreticians and practitioners value 'good ideas' and 'good practice,' respectively, and that this forms a barrier between them. The barrier seems to concern two highly different educational contexts: the 'ivory tower' of the university and the 'trenches' of the school building and its individual classrooms.

We have doubts as to whether the foregoing two contexts are reconcilable; alternatively, we propose that theoreticians and practitioners do hold similar values when questions are raised regarding alleged differences between theory and practice. And we further propose that these similarities are rooted in common epistemological frameworks and biases. These similarities are visible in Connelly and Clandinin's (1988) suggestions. Both theoretician and practitioner honour the truth value of categorical knowledge as supported by transcendental cognition, and, it follows, they both utilize the latter in their attempt to attain the former. As we showed in the section on transcendental cognition, metaphor as a vehicle of thought is part of a philosophical lineage that unifies subjective and objective realm. Connelly and Clandinin attempt to show that theory and practice may be unified through the use of appropriate principles, strategies, and tactics. For example, they advise the practitioner to pose the following two questions:

- What does this stakeholder want me to do?
- What is the reason (the idea) that this stakeholder gives for asking me to do this? (p. 89, italics in original)

They conclude by privileging personal knowledge as a useful approach to such integration, and they advocate the use of Aristotelian epistemology. The practical context, in their view, constitutes 'a kind of proof', and the verification of this proof privileges praxis over theory. According to the principles of categorical knowledge as established by Aristotle, theoretical speculation should be modified according to the shifting exigencies of the practical world. 'The essential task of the dialectic', Connelly and Clandinin conclude, 'is to resolve oppositions' (p. 95). The goal, then, is to involve researchers and practitioners as co-participants in the study of intentions, purposes, predispositions, and practices. The recovery of the meaning of curriculum, therefore, involves uniting both researcher and practitioner in a common plan dedicated to attaining a common goal.

We remain sceptical of the possibility of such a unification both in theoretical and in practical terms. Part of our scepticism comes from our concern over a theory of metaphor and a methodology for problem solving that is premised on the construction of linear paths of topical thinking. We especially have reservations as to the value of this categorical epistemology with regard to its evaluation of 'truth'. In short, what is the basis for the commitment to the truth-value of categorical knowledge and its accompanying methodologies of acquisition/mediation? In the final section of this chapter, we propose a more radical perspective on personal knowledge – one that Nietzsche elaborated upon and that cares little for strategies of mediation.

Aphoristic knowledge and the fragmentary language of babel

> Of all that is written I love only what a man has written with his blood. Write with blood, and you will experience that blood as spirit. . . . Whosoever writes in blood and aphorisms does not want to be read but to be learned by heart. In the mountains the shortest way is from peak to peak: but for that one must have long legs. Aphorisms should be peaks – and those who are addressed, tall and lofty.
>
> (Nietzsche 1966, p. 40)

We remain curious as to why 'a babble of voices' (Connelly and Clandinin, 1988, p. 83) poses a threat to the academic curriculum. Why must babble be harnessed within categorical terms before it is perceived as legitimate? It might be useful, given the academy's preference for transcendental cognition and categorically structured knowledge, to investigate a Nietzschean perspective on metaphor and knowledge (1995) – a perspective that does not mandate strategies of reflective unification or categorical knowledge. This investigation may open paths whereby practice could be expressed without the necessity of some theoretical vehicle of mediation. Until Nietzsche, the theory of metaphor depended on interpreting human essence as a transcendental entity (a religious soul, a cognitive mind, or a reflective consciousness) that has the power to produce and to manipulate knowledge. Thinking, as articulated through interactive reflection, amounts to the metaphorical equivalent of feeling, intuitive seeing, and speaking or acting. First, the object of desire is perceived (i.e. it is visualized internally), then the abstract is vocalized and implemented in practice. It is taken for granted that the teacher is a conscious, thinking agent capable of accomplishing these tasks and that metaphor facilitates transference between the conscious and subconscious realms. Such a dialectical structure requires the constant refinement of strategies that seek to unify the subjective and the objective, the theoretical and the practical, as was evident in Hegel and, more recently, in Lakoff and Johnson.

According to Nietzsche, we imagine the existence of other things by analogy; that is, anthropomorphically (Stack 1990, p. 4). In this perspective, knowledge is comprised of socially determined conventions that are communicated through the use of customary metaphorical signs. Over a period of time certain linguistic habits become canonical and are always used when describing practices. Language, therefore, cannot be expected to correspond accurately to lived experience, and metaphor cannot be expected to be a dependable vehicle for the transference of authoritative knowledge. There is no transcendental intuition from which experience may be expounded.

Johnson's (1980) history of metaphor makes it clear that Nietzsche was attempting to counter the long heritage that has marginalized rhetoric and emotions, separating them from the process involved in generating truth claims. In Nietzsche's terms, metaphors are not involved in conducting transferences between meaning gestalts; rather, they spring from a primordial protosynthesis of physical/emotional sensations (Sallis 1989, p. 45). From a research perspective, then, it is not the rational exercise of logical and categorical thinking that should concern us as educators, but the degree to which we can come to terms with our fundamental relationship to physical and emotional consciousness. Nietzsche's anthropomorphic mode of thought is affective and egocentric even when it is 'trained' to pattern itself according to social rituals (including academic research methodologies). From this hyper-organic perspective, metaphor still serves a purpose, but it is not to bridge the chasm between consciousness and the theoretically conceived objective world. Metaphor is not a vehicle that drives towards rational clarity; rather, it is the totality of all figurative rhetoric and springs from a basic connection between the body's needs and passions and the earth to which it is inextricably connected.

Learning, for Nietzsche, might be viewed vegetatively as if one is cultivating the soul (see Nietzsche, 1982, p. 561). Language merely perpetuates conceptual schemata that abstract, simplify, and incorporates fallacious identities (Lakoff and Johnson's 'gestalts') for pragmatic use. Researchers seem to be much more concerned with organizing and legislating the epistemological boundaries of these schemata than they are with directly confronting the body's passions, not to mention those passions' relationship to the teaching and learning process. Such a confrontation de-emphasizes knowledge acquisition and emphasizes wisdom and its development, a capacity which we believe may be appropriate for considering the craft of teaching.

Learning to teach may be a pragmatic challenge, and the quest for authoritative, unified knowledge of the process that it entails may be elusive. We suggest that the researcher's desire to articulate teacher development and its relationship to knowledge through an analysis of metaphorical mediation and categorical knowledge cannot be fulfilled. Such a desire is as old as the notion of metaphor as a streamlined vehicle of consciousness. It descends from a desire to somehow grasp and control the flux of experience. A more authentic relationship to experience may produce novel perspectives on how one learns to teach. 'Novel perspectives' will necessarily be represented in different forms from those to which we are accustomed. Following Nietzsche, who attempted to articulate his perspective aphoristically, we offer an anti-structural perspective (the 'tower of Babel') on teacher development – one that originates in Nietzsche's highly personal style (1878, 1881, 1882).

Nietzsche's educational challenge: self-overcoming

In a letter to Georg Brandes, dated 19 April 1888, Nietzsche wrote that 'the person who does not find himself addressed personally by my work will probably have nothing to do with me' (Breazeale 1998, p. 1). Fourteen years earlier, Nietzsche had written that the only valid critique of a philosophy concerns whether or not one can live in accordance with it (Nietzsche 1983, p. 187). Nietzsche was writing to himself and speculating on his own educational agenda; in essence, he was outlining and undergoing a program of personal research. It is not possible to imitate Nietzsche's personal agenda when one is in pursuit of one's own perspective. It is possible, however, to use Nietzsche's journey as an inspiration for reconsidering one's own path.

As in the usual academic tradition, such research begins by framing a context within which to locate one's study. But in this case, the context includes not only published secondary materials, but also one's own biography, which must be (re)evaluated along with any 'facts' that one may find. The methodology called for by such a programme of learning assumes a distinctive Nietzschean notion of self-concept – one that is balanced between essentialist and existentialist extremes.

Zarathustra's problem of 'self-overcoming' is related directly to his problem with temporality. In the prologue of *Zarathustra*, Nietzsche attacks the 'grave view' of the passage of time and its movement towards consummation

(Lampert 1986, p. 2). This attack is transferable to the 'grave view' of learning as a recurrent generation of dialectical thinking. Specifically, it is an attack on the concept of experience as a recurrent, forward moving rhythm that can be schematized as a progressive journey towards some specific end. It is for this reason that Nietzsche refers to aphoristic thinking as stepping from 'peak to peak' rather than as following a dialectical path. The fragmentary thinking of 'long legs,' which take the shortest route to knowledge, requires a different conception of thinking. It relates to problem posing rather than to problem solving. Generally, the rhythm of experience is interpreted in a dialectical fashion and the process of thinking is mediated through metaphor. This leads to severely limiting the possible paths of thinking as all methodologies can begin to resemble one another. This desire for correct and common understanding has religious undertones, but it originates in Socratic Platonism, specifically in the allegory of the devoted learner who, by following an ascending path, strives for a glimpse of the ultimate ideal of moral virtue.

Nietzsche calls for a new form of understanding – one that is more loyal to the body's obvious connection to earthly processes. The Nietzschean 'self' is a middle ground between the two extremes of essentialism and existentialism (Breazeale, 1998). Nietzsche proposes 'the kernel' as a metaphor of being (p. 11). And, of course, kernels must be germinated in order to grow. Unless held back by negative external circumstances, a germinated kernel will sprout. For Nietzsche, such negative external circumstances include transcendental cognition and the dialectic. Beginning with essentials, one must make a critical inventory, not of what one's peers value, but of what one values for one's self. Nietzsche refers to these values as 'idols' (1983, p. 129). Many may be reluctant to conduct such an inventory, for it demands honesty and may involve difficult admissions. Nietzsche concedes that 'writing in blood' is not for everyone, however, he promises rewards to those who can do it (p. 143).

In order to satisfy the anti-essentialist extreme, one must collect, order, and destroy former values; in order to satisfy the existential extreme, one must cultivate one's true self. And if one wishes to be a philosopher in Nietzsche's sense, then one must become so through one's own striving. This involves renouncing the outer circumstances that impede development. The degree to which renunciation takes place measures the degree to which the way is made clear for the revaluation of those values committed to transcendental cognition and dialectical problem solving. To learn, we must overcome the 'self,' and for this we require the assistance of educators.

Two bodies of data are relevant to self-overcoming. The first is one's own biography, which often leads one to be contemptuous of one's cultural milieu and its values. We could say that this paper is intended to bring its readers to see transcendental cognition and dialectics as constraints on thinking and so to feel contempt for them. The second body of data is the philosophical tradition that has supplied the context for knowledge within the discipline of study. Begin by 'cleaning house,' by examining the texts that reared you as a researcher within the epistemologically 'common' place. Make an inventory of your values, including those that taught you the meaning of your life (Nietzsche 1983, p. 129). Be relentless in your exhumation, and be honest about everything, especially when it hurts. Carry on until you begin to admit to thinking the bitterest truth of all: knowledge has no 'truth value.'

In Nietzsche's terms, then, one must paint a new existential picture of life, and this can be done in one's writing. Philosophical language is a significant medium within which to build the bridge to aphoristic, or fragmentary, thinking. However, our immersion in such philosophical language is, at this stage, contained within a specific linguistic mode – one that seeks to grasp the outline of objects of perception through some form of mediation. Since Nietzsche believed that we think in terms of analogy (between ourselves and an anthropomorphic world), our investigation should begin with a critical examination of our own research texts.

Conclusion: towards a place for fragmentation in university curriculum writing

Nietzsche, a trained philologist, taught classics and philosophy at the University of Basel, Switzerland, from 1869 to 1876. According to Nietzsche, if one document's one's own development, then one avoids the dialectical path of thinking and pursues an impetuous and aleatory notion of knowledge development. His penchant for this form of development explains his attempt to articulate his research in the form of thousands of fragmentary aphorisms, a style common to the Presocratic philosophers. Between 1878 and 1888, Nietzsche composed at least 5,000 aphorisms in published texts and unpublished notebooks. For Nietzsche, this had to do with engaging in a process of self-directed transfiguration. Much of his educational 'training' took place within the walls of esteemed research and teaching universities. Most of his writing, however, took place after he left the university setting (due to protracted illness and long-term disability). He was at liberty, some might say, to write what he chose regardless of his peers and colleagues.

We recommend a sympathetic reading of the Nietzschean perspective, for it could lead to novel interpretations of teaching and learning within the university setting. For this to be so, however, we must expect increased fragmentation in the expression of research practices, and these expressions may be initially shocking to some. One of Nietzsche's pedagogical projects was to fuel readers' doubts about the morality within which they had been raised (Higgins, 1987, p. 45). With regard to this, he is often misinterpreted. Nietzsche attacked the moral commitment to propositional and dialectic knowledge. He maintained that our allegiance to the truth value of knowledge was habitual, not unlike our allegiance to living a religious life style even after our belief in a deity has been long forsaken. What is required is a change in habits and practices. Our dedication to transcendental cognition through metaphor and dialectic thinking is simply an old habit.

Nietzsche's writings do not claim to provide universal or permanently useful knowledge (Strong, 1988, p. 132). Unlike the analytic tool of the dialectic, there is nothing one can 'do' with an aphorism. But any utilitarian dismissal of Nietzsche misses the point of his works. Like Nietzsche, we argue that, to a large degree, our research is limited by a dominant linguistic mode and by a pervasive orientation towards transcendental, dialectical thinking. In many ways, our research is a repetitive faith in old cognitive habits. Nietzsche's style begins the project of undermining that faith and its morality, thus opening the way to experimentation in the fragmentary. It is time to explore where this way of thinking may lead us.

References

Andrews, S. V. (1990) 'A Student's insights: windows on the reflective classroom.' *Contemporary Education* 61(2).

Aristotle (1941) *Poetics*, trans. I. Bywater, in M. McKeon (ed.) *Introduction to Aristotle*, New York: Random.

—— (1947) *Topics*, trans. W. A. Pickard-Cambridge, in R. McKeon (ed.) *The Basic Works of Aristotle*, New York: Random.

—— (1962) *Nicomachean Ethics*, trans. M. Ostwald, New York: Liberal Arts.

Ayers, W. (1988) 'Fact or fancy: the knowledge base quest in teacher education', *Journal of Teacher Education* 39(5): 24–9.

Bell, J. S. (1993) 'Finding the commonplaces of literacy', *Curriculum Inquiry* 23(2): 131–53.

Ben-Peretz, M. (1991) 'Professional Thinking in Guided Practice', paper presented at the annual meeting of the American Educational Research Association, Chicago, IL.

Breazeale, D. (1998) 'Becoming who one is: notes on Schopenhauer as educator', *New Nietzsche Studies,* 2(3 and 4): 1–25.

Bullough, R. V., Jr. and Stokes, D. K. (1994) 'Analyzing personal teaching metaphors in preservice teacher education as a means for encouraging professional development', *American Educational Research Journal* 31(1): 197–224.

Calgren, I., and Lindblad, S. (1991) 'On teachers' practical reasoning and professional knowledge: considering conceptions of context in teacher thinking', Paper presented at the annual meeting of the American Educational Research Association, Chicago, IL.

Carter, K. (1993) 'The place of story in the study of teaching and teacher education.' *Educational Researcher* 22(1): 5–12.

Collins, E. and Green, J. (1990) 'Metaphors: the construction of a perspective', *Theory into Practice* 29(2): 71–7.

Connelly, F. M. and Clandinin, D. J. (1988) *Teachers as Curriculum Planners: Narratives of Experience*, Toronto: OISE Press and New York: Teachers College Press.

Dewey, J. (1938) *Experience and Nature*, New York: Collier.

Doyle, W. (1985) 'Learning to teach: an emerging direction in research on preservice teacher education', *Journal of Teacher Education* 36(1): 31–2.

Elliott, R. (1984) 'Metaphor, imagination, and conceptions of education', in R. Elliott (ed.) *Metaphors of Education*, London: Heinemann.

Enns, R. (1982) 'Crisis research in curriculum policy making', PhD dissertation, University of Toronto.

Freire, P. (1971) *Pedagogy of the Oppressed*, London: Penguin.

Giroux, H. (1989) *Critical Pedagogy, the State, and Cultural Struggle*, Albany: SUNY.

—— (1992) *Border Crossings: Cultural Workers and the Politics of Education*, New York: Falmer.

Hegel, G. W. F. (1983) *Lectures on the History of Philosophy*, vol. 2. trans. E. S. Haldane and F. Simson. New Jersey: Humanities.

Higgins, K. M. (1987) *Nietzsche's Zarathustra*, Philadelphia: Temple University Press.
Johnson, M. (1980) *Philosophical Perspectives on Metaphor*, Minneapolis: University of Minnesota Press.
Lakoff, G. (1992a) 'Multiple selves: the metaphorical models of the self inherent in our conceptual system', paper presented at the Conference of the Mellon Colloquium on the Self, May, Atlanta, GA.
—— (1992b) 'Metaphor: The Language of the unconscious', paper delivered for the Association for the Study of Dreams, June, University of California, Santa Cruz, CA.
Lakoff, G. and Johnson, M. (1980) *Metaphors We Live By*, Chicago: Chicago University Press.
Lampert, L. (1986) *Nietzsche's Teaching: An Interpretation of* Thus Spoke Zarathustra', New Haven: Yale University Press.
Martin, J. and Kompf, M. (1996) 'Teaching in inclusive classroom settings: the use of journals and concept mapping techniques', in M. Kompf, R. Bond, D. Dworet, and T. Boak (eds) *Changing Research and Practice: Teachers' Professionalism, Identities, and Knowledge*, New York: Falmer.
Nietzsche, F. (1966) *Thus Spoke Zarathustra: A Book for All and None*, trans. W. Kaufmann. London: Penguin.
—— [1882] (1974) *A Philosophy of Joy*, trans. W. Kaufmann, New York: Vintage.
—— [1881] (1982) *Daybreak: Thoughts on the Prejudices of Morality*, trans. R. J. Hollingdale, Cambridge, MA: Cambridge University Press.
—— (1983) 'Schopenhauer as educator', in R. J. Hollingdale (ed.) *Untimely Meditations*, Cambridge: Cambridge University Press.
—— [1878] (1984) *Human, All Too Human: A Book for Free Spirits*, trans. M. Faber, Lincoln, NE: University of Nebraska Press.
—— (1995) 'On the truth and lies in a nonmoral sense', in trans. D. Breazeale (ed.) *Philosophy and Truth: Selections from Nietzsche's Notebooks of the Early 1970s*, New Jersey: Humanities.
Oakeshott, M. (1975) 'Education: the engagement and its frustration', in R. Dearden, P. Hirst, and R.S. Peters (eds) *Education and the Development of Reason*, London: RKP.
Orton, R.E. (1997) 'Toward an aristotelian model of teacher reasoning', *Journal of Curriculum Studies,* 29(5): 569–83.
Peters, R. S. (1965) 'Education as Initiation', in R. Archambault (ed.) *Philosophical Analysis and Education*, London: RKP.
Sallis, C. F. (1989) 'The myth of reason: Hegel's logic as a speculative tropology', PhD dissertation, Graduate Institute of Liberal Arts, Emory University, Atlanta, GA.
Schimmel, A. (1975) *Mystical Dimensions of Islam*. Chapel Hill, NC: University of North Carolina Press.
Schon, D. A. (1983) *The Reflective Practitioner*, New York: Basic
—— (1987) *Educating the Reflective Practitioner*, San Francisco: Jossey-Bass.
Schwab, J. J. 1962. 'The teaching of science as inquiry', in J. J. Schwab and P. Brandwein (eds) *The Teaching of Science*, Cambridge: Cambridge University Press.
Sfard, A. (1998) 'Two metaphors for learning and the dangers of choosing just on', *Educational Researcher* 27(2): 4–13.
Shulman, L. (1987) 'Knowledge and teaching: foundations of the new reform', *Harvard Educational Review* 57(1): 1–22.
Smith, R. (1995) 'Logic', in J. Barnes (ed.) *The Cambridge Companion to Aristotle*, Cambridge: Cambridge University Press.
Stack, G. (1990) *Nietzsche: Man, Knowledge, and Will to Power*, Durango, CO: Hollowbrook.

Strong, T. B. 1988. *Friedrich Nietzsche and the Politics of Transfiguration*, Berkeley: University of California Press.
Toulmin, S. (1990) *Cosmopolis: The Hidden Agenda of Modernity*, New York: Free Press.
White, H. (1973) *Metahistory: The Historical Imagination in Nineteenth-Century Europe*, Baltimore: Johns Hopkins University Press.

Chapter 4

Navigating through pedagogical practice

Teachers' epistemological stance towards pupils

Jukka Husu

Introduction

A widely accepted explanation of the practice of teaching is that it requires an understanding of specific cases and unique situations. According to such a view, this practical know-how is mostly built up by teachers in the field as they cope with the daily challenges of teaching and as they attempt to develop their professional practice. It is derived largely from their own experiences and interpretations and it is mainly formulated in concrete and context-related terms. In the field of teacher knowledge it has been referred to as craft knowledge (Leinhart, 1990; Grimmet and MacKinnon, 1992), practical knowledge (Elbaz, 1983; Johnson, 1984), personal practical knowledge (Clandinin, 1985) and as the professional knowledge landscape (Clandinin and Connelly, 1995). Practical knowledge emphasizes its experiential origins (Handal and Lauvas, 1987) and implicit nature (Wagner and Sternberg, 1985; Clark and Peterson, 1986; Freeman, 1991) and it tends to build up in teachers' minds. This stance considers a teacher's knowledge not as a property of formal propositions but instead as a property of a mind constantly relating to action.

Stich (1990) has critized philosophers for holding epistemological expectations that are simply unattainable, blaming us for using faulty reasoning that can really only be shown to be faulty through distanced, *ex post facto*, reflective analysis. Instead, Stich suggests that we should adopt a naturalized epistemology, in which we move away from blaming people for being unable to meet analytic epistemic standards and move towards appreciating the variety of human reason (see McCadden, 1998). Eisner (1998) encourages us to take a stand for alternative epistemologies in order to understand the ways in which pupils and teachers make sense out of the world. According to him, even epistemology as a concept might be too severe because '"[e]pistemology" in Greek philosophy refers to true and certain knowledge. *Phronesis*, wise practical judgement, is being seen increasingly as a more reasonable orientation to the ways in which human action can be studied and revealed' (p. 34, italics in original).

The nature of practical knowing

Dewey (1931) rejected any conception of the mind that regards mind as isolated from persons and things. According to him, 'Mind is primarily a verb. It denotes all the ways in which we deal consciously and expressly with situations in which we find ourselves' (Dewey, 1931, p. 263). As Greene (1994, p. 435) argues, this stance leads to 'viewing knowing primarily as a [personal] search for the meaning of things with respect to acts performed and with respect to the consequences of those acts when performed'. Thus, knowing is what is obtained by acting to resolve practical situations. As such:

> [knowing is not] independent of who and what one is as a person. It is, instead, an organic property of being human, of acting in thoughtful and discerning ways. . . . to know is a form of competence, an ability to navigate the puzzlements and predicaments of life with moral and intellectual surefootedness . . .
>
> Fenstermacher and Sanger, 1998, p. 471

Practical knowing must work for the person in such a way that it secures a method for action. In the case of teachers, practical knowledge seems to offer them guidelines as to what will probably be regarded most useful and effective in the particular contexts in which they are working. As Marland (1998, p. 15) notes, its utility is reflected in teachers' professional attitude: teachers place little faith in researchers and the research enterprise for knowledge about how to teach. Instead, they draw heavily on their practical know-how. From a research perspective, teachers have learned to live with a 'lesser form of knowledge' and knowing (see Labaree, 1998). According to Coulter (1999), academic teacher research and field-working teachers still seem like two solitudes that do not meet. Both parties lack a kind of dialogue from which they would profit. Zeichner (1995, p. 154) makes this point by stating that:

> [D]espite isolated examples of instances where teacher research and academic research have crossed the borders that divide them, they have essentially been irrelevant to each other. For the most part, educational researchers ignore teachers and teachers ignore researchers right back.

Handal and Lauvas (1987) argue that practical knowing is the strongest determining factor in teachers' educational practice: '[it is] a person's private, integrated but ever changing system of knowledge, experience and values which is relevant to teaching practice at any particular time' (p. 9). Sanders and McCutcheon (1987) speak about 'conceptual structures and visions that provide teachers with reasons for acting as they do' (p. 52).

This thrust to practice originates from the nature of the practical problems in teachers' work. As Schwab (1971) emphasized, a vast majority of educational problems cannot be solved procedurally by applying a uniquely suitable formula or technique. Instead, solutions to them must be found by an interactive consideration of means and ends. Practical problems present many kinds of complexity. As Gauthier (1963) has remarked, 'the sphere of the practical is necessarily the sphere of the uncertain' (p. 1). A practical problem is 'a problem about what to do . . . whose final solution is found only in doing something, in acting' (p. 49). Practical problems are the kinds of problems teachers face all the time, and in fact, teachers are quite good at solving them, or at least learning to live with them (Lampert, 1985).

The justification of practical knowing

The traditional and propositional view of knowledge requires that to know *x*, one must have a justified, true belief that *x* is so. Is there a parallel to such conditions regarding practical knowing? Apparently not, because the process of practical knowing 'can scarcely be appraised as either true or false; for it is not clear what the basis of the assessment would be, or what kind of evidence should be decisive' (Hampshire, 1959, p. 167). However, Carr (1981) has taken up the challenge of providing a basis of assessment for practical knowledge situations. He proposes three conditions (similar to the justified, true belief conditions of propositional knowledge). Following his argumentative reasoning, for one to know how to do teaching, one must

- entertain teaching as a purpose,
- be acquainted with a set of practical procedures for successful teaching, and
- exhibit recognizable success at teaching.

Carr, 1981, p. 58

Entertaining teaching presupposes expressions of deliberative purposes, intentionality. Being acquainted with a set of practical procedures for successful teaching is a vital condition for practical knowing, but the final condition involves exhibiting recognizable success at teaching. This condition is analogous to the truth condition of a propositional knowledge claim. However, in the case of the practical knowledge of teaching, what one knows how to do is not a proposition but an action and thus can be neither true nor false. Therefore, in the case of practical knowing, the concept of satisfactoriness should be regarded as the validating principle. 'Practical knowledge seeks satisfactory ways to adapt the world to often complex human purposes' . . . [and practical reasoning] . . . 'is concerned with *making truth* rather than discovering it' (Carr, 1981, p. 60, italics in original).

Practical knowledge must work for the person in such a way that it secures a method for action. Haak (1996) emphasizes that this 'knowing is not isolated from practice but is itself a kind of practice – to be judged, like other practices, by its purposive success rather than by some supposed standard of accuracy of reflection of its objects' (p. 652). Thus, knowledge is obtained by facing and acting to resolve indeterminate situations by using workable methods and techniques. Knowledge must work for the person in a way that empowers the person. Practical knowledge 'embraces this pragmatic orientation towards action' (Fenstermacher and Sanger, 1998, p. 471).

This orientation is a certain mental state. Aristotle spoke in his *Nicomachean Ethics* (VI 5a 30) of 'practical wisdom' which he described as a 'reasoned state'. According to Anscombe (1957), this reasoned state is 'a certain sort of general capacity in a particular field' (p. 88). With the help of this capacity, teachers are able to perform in their profession.

Research area and tasks

So far, our analysis has shown that teachers' practical knowing is mainly formulated in concrete and context-related terms. It deals with teachers' lived experiences (van Manen, 1990), and its statements are essentially perceptual rather than conceptual. According to Kessels and Korthagen (1996), statements concerning perceptions and possible actions tend to be loose and indefinite by nature. In *Nicomachean Ethics* (VI, 1103b–04a), Aristotle views this kind of knowing as *phronesis*, according to which '[e]very statement concerning matters of practice ought to be said in outline and not with precision . . .' because '. . . statements should be demanded in a way appropriate to the matter at hand'. And in practice, the matter at hand in educational situations tends to be imprecise by nature.

However, the perception we are now talking about is not just normal sensory perception. *Phronesis* deals with more than meets the eye. It is a sort of capacity that is developed through being and acting in educational situations. The way teachers perceive their practice recasts their knowing from formal reasoning and reflection upon action to a complex set of ways of thinking about what it means to be a teacher (Jackson, 1968, 1986; Jackson *et al.*, 1993; Hansen, 1995; Nias, 1989). When knowledge is viewed from the perspective of *phronesis*, we need to define teachers' knowing substantially in terms of their personal experiences and their reported deeds and results.

The 'knowing how' situations of practical knowledge do not always lend themselves easily to verbal articulation. However, this is not to imply that practical knowledge is devoid of conceptual content. Ross (1988) has elaborated the employment of concepts in practical thinking. According to him, even if the agent may be unable to express his activities in verbal concepts, 'he employs them in the judgements he renders and the decisions he makes' (p. 24).

Therefore, we need descriptions and interpretations that are adequate enough to reveal the structures of the experiential meanings which teachers report. As a result, if we succeed, we will get a description or interpretation that we can acknowledge. We can recognize it as a kind of description or interpretation that helps us to understand the thoughts and experiences of others, as well as our own. van Manen (1990, p. 27) speaks of the 'phenomenological nod' which means that a good description or interpretation is collected by lived experience, and helps to recollect lived experience.

In general, this chapter aims at identifying teachers' practical ways of knowing. In particular, it focuses on developing descriptive and interpretative categories within which teachers relate to their pupils.

Narrative interviews

The study was conducted by means of a narrative interview (Mishler, 1986, pp. 75–87; Cortazzi, 1993, pp. 55–6). The aim is to get as accurate and authentic as possible a picture of justifications underlying teachers' interactive ways of knowing their practice. According to Connelly and Clandinin (1990), the study of narrative is the study of the ways humans experience the world. It allows teachers' 'voices' (Goodson, 1992; Clandinin, 1992) to be heard and it emphasizes the need for teachers to talk about their experiences and perspectives on teaching in their own words.

The narrative interview focused on the professional character of the teachers' work. The concept of professional character was used as a description of practice. It describes the manner of conduct within an occupation, how its members integrate their obligations with their knowledge and skills. The narrative interview of professional character consisted of three related themes: (1) themes of teachers' teaching and students' learning activities; (2) themes of social relationships within the profession; and (3) themes of teachers' professional 'selves'. The first theme of teaching and learning aimed at explaining how teachers had organized teaching in their classrooms, what kind of student activity teachers preferred and for what reasons. The way teachers perceived their students in general, how they talked about them, was also equally important. The second theme of social relationships focused on collegial relations and relations with parents and the surrounding local community, how teachers shared with their colleagues the tasks of teaching in their schools. Our inquiry focused on the prevailing school culture, how it supported or hindered teachers' professional tasks. The third theme of our narrative interview aimed at looking into the connection between the teachers' views of themselves and their ideas about teaching in general. We aimed at investigating how teachers' teaching activities were related to their personal values, how teachers perceived themselves as translators of personal values into specific behaviors in their classrooms.

Twenty-nine elementary school teachers (twenty females/nine males) in the capital area of Helsinki were interviewed. The interviews took 1½–2 hours per teacher and were conducted by the author. The data are rich and diverse and in many cases they resemble a sort of authentic conversation between the teacher and the researcher. After each interview had been carried out the interviewer noted the location and the extent to which the respondent was interested in the themes. A great majority of the respondents were 'typed' with positive features (i.e. 'very interested') as well as positive attitudes ('cordial, warm, open').

Interview data analysis

All the interviews were recorded and later transcribed. All the materials were translated from Finnish into English with the help of a native English speaker. The qualitative analysis was a four-fold process:

- Summarizing and organizing the data: the data were coded and analytical

notes were written in order to find linkages to various frameworks of interpretation. Tentative coding categories were tried out in order to find a set that was suitable.
- Reorganizing and aggregating the data: searching for relationships in the data and finding out where the emphasis and gaps in the data were. Identifying major themes in the data.
- Developing and testing concepts to construct an explanatory framework: testing various interpretative concepts and reducing the bulk of the data for analysis.
- Finally, the data were integrated into the explanatory framework.

It turned out, as Bruner (1996) has argued, that the narrative construal of the data were surprisingly difficult to examine and present – but in a rather unique way. As Bruner notes, the dilemma comes from the fact that 'narrative realities are too ubiquitous, their construction too habitual or automatic to be accessible to easy inspection. . . . [the problem is] how to become aware of what we easily do automatically' (p. 146). McCadden (1998, p. 77) has also noted that teachers' understanding of their doings in pedagogical situations seems wavering: teachers express concern that their pupils succeed in school and in other nonscholastic social arenas, but they tend to express their doings in their general language of behavioural appropriateness and classroom management. Teachers seem to '"talk around" social practices, and in the act *mean*' (Gee, 1992, p. 12). Therefore, the study of meanings is not only the study of heads; it is the study of social practices and cultural models that imply teachers' acts and thoughts.

Ways of being in practice – the nonscholastic stance

Being themselves

In our data, when teachers talked about instances of their practice, they were talking about themselves. Events seemed to be filtered through the person of the teacher. Teachers used themselves as tools to manage both the problems and the possibilities of their work. To a great extent teacher talk contained self-referential comments. Throughout the data, aspects of the self repeatedly emerged as a central experience in the teachers' thinking, even though each 'self' was different.

The data show that these self-descriptive statements are often formulated in terms of the general beliefs and images that govern teachers' professional behaviour. These statements are often used to justify both the general approach to the teaching profession and the particular practices of teachers in their classrooms.

Teachers tend to justify their ideas and actions according to the possibilities of 'being themselves' in the classroom. Many saw little distinction between themselves at work and outside of it; as one said, 'What happens to you outside school as a person can't be separated from what happens to you as a teacher in the classroom.' Teachers often experienced the blurring of personal and professional boundaries as very satisfying. They felt a sense of unity with the school, particularly with their classes.

Teachers did not separate their own moral character and their professional persona from each other. Nash (1996) talks about the 'thick' language of moral character and acknowledges the importance of feelings and intuitions in the decision-making process. In a moral dilemma related to sensitive matters, a female teacher made her final decision based on her intuition and feelings:

> First I thought that it might be better not to ask this pupil a question, but then I felt that the pupil might find me ignorant if I did not ask her anything. This kind of sensitive matter might not belong to a teachers' work, but you cannot ignore such things if you work with pupils. I wanted to show the girl that I cared. I felt that she needed caring from me (female, 20 years of teaching experience).

Social selves

In the person of the teacher, pedagogical knowledge is justified according to the ideas that are meaningful to the teacher himself/herself. Claiming that those ideas are often intuitive by nature does not mean that they are unsound for the practice of teaching. Rather, the teachers present and justify pedagogical ideas in a way that is socially useful. Teachers have learned this 'language of practice' in classrooms and staff rooms together with their pupils and their peers. This indicates that teachers' knowledge is justified much in the same way as they experience the people and things with which they come in contact. Accordingly, teachers' 'selves' in the processes of justification are inescapably social. The main basis for legitimating ideas and actions seems to be their value for the classroom. The experience that 'it works' seems to be the most important criterion for justifying ideas and actions in a teacher's personal agenda. The same teacher continued:

> According to my own view, I see that I have progressed quite well and I am pleased with the situation. And now I am not talking only about myself. According to my experiences the pupils also feel the way I do . . . During our discussions I have told my pupils that I can't go back to the old days and old ways of teaching and they have told me that neither can they.

The main basis for legitimating ideas and actions seems to be their value for the classroom. According to the teachers, the 'others' that matter the most are their pupils. Ultimately, the teacher's ideas and actions are justified by how well they work with pupils. However, it is not only a matter of formal teaching. Many teachers report that their personal agenda must help to 'establish all in all a good relationship with the pupils'.

They also stated that 'a teacher must get co-operation from the pupils', and 'teaching is a joint effort between you and them'. Teachers' pedagogical ideas and actions were often justified by their experienced regard for teacher-pupil relationships.

One of the most often-used arguments in teachers' justifications for their actions in moral conflicts was the best interest of a child. In dilemmas that involved colleagues or parents, the teachers reported that they took the side of their pupils. In conflicts between pupils, the teachers advocated the rights of the weaker party. One teacher justified this decision in the following way:

> But I think it was right to take the side of the weaker pupil. I thought that I am strong and I have to protect the weak. I also have more experience than some other teachers and I thought it is my responsibility as a strong person to protect the rights of weak pupils (female, 15 years of teaching experience).

Commitment and hopefulness

Many teachers felt that they were committed to their work. The notion of 'commitment' was obviously central to how teachers reasoned and justified their pedagogical ideas and actions. However, they did not use the concept of 'commitment' frequently in their talk. Rather, teachers reported the amount and quality of thought and energy they put into their work. One teacher said: 'Now I have worked with these pupils for over five years and I am gradually starting to see where all my efforts are leading us. And it is quite akin to what I hoped for' (female, 9 years of teaching experience). Teachers are not only committed to their pupils. They also care about the improvement of their school and they strive to reach higher professional standards in their own work. When teachers talk about their pedagogical agenda, they seem to feel that their personal strivings serve as adequate justifications for their actions. Still, it looks as if their intuitive high hopes are often placed above the reasoned facts. One teacher explained, 'I am not at all sure about the way I am teaching my class. Ultimately, I can only hope that it will bring some good results' (male, 7 years of teaching experience).

The commitment to teach calls for hope. Often it requires placing personally relevant and optimistic beliefs above the facts. Zeuli and Buchmann (1988) call it a 'triumph of hope' in teachers' thinking. According to them, as a basis for action, 'the hope that pupils can learn and change must be upheld whenever test scores, the opinions of parents, or even the first hand experiences of the teacher may imply the contrary' (p. 142). The primacy of spontaneous feelings of hope over reasoned experiences is justified, not because they can fit with our data, but because teachers think that their hopes can create new and more desirable results in their pupils and in themselves, too. As one teacher said: 'Even if you can't see the positive results, you must still hope for the best' (female, 12 years of teaching experience).

This hopefulness plays a moral role in teachers' thinking. It can be seen in two ways: on the one hand, as a relatively passive willingness to wait and see how things turn out and, on the other hand, as a more active tendency to foster pupils' growth. About the former, one teacher said: 'You must give your pupils and yourself as a teacher enough time to develop' (Male, 17 years of teaching experience). Another teacher commented on the latter: '[As a teacher] you just can't sit still and wait, you have to help your pupils [in their growth]' (female, 8 years of teaching experience). Elbaz (1992) stresses that this hopefulness in teachers' thinking should not be interpreted merely as naive or sentimental. It rests not on teachers' idealized images of their work but often on a detailed perception of their pupils' life in their classrooms. Accordingly, teachers (hope to!) know more than they can say (even to themselves!).

Ways of acting in practice – the organizational stance

Rules and regulations of practice

In analysing the organizational stance and to identify its structure, we are at first inclined to look for some straight reasonings that can be read in the data. One teacher stated:

> When it is the question of my pupils' safety, I always prefer clear and clean-cut rules and guidelines on how to act in those situations. And that is because I have seen what can happen if you don't do it (female, 5 years of teaching experience).

The statement is direct and its content is simple: as a teacher you must protect your pupils from getting into accidents and getting injured. The teacher does this by giving 'clear and clean-cut rules' to her pupils and ensures that her pupils act accordingly. In the case of safety issues, this is the most common rule of practice which teachers use. The reasoning here goes along a single line: if a teacher does not do her work properly, she might cause accidents and injuries to her pupils. Therefore, the single causal line in reasoning is included in the rule of practice: give clear and clean-cut rules and guidelines to your pupils.

The rule of practice is simply what the terms suggest: a brief, clearly formulated statement of what to do in a particular situation frequently encountered in practice (Elbaz, 1983, p. 132). In the case of a safety rule, the rule of practice can be applied to broader situations, but the rules of practice can also be highly specific, relating to how to deal with conflicts a teacher faces with a pupil, for instance. As one teacher reported:

> I have one pupil who really gets on my nerves. He just can't sit still and wait his turn. He wants to be noticed immediately; he can't stand the fact that there are others in the classroom, too. What I have tried to practise with him is that he will get my attention after I have finished my instructions and the other pupils have made their comments on the subject at hand (female, 5 years of teaching experience).

Here, too, the reasoning goes along a single line: the pupil must wait his turn. Only then can he get attention from the teacher. In this case, the single causal line in the teacher's reasoning is included in the rule of practice: in the classroom, pupils must learn to wait their turn.

The data included an instance where there was a pupil whom the teacher described as 'the weakest pupil in the class', who refused to go into a small group with a fat girl. He had said aloud: 'I will not work with a person like that, I cannot learn anything with her.' The teacher said that this kind of situation is very typical and repeats itself every single day. According to the teacher, pupils are cruel to each other and use very hurtful language in evaluating each other's appearance and skills. The teacher did not say anything at the moment this episode happened, but she asked both pupils involved to stay after class. The teacher discussed the episode with these two pupils; however, they did not find any solution then. The teacher asked the pupils to come and talk to her the next day in the teachers' room before classes began. The teacher justified her rule of practice of involving herself in situations like this: 'I think this is very important; always pay attention to these kinds of episodes and do not let them go unnoticed' (Female, 10 years of teaching practice).

In all our cases, the rules and regulations of practice seemed to necessitate both thinking the practical matter through and acting according to the rules. The rules and regulations of practice were justified because they met the standards of the smooth practical action held by the teacher. However, teachers did not argue that their rules are unique and superior to some alternative rules held by other teachers. Since teachers and situations vary, the rules must vary, too.

Principles of practice

The organizational stance also consists of more inclusive statements. One teacher commented:

> I do not have a huge amount of pedagogical ideas guiding my work with my pupils. I'll try to be fair and honest towards every one of them; I try to guide them to do their work in an appropriate manner and so on . . . but all this can happen only if they really like to come to school and your classroom. If you [as a teacher] have failed to create that sort of good mood among your pupils, then even a great many of your sincere efforts are useless. And as a teacher you must yourself act accordingly (male, 12 years of teaching experience).

Compared to the rules and regulations of practice, this statement is more comprehensive. Here, the reasoning does not follow one procedural technique, as was the case in the rules and regulations presented earlier. Instead of one formula, the statement now consists of multiple rules. We can identify at least three rules and regulations of practice. First, when the teacher states that he tries to 'be fair and honest towards every one of them', he expresses his rule of justice; second, the comment 'to guide them to do their work in an appropriate manner' refers to the rule of diligence; third, the rule of a moral example is exemplified in the expression 'as a teacher you must yourself act accordingly'. As presented earlier, each of these three rules of practice can be justified separately by its own external evidence. However, here the three rules of practice find their justification in the statement 'all this can only happen if they (the pupils) really like to come to school and your classroom'. This statement is more inclusive than the rules and it implies what the teacher should do and how it should be done in a given range of practical situations. The above three rules find their justification in this more general principle of 'pupils' pleasure in attending'.

This principle of pupils' pleasure in attending gives the teacher a good reason to act according to the three rules that are related to the principle. But the rules must be practised in a manner that accords itself with the pedagogical idea and the agenda of the principle. It is the practical principle of pupils' pleasure in attending that justifies the three rules. And vice versa, what finally makes sense for the teacher is that the rule of justice, the rule of diligence, and the rule of moral example are practised according to the principle of pupils' pleasure in attending.

According to organizational stance, justification can take place when reasoning may show that 'an action is the reasonable thing to do, an obvious thing to do, or the only thing to do under the circumstances' (Fenstermacher, 1994, p. 44). Each of these is a contribution to the justification of the organizational stance. Notwithstanding, the evidence supporting the organizational stance must come from the practice itself. The rules and principles are justified because they have proven their worth and have therefore been approved. Teachers think, both implicitly and explicitly, that their organizational stance work. And because it works, teachers act accordingly. Teachers are justified in reasoning that there is a connection between their organizational stance and its supposed or intended outcomes.

The organizational stance seems to be socially constructed in that it emerges from years of experience in school settings. It is a way teachers have found to be effective in problematic situations. The real-time constraints on teachers articulate a professional need: a successful teacher is one who, among other things, acquires a strong organizational stance toward his/her professional tasks and duties. The stance sets a strong organizational power to often chaotic practices in the classroom.

An epistemological stance – not a method but a manner of knowing

In looking for justifying evidence, we were not interested primarily in statements having an external form. Rather, we concentrated on determining how such statements operated in structuring teachers' ways of knowing. Our data indicated that teachers used two different kinds of justifications in structuring their practical knowing (Husu, 2000) However, as presented above, practical knowing is an interrelated entity, a general capacity. As Anscombe (1957) emphasized, practical performance 'has a special procedure or manner, not special antecedents' (p. 32). In order to present this entity, the conceptual frameworks of both the nonscholastic stance and the organizational stance should be brought together. Figure 4.1 presents the combination.

As already noted, presentation of the conceptual framework does not claim that every aspect of teachers' ways of knowing can be slotted into one or another of the aforementioned categories. The boundaries between the categories are often obscure and in many cases the categories are interrelated. When the case of practical knowing is vaguely felt or of a complex nature and not easily translated into specific actions, we may be unsure where to place it. We may face descriptions which we can simultaneously place in two categories. But perhaps, as Reid (1979) wisely tells us, 'the solution will come through shunting the problem back and forth, looking at it now in one light, now in another' (p. 191). In the beginning, some cases of teaching may be analysed in a procedural fashion by studying the rules and principles on which they are probably based. This may lead us to some insights on how to interpret the practice of teaching (Husu, 1998, 2000; Kansanen *et al.*, 2000). In turn, these considerations can become the grounds for a process of uncertain reasonings about the losses and gains that are beyond the reach of procedural analysis.

Non-scholastic stance interacts with teachers' more procedural ways of acting. As argued above, when teachers talked about their pupils, they simultaneously talked about themselves, too. The events relating to the pupils were filtered through the person of the teacher. Teachers used themselves as tools to manage their work with their pupils, and a large proportion of teacher talk contained self-referential comments. The aspects of self emerged quite implicitly, without much conscious thinking, in teachers' ways of knowing. Teachers' ways of being provided the overall context of thought seemed to regulate the determination of more procedural reasonings.

This accords with Dewey's (1926/1984) notions concerning people's selective attention and its intuitive base. He maintained that our primary relation to reality is not cognitive. Rather, the experience of the situation, i.e. what is perceived from the contextual whole, is immediate. According to him, the word 'intuition' describes that 'qualitativeness underlying all the details of explicit reasoning' (Dewey, 1926/1984, p. 249). This intuitive background may be

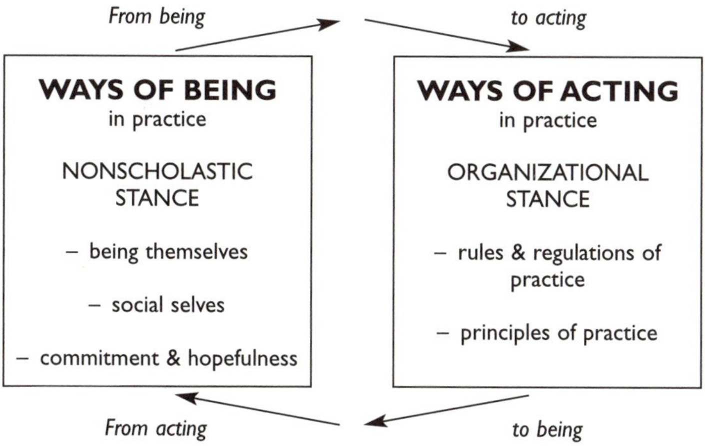

Figure 4.1 Ways to justify teachers' practical knowing.

relatively simple and unexpressed and yet penetrating; it often underlies the definite ideas which form the basis for explicit reasons and justifications. However, it directs attention and thereby determines what is perceived. For example, hopefulness and commitment set a teacher's mind to seek 'weak signals' to prove that at least some learning and progress have taken place in their pupils. It often implies that some personally relevant and optimistic beliefs are placed above 'the reasoned facts' of explicit and formal reasoning. But without hopefulness and commitment, those 'weak signals' of learning and progress would not even be recognized. Therefore, the intuitive, uncertain aspects of teachers' practical knowing are crucially important: they justify and compel teachers to perceive their pupils with great care.

Conclusion

Fenstermacher (1994, p. 3) reviewed conceptions of knowledge in published research on teaching. At the end of his review, he left readers with a challenge to show not only that teachers think, believe or have opinions, but also to investigate what teachers know, and especially, how they know. This chapter attempts to tackle that epistemological challenge. But, instead of giving formal and direct solutions that lead to better teachers and teaching, its answers are expressed provisionally. Based on the findings, these answers depend on three features of teachers' practical knowing. First of all, teachers' practical knowing is characterized by the constant interplay of procedural and uncertain ways of knowing. Second, they depend on the ways knowledge is formed and expressed in the school contexts in which teachers work and live. The data and continuing conversations with teachers have reminded us of the immense complexity of the social contexts of teachers' ways of knowing. Third, they depend on the authority of the person. The ways of being presuppose that teachers' personal values and understandings are used as the standards to test the claims of knowing.

In sum, and loosely interpreting Heidegger's (1962) ideas, teachers' being-in-the-pedagogical-world can be characterized as unexplicit and non-representational understanding that comes about through shared everyday skills and practices into which teachers have become socialized (Dreyfus, 1991, p. 4). This being-in-the-pedagogical-world that arises through this shared, social background seems to be the basis for teaching activity.

References

Anscombe, G. (1957) *Intention*, Oxford: Basil Blackwell.

Aristotle (1975) *The Nicomachean Ethics, Books I–X*. London: Oxford University Press.

Bruner, J. (1996) *The Culture of Education*, Cambridge, MA: Harvard University Press.

Carr, D. (1981) 'Knowledge in practice', *American Philosophical Quarterly*, *18*(1), 53–61.

Clandinin, D. (1985) 'Personal practical knowledge: a study of teachers' classroom images', *Curriculum Inquiry*, 15(4), 361–85.

—— (1992) 'Creating spaces for teachers' voices', *The Journal of Educational Thought* 26(1), 59–61.

Clandinin, D. and Connelly, M. (1995) Te*achers' Professional Knowledge Landscapes*, New York: Teachers College Press.
Clark, C. and Peterson, P. (1986) 'Teachers' thought processes', in M. Wittrock (ed.) *Handbook of Research on Teaching*, New York: Macmillan.
Connelly, F., and Clandinin, D. (1990) 'Stories of experience and narrative inquiry', *Educational Researcher* 19(5), 2–14.
Cortazzi, M. (1993) *Narrative Analysis*, London: Falmer Press.
Coulter, D. (1999) 'The epic and the novel: dialogism and teacher research', *Educational Researcher* 28(3), 4–13.
Dewey, J. (1931) *Art as Experience*, New York: Minton, Balch.
—— (1926/1984) *Affective Thought*, Carbondale: Southern Illinois University Press.
Dreyfus, H. (1991) *Being-in-the-World: A Commentary on Heidegger's Being and Time, Division I*, Cambridge, MA: MIT Press.
Eisner, E. W. (1998) '"The vision thing": educational research and AERA in the 21st century', *Educational Researcher* 27(9), 33–5.
Elbaz, F. (1983) *Teacher Thinking: A Study of Practical Knowledge*, London: Croom Helm.
—— (1992) 'Hope, attentiveness, and caring for difference: the moral voice in teaching', *Teaching and Teacher Education* 8(5/6): 421–32.
Fenstermacher, G. (1994) 'The knower and the known: the nature of knowledge in research on teaching', *Review of Research in Education* 20: 3–56.
Fenstermacher, G. and Sanger, M. (1998) 'What is the significance of John Dewey's approach to the problem of knowledge?', *Elementary School Journal* 98(5): 467–78.
Freeman, D. (1991) '"To make the tacit explicit": Teacher education, emerging discourse, and conceptions of teaching', *Teaching and Teacher Education* 7(5/6): 439–54.
Gauthier, D. P. (1963) *Practical Reasoning: The Structure and Foundations of Prudential and Moral Arguments and their Exemplifications in Discourse*, London: Oxford University Press.
Gee, J. P. (1992) *The Social Mind: Language, Ideology, and Social Practice*. New York: Bergin and Garvey.
Goodson, I. (1992) 'Sponsoring the teacher's voice: teacher's lives and teacher development', in A. Hargreaves and M. Fullan (eds.) *Understanding Teacher Development*, New York: Teachers College Press.
Greene, M. (1994) 'Epistemology and educational research: the influence of recent approaches to knowledge', *Review of Research in Education* 20: 423–64.
Grimmet, P. and MacKinnon, A. (1992) 'Craft knowledge and the education of teachers', *Review of Research in Education* 18: 358–456.
Haak, S. (1996) 'Pragmatism', in N. Bunnin and E. P. Tsui-James (eds) *The Blackwell Companion to Philosophy* , Cambridge, MA: Blackwell.
Hampshire, S. (1959) *Thought and Action*. London: Chatto and Windus.
Handal, G. and Lauvas, P. (1987) *Promoting Reflective Teaching: Supervision in Practice*. Milton Keynes: SRHE and Open University Educational Enterprises.
Hansen, D. (1995) *The Call to Teach*, New York: Teachers College Press.
Heidegger, M. (1962) *Being and Time*, San Francisco, CA: Harper San Francisco.
Husu, J. (1998) 'Two ways to justify teachers' practical knowing', *REFLECT – The Journal of Reflection in Learning and Teaching* 4(2): 26–31.
Husu, J. (2000) 'How teachers justify their practical knowing. Conceptualizing general and relative justifications', *Asia-Pacific Journal of Teacher Education and Development* 3(1): 163–86.
Jackson, P. (1968) *Life in Classrooms*, New York: Holt, Rinehart and Winston.

Jackson, P. (1986) *The Practice of Teaching*, New York: Teachers College Press.
Jackson, P., Boostrom, R. and Hansen, D. (1993) *The Moral Life of Schools*, San Fransisco, CA: Jossey-Bass.
Johnson, M. (1984) 'Review of teacher thinking: a study of practical knowledge', *Curriculum Inquiry* 14(4): 465–8.
Kansanen, P., Tirri, K., Meri, M., Krokfors, L., Husu, J. and Jyrhämä, R. (2000) *Teachers' Pedagogical Thinking: Theoretical landscapes, practical challenges*, New York: Peter Lang.
Kessels, J. P. A. M. and Korthagen, F. A. J. (1996) 'The relationship between theory and practice: Back to the classics', *Educational Researcher* 25(3): 17–22.
Labaree, D. F. (1998) 'Living with a lesser form of knowledge', *Educational Researcher* 27(8): 4–12.
Lampert, M. (1985) 'How do teachers manage to teach? Perspectives on problems in practice', *Harward Educational Review* 55(2): 178–94.
Leinhart, M. (1990) 'Capturing the craft knowledge in teaching', *Educational Researcher* 19(2): 18–25.
Marland, P. (1998) 'Teachers' practical theories: implications for preservice teacher education', *Asia-Pacific Journal of Teacher Education & Development* 1(2): 15–23.
McCadden. B. M. (1998) *It's Hard to be Good. Moral Complexity, Construction, and Connection in a Kindergarten Classroom*. New York: Peter Lang.
Mishler, E. (1986) *Research Interviewing: Context and Narrative*, Cambridge, MA: Harvard University Press.
Nash, R. (1996) *The 'Real World' Ethics*, New York: Teachers College Press.
Nias, J. (1989) *Primary Teachers Talking. A Study of Teaching as Work*, London: Routledge.
Reid, W. (1979) 'Practical reasoning and curriculum theory: in search of a new paradigm', *Curriculum Inquiry* 9(3): 187–207.
Ross, S. (1988) *Persons, Minds and Bodies: A Transcultural Dialogue Amongst Physical Education, Philosophy, and Social Sciences*, Toronto, ON: University of Canada Press.
Sanders, D. and McCutcheon, G. (1987) 'The development of practical theories of teaching', *Journal of Curriculum and Supervision* 2: 50–67.
Schwab, J. J. (1971) 'The practical: arts of eclectic", *School Review* 79(4): 493–542.
Stich, P. P. (1990) *The Fragmentation of Reason: Preface to a Pragmatic Theory of Cognitive Evaluation*, Cambridge, MA: The MIT Press.
van Manen, M. (1990) *Researching Lived Experience. Human Science for an Action Sensitive Pedagogy*, London, ON, The Althouse Press.
Wagner, R. and Sternberg, R. (1985) 'Practical intelligence in real-world pursuits: the role of tacit knowledge', *Journal of Personality and Social Psychology* 49(2): 436–58.
Zeichner, K. (1995) 'Beyond the divide of teacher research and academic research', *Teachers and Teaching: Theory and Practice* 1(2): 153–72.
Zeuli, J. and Buchmann, M. (1988) 'Implementation of teacher-thinking research as curriculum deliberation', *Journal of Curriculum Studies* 20(2): 141–54.

Chapter 5

Teaching and learning in the new millennium

Peter Woods

Introduction

Teaching and learning are currently high on everyone's agenda. In the UK, as in many other countries, there is a national drive for 'improved' teaching and learning, which has added urgency from the need for national competitiveness and well-being, concern at the performance of British children and workers compared to those in Germany, Switzerland, and, until recently, countries in the Pacific Rim, and vague feelings that things ought to be different in the new millennium. Developing also is a renewed focus on learning. We have 'learning schools', 'learning organizations', 'learning communities', 'learning societies', 'lifelong learning', and even a 'learning age'. Suddenly everybody, every group and every institution is learning.

Clearly, this interest in 'teaching' and 'learning' embraces a large number of issues, some of them not directly concerned with pedagogy. Campbell (1998, p. 98), for example, has argued that the 'obsession' with pedagogy since 1992 has been yet another attempt to deflect criticism of problems emanating from the National Curriculum and of resource on to the teacher. However, it is a good opportunity for a review of teaching approach in the light of current circumstances. I want to argue the case for a creative, child-centred, progressive pedagogy. The term 'progressivism' has become discredited, it being alleged that it has been responsible for a decline in educational standards, but the principles upon which it has been understood to be based are, in my view, not only still relevant, but becoming ever more so.

Child-centredness reconstructed

Much of the debate on teaching has been conducted in terms of polarities or dichotomies: traditional versus progressive; child-centred versus curriculum or teacher-centred; instruction versus discovery; holism versus compartmentalization; individual versus whole class teaching; phonics versus good books; managerialism – professionalism; economic rationalism – humanism. Polarities give something to hang the debate around, one can make points more sharply by contrasting them with opposites. Unfortunately, they give rise to false arguments, and ultimately, are counter-productive. They are products, it has been argued, of modernist thinking, which overlook the complexities, uncertainties and inconsistencies of life as it is lived at the turn of the century (Hargreaves, 1994). When researchers get down to investigating what teachers actually do, they find their practice much more complicated, featuring a mixture of elements that cannot be represented in a simplistic, polarized way (Bennett, 1976; Francis, 1986; Galton, 1989). Teachers' practice might be informed by certain principles, but loosely, and variably, being influenced by social and cultural context, personal biography, and professional experience (Sugrue, 1997; see also Day and Hadfield, 1995; Gipps *et al.*, 1999). At the same time, there is strong evidence of the efficacy of child-directed learning (e.g. Sylva, 1998). Even the Office for Standards in Education (Ofsted) (1993) has stressed the need for balance for young children between self-directed learning and teacher-directed activities. In one of the most detailed recent studies of primary teaching, conducted in the Republic of Ireland, Sugrue (1997, p. 222) concludes:

> Child-centred teaching retains an uncertainty, a tentativeness which allows the magic of childhood and the thrill of discovery to manifest itself in contrast with the predictability and certainty of finding right answers. It is unapologetically optimistic about human nature, but not in any sloppy sentimental sense. It seeks to face the future with confidence and recognizes that it is necessary to instil confidence into learners that is self-assured but not arrogant; it is task-oriented but creates spaces for humour, spontaneity, dialogue and individual initiative, yet recognizes that social development is an investment in learners' and societies' futures also. It recognizes that paying attention to relationships is not merely an instrumental necessity for more effective cognitive development, but that they have educational importance in their own right, for moral formation and responsible citizenship.

To these ends, Sugrue (p. 227) argues, child-centred practice needs reconstructing and revitalising.

Creative teaching

I see the 'creative teaching' identified in my research, and that of my colleagues, of the last 12 years as such a 'reconstructed progressivism'. At the beginning of this research, I argued that the time was ripe for a reassertion of teacher independence and inventiveness. At the height of Thatcherism (especially the application of market principles to education), 'visions were off the agenda' for teachers (Barker, 1987), and only 'systems' people seemed to be needed (Brighouse, 1987). Yet I had just completed research in primary schools, admittedly conducted mainly pre-1988, that had demonstrated, echoing Sugrue,

- the magic, thrill, excitement, enthusiasm, joy of teaching and learning (derived from what Michael Barber calls 'the sense of idealism which is at the core of all good teaching', in Day, 1997, p. 52)

- the charismatic qualities of educators involved, who included other personnel as well as teachers
- the democratization of the teaching–learning process
- the creation of classroom atmospheres
- emotional connections between teachers and pupils
- a mix of discourses and styles
- uncommon accomplishment

(Woods, 1990, 1993)

Teachers used their skills of invention and innovation to find 'ways through' to pupil learning, to orchestrate conflictual elements in the teacher role, to resolve satisfactorily the many dilemmas thrown up in the classroom from moment to moment, to improvise and employ all moments of the day to optimize learning, and, not least, to cope with the many pressures and constraints. Since then, the growth in the last of these – the pressures and constraints – have tested teachers' creativity to the full. Our own work has oscillated between documenting teachers' continuing ingenuity and a certain re- and en-skilling on the one hand, and their deskilling and deprofessionalization on the other. As with progressivism–traditionalism, it is not a case of either/or. There are elements of each in the typical primary teacher's experience. However depressed we might have felt from time to time, as we have done during our researches on school inspections and on teacher stress, there are the occasional uplifting moments, for example, in finding the continuance of creative teaching in some areas, the appropriation of the National Curriculum by some schools and teachers, and the cultivation of child-centred values in a new context (see Woods, 1995; also Pollard *et al.*, 1994). Webb and Vulliamy (1996) conclude that, despite overwork and stress:

> Many (teachers) have come through the last five years clearer about their educational beliefs, recognising what is worth fighting for in primary education and what needs to change, more politically aware of how to go about this at the micro and macro level and possessing more self-confidence and communication skills. (p. 163)

In one instance, we discovered a school which seemed to rise above competing discourses. The Ofsted Report (1997) on Coombes County Infant and Nursery School, a paradigm case of a 'creative' school (see Woods, 1995, 1999), concluded that 'the school provides an exceptional standard of education, which not only pushes the boundaries of imaginative teaching but ensures pupils achieve well in all areas of learning'.

Creative learning

I depicted creative teaching as having four main properties: innovation, ownership, control and relevance (Woods, 1990). Creative teaching leads to creative learning (Jeffrey and Woods, 1997; Woods *et al.*, 1999) in the following ways:

- innovation. Something new is created. A major change has taken place in the pupil – a new skill mastered, new insight gained, new understanding realized, new significant knowledge acquired, new ways round a problem found. A radical shift is indicated, as opposed to more gradual, cumulative learning, with which it is complementary. Jenkins (1999) noted that:

  > It is a paradox that while science is one of the supremely creative, imaginative and successful achievements of the human race, school science is often perceived by pupils as dull and repetitive, with laboratory work reduced to little more than a lengthy elaboration of the obvious. Every effort should be made, therefore, to help pupils capture something of the flavour of science as a disciplined, creative activity (p. 6) (In other words, for pupils to be innovative, not just receptive.)

- ownership of knowledge. Pupils learn for themselves, not simply for 'tests' or for others. Creative learning is internalized, and makes a difference to the pupil's self. Clayden *et al.* (1994) are concerned about pupils acquiring 'bodies of inert knowledge' (p. 172), a fear many have expressed in the wake of an overloaded National Curriculum (e.g. Campbell, 1993) and the official approach to its transmission. Clayden *et al.* (1994) cast knowledge as the working practices of a domain or discipline, and learning as enculturation into these practices . . . (This puts) the pupil into the engine room, as it were, of knowledge creation. (p. 172).

- control of learning processes. The pupil is self-motivated, not governed by extrinsic factors, or purely task-oriented exercises (Apple, 1986). John Abbott (1999) tells a story of how he learnt to be an expert woodcarver from an old seaman, who had taught himself the skill in any spare time he had from his job of shovelling coal into the boilers of battleships. Abbott became skilled enough at woodcarving to represent the UK in an international exhibition. But woodwork, let alone woodcarving, was not on the curriculum of his school, and was consequently of very low status. Latin was on the curriculum, and was supremely important, because in those days you needed it to get into university. Abbott failed his Latin three times. He says:

  > If I was good enough to beat everybody else at woodcarving, I rationalised, why couldn't I learn Latin? The answer appeared simple – I wasn't in charge. So that afternoon I went to my Latin teacher and explained that I wouldn't come to any more of his lessons. I would teach myself. For six weeks nobody knew what to do with me; but that didn't matter. I memorised vast chunks of Caesar's Gaelic War and Virgil's Aeneid. Night after night I lay awake testing myself on conjugations and declensions. And of course I passed Latin. Six months later I had forgotten most of it . . . but I still woodcarve! (p. 5)

Here we have control, but not ownership in the case of Latin, whereas the woodcarving has both. Better of course to have one than neither, for one could argue that control in this instance unlocked the way to ownership in the future

– it did get him in to university. Other examples are at hand in the review commissioned in 1998 by the DfEE of research into thinking skills and their role in the learning process. Among the conclusions, McGuiness (1999) notes: 'Developing thinking skills is supported by theories of cognition which see learners as active creators of their knowledge and frameworks of interpretation. Learning is about searching out meaning and imposing structure' (p. 2). Focusing on thinking skills in the classroom is important because it supports active cognitive processing which makes for better learning. It equips pupils to go beyond the information given, to deal systematically yet flexibly with novel problems and situations, to adopt a critical attitude to information and argument as well as to communicate effectively (p. 2).

Yet another example of ownership and control is given in an RSA (Royal Society of Arts) report, where Bayliss (1999) proposes a competence or skills led curriculum, involving open and individual negotiation of learning targets between teacher and learner. Competence here is 'the ability to understand and to do' – ownership and control. The Report proposes five broad competences: for learning, citizenship, relating to people, managing situations, and managing information. One headteacher welcomed the emphasis on skills, giving the example of GNVQs (vocational qualifications), where in her school there had been 'dramatic successes at post-16 amongst previously unmotivated children'. 'It seems it would be more sensible to 'tease out' these key skills, and to show that as well as literacy and numeracy people need to be able to use their brains'. Tamsin Imison, quoted in *Guardian Education*, 15 June 1999, p. 3.

- relevance. We have discussed the notion of 'relevance' in a general context in a study (Woods and Jeffrey, 1996), where we considered how teachers strove to construct knowledge that is meaningful within the child's frame of reference (see Donaldson, 1978). We described teachers' strategies in sharing and creating knowledge, stimulating 'possibility knowledge' through imagination, utilizing children's 'prior knowledge', and developing 'common knowledge' (Edwards and Mercer, 1987). If knowledge conveyed to the children is relevant to their concerns (Woods, 1995, p. 2) and reflects their societal and cultural knowledge (Woods and Jeffrey, 1997, p. 1), then it is more easily internalized by the child, developing into 'personal knowledge' (Woods and Jeffrey, 1996, p. 116). We might posit some alternative notions of 'relevance' (see Fielding, 1999). Teachers might feel obliged to try to deliver the prescribed National Curriculum and to 'teach to tests', regardless of whether they are serving the causes of 'common' or 'personal' knowledge or not (Parker-Rees, 1997). The relevance here is to some others' conception of pupils' and society's needs. Chris Woodhead (1995), formerly HM Chief Inspector of Schools in England, criticized the belief that 'education must be relevant to the immediate needs and interests of pupils', arguing that 'Our school curriculum must provide young people with the knowledge and skills they need to function effectively in adult working life'. Apart from the fact that this speaks to only one aim of education, it might be argued that relevance to 'immediate needs and interests' – and in particular pupil cultures – is a desirable aid towards that adult state. As Martin and Stuart-Smith

> (1998, p. 251) have shown, 'children are affected by the relevance and cultural nearness of what they are learning about' (see also Ferdman, 1990; Kress, 1997; Jeevanantham, 1998). We developed this argument in considering the application of relevance to different situations and within different aspects of the overall curriculum in relation to young bilingual learners (Woods *et al.*, 1999). Their teachers sought to establish relevance in various ways: encouraging children's play; starting with the child; developing home-school links; revisiting topics and skills; 'teaching in the margins'; and through spontaneous reaction to children's interests.

Considering the relationship among these criteria, we conclude that the higher the relevance of teaching to children's lives, worlds, cultures and interests, the more likelihood there is that pupils will have control of their own learning processes. Relevance aids identification, motivation, excitement and enthusiasm. Control, in turn, leads to ownership of the knowledge that results. If relevance, control and ownership apply, the greater the chance of creative learning resulting – something new is created, there is significant change or 'transformation' in the pupil – i.e. innovation.

The Need for Creative Learning

I consider a focus on creative learning important for a number of reasons.

First, it is eminently suited to the multiple needs of life in thetwenty-first century, which call for skills of adaptation, flexibility, initiative, and the ability to use knowledge on a different scale than has been realized hitherto. There has been the enormous expansion of information and communication technologies, which augment our connectedness and interdependence. Bentley (1998, p. 3) argues:

> To make sense of these connections, to turn them into opportunities rather than threats, we must use information to create, share and use knowledge. The explosion of information means that much of it is useless and trivial, requiring us to sort and synthesize, to spot connections that matter, to distinguish meaningful messages from the noise that surrounds them. . . . To make full use of the resources that an information society offers, we must be able to handle the overload, to develop capacities which can make sense of it all without screening out things that might be valuable.

Stephen Heppell (in Levis, 1999, p. 31) argues that computers emphasize the need for a change from the notational, factory system of digesting information and reproducing it in examinations. Instead of looking at the product, we should focus on the process – how children learn.

> Children are active learners . . . and need to use their computers primarily as learning tools not as teaching machines. They learn with a computer, not from a computer. Software tools should empower them as contributors rather than simply empower them to explore others' work: authoring as well as browsing, annotating as well as selecting.

What's the use, he says, of having all this wonderfully dexterous and expensive equipment if we 'simply use it to deliver the traditional curriculum . . . of having great tools but only mundane targets?'

Second, work patterns are undergoing a revolution. Day (1997) argues the 'need for more highly educated motivated employees who are able to use more autonomy in applying skills in combination with flexible technology and work processes' (p. 48). Charles Handy (1998) feels, in the light of more short-term contracts and fewer career jobs, that:

> careers will become more variegated. . . . It will increasingly be the individual's responsibility to make sure that the opportunities on offer add up to a sensible career path. . . . Education in these circumstances becomes an investment, wide experience an asset provided it is wide and not shallow (p. 125).

Handy (1999) predicts:

> There are going to be many opportunities, many choices, and that's wonderful if you have competence or skills. If you are sure of yourself, know what you want to be and what you want to do. If you can promote yourself, if you're good with people, if you're prepared to take responsibility, prepared to work on your own, can be trusted and are willing to trust other people. And it's going to be absolute hell if you can't do any of those things. (p. 3)

There's no time, he argues, for one to acquire these attributes in work, as in the past:

> They expect you to come fully equipped. And fully equipped means not only having basic skills and 'A' levels and maybe degrees even, but all kinds of other qualities [*Handy lists self-confidence, self-discipline, trustworthiness, honesty, openness, being good with people, and also* –] They want you to be courageous and imaginative. They want you to be able to take risks and to learn when the risks go wrong. (p. 3)

You can read these sorts of things about many other countries. Day (1997, p. 50) quotes from a Canadian Ministry of Education document on 'Year 2000 Framework Learning':

> In view of the new social and economic realities, *all* students, regardless of their immediate plans following school, will need to develop a flexibility and versatility undreamed of by previous generations. Increasingly, they will need to be able to employ critical and creative thinking skills to solve problems and make decisions.
>
> Ministry of Education 1991, p. 2

Third, a third major area of change is the family, the former bedrock of social stability. Family formations have become much more variable. The traditional family represents only 40 per cent of such groupings; and the number of single parent families continues to rise. More than one-third of marriages end in divorce. In 1998, nearly one in four households was headed by a single parent. In 1971, it was 1/13, and most single mothers were either widowed or separated. In 1998, 40 per cent of lone mothers had never married. What the changes in work and family mean is that we have lost the security of scheduled status passages, which guide us on how to behave, how to feel, how to cope through key transitions in life. We are increasingly thrown back on our own resources. We need to strengthen our strategical and biographical competence.

Fourth, despite its efficacy and increasing relevance, there are signs that creative teaching and learning are becoming increasingly squeezed in the intensification that has taken place throughout education in recent years (Apple, 1986). There is less time and space for teacher experimentation, more prescriptive curricula and assessment, and pressure for more whole-class teaching. The trend is towards traditionalism. Galton *et al.* (1999), comparing teacher pedagogy in primary schools in 1976 with that of 1996, conclude that teachers today talk even more and children listen more. Teachers do less of their personal work in the classroom, such as marking, but they still talk at children, making statements, rarely using challenging questions or asking for speculation. Teachers today feel obliged to 'deliver' a curriculum and consequently they still maintain a low level of pupil participation. Francis and Grindle (1998) also demonstrate a move back to more traditional teaching styles. This is all within the context of the growing emphasis on 'performativity' (Ball, 1998; Broadfoot, 1998), an ideology of 'performance' with fixed goals, task analysis and testing, and the exclusion of any alternative view. Lauder *et al.* (1998, p. 15) speak of the cultivation of a 'trained incapacity to think openly and critically' (see also, Ball, 1999). This all reflects the shift in emphasis in official policy in recent years from the liberal and egalitarian view of the 1960s and 1970s (an 'empowering' ideology) to one dominated by economic considerations, focusing on the need for a highly skilled work force to enable the country to compete successfully in the global economy. While few would dispute this as a worthy aim, some fear the marginalization of other equally worthy aims, such as the fostering of qualities of independence and autonomy, of self-awareness and development of identity, of critical and creative capacity, of cultural and artistic appreciation, of other- as well as self-regard, of emotional maturity, of moral responsibility, of social and political conscience, of benefits that stem from development of one's full range of abilities, and qualities of integration whereby the various domains of one's life enrich each other.

Morrison (1989, p. 14) argues that 'Primary education should continue its support of the aesthetic, creative and reflective areas of children's experience as one of the 'basics', providing a counter to the positivistic, technicist rationality and mentality seen . . . to be so detrimental to contemporary society.' This sentiment was echoed in the 1999 report by the National Advisory Committee on Creative and Cultural Education. Among their key recommendations were:

- Creative and cultural education should be explicitly recognized and provided for in the curriculum, in pupil assessment and in school inspection
- Teachers should be trained to use methods and materials which help develop young people's creative abilities and cultural understanding
- Innovative approaches to funding creative activity in schools should be explored.

The report was welcomed by the Education Secretary of State, David Blunkett, who said he had set up the Committee because:

> I was concerned that pupils should not only be equipped with the basic skills of literacy and numeracy, but should also have opportunities to develop their creative potential. . . . The Government wants to develop young people's capacity for original ideas. . . . The revised curriculum [ie The National Curriculum reviewed for the year 2000] will offer teachers more flexibility in their delivery of the curriculum with more opportunities for pupils to explore their creative potential. The increased emphasis which will be placed on thinking skills in the revised curriculum will also enable pupils to focus more on their creative talents.
>
> quoted in DfEE, 1999, p. 1.

The Government has recently moved in the direction of creativity, instituting a full programme of arts and music for all, more flexibility for teachers to explore children's creative potential and more emphasis on thinking skills. However, Kenneth Robinson, the chair of the National Advisory Committee on Creative and Cultural Education, felt 'the government's plan would not be enough to restore creative energy to the classroom' (*The Guardian*, 15 May 1999). This committee would like to see provision for creative and cultural education in the curriculum improved; teachers given access to materials and training necessary to promote creativity; and creative partnerships encouraged between schools and other agencies, such as businesses and community organizations.

Finally, creative learning is indicated from the child's view. Children are naturally inventive and playful. Grainger and Goouch (1999, p. 19) attest: 'The playful irreverence and inventiveness of the early years are energetic forces in their language and as such deserve further recognition, exploration and development.' They feel Bakhtin's (1968, p. 135) notion of 'carnival' celebrating 'temporary liberation from the prevailing truth and from the established order' can be applied to children's ability to subvert convention, through, for example, literature, role play, playground sub-cultures, humour. These subversive encounters, according to Grainger and Goouch (1999, p. 19), 'provoke vitality, emotional engagement and active involvement in learning'.

It is a small step from here to an empowerment point. Is it not important for pupils' voices to be heard in matters concerning their own learning? Too often they are treated as ciphers, things 'to be done to' by the prescription of others, the efficacy of which is totally judged by others (see Qvortrup, 1990). A great deal of research, too, has treated young children as deficient, instead of countenancing the deficiencies of their own research assumptions (see

Deloach and Brown, 1987). Primary pupils are well able to articulate their views on new developments (Pollard *et al.*, 1997). Who are better qualified to speak of their own learning? Nias (1989) says, 'teachers rely in the last resort for recognition upon their pupils, for no one else knows, or can know, how effectively they have taught' (see also Guba and Lincoln, 1981; Riseborough, 1985; Sikes et al, 1985; Morgan and Morris, 1999).

Contexts for creative learning

A reconstructed progressivism would embrace all knowledge, not just that learnt at school through the National Curriculum. Child-centred teachers teach the whole child, for life, not just the student for the National Curriculum and short-term goals like SATs. This involves long-term, qualitative measures of assessment, an important part of which is done by the student. And it is effective for all – students, teachers, parents, governors, and others.

One implication of this is diversification, rather than what Caldwell (1997) calls a 'factory system', turning out standardized products in the contextual grip of 'categoric' assessment (Broadfoot, 1998). We are in danger of becoming locked in the sort of organizational straitjacket which bedevilled Japanese education until recently. Interestingly, Japan now seems intent on breaking out of this, and diversifying curriculum and schools. Shimahara (1997) reports on the introduction of innovative schools, such as comprehensive high schools, schools for international studies, schools for information science, economics, etc, which vary in their programmes and approaches. It is indeed curious that 'what has been seen as the solution in Britain (ie uniformity and standardization) is . . . seen as one of the greatest problems in Japan' (pp. 102–3). There is a danger here that some forms of diversification would reintroduce selection. Structural safeguards (for example, diversification within and across a number of linked comprehensive schools, allowances for the development of aptitudes and abilities at different ages) can ensure that it is done in the interests of opportunities for all, and for both child and society.

A second implication is communitization. One context well suited to a reconstructed child-centredness, and well honed to the needs of the twenty-first century is that of the learning community (Retallick *et al.*, 1999). In the learning community, all are teachers and all are learners, members of the general community included. There is a holistic approach to knowledge, there is common ownership of knowledge, progressive development and continuous renewal, and shared and democratic leadership. It is not surprising that those involved in Apple and Beane's (1999, p. 11) 'democratic schools' see themselves as 'participants in communities of learning'. We have urged the potential in this idea especially in areas of ethnic mix (Woods *et al.*, 1999). It would involve the school moving outwards to its community in order to create an interactive, collaborative culture, counteracting the hierarchical relationships of the traditional order (Cocklin *et al.*, 1996), and parental reserve and caution at challenging teachers' professionalism. In this way, those same elements of ownership, control and relevance characteristic of creative teaching and learning make the community an innovative educational force. Excellent examples of such communities working in inner city areas are given in Searle (1998) and in Retallick *et al.* (1999).

Bentley (1998) refers to 'neighbourhood learning centres', 'offering learning opportunities to a wide range of people in their local areas. . . . Schools will become brokers as well as providers, forging partnerships with employers, voluntary and religious organizations, parents and young people, to extend and enhance opportunities for learning' (p. 6). The telecommunications revolution aids this development since it is breaking down the boundaries which have traditionally surrounded school. Day (1997, p. 56) argues that: 'Schooling will become more of a partnership and "learning contracts" between teachers, pupils and parents will become established on a more explicit basis. . . . Learning, if not teaching, will become everybody's business.'

Another variation is offered by Handy (1999, p. 5), who suggests stopping school at 2 p.m. and 'handing the kids over to a community faculty to do all kinds of things that will bring forth their other kinds of intelligences'. Other kinds of intelligences, that is, than are fostered by formal schooling. Certain initiatives around the edges of mainstream schooling, such as the Prince's Trust Study Support programme, are ministering to this need for independent, meaningful learning, and making connections between learning in the various different domains of life (see Bentley, 1998, pp. 30–1).

Lifelong and lifewide learning

This brings me to lifelong and lifewide learning. We already have a considerable head of steam on this rhetorically, encapsulated in the notion of the 'Learning Society', reflected in the Government's 1998 policy document on 'The Learning Age', and various initiatives from other organisations (see Broadfoot, 1998, p. 158). In the 'Learning Society':

> Learners are empowered to want, and to be able, to manage their own learning in a highly individualistic manner . . . there will be fewer and fewer designated spaces and times, defined outcomes or prescribed bodies of knowledge. . . . The vision calls for resilient and flexible learners, whose intrinsic motivation and mastery orientation will provide the foundation of future national economic and social development.

However, a recent report, containing advice to the Government following their policy document, said a huge shift in the country's culture was essential to instil a craving for learning in every adult and child. But at present, the Report notes, 'to some, the notion of 'lifelong learning' sounds more like a penal sentence than an invitation to pleasure, achievement and progress'. There has been little progress, as yet, toward creating a learning society. We have in mind a determined and imaginative initiative to parallel those mounted for educational standards and healthy living. . . . Structures, procedures, language, curricula, learning environments, teaching methods and systems of support for learners, will all need modifying (TES, 21 May 1999, p. 35). Broadfoot concurs, arguing that the effect of the educational policies of the present, as well as the previous government, has been to 'turn the clock backwards' (1998, p. 159), reinforcing 'traditionalist conceptions of teaching and learning which are associated with a greater instrumentalism on the part of pupils', and making pupils 'more dependent on the teacher and less ready and able to engage in 'deep' learning' (Broadfoot and Pollard, 1998).

In the first report of a major research programme on 'The Learning Society' (Coffield, 1998), contributors raise the issue of what is to count as learning. Some argue that it is 'all learning', another that it refers 'only to significant changes in capability or understanding' (similar to 'creative learning'), another that it should include the 'commitment of the individual to both the group and the wider organisation'. Others emphasize informal learning. Eraut *et al.*, for example, conclude that 'learning from formal education and training . . . is often of only secondary importance'; and Ashton notes in his study that 'training was an infrequent activity but learning was an everyday occurrence' (quoted in Coffield, 1998, p. 3). Contributors also note the need for 'open, trusting relationships among colleagues at work to enable informal learning to thrive' (p. 4), but that there are a number of structural impediments to this, such as competition, downsizing and delayering. This research is showing how we need to bring to greater prominence 'the more informal skills of mentoring, coaching and collaborative learning in teams' as opposed to more formal transmission of knowledge; the importance of informal learning at work, 'the sheer amount of learning from other people, rather than, say, from manuals or formal training sessions (p. 5).

I want to complement the research on learning at work by considering learning at leisure, and specifically by reference to what might seem at first glance a rather delinquent activity – banger-racing ('bangers' are old, battered cars). This might seem an almost trivial example if 'education' refers to what goes on in formal schools and other formal institutions of learning – but it has a great deal of relevance, I would suggest, if it were connected to creative teaching and learning communities, and if seen in the context of the 'learning society'. I did some research on this activity in the 1980s, and I draw on this here.

Banger-racing had not only provided opportunities for the drivers – for some of them it had been a redemption. Brian, for example, told me that as a schoolboy he always wanted to be a racing driver, but working six days a week he never had the chance. Then, at the age of 35, he discovered this sport and joined the Bedford Banger Club,'picking the bits and pieces up from the rest of the team'. Colin, in the following extract, shows how he has successfully taken up a hobby involving mechanics, against the advice given him at school by a careers adviser:

> I remember when I first left school I wanted to be a mechanic, and we had a chap come and interview us at school, and he asked me what I would like to do. I said, 'I'd like to be a mechanic', and he asked me one question. He said, 'Tell me how you put a front wheel on a bike.' I said, 'You shove it in and do the nuts up.' And he said, 'Would you like to do anything else?' I said, 'Why?' He said, 'Well I think you'd better leave it for the time being.'

> And I never was a mechanic, but now I've picked things up at banger-racing and I know a bit about cars' engines for my own benefit of racing, and I enjoy racing my own cars what I build myself, and that's how I get along.

It is clear, too, that many have not, and would not have, learned these things anywhere else: 'All I've learned about mechanics is what I've learned through banger-racing really' (Brian). Andy tells us, 'I used to race motorcycles years ago in scrambles. But I hadn't really that much knowledge on cars. I knew how they worked but I'd never worked on cars before.' What is remarkable, perhaps, is the unsystematic, but thorough, acquisition of knowledge. As Toddy says, 'These are not the sort of things you learn at school. This is something you pick up. I mean, I couldn't have changed a gearbox here 12 years ago. I take it to bits now without thinking about it.'

There is always something new. Charles tells us,'I've been in this ten years, and I'm still learning. There's always something to learn, you know you never learn everything.' In a similar vein Andy says, 'Every race is different. You never get a race that's the same because the hazards are different.'

To a large extent the participants generate their own special knowledge and tricks of the trade. They are masters of improvization. If something needs doing, there is a way of doing it. No problem is insoluble. Someone will find an answer. Much as work cultures develop, so the participants here have developed a distinctive culture, with its own language, symbols, way of doing things, unwritten rules and codes of behaviour, and structured networks among the drivers. Some drivers belong to teams, which act as support groups for car preparation during the week, and provide a basis of other social activity occasionally; and there is still largely friendly rivalry between them, though most contests are run on an individual basis.

People learn through the community by various means. You 'beg, steal or borrow' (Charles), and 'pick people's brains, watch what other people do, trial and error, you learn as you go' (Toddy). Andy says:

> You find out the hard way. You do something you think is a good idea, and you find it's a disaster. The whole of the wiring will burn out, for example. Or you'll have to experiment to find the best place to route the petrol lines through. And also when you get the chance you look under somebody else's bonnet, and see what they've got!

Colin recalls 'scrounging a steering box' so he could take part in a final. Brian points to '101 silly little things you pick up, like taping the plugs on.' In this way experts are made.

There is more to activities like this than 'recreation', if you use that word in the sense of an amusing and relaxing sideline to the main business of life. We are talking about, rather, creation of one's powers, abilities and aspirations, all of which may be unfulfilled in other walks of life. The chances are that this will increasingly become the case as some forms of work become even more automated and systematized, and as the time spent at work diminishes. Hobbies and interests then may offer the best chance of realizing our aims, and of being the sort of person we wish to be, whether the hobby be photography, hi-fi, drama, gardening, pigeon-fancying, ballroom-dancing, music, growing leeks, whippet-racing, pottery, fishing, or whatever. This adds to the argument for less school, more community involvement, and more diversification.

I am not saying that banger-racing as such should be part of the National Curriculum, which is crowded enough already (although it is tempting, just for one thing, to think of the literacies involved – notes passed around among them, programmes, specifications. Toddy's house was full of motoring magazines, some of them of the most amazing complexity and technical jargon). It is more an attitude of mind, the approach, the expansiveness, inclusiveness and self-searching that is important. Unfortunately, a recent Green Paper, while paying lip service to the 'Learning Society', still seemed mainly concerned with the economic factor. Learning here is about employability. As Frade (1996) puts it education has been 'publicly redefined as a mere instrument of the economy' (quoted in Coffield, 1999, p. 34).

Bearing this in mind, we have to be cautious about official pronouncements on the 'learning society', recalling the point made earlier about alternative discourses. Coffield (1999, pp. 8–9) outlines four models of the 'learning society':

1. The skill growth model, which emphasizes re-skilling and re-training.
2. The personal development model, which involves self-fulfilment in all areas of life.
3. The social learning model, to do with the development of networks, and of civil society.
4. The social control model. Here, lifelong learning is seen by government and others as 'the solution to a wide range of economic, social and political problems'. How long will it be, Coffield wonders, before we see the advertising slogan "You will learn, and what's more, you will enjoy it" (pp. 10–11). He concludes:

   > . . . behind the benevolent intentions and the high flown rhetoric, lifelong learning, the learning society and the learning organisation are all being propounded to induce individuals to become more or less willing participants in learning for life and to bear an increasing proportion of the costs of such learning without end. (p. 11)

It is easy to see how the first three models – skills, personal and social development – apply to banger-racing as I have described it. This blend meets the requirements of education in the twenty-first century as some see it. The Institute for Public Policy Research (IPPR) (1993), for example, sees the need for a blend of 'distinctive individualism' and 'the capacity for harmonious co-operation', together with 'the acquisition of knowledge, skills, attitudes and appropriate patterns of behaviour' (pp. 8–12, quoted in McCulloch, 1997, p. 23). Has this to operate outside our formal educational institutions? In all the debate about raising standards of education the current official policy line seems to miss the point. It is one about human self-realization. Too often school suppresses or oppresses the self. Amongst the reminder notices of this I have on my study wall is a quote from Valerie Walkerdine (1989, p. 267):

> A woman teacher, one of my students, receives a well-deserved distinction for her Master's degree. She received more or less straight 'A's for all her work, but still she cannot believe that the distinction belongs to her; it is though the person with her name exists somewhere else, outside her body: this powerful person that she cannot recognize as herself. Instead, she feels that she is hopeless, consistently panics about her performance and appears to have little confidence in herself . . . I am sure that this story has resonances for many women.

I would think for quite a few men, too – people who have internalized an inferior or indifferent academic or intellectual identity through their experiences at school. This is not to say that many have not found fulfilment through the state system. But I know through my experience at the Open University (the university of the 'second chance') over 27 years that there are many who have not, and who, like Walkerdine's student, have held vastly underrated views of their own abilities and of their identities.

This is one way of seeing the need for people to unlearn and to relearn. To help them to do so, teachers also need to unlearn and relearn, and schools need to deschool and reschool in a wholesale review of pedagogy, curricula, and organizational contexts. Not least, governments need to formulate policy that facilitates and promotes, rather than constrains and reverses such a review.

Bibliography

Abbott, J. (1999) 'Battery hens or free range chickens: What type of education for what type of world?' Speech delivered at North of England Conference, Sunderland, January.

Alexander, R. (1992) *Policy and Practice in Primary Education*, London, Routledge.

—— (1997) 'International comparisons and the quality of primary teaching' in C. Cullingford (ed.) *The Politics of Primary Education,* Buckingham, Open University Press.

Alexander, R., Willcocks, J. and Nelson, N. (1995) 'Discourse, pedagogy and the National Curriculum: change and continuity in primary schools', *Research Papers in Education* 11(1): 81–120.

Apple, M. W. (1986) *Teachers and Texts: a Political Economy of Class and Gender Relations in Education*, New York: Routledge and Kegan Paul.

Apple, M. W. and Beane, J. A. (1999) *Democratic Schools; Lessons From the Chalkface,* London, Open University Press.

Bakhtin, M. (1968) *Rabelais and His World,* Cambridge, MA: Harvard University Press.

Ball, S. (1998) 'Performativity and fragmentation in 'Postmodern Schooling'', in J. Carter (ed.) *Postmodernity and Fragmentation of Welfare*, London: Routledge.

Ball, S. J. (1999) 'Labour, learning and the economy: a 'policy sociology' perspective', *Cambridge Journal of Education* 29(2): 195–206.

Barker, B. (1987) 'Visions are off the agenda', *The Times Educational Supplement*, 3 December, p. 4.

Bayliss, V. (1999) *Opening Minds*, London: Royal Society of Arts.

Bennett, N. (1976) *Teaching Styles and Pupil Progress*, London: Open Books.
—— (1997) 'Voyages of discovery: changing perspectives in research on primary school practice', in C. Cullingford (ed.) *The Politics of Primary Education,* Buckingham, Open University Press.
Bentley, T. (1998) *Learning Beyond the Classroom: Education for a Changing World,* London: Routledge.
Bonnett, M. (1996) '"New" ERA values and the teacher–pupil relationship as a form of the poetic', *British Journal of Educational studies* 44(1): 27–41.
Brighouse, T. (1987) 'Goodbye to the head and the history man', *Guardian*, 21 July, p. 11.
Broadfoot, P. (1998) 'Quality standards and control in higher education: what price life-long learning?', *International Studies in Sociology of Education* 8(2): 155–81.
Broadfoot, P. and Osborn, M. with Gilly, M. and Paillet, A. (1988) 'What professional responsibility means to teachers: national contexts and classroom constants', *British Journal of Sociology of Education* 9(3): 265–87.
Broadfoot, P. and Pollard, A. (1998) 'Categories, standards and instrumentalism: the changing discourse of assessment policy in English primary education', paper given at The American Educational Research Association Conference, San Diego, April.
Caldwell, B. J. (1997) 'The impact of self-management and self-government on professional cultures of teaching: a strategic analysis for the twenty-first century', in A. Hargreaves and R. Evans (eds) *Beyond Educational Reform: Bringing Teachers Back In,* London: Open University Press.
Campbell, R. J. (1993) 'The National Curriculum in primary schools: a dream at conception, a nightmare at delivery', in C. Chitty and B. Simon (eds) *Education Answers Back: Critical Responses to Government Policy*, London: Lawrence and Wishart.
—— (1998) 'Broader thinking about the primary school curriculum", in N. Tester (ed.) *Take Care, Mr Blunkett*, London: ATL.
Clayden, E., Desforges, C., Mills, C. and Rawson, W. (1994) 'Authentic activity and learning', *British Journal of Educational Studies* 32(2): 163–73.
Cocklin, B., Retallick, J. and Coombe, K. (1996) 'Learning communities in Australian schools: case studies from rural New South Wales', paper presented at The European Conference on Educational Research, University of Seville, 25–8 September.
Coffield, F. (ed.) (1998) 'Learning at Work', *ESRC Learning Society series, 1*, University of Bristol: The Policy Press.
—— (1999) 'Why's the beer always stronger up North?' Studies of lifelong learning in Europe, *ESRC Learning Society series, 2*, University of Bristol: The Policy Press.
Cox, B. (1998) (ed.) *Literacy is not Enough: Essays on the Importance of Reading,* Manchester, Manchester University Press and Book Trust.
Day, C. (1997) 'Teachers in the twenty-first century: time to renew the vision', in A. Hargreaves and R. Evans (eds) *Beyond Educational Reform: Bringing Teachers Back In,* London: Open University Press.
Day, C. and Hadfield, M. (1995) 'Metaphors for movement: accounts of professional development', paper presented at ECER Conference, Bath.
Deloache, J. S. and Brown, A. L. (1987) 'The early emergence of planning skills in young children', in J. Bruner and H. Haste (eds.) Making Sense, London: Methuen.
Department for Education and Employment (DfEE) (1998) *The National Literacy Strategy: Literacy Training Pack,* London: DfEE.
—— (1999) 'Encourage creativity in schools says new report', DfEE paper 215/99, London, DfEE, 14 May.
Donaldson, M. (1978) *Children's Minds*, London: Fontana.
Edwards, D. and Mercer, N. (1987) *Common Knowledge: the Development of Understanding in the Classroom*, London, Methuen.

Ferdman, B. M. (1990) 'Literacy and cultural identity', *Harvard Educational Review* 60: 181–204.

Fielding, M. (1999) 'Target setting, policy pathology and student perspectives: learning to labour in new times', *Cambridge Journal of Education* 29(2): 277–87.

Frade, C. (1996) *Education and Training Policies in the UK,* the DELILAH Project, TSER Programme, Brussels: DGXII, EC.

Francis, L.J. (1986) *Partnership in Rural Education: Church Schools and Teacher Attitudes,* London: Collins Liturgical Publications.

Francis, L. J and Grindle, Z. (1998) 'Whatever happened to progressive education? A comparison of primary school teachers' attitudes in 1982 and 1996', *Educational Studies,* 24(3): 269–79.

Galton, M. (1989) *Teaching in the Primary School*, London, David Fulton Publishers.

Galton, M., Hargreaves, L., Comber, C., Wall, D. and Pell, T. (1999) 'Changes in patterns of teacher interaction in primary classrooms: 1976–96', *British Educational Research Journal* 25(1): 23–37.

Gipps, C., McCallum, B. and Brown, M. (1999) 'Primary teachers' beliefs about teaching and learning', *The Curriculum Journal,* 10(1): 123–34.

Grainger, G. and Goouch, K. (1999) 'Young children and playful language', in T. David (ed.) *Teaching Young Children,* London: Paul Chapman Publishing Ltd.

Guba, E. G. and Lincoln, Y. S. (1981) *Effective Evaluation*, San Francisco: Jossey-Bass.

Handy, C. (1998) *The Age of Unreason*, London: Business Books Ltd.

—— (1999) 'The world around the corner: How best to prepare for it', speech delivered at North of England Conference, Sunderland, January.

Hargreaves, A. H. (1994) *Changing Teachers, Changing Times*, London: Cassell.

—— (1998) 'The emotional practice of teaching', *Teaching and Teacher Education,* 14(8): 835–54.

—— (1996) 'Teaching as a research-based profession: possibilities and prospects', *The Teacher Training Agency Annual Lecture,* mimeo.

Hillage, J., Pearson, R., Anderson, A. and Tamkin, P. (1998) *Excellence in Research in Schools,* DfEE Research Report no. 74, London: HMSO.

Institute for Public Policy Research (IPPR) (1993) *Education: A Different Vision. An Alternative White Paper*. London: IPPR.

Jeevanantham, L. S. (1998) 'Curriculum content: a quest for relevance', *Curriculum Studies,* 6(2):. 217–30.

Jeffrey, R. and Woods, P. (1997) 'The relevance of creative teaching: pupils' views', in A. Pollard, D. Thiessen and A. Filer (eds.) *Children and their Curriculum: The Perspectives of Primary and Elementary School Children,* Lewes: Falmer.

Jenkins, E. (1999) 'School science and the creative and cultural development of young people', speech delivered at North of England Conference, Sunderland, January.

Kress, G. (1997) *Before Writing: Rethinking the Paths to Literacy,* London: Routledge.

Lauder, H., Jamieson, I. and Wikeley, F. (1998) 'Models of effective schools: limits and capabilities' in R. Slee, G. Weiner and S. Tomlinson (eds) *School Effectiveness for Whom? Challenges to the School Effectiveness and School Improvement Movements,* London: Falmer Press.

Levis, N. (1999) 'Technology's tool for active learning', *Times Educational Supplement, 4* June, p. 31.

Mac an Ghaill, M. (1992) 'Student perspectives on curriculum innovation and change in an English Secondary School: an empirical study', *British Educational Research Journal*, 18(3): 221–34.

—— (1994) *The Making of Men*, Buckingham: Open University Press.

McCulloch, G. (1997) 'Marketing the millennium: Education for the 21st century', in A.

Hargreaves and R. Evans (eds) *Beyond Educational Reform: Bringing Teachers Back In,* London, Open University Press.
McGuiness, C. (1999) 'From thinking skills to thinking classrooms', (DfEE) *Department for Education and Employment Research Briefs*, Research Report No. 115, London: DfEE.
Martin, D. and Stuart-Smith, J. (1998) 'Exploring bilingual children's perceptions of being bilingual and biliterate: Implications for educational provision', *British Journal of Sociology of Education* 19(2): 237–54.
Morgan, C. and Morris, G. (1999) *Good Teaching and Learning: Pupils and Teachers Speak*, Buckingham: Open University Press.
Morrison, K. (1989) 'Bringing progressivism into a critical theory of education', *British Journal of Sociology of Education* (1): 3–18.
National Advisory Committee on Creative and Cultural Education (NACCCE) (1999) *All Our Futures: Creativity, Culture and Education,* London: DfEE.
Newman, J. and Clarke, J. (1994) 'Going about our business? The managerialisation of public services', in J. Clarke, A. Cochrane and E. McLaughlin (eds) *Managing Social Policy*, London: Sage.
Nias, J. (1989) *Primary Teachers Talking: a Study of Teaching as Work*, London: Routledge.
Nixon, J. (1999) 'Teachers, writers, professionals. Is there anybody out there?' *British Journal of Sociology of Education,* 20(2): 207–21.
Ofsted, (1993) *First Class,* London.
Palmer, S. (1997) 'Magnetised by Mr Enthusiasm', *Time Education Supplement, Primary Update*, London, Times Newspapers, 24 January, p. 9.
Parker-Rees, R. (1997) 'The tale of a task: learning beyond the map' in A. Pollard, D. Thiessen and A. Filer (eds) *Children and their Curriculum: The Perspectives of Primary and Elementary School Children*, London: Falmer Press.
Pollard, A., Broadfoot, P., Croll, P., Osborn, M. and Abbott, D. (1994) *Changing English Primary Schools? The Impact of the Education Reform Act at Key Stage One*, London: Cassell.
Pollard, A., Thiessen, D. and Filer, A. (1997) *Children and their Curriculum: The Perspectives of Primary and Elementary School Children,* Lewes: Falmer.
Qvortrup, J. (1990) 'A voice for children in statistical and social accounting: a plea for children's right to be heard', in A. James and A. Prout (eds) *Constructing and Reconstructing Childhood,* London: Falmer Press.
Retallick, J., Cocklin, B. and Coombe K. (eds) (1999) *Learning Communities in Education*, London: Routledge.
Riseborough, G. F. (1981) 'Teacher careers and comprehensive schooling: an empirical Study', *Sociology* 15(3): 352–81.
—— (1985) 'Pupils, teachers' careers and schooling: an empirical study', in S. J. Ball and I. F. Goodson (eds) *Teachers' Lives and Careers,* Lewes: Falmer Press.
Searle, C. (1998) *None But Our Words: Critical Literacy in Classroom and Community*, Buckingham, Open University Press.
Shimahara, N. K. (1997) 'Japanese lessons for educational reform', in A. Hargreaves and R. Evans (eds) *Beyond Educational Reform: Bringing Teachers Back In,* London: Open University Press.
Sikes, P., Measor, L. and Woods, P. (1985) *Teacher Careers: Crises and Continuities*, Lewes: Falmer Press.
Silcock, P. (1993) 'Towards a new progressivism in primary school education', *Educational Studies* 19(1): 107–21.
Sugrue, C. (1997) *Complexities of Teaching: Child-Centred Perspectives*, London: Falmer Press.

Sylva, K. (1998) 'Too formal too soon?' Keynote address presented at the Islington Early Years' Conference, Building on Best practice in the Early Years, 9 July.
Tooley, J. and Darby, D. (1998) *Educational Research: A Critique,* London: Office for Standards in Education.
Tyler, S. (1986) 'Post-modern ethnography: from document of the occult to occult document', in J. Clifford and G. Marcus (eds) *Writing Culture*, Berkeley, CA: University of California Press.
Walkerdine, V. (1989) 'Femininity as performance', *Oxford Review of Education,* 15(13): 267–79.
Webb, R. and Vulliamy, G. (1996) *Roles and Responsibilities in the Primary School*, Buckingham: Open University Press.
Woodhead, C. (1995) *Annual Lecture of HM Chief Inspector of Schools*, London, Ofsted.
Woods, P (1990) *Teacher Skills and Strategies*, Lewes: Falmer Press.
—— (1993) *Critical Events in Teaching and Learning*, London: Falmer Press.
—— (1995) *Creative Teachers in Primary Schools*, Buckingham: The Open University Press.
—— (1999) 'Talking about coombes: features of a learning community' in J. Retallick, B. Cocklin, and K. Coombe (eds) *Learning Communities in Education,* London, Routledge.
Woods, P. and Jeffrey, R. (1996) *Teachable Moments: The Art of Teaching in Primary School,* Buckingham: Open University Press.
—— (1997) 'Creative teaching in the Primary National Curriculum', in G. Helsby and G. McCulloch (eds) *Teachers and the National Curriculum,* London: Cassell.
Woods, P. and Wenham, P. (1994) 'Teaching, and researching the teaching of, a history topic: an experiment in collaboration', *The Curriculum Journal* 5(2): 133–61.
Woods, P., Boyle, M. and Hubbard, N. (1999) *Multicultural Children in The Early Years: Creative Teaching and Meaningful Learning,* Clevedon: Multilingual Matters.

Section 2

Sites and sources

Chapter 6

Sites and sources of teachers' learning

Milbrey W. McLaughlin

Complicating questions of what teachers need to know and how they learn it

The policy community seldom makes problematic the question of what teachers need to know in order to improve their practice. Reformers and publics impatient with disappointing student outcomes cast requirements for teachers' learning in relatively simple terms – more or different content knowledge. For instance, we hear: Teachers need technical skills to work effectively with their students in the information age. Teachers need to be up-to-date in their subject area. Teachers at all levels and across disciplines need to be able to teach reading. In policy circles, 'knowing more' often is treated synonymously with 'teaching better'. (Cochran-Smith and Lytle, 1999).

Certainly, knowledge of new practices is essential for teachers to improve instruction for today's classrooms and prepare students for a productive role in the twenty-first century workforce. Yet more or better content knowledge by itself cannot necessarily accomplish much. For one, simply having more and better knowledge resources available does not mean that teachers will or can use them effectively in their classrooms. But equally as important, teachers require more than content knowledge to construct the sorts of educational environments reformers hope for and contemporary students need. For example, teachers need to know how to engage students in content knowledge, how to allocate time and attention, how to articulate standards appropriate for practice. Teachers need to know where to place instructional priority, how students are responding to their classroom choices, how to make adjustments when student achievement disappoints. Treating 'knowledge' as a generic concept fails to provide useful guidance to either policymakers or practitioners.

Conceptions of teachers' learning that inform policy and practice are similarly underdeveloped (Bransford *et al.*, 1999). Research on teachers' learning generally is decontextualized and silent on the question of environments that stimulate or frustrate it. Relatively little research looks at how sites and sources of teachers' learning affect teachers' ability and motivation to learn and use new knowledge. Likewise, research on teachers' learning typically is more concerned about the content of teachers' learning than with the processes mulate, support and sustain it.

This paper draws on one initiative's experience with evidence-based reform to describe how multiple forms of knowledge intersect with each other practically and theoretically. It presents a picture of how teachers are organized within a community of learners and how that community relates to its external environment.

I start from the position that reform initiatives aimed at improving teaching and learning involve distinctly different forms of knowledge, and that these forms of knowledge are generated at different sites and play strategically different roles in teachers' learning and change. I then turn to the character of school communities of practice as both medium and context for teachers' knowledge use, generation, learning and change. This descriptive analysis highlights ways in which policy can affect teachers' learning and support the knowledge they find useful as they seek to make change at their school and in their classrooms.

What kinds of knowledge do teachers need to improve their practice?

Marilyn Cochran-Smith and Susan Lytle (1999) distinguish among three substantively and strategically different conceptions of the knowledge associated with teachers' learning and change: knowledge for practice, knowledge of practice, and knowledge in practice. Cochran-Smith and Lytle define knowledge for practice as the formal knowledge and theory generated by researchers and university-based scholars. Some of this external knowledge comprises new programs or strategies – for example, Success for All, or Reading Recovery programmes are examples of such university-produced knowledge for practice. Other externally developed knowledge for practice involves new theories of learning or instruction, such as reciprocal teaching, cooperative learning, or peer instruction. Knowledge for practice also includes assessments, strategies for research and evaluation, or other inquiry tools such as running records to score students' reading progress.

Knowledge of practice conveys yet another form of knowledge and image of teachers' learning. This second form of knowledge comprises neither formal nor practical knowledge. Knowledge of practice is generated when teachers treat their own classrooms and schools as sites of inquiry and examine them in terms of such broader social and political issues as equity, patterns of student achievement, or school supports for students' futures. Knowledge of practice may be produced by teachers themselves, or may involve data and analysis provided by outside evaluators or researchers – working with or without teachers' involvement.

Knowledge in practice – a third kind of knowledge – is what teachers come to understand as they reflect on their practice, and is situated in their own classrooms. It is practical knowledge. Action research and other forms of classroom-based inquiry support teachers' learning of this sort. Knowledge in practice is individual knowledge, stimulated by teachers' own questions about their own classrooms. (Knowledge in practice, as used in this paper, is the product of deliberate inquiry rather than the tacit knowledge born of experience.)

Calls for reform in teaching and learning implicate all three forms of knowledge. Without knowledge for practice, teachers lack the new ideas, skills and perspectives they need to evaluate, enrich or change their practices. Yet, without knowledge of practice, teachers are constrained in their ability to exploit external knowledge, situate it in their particular school workplace, or even understand the need for new ways of doing things. Teachers often do not know what they need to know to address questions of whole school change and to move a faculty forward in a consistent manner. Knowledge of practice enables a faculty to see problem areas in their practice, and to identify opportunities for inquiry and innovation. Knowledge of practice points a faculty to needed external resources and areas for internal improvement.

However absent teachers' knowledge in practice, new ideas may have only uneven or marginal effects on individual classrooms, since they may not reflect the needs and issues specific to any one classroom setting, or since any individual teacher may or may not be interested in how his classroom is located in school-level data. Knowledge in practice informs individual teacher action and reflection, and guides teachers in tailoring resources to best support their everyday work.

Engaging multiple forms of knowledge

Most strategies or policies concerned with enhancing teachers' knowledge and learning are single-focus and disjoint. Research and Development efforts aim to provide teachers with the latest in best practices but pay little attention to teachers' motivation or capacity to use that knowledge or sustain changes associated with it. Action researchers focus on teacher-produced knowledge about their classrooms. Yet these individual efforts are seldom seen in terms of the broader school context, or as parts of a whole picture of practice at a site. Reform strategies such as site-based management or school improvement programmes centre attention on school-level knowledge for action, but focus little if at all on the content of those changes and the knowledge resources necessary to support them.

What would a strategy look like that attended simultaneously to all three knowledge domains as sites and sources of teachers' learning? The Bay Area School Reform Collaborative (BASRC) provides the opportunity to see how different forms of knowledge can or do work together to support teachers' learning and change.[1] BASRC, a 5–year reform effort involving schools throughout the 118 district Bay Area region, seeks to 'reculture' schools in ways that support whole school reform.

BASRC strategies aim to change the way schools do business. Merrill Vargo, BASRC's executive director, likes to ask people to complete the sentence: 'The problem with schools today is . . .' BASRC's design for reform finishes the sentence 'their culture' and posits a missing element in schools' cultures as evidence-based decision making centred on a focused reform effort. BASRC's overall strategy uses a cycle of inquiry to inform school reform efforts, and marshals diverse forms of knowledge to support teachers' learning and change.

The initiative exposes teachers to diverse forms of knowledge for practice. Much of it is content knowledge – resources and technical assistance in such domains as literacy, mathematics, technology and writing. These knowledge resources generally are carried to schools and teachers through so-called Support Providers, organizations contracted by Leadership Schools using their BASRC funds.

The initiative also attends to the learning skills that teachers will need in order to make effective use of that content knowledge. In an effort to foster teachers' capacity and comfort in generating knowledge of, teachers receive training in asking probing questions, in developing an accountability framework to guide their school's cycle of inquiry, and in constructing standards against which to measure their school's progress in their focused reform effort. They practice these skills in many BASRC events. For example, regional meetings of hundreds of Bay Area teachers, administrators, parents, support providers and funders were convened to score schools' portfolio applications for BASRC Leadership School status. Subsequently, regional preparation and reviews Leadership Schools' Reports of Progress immersed teachers in the use of rubrics to evaluate the process on five dimensions of whole school change.

A number of teachers told us that evaluating the portfolios with teachers from around the Bay Area 'was the best professional development I have ever had'. One said, for instance, 'Just reading about other schools and using that rubric forced us to use it well. It taught me about standards and accountability, skill I could take back to my school.' Critical friends visits – a BASRC strategy that brings two or three schools together to consider each others' practice – involve teachers in both giving and receiving critique of practice and school culture. As one teacher put it, '(our Critical Friends) enabled us to look at evidence from a different perspective; we learned about gaps and about what we didn't know'. Affinity groups engaged teachers from across the region in research on topics of their choosing. Through summer institutes for faculty teams from Leadership Schools, BASRC gave teachers tools in other areas important to their success in generating knowledge of practice in their schools – how to run a meeting, how to facilitate a discussion, how to deal with the 'politics of data'.

Teachers' skill in and experience with generating knowledge of and in practice was stimulated initially by their schools' preparation of the Portfolio Application for Leadership School status. BASRC required schools to provide evidence of their status along five dimensions of whole school change and in support of the 'focused effort' they selected to frame their reform efforts. Subsequently, BASRC required that each Leadership School develop and carry out a 'Cycle of Inquiry' to inform their school's reform efforts and to provide data for what BASRC calls an 'accountability event', where the school reports its progress annually to its community – faculty and parents.

BASRC's strategy places as much emphasis on developing teachers' learning and inquiry skills as it did on connecting them with relevant content knowledge. These tools and learning skills, BASRC hoped, would equip teachers to begin to ask questions about their own practices, gather evidence to address those questions, and situate reform efforts in their analyses. In other words, BASRC provided teachers with exposure to and practice with the skills and experience they would need to generate knowledge of and in practice at their own school site.

How did teachers use new knowledge to support learning and change?

What happened as a result of BASRC's efforts to reculture schools around habits of inquiry and whole school change? Across BASRC Leadership Schools we observe different patterns and processes of teachers' knowledge use, and so of their learning, change efforts and outcomes associated with them.

Not all schools or teachers were able to receive or use knowledge resources in the same way; schools and teachers also differed in the ways in which they approached engaging or generating forms of knowledge in their reform efforts. Some teachers or schools were relatively sophisticated in their thinking about inquiry-based reforms; some teachers wondered out loud 'What's data?' Few schools had experience with the school-based cycle of inquiry and accountability BASRC required – they were experienced in accounting for compliance's sake, but not for their own community of practice.

Over the course of the initiative's 4 years, we have begun to see in Leadership Schools different overall patterns of teachers' knowledge use as well as varied patterns of relations among forms of knowledge. Associated with these different patterns of knowledge generation and use, we find different consequences in terms of changed practices at school and classroom levels. Four general patterns emerged across BASRC Leadership Schools: First Steps, Beginning Inquiry, Getting Comfortable with Inquiry, A Cycle of Inquiry. I sketch them below and highlight the processes of knowledge use and learning we observed in Leadership Schools.

First steps in using knowledge to support learning and change

One pattern could be called 'First Steps' (Figure 6.1). For some Leadership Schools, BASRC involvement comprised the faculty's first efforts to think about whole school change – either in substantive or strategic terms. First steps were apparent especially in secondary schools where schools rarely thought in whole school terms, but rather in terms of departments, student academic placements or grade levels. Common to secondary schools are so-called Christmas Tree reform efforts, which collect multiple but usually unrelated reform efforts.

The evidence and inquiry BASRC requires of its Leadership Schools was both foreign and threatening to many teachers. 'Why are we doing this data collection stuff?' one teacher asked as she began her involvement with BASRC and was introduced to expectations for assessment and analysis. 'We're not methodologists', said another. This teacher, like many if not most of her colleagues, knew nothing about how to develop standards for assessment, how to go about systematic inquiry into the consequences of practice, or even how to construct the indicators that would be most meaningful to practice and action.

In schools taking their first steps towards whole school change based on a cycle of inquiry, teachers engaged support providers to provide assistance with their focused effort and made tentative, usually difficult and painful, efforts to think about what evidence and inquiry at the school level would mean or require. Teachers in these schools attended BASRC workshops on accountability and standards, but often found them inadequate in the light of their inexperience and anxiety about inquiry at the school level. These faculties often turned to their support providers for help with figuring out what measures would be meaningful in their schools, and strategies for collecting evidence about their work.

A major element frustrating the inquiry process in 'first step' schools was a contrary normative climate of the school which made teachers' work and student outcomes largely a private matter, and cast accountability as something done to, not for, the school. As the solid arrow in Figure 6.1 suggests, the learning most evident as schools began their journey as Leadership Schools was about new forms of practice. For many teachers, it was the first time in many years they had taken a hard look at what they were doing and thought about alternatives. For example a veteran teacher, working in a tough elementary school setting told us that BASRC

> opened my mind to certain strategies – and I have been teaching for more than a quarter century . . . but I didn't realize there were other outlets – that I could use much better strategies. So I became a strategy-seeker. . . . I was open to the fact that it's not my way or the highway any more. I am opening up new approaches to my students . . .

Another teacher commented on the expanded view of her work and career promoted by BASRC's various assemblies, institutes and other learning

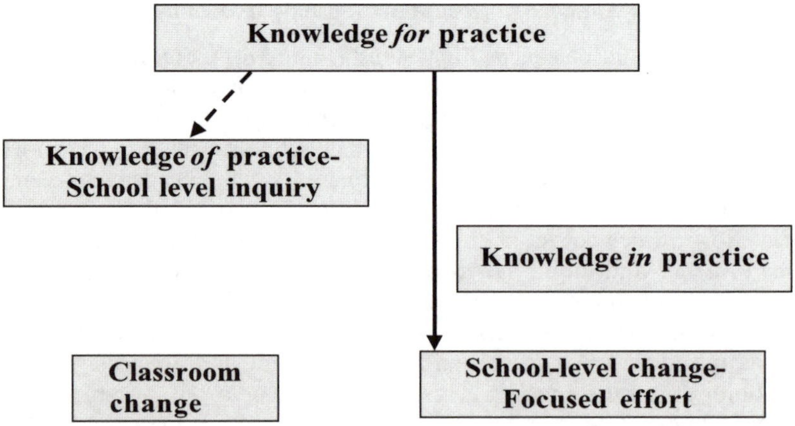

Figure 6.1 First steps.

opportunities: 'Being a part of BASRC has forced me to see some areas of professional growth that I wasn't aware of before.' Another said: 'BASRC has provided the intellectual challenge that I need in my work. A couple of years ago, I was really thinking [of leaving teaching] and BASRC was a good vehicle for me to get recommitted . . . so now it's become challenging and intense.'

As these comments suggest, in schools just getting started with the challenges of using and generating knowledge, much of the 'learning' we heard about was at individual rather than at school levels. Notice, too, that sources of knowledge for teachers in 'first steps' schools were external, located in BASRC workshops or institutes, or brought into the school by the Support Providers hired with BASRC funds.

Beginning school-level inquiry and change

For many if not most of the BASRC Leadership Schools, their BASRC involvement was their first venture into looking at their school-level practice. A second pattern we observed in Leadership Schools could be called 'Beginning school-level inquiry and change.' (Figure 6.2).

These schools had started with their cycle of inquiry, and were struggling with questions about appropriate indicators for their focused effort, sources of data, and strategies for data collection. We see norms about evidence and uses of data changing from the culture of privativism seen in First Steps schools, to openness on the faculty's part to consider new ways of looking at their practice at the school level. Teachers in schools just beginning remark on what they have learned about the power of data to illuminate their own practice and student accomplishments school wide.

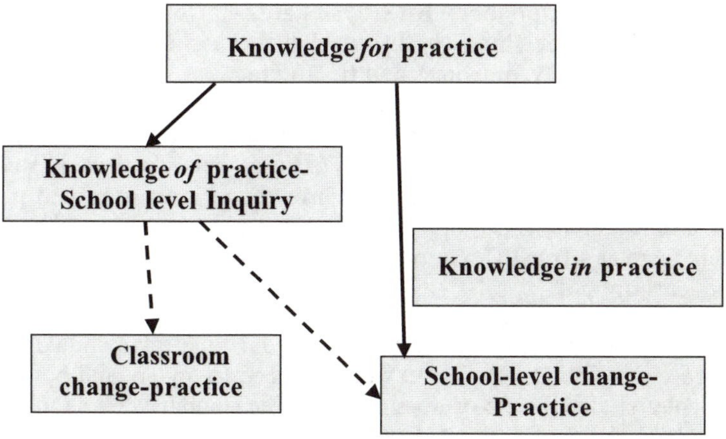

Figure 6.2 Beginning school-level inquiry and change.

> We are starting to ask what are our data and inquiry strategies really telling us about our children? What do we want to know about our children? We have finally been able to ask ourselves: What do we really want them to know about and be able to do when they go out the door at the end of the year?

Teachers in schools just beginning substantive engagement with a cycle of inquiry were having some of their first conversations about data, using new language, and working to generate evidence of practice as a faculty.

In many of the Leadership Schools at this point, teachers tell us that this was the first time that 'every single teacher' had some form of assessment data for his or her class, and that for the first time, baseline data were collected across the school. Teachers also point to the changed lens they have now:

> I never could see what a good school this is because I was so into my own classroom. I never had the broad picture. And until I saw that, when I could really sit down and see the whole school, that's when the light went on. You know, we have some holes, we have some gaps, but boy, we're okay!

In schools described by 'Beginning school-level inquiry' we saw how BASRC affiliation helped faculty deal with the politics of data.

> The data part of this has been hard for our school . . . a real challenge . . . we have some teachers who will pass any child who breathes. We have to be very creative in how we look at data . . . BASRC is a real help [as a shield]. BASRC says 'data, data, data'.

BASRC's requirements about evidence and accountability allowed teachers eager to generate knowledge of practice make objective fact of what before had been seen as personal and subjective evaluation, where it was seen at all – most especially problematic evidence about particular classrooms or student groups. Teachers commented on how BASRC's status as 'outsider' and BASRC requirements for Leadership Schools enabled their schools to wade into the difficult waters of equity, outcomes and ties to practice.

Where schools began to see the value in site-level data, most remarkable to us was the shift in teachers' discourse. The language of inquiry and data thread through faculty conversations. Teachers use evidence-based standards comfortably, and we hear new standards brought to evaluation and planning sessions. For example, this snippet of conversation among members of the leadership team at a BASRC school reflects serious effort to take a hard look at data and learn from it:

> Do all students meet or exceed the standards? What plan should we make to figure out who isn't or is and why? We need to understand how to say a particular student meets or does not meet the standard. We should be able to explain why one child got a particular stamp on their head and another did not. If standards aren't understood by teachers, then it's a problem for our school.

We would not have heard this conversation among this faculty the year before, when they were grappling with how to address new expectations for accountability and decision-making associated with their Leadership School status. We hear this discourse as evidence of the emergence of a 'community of explanation', where teachers share language and understandings about the meanings of evidence and social facts.[2]

In some 'beginning inquiry' schools, these conversations have started to make their way into change in practice at school or classroom levels, but as the dotted arrow in Figure 6.2 suggests, these effects were the exception. The problem most pressing in terms of knowledge generation and use in 'beginning inquiry' schools is the character of the community of practice in the school. Many reform-minded faculties in these schools wrestled with rifts in their community; not all teachers bought into the 'whole school' character of the reform. Moreover, in some schools – most especially high schools – reform leaders acknowledge that not all of their colleagues really believed that 'all students could perform at challenging standards', a central tenet of BASRC's whole school reform vision.

In these schools, the community of explanation was emergent only, since teachers viewed the same disappointing data about student performance in different ways – some see it as a warrant to re-examine practice and others view it as evidence about students' abilities and motivation. Yet, in schools such as these, the sites and sources of teachers' knowledge and learning are moving, if only in tentative ways, inside the school. Outside knowledge resources remain important to teachers' thoughts about how to change, but energy in these communities focused more at this stage on establishing priorities for data collection and reform.

Getting comfortable and capable with data

A third pattern of relations among knowledge, learning and change could be called 'Getting comfortable and capable with data'. (Figure 6.3). Some Leadership Schools entered the Initiative already comfortable with inquiry and experienced with school-level reform.[3]

But for most of the Leadership Schools where we found faculty comfortable with using evidence from their own inquiry to rethink their practices, we saw significant learning on the part of individual teachers and the faculty as a whole. We also found faculty struggling with their inquiry processes, but around different issues than were schools less experienced with inquiry. In some schools, the most important learning was about inquiry itself. For example, at the end of their first year of inquiry a high school faculty realized that they had chosen the wrong measures to assess their focused effort. In their second year, they returned to questions of indicators and evidence, but with concrete experience about internal validity to guide their decisions.

In this and other schools, we saw that the cycle of inquiry often was not sequential as a 'cycle' image might imply. Faculty had to revisit first questions before proceeding to data collection and analysis. Faculty gained confidence and competence as data collectors and analysts. One teacher said, for instance:

'It's hard to know what is good evidence. But the more you do it, the more you are able to identify what's good evidence.'

An elementary school teacher's remark speaks volumes about the new knowledge and skill teachers have acquired through BASRC, in this instance the reading assessment tool of running records.

> It will be interesting to compare running records across teachers to see whether the evaluations are reliable – we all need to be speaking the same language and looking at kids work in the same way . . . next year we want to get people to the table understanding data . . . it will be a 'so what' year. We have been working on collecting data to take action.

In many schools, we see that the results of their inquiry process have led to new knowledge and understandings about practice in their school and classrooms. For example, an elementary school faculty looking at student work samples based on BASRC rubrics saw both examples of 'high levels' of instruction in some classrooms, but also identified issues of co-ordination within and across grade levels. Based on this knowledge the faculty took steps to 'evaluate where our kids are and what we are going to do to move them forward'.

Teachers' new knowledge of their practice motivated more inquiry and commitment in some instances. Faculty in a number of Leadership Schools told us that 'there is a lot of buy-in [to reform] from doing these assessments'. Teachers formerly resistant to collecting baseline data, or engaging in the assessment effort at all, are energized by seeing growth in their students as well as by identification of concrete problem areas for the school to grapple with. What had been generic 'problems' became more concrete – they took on names

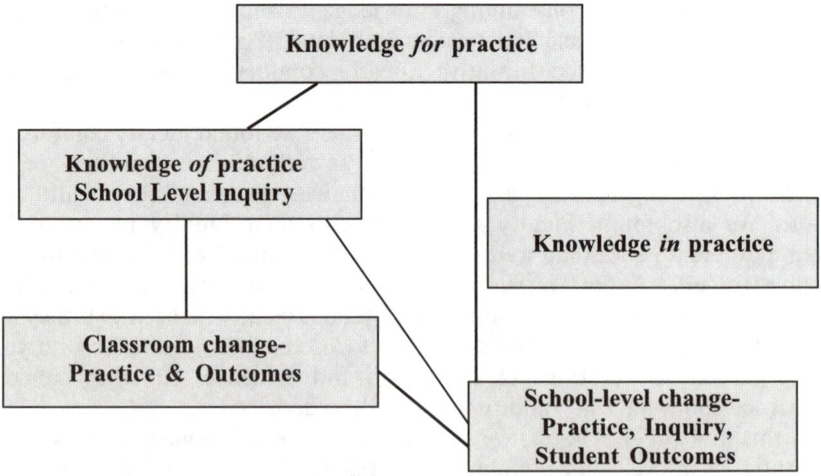

Figure 6.3 Getting comfortable and capable with data and reform processes.

and faces. They also became more amenable to action as teachers began to agree on the nature of the issues facing the school and a range of possible responses. Teachers in schools comfortable with new learning skills and norms of discourse readily admit that such conversations did not and could not have taken place prior to their involvement with BASRC – nor could have expressions of collective responsibility for all students in the school.

This teacher's comment makes apparent, for instance, how teachers' problem-solving skills developed though the BASRC rubrics can affect faculty discourse and attention:

> We gave a writing sample to all students last fall. All staff learned how to score it. From that experience, all teachers, even art teachers, realized how important writing is. It was interesting to hear history teachers debate with the art teacher about whether [student work] was a 3 or a 4 [on a rubric of 1 to 4, with 4 being high]

An elementary school made substantial progress in their students' achievement once they disaggregated scores by ethnicity and re-evaluated the literacy programs they were using. In 2 years, the school's Limited English Proficient students moved from 44 per cent scoring at grade levels on a reading comprehension test to 73 per cent achieving at or above grade level. In this and in other Leadership Schools, we find positive signs that changes in practices at school and classroom levels are reflected in student achievement. Eleven of the first cohort of fourteen Leadership Schools report student achievement gains in their annual Review of Progress.[4]

Sites and sources of teachers' learning found in these schools 'Getting Comfortable' are both internal and external. Faculties have begun to internalize norms of inquiry and habits of evidence. Teachers ask for data to support decisions and inform discussions about practice. By their language and action, faculty in schools described by these relationships between knowledge, learning and change appear to have become communities of explanation (Freeman 1999).

Cycle of inquiry, learning and change

In a few of the Leadership Schools we see a fourth pattern of relations between knowledge generation, use and change. In these schools, the Cycle of Inquiry has begun to mature into an accepted, iterative process of data collection, analysis, reflection, and change. These schools function as 'learning organizations', and themselves constitute teachers' essential site and source of learning.

As the double-headed arrows in Figure 6.4 suggest, learning is ongoing and recurrent and the three forms of knowledge are strategically interrelated. These schools appear to be 'recultured' in the way BASRC's theory of change envisioned. The whole school is both the site of inquiry and the focus for change; the community of explanation incorporates most of the faculty, not just a smaller group of reformers. Discourse about students' standard-based achievement and expectations about evidence are everyday rather than

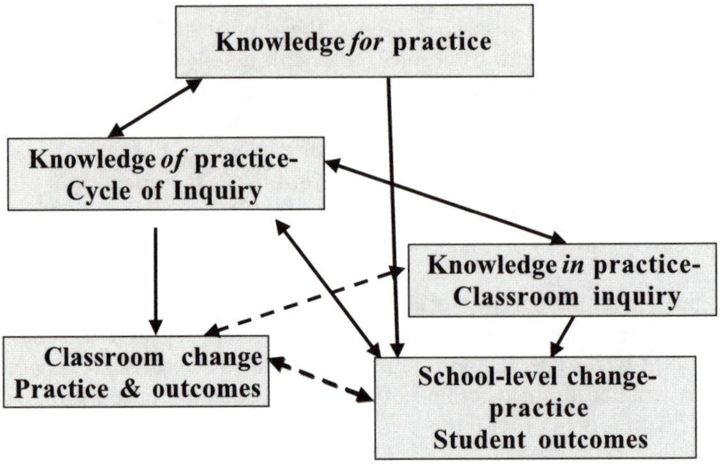

Figure 6.4 Cycle of inquiry, learning and change.

exceptional. The sites and sources of learning are internal and external – and mutually informing.

Knowledge for practice is both sought and filtered through knowledge of practice. Teachers' new knowledge of their practice enables them to see ways in which they need to improve, and the kinds of resources [or knowledge for practice] they need to begin making those improvements. One teacher commented, for example, that the links between their focused effort on literacy, and their students' work has allowed them to 'see connections' they had not seen before, and make much more specific demands for assistance from their support provider.

Teachers in such schools have become particular and demanding in terms of what their school needs by way of knowledge resources from the outside, and in what form they should be provided. Knowledge of their practice has made them more powerful as consumers, as the double-headed arrow implies.

We observe a number of other things in schools whose patterns of relations among knowledge, learning and change resembles those depicted in Figure 6.4. We see that teachers' generation and use of knowledge of practice often comes before systematic production of knowledge in practice. A hunch based in this observation is that the collective experience of inquiry at the school level may stimulate more inquiry at the classroom level. Teachers' involvement with and acceptance of inquiry at the school level both lends cachet to the norms and mental attitude teachers need to do the work in their own classrooms, and provides the experience, skills, and comfort necessary to ask tough questions of one's own practice – and to share the results.

In a few schools, school level inquiry is making its way into classroom-based inquiry and change. For example, a high school science teacher who had long assumed the disappointing achievement of many students in his culturally-diverse classes was a consequence of indifference or laziness, was provoked by literacy data collected at the school level to take a look at his own class through that lens. What he found forced him to fundamentally re-evaluate his practice. He discovered that a significant number of students in his science classes read at a level insufficient to grasp the material. Yet, as the dashed arrow suggests, teachers' systematic collection and analysis of their classroom data to inform both their practice and school-level decision-making is not yet routine in any BASRC Leadership School.

In schools comfortable with inquiry, we also find instances of teachers using inquiry tools to address issues that confront the school. For example, in the face of concern about the relationship between the assessments the state was soon to require, and those the school was using to assess their progress, a teacher did research on the overlap, congruence and conflict between them. She found 'potentials for overlap and a different way of looking at this' and so turned a problem into an opportunity for the school to deepen its work. This teacher's response to a challenge signals an inquiry stance new to the school and extraordinary in most communities of practice.

The inquiry and action we see in Leadership Schools comfortable and confident with learning from their own site and practice are contrary to the norms of privacy and individualism characteristic of schoolteaching (Lortie, 1975). They mark a changed school culture, and generate a number of questions based on institutional traditions. Why would such things as portfolio readings or critical friends' visits translate into new forms of inquiry at the school level? Why would site level data about problematic patterns of achievement among students encourage teachers to face up to their own effectiveness and look at the gap in their classrooms between intention and accomplishment? Why would teachers expose their own uneven student results to their colleagues?

Communities of practice

We find some answers to these questions in the character of the school's community of practice and relations among teachers. These communities of practice have become communities of explanation by virtue of their collective inquiry; they also are learning communities where reflection about current practice and habits of inquiry prompt change at schools and classroom levels. They are communities of teacher learners where learning and change are a social process of active participation in inquiry. (Rogoff, 1994; Wenger, 1998).

BASRC Leadership Schools suggest how patterns of knowledge use and learning define the culture of the community of practice at the school-level (see Figure 6.5). We see seven interrelated elements of the school's community of practice that influence whether or how teachers could use knowledge for practice, whether or how they developed knowledge of or in practice.

In schools where we find teachers using data about their students and their practice to inform their decisions about directions for their school and about the sorts of external resources that would be most useful, we find that a majority of the faculty hold clear and shared goals for their students and their performance as a faculty. Faculty conversations about priorities for their school's reform effort, evidence to support their strategy, portfolio application and designing a cycle of inquiry to assess their progress fostered clarity and buy-in on school goals. They also stimulated active communication within the faculty, across grade levels and departments. Faculty communication continued to address these classroom-specific concerns, of course, but in addition regularly engaged whole school issues, most especially patterns of student performance and faculty responses to disparities by students' ethnicity.

Communities of teacher learners explicitly adopted what Cochran-Smith and Lytle (1999) call an inquiry stance towards their own practice as well as towards their broader workplace environment. In these communities we found instances where 'problems' were transformed from 'immutable facts' to subjects for inquiry and problem solving. This transformation was most apparent in high school faculties where explanation for poor student performance moved from those based on beliefs about students' attitudes, backgrounds or capacities to the 'fit' between what their students needed to learn and achieve and what was provided them.

Communities of teacher learners possessed and used a number of resources. They developed the learning skills necessary to pursue inquiry and analyse evidence; they had a growing body of knowledge about aspects of their practice and continued to add to that understanding. These skills and knowledge were broadly distributed across the faculty community, not merely the assets of an isolated sub-group of teachers.

Communities of teacher learners also had a store of knowledge about 'best practices' and were able to distinguish on technical grounds among alternative

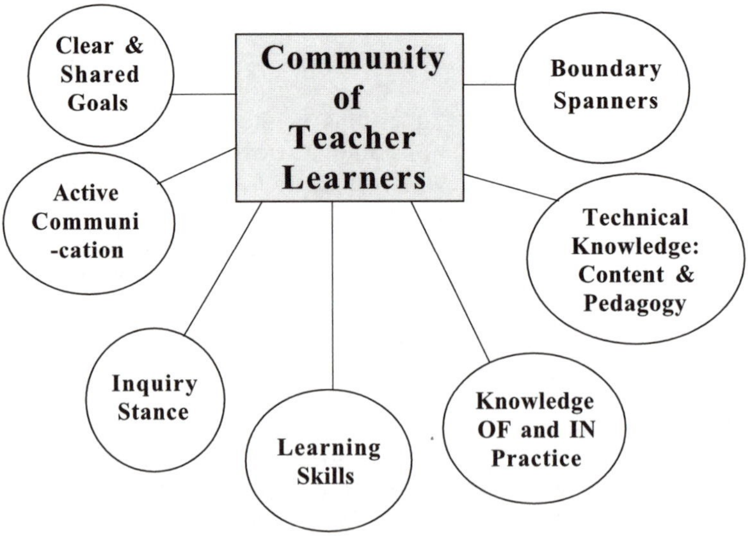

Figure 6.5 A community of teacher learners at the school-level.

practices available to them. They knew not only what kinds of resources best suited their school, they also knew where to build or rebuild their own core technical capacity. This technical knowledge, combined with knowledge of their school site and classrooms, combined to make teachers adept at evaluating the kind and quality of knowledge for practice available to the school, and was central to what Donald Schon (1983) called the 'reflective transfer' of knowledge from outside the school.

Finally, communities of teacher learners were communities open to the environment. In one or another form, they had boundary spanners, individuals active in the context outside the school who brought new ideas as well as challenges into the community.

These elements of the communities of teacher learners we encountered among BASRC Leadership Schools were mutually reinforcing and deeply interdependent. Technical skills alone did not enable a community of practice to be learners, or teacher learners to make productive change in their practice. Teachers required common values about inquiry, goals for their school, and shared conceptions of 'good' work and a 'good' colleague.

The high levels of social participation are signal to communities of teacher learners (see Rogoff, 1994; Wenger, 1999). We saw how communication and co-ordination among teachers extended the shared understanding (or community of explanation in Donald Freeman's terms) that generated both action and inquiry. Communities of teacher learners used active participation to forge common ground about the meaning of the evidence they generated, and agreements about a course of action at both individual and organizational levels. Further, the teachers' quest for shared goals and common perceptions of the facts of the matter, involved both individual accommodation and learning. Individual teachers' learning, in this sense, is part and parcel of their involvement in reflecting on and inquiring into the practices of their school community.

BASRC's strategy stimulates communities of teacher learners

Many of these elements of a community of practice where teachers are learners often are thought to be outside the purview of policy, and to operate in the domain of school leadership – most particularly, school-level clear goals, communication, stance towards learning and inquiry. Certainly, we find, with the rest of the research community, that leadership matters. Strong principals were a feature of almost all of the Leadership Schools successful in forging new relationships, making progress with a Cycle of Inquiry and whole school change. However, we also find clear evidence in our interviews, observations and surveys of BASRC's influence on the development and functioning of all elements of communities of teacher learners in Leadership Schools.

A number of principals note change in their faculty's norms of communication and attitudes of sharing and exchange. One said, for example: 'I see my staff asking one another more questions. They check things out from the resource lab. A teacher will walk in to get materials, have a dialogue with the teachers and before you know it, one will be stopping by another's classroom.'

Principals' survey responses also credit BASRC involvement with substantial change on a number of critical dimensions of teacher community. 'High standards for all students', 'Teachers' consensus' on student outcomes and areas for whole school change tap the presence of 'Clear and shared goals' depicted in Figure 6.5. Similarly, 'Teacher leadership' and 'Staff discussions' tap dimensions of active communication among faculty. 'Working with outside change agents' provides an indicator of 'Boundary spanning', and 'use of data as a basis for decision-making' captures principals' views about change in their faculty's inquiry stance, learning skills, and knowledge both about their practice and appropriate resources to enhance their work (Table 6.1).

Principals also report that they have some distance to go in order for their schools to be characterized by a community of teacher learners.

In a nutshell, Leadership School principals say that their school's involvement with BASRC has resulted in important changes in their schools' cultures – but that especially in the area of 'consistent standards for all students', and inquiry stance, much change has yet to take place (Table 6.2).

Support providers also see new, stronger communities of practice taking form in Leadership Schools. One said, for example:

> What difference do I see in BASRC schools? The main difference I see is that those schools and the district, to a lesser extent, are slowly turning towards gathering and using evidence in a formal accountability system. I think teachers, individuals, have been turning that way. . . . And it's been neat to get a whole school community to pay attention and give [data and consequences] that level of priority.

Teachers' comments and our observations of faculty meetings and planning sessions point to the emergence of a significantly different community of practice in many Leadership Schools. These new communities of practice have formed around the knowledge resources associated with BASRC – new skills and capacities, new knowledge of the school as an educational setting – and the community itself serves as a resource to generate new practices and invent ideas for reform. A number of teachers commented, for example, on how the diverse perspectives within their community enable them to see gaps in understanding that would otherwise be invisible. One said, for example:

> I know that I'm not perfect, but my standards are higher because of my colleagues. Also, I found out that there are many different ways to do something amazingly well . . . [through our teacher community] I found out that a person who writes a whole lot differently from me can be amazingly successful . . . and although I found out that I need to improve a lot I also found a couple of ways that work.

Teachers also comment on the power of distributed expertise within the teacher community. One middle school teacher said, for example:

Table 6.1 Leadership school principals' report of changes associated with BASRC involvement (N=63).

	Strongly Disagree				*Strongly Agree*
High standards for all students	0%	0%	10%	62%	28%
Teachers' consensus on desired student learning outcomes	0%	0%	10%	53%	37%
Teachers' consensus on needed areas for whole school change	0%	0%	3%	52%	45%
Teacher leadership	0%	0%	10%	47%	44%
Staff discussions of teaching and learning	0%	0%	5%	49%	46%
Working with outside change agents to support reform goals	0%	0%	12%	53%	35%
Use of data as a basis for decision making	0%	0%	8%	50%	42%

Note: These data are from a Winter 1999 survey of all Leadership School principals.

Table 6.2 Principals' report of existing conditions in leadership schools (N=63).

	Strongly Disagree				*Strongly Agree*
This school has high standards for all students	0%	3%	21%	49%	27%
This school has consistent standards for all students	5%	14%	44%	29%	8%
Teachers are engaged in systematic analysis of student data	2%	8%	27%	38%	27%
Teachers in this school regularly examine school performance	2%	16%	22%	41%	20%
Teachers take steps to solveproblems, they don't just talk about them	3%	8%	23%	30%	36%

> By sticking together, someone comes up with something and we try it. When you start in this [teaching] business you are isolated and think in the box. [Because of the teacher community in my school,] I have learned to think outside the box. We have hit a lot of curves, but we feel like we are a group that can work through them. When you talk together it is a powerful problem-solving group. There are things to be gained from this [community of practice] that cannot be gained from working alone.

Many teachers attribute the stronger teacher learning communities at their schools to the tools and processes they learned at BASRC's Summer Institutes, most especially skills in facilitation, reflective dialogue and conflict resolution –

pragmatic skills important both to generating new knowledge and understanding about practice and in making effective use of the knowledge resources available to members of the Bay Area School Reform Collaborative.

Lessons for policy about sites and sources of teachers' learning

This chapter began by complicating questions of what teachers need to know in order to improve practice and how they can learn it. It draws upon our evaluation of BASRC to provide elements of a descriptive theory of how different forms of knowledge relate to one another, how teachers interact with these forms of knowledge and with each other to foster learning and change.[5] The patterns of knowledge use and elements of teachers' learning communities associated with BASRC's experience contain important lessons for reformers.

Patterns of knowledge use

Looking across the different patterns of knowledge use and generation in BASRC Leadership Schools, it is evident that forms of knowledge are path dependent. We notice that the knowledge teachers bring into the school and the knowledge and learning generated at the school site builds on what they know and can do. Wesley Cohen and Daniel Levinthal (1990) use the term 'absorptive capacity' to signal the critical role prior knowledge plays in an organization's ability to use external knowledge to remain vigorous and stay ahead of the competition. Their conception of how organizations identify and use knowledge corresponds with our observation that what teachers already know mediates between external knowledge and teachers' capacity to use it effectively – or even to recognize – relevant external knowledge resources.

This view of knowledge, teachers' learning and educational change makes it evident why 'solutions' cannot be 'imported' into schools or classrooms with any significant effect if internal capacity in the form of prior knowledge is not already there. Without foundational, situated knowledge of and in practice, teachers lack effective hooks to pull new ideas into their workplace. In other words, what teachers know about their own practices, and about their school as an educational environment, shapes fundamentally what and how much they can learn from knowledge for practice.

These diverse but interrelated images of knowledge complicate policy investments in teachers' knowledge since they implicate different sites and supports for teachers' learning. A successful school reform effort, in this view, would need to supply or foster knowledge of all three sorts – for, of and in practice – in order for teachers to learn what they need to know to initiate, deepen and sustain change.

Communities of practice

A description of relations in a community of practice illuminates age-old problems of knowledge use. Change agents and reformers have long been frustrated that teachers too often make little or only superficial use of the knowledge resources available to them. Knowledge resources evidently are not self-enacting nor do they necessarily engender learning. And learning does not necessarily lead to productive change in practice. What happens to knowledge brought into or produced by a community of practice depends fundamentally on the character of that community and relations among its members.

BASRC's experience highlights the many ways in which a community of practice is both the medium and source of learning, reflection and new knowledge about practice. It also illustrates the situated character of the community of explanation created at a school. In each of the Leadership Schools where we found a community of teacher learners we found a community of explanation – we heard language and understandings particular to and shared by that community.

One important implication of the central role we see for communities of practice is their centrality to reformers' visions of how to stimulate and sustain change. Policies need to consider how strategies can provide occasions, tools and resources for building a community of teacher learners. BASRC's design is remarkable in that it provides teachers with the tools they need to learn how to learn, to forge new conversations and accommodation among faculty, and with a 'focused effort', the work essential to constructing shared goals and understandings. Few reform policies keep communities of practice in their vision or acknowledge the pivotal role of a community of explanation to knowledge use, learning and change.

Another important implication of the situated character of these communities is that they cannot simply be regrouped or combined with other communities without attention to the [re]building of shared understanding and language. Policies aiming to bring different communities of explanation together – be they different school communities or more obviously diverse communities such as researchers and practitioners, policy makers and practitioners, or knowledge providers and knowledge users – must attend at the outset to building common understandings. BASRC accomplished some of this in its first years through the Portfolio Review process, where parents, educators, researchers, business people and others first spent time together calibrating their responses to schools' portfolios and talking about why they saw the same evidence in divergent ways. Only after some level of mutual understanding was achieved did the group move on to their common work. Teachers' assessments of these Portfolio Reviews as 'the best professional development I've ever had' lay in the process of participation and joint sensemaking it entailed. These strategies for developing shared understandings and standards for good work not only created new communities of explanation among individuals based in other ones, they also play a critical role in generating a regional understanding of the goals and elements of school reform in the Bay Area. BASRC experience illuminates the trap of de facto assumptions about common language and explanations across communities of practice. Simply convening stakeholders from different organizational or institutional communities may be efficient, but will probably accomplish little by way of learning and progress without opportunity for them first to have conversations about their different perspectives and understandings.

A related lesson: BASRC's experience also suggests how teachers' participation in multiple communities of practice/explanation can promote more durable structures for knowing and learning. Teachers from Leadership Schools who have participated in conversations throughout the region have been able to hear multiple perspectives on practice and reform and integrate them into their own. Participation in multiple stakeholder groups enables teachers to take them into account as they go about work in their own school communities. Access to multiple communities makes teachers' own understandings more durable because they are more cosmopolitan and so less vulnerable to external 'shocks' to their beliefs such as new or contradictory ideas about practice.

BASRC's experience and the practical theory of learning it suggests stand in direct contrast to professional development or school reform policies that frame teachers' learning as solely an individual matter. We see in BASRC Leadership Schools that learning is a social process, where the process in critical ways is the product, and where the knowledge generated by the community is more than a sum of individuals' learning. Communities of practice generate knowledge and understanding that is different in kind from that produced by individuals alone. Likewise, individuals' learning is a matter of their participation in a community of practice engaged in reflection and inquiry. In summary, observations of relations among teachers and forms of knowledge in BASRC schools suggest a different perspective for policy, one rooted in communities of practice as sites and sources of teachers' learning.

Notes

1 The Center for Research on the Context of Teaching at Stanford University's School of Education has evaluated BASRC since 1996.
2 Donald Freeman (1999) elaborates the notion of 'community of explanation' and ways in which it is congruent with but different from a community of practice.
3 Many of these schools had received funds under an earlier California reform effort that was a significant BASRC ancestor in its focus on inquiry and whole school change: Senate Bill 1274.
4 Two of the remaining schools also report gains in student achievement but since they have only 2 years, rather than the required 3 years, of data using the same measures, their growth cannot yet be 'counted'. The third school reports neither decline nor growth, but is 'holding steady'.
5 Thank you to Donald Freeman (1999) for reminding me about the value of descriptive theory as policy guide.

References

Bransford, J. D., Brown, A. L. and Cocking, Rodney R. (1999) *How People Learn: Brain, Mind, Experience and School*. Washington, DC: National Academy Press.

Center for Research on the Context of Teaching. (1997, 1998, 1999) *Assessing Results: The Bay Area School Reform Collaborative*. School of Education, Stanford University.

Cochran-Smith, M. and Lytle, S. L. (1999) Relationships of knowledge and practice: 'Teacher learning in communities', A. Iran-Nejad and C. D. Pearson (eds) *Review of*

Research in Education, Vol. 24, Washington, DC: American Educational Research Association.

Cohen, W. M. and Levinthal, D. A. (1990) 'Absorptive capacity: a new perspective on learning and innovation', *Administrative Science Quarterly* 35: 128–52.

Freeman, D. (1999) 'Towards a descriptive theory of teacher learning and change', paper given at the International Study Association on Teachers and Teaching (ISATT) Conference, Dublin, Ireland, July.

Lortie, D. (1975) *Schoolteacher: a sociological study*, Chicago: University of Chicago Press.

Rogoff, B. (1994) 'Developing understanding of the idea of communities of learners', *Mind, Culture and Activity*. 1(4): 209–29.

Schon, D. A. (1983) *The Reflective Practitioner*, New York: Basic Books.

Wenger, E. (1998) *Communities of Practice*, New York: Cambridge University Press.

Chapter 7

Professional development as 'interference'?

Insights from the Reading Recovery in-service course

Jane Ashdown

Introduction

The continuing professional development of teachers has become increasingly associated with educational change particularly in terms of school reform efforts and improving student achievement (Thompson and Zeuli, 1999; Elmore and Burney, 1999). Indeed, it is sometimes touted as the solution for the problems of contemporary schooling, where a designated number of hours spent in professional development may be mandated by local and state education authorities. As a result, the nature and effectiveness of professional development, particularly with regard to student outcomes, is under increasing scrutiny. Given the greater focus of attention professional development is receiving, we need to keep refining our insights into how it works and where it fails.

Studies suggest that teacher involvement in professional development increases motivation and commitment to learn and therefore is an essential component of effective professional development (Guskey, 1995; Hawley and Valli, 1999). However researchers and teachers have reported on tensions between individual teachers' perceived needs for self-improvement and system demands of teachers for changes in curriculum and teaching approaches (Bell, 1991; Richardson, 1992). Such tensions have been categorized as 'dissonance' a 'lack of congruence' 'resistance,' or 'discontinuities'. Fullan (1993) argues that conflict cannot be avoided in successful change efforts. However, his advocacy for conflict – he describes it as 'essential' – does not necessarily account for the toll that the tensions, stress, and uneasiness typically associated with conflict, takes on individual teachers. Social and cultural norms might aggravate the situation for teachers, who are not accustomed to the kind of arguments and disagreements that Fullan extolls as part of the change process (p.27).

Rather than ignore these emotions, the purpose of this article is to take a closer look at the nature of the tensions teachers report experiencing in one particular professional development setting – the Reading Recovery in-service course. The pressure on teachers to change may mean their points of view about the negative aspects of professional development, gets ignored. However, teachers as individuals carry the responsibility for executing change within the school as an organizational context. Finding an appropriate mix of organizational and individual processes to support change can be elusive, create tensions, and limit reform possibilities (Guskey, 1995). The term 'tension' is used here broadly to encompass the emotions of strain and pressure experienced when a person encounters demands for change. It is assumed that a clearer description and analysis of such tensions (1) can contribute to evaluations of professional development which are inclusive of teachers' less positive, and more skeptical perspectives; (2) can contribute to future planning of in-service opportunities for teachers which address the complexities of teachers' perceptions of their professional development needs and; (3) help identify directions for further research.

Reading Recovery is an early literacy intervention for 'at-risk' first grade students (6-year-old students) which is implemented as part of a school or school system's drive to improve students' literacy achievement. Its key design features are daily, one-to-one tutoring of the lowest performing students, an emphasis on short-term instruction and accelerated learning, and (in the USA) an on-going, national evaluation. The Reading Recovery in-service for teachers, which is also a key element of its design, is a useful case example for considering the tensions and stresses generated by professional development. It operates within a standard framework which focuses on the activity of teaching, not only on discussion or transmission of information. Teachers typically respond positively to this in-service, finding it stimulating, challenging and rewarding (Browne *et al.*, 1997). However, as participants, teachers may encounter new attitudes towards, and expectations about, what is possible for 'at-risk' students. Encouragement to change long-held assumptions about children's learning, and to teach 'hard-to-teach' children more effectively, can increase pressures on teachers and so in contrast to the typically positive experiences of teachers who complete the in-service course, one teacher described her experience as one of 'pressure,' uneasiness' and 'continual stress' (Barnes, 1997). Whilst much attention has been paid to the impact and effectiveness of Reading Recovery on children's literacy achievement (Lyons, 1998; Shanahan and Barr, 1995), and the potential contribution of the design of the in-service to the program's outcomes with students (Pinnell *et al.*, 1994), a broader evaluation of the impact of Reading Recovery on the professional lives of teachers has received much less scrutiny. It is anticipated that this paper will make a contribution in that respect.

Theories from studies in organizational learning (Agyris and Schon, 1996) and in human psychological development (Britzman, 1998) will be drawn on for explanations of 'tensions' which teachers may experience in professional development contexts. This will be supported by evidence from written evaluations completed by over 100 teachers, in fourteen different school districts, after undertaking the year-long in-service course (1997–8) to become Reading Recovery teachers.

Theoretical frameworks

Organizational learning

A description and analysis of the tensions that arise in the context of professional development is informed by organizational learning theories.

Organizational learning theories include an account of inter-group and interpersonal conflicts which arise when organizations embark on making changes in response to perceived needs. Although the following example from Agyris and Schon (1996) concerns a chemical company, there are parallels with schools as organizations.

> Consider a chemical firm . . . which has created its new R&D division in response to the perceived imperative for growth in sales and earnings and the belief that these are to be generated through internally managed technological innovation. However, the new division, generates technologies that do not fit the corporation's familiar pattern of operations. In order to exploit some of these technologies, the corporation may have to turn from the production of intermediate materials, with which it is familiar, to the manufacture and distribution of consumer products with which it is unfamiliar. . . . And these requirements for change come into conflict with another sort of corporate norm, one that requires predictability in the management of corporate affairs. (p. 22)

This account can be paralleled in an education setting as follows. Reading Recovery is likely to be introduced into a school as part of a response to concerns about children's poor literacy performance. However, as a 'technology', that is, a system of teacher professional development and intensive, short-term tutoring for children, it may not fit with the school's familiar predictable, pattern of operation. This pattern might, for example, include reliance on long-term remedial reading instruction, and lower expectations for certain children. However, this reliance will be challenged through participation in the Reading Recovery in-service course. Modifying, or giving up such patterns of operation, and adapting to new norms, can generate conflicts between individual teachers or groups of teachers or between the school and the school district.

What such conflicts reveal, according to Agyris and Schon (1996) are various 'theories-of-action' held by individuals or organizations. In the Reading Recovery example described above, its introduction into a school may fit with the school's 'espoused theory' of a need for improved student literacy performance. However, its introduction may also reveal implicit 'theories-in-use' held by individual teachers or by the school as a whole, about different achievement expectations for different groups of children and about teachers' responsibilities toward those children. Tensions which may arise between individual teachers, or between teachers and a school system concerning perceptions of the need for change and the purpose of professional development in fostering it, may be explained as resulting from differences in 'theories-of-action,' both espoused and tacit, which are driving the perceptions of all concerned.

An individual teacher participating in the Reading Recovery in-service course may be caught in this clash of theories-in-action and in a struggle to resolve such conflicts. Resolving these conflicting perspectives may, in the example described above, result in improved capacity to raise the performance of some low achieving children, but no major re-evaluation of the schools' responsibilities to ensure high expectations and achievements for all children. The latter would require the kind of 'double-loop' rather than 'single-loop' learning which would lead to changes in the underlying value system and norms of operating that the school has been accustomed to.

Education as interference

Whilst schools and school systems are the organizations involved in Reading Recovery, it is individual teachers who participate in the in-service course. A better understanding of the personal impact of this experience on teachers may be possible if we draw on explorations of human psychological development. Britzman (1998) begins her psychoanalytic inquiry into learning with the work of Anna Freud. Miss Freud described the relations between student and teacher as a never-ending battle, as the wishes of education clash with the wishes of the child. Britzman explores this clash of wishes and desires and broadly addresses the problems posed by learning for individuals, child or adult. These problems are described through the lens of Anna Freud's concept of education as 'interference.' Britzman writes:

> There is nothing else it [education] can do, for it demands of students and teachers that each come to something, make something more of themselves. The problem is that the demand can be felt as too much and too little. The demand can come too early and too late. (1998, p. 10)

This concept of education as interference lends itself to a characterization of the tensions generated by professional development, which may be simultaneously welcomed by individual teachers, initiated by them, resisted by them and imposed on them. The value of this framework is that it offers a context for considering personal and ethical dimensions of professional development. Britzman (1998) raises this herself when she asks: 'With what does education interfere? What interferes with education? What types of interference can we consider, and how much interference becomes felt as too much?' . . . Can there be an ethic of interference?' (p. 6)

This concept of education as interference can work in a number of directions. The teacher who is required to undertake an in-service course may perceive both the requirement and the course itself as unwelcome 'interference' in his/her professional life. On the other hand teachers' may be actively seeking 'interference' (in the form of professional development) with the habitual instructional practices that they have become all too familiar with over the years, and yet not be afforded opportunities to expand and refine their skills and knowledge base. Or, in another scenario, a principal in a school may feel obligated to 'interfere' with a particular teacher's teaching, by insisting on participation in professional development, because there is serious risk to children's learning.

In summary, understanding teachers' perceptions of the impact of professional development on their lives, particularly where those perceptions are characterized by resistance and tensions, may be helped by theories of organizational and individual learning.

Background to the Reading Recovery in-service course

Reading Recovery is an early literacy intervention which targets first-grade children (6–7 years old) who are experiencing difficulties learning to read and write, and who perform in the lowest 20 per cent of their class. Children who participate in this programme receive daily, 30 minute lessons, one-on-one ,with a teacher who is specially trained for this intensive literacy tutoring. Teachers who provide this service complete a year-long, graduate-level course, accredited through a local university or college and offered in their own school district, or one nearby. Teachers attend the course after school, but start tutoring children right away so that they are simultaneously participating in the course and learning how to identify and teach children with particular literacy difficulties. The Reading Recovery courses delivered in the USA are similar in design to INSET (In-Service Education and Training) described by Day (1999) as 'a planned series of events or extended programme of accredited or non-accredited learning' (p.131). Beyond the initial in-service course, Reading Recovery teachers continue to meet periodically for professional development. There are a number of distinctive features to this in-service and the contexts within which it occurs, which make it worthy of further attention in relation to teachers' perceptions about the nature of its impact on them.

Table 7.1 Features of the Reading Recovery in-service course compared with other professional development.

Features/service	*Traditional school/district based professional development*	*District based reading recovery in-service*
Time	Periodic; 1–3 day workshops.	21/2 hour, weekly, after school; 20–30 weeks.
Participants	Varies from 10–100.	Limited to 8–12 teachers.
Materials	Videos; overheads; resource books; handouts; materials to use with children.	Resource books; guidesheets; books to use with children.
Provider	External agency.	In-district teacher leader with external University support.
Location	School auditorium; library, classroom; district office.	Specifically adapted classroom with one-way observation mirror.
Orientation to learning	Lecture/presentation; group activities; possible in-school follow-up; periodic practice.	Direct observation and discussion; evaluating teaching; group discussion; follow-up, in-school observations; colleague visits; daily practice of teaching.

Distinctive organizational features of the Reading Recovery in-service

Table 7.1 indicates specific features with regard to time, participants, materials, providers, location and orientation, which may differentiate Reading Recovery from other kinds of school-based professional development previously undertaken by teachers.

These distinctive features speak of potential conflicts in expectations which teachers experience through their participation in the Reading Recovery in-service as compared to previous staff development experiences. For example, half-day staff development workshops in school, which may be mandated by the school system's leadership, may include discussion about teaching, but the Reading Recovery course includes direct observation and evaluation of teaching, as it occurs behind a one-way viewing mirror. Making teaching an object of public scrutiny can be disturbing and uncomfortable, if previously teaching has only been the subject of talk. A teacher may openly espouse a desire to improve his/her ability to teach reading to low-performing children through peer feedback, but tacitly believe teaching is a private activity which he/she should be allowed to get on with, without outside interference. Even if the teacher resolves these conflicts in differing perceptions of teaching, through discussion with colleagues in the Reading Recovery in-service course, he/she may still experience conflict with colleagues' beliefs and perceptions in his/her school. This is an example of the intersection of potential mismatches between individuals' (teachers) and organizations' (schools or school systems) theories of action, as conflicting espoused, and tacit, assumptions are revealed, in a professional development setting.

On the other hand the Reading Recovery course framework is determined by external agencies, the accrediting university and the Reading Recovery Council of North America, which governs professional standards and guidelines for the operation of Reading Recovery. Day (1999) identifies similar constraints about the INSET model, where teachers have less choice over what they learn (p.133). Teachers participating in Reading Recovery may have previously experienced more control over agenda-setting in other professional development settings.

Distinctive organizational contexts for the Reading Recovery in-service

The broader organizational contexts within which Reading Recovery is implemented may also influence how a teacher experiences the in-service course which accompanies the program. Table 7.2 indicates some of the contrasting features of the contexts at the school district and school building levels which may characterize the implementation of Reading Recovery.

The following account is an illustration of how the above contrasting features may be in evidence and interact within school and district contexts. A school district's leadership team may designate Reading Recovery as a 'safety-net' provision within a comprehensive early literacy plan, and mandate its adoption in all elementary schools. Whilst some schools may embrace this decision, others may resent its imposition. Among staff at the school level there may be teachers who eagerly volunteer to participate and who are selected for

Table 7.2 Contrasting features of Reading Recovery implementation.

Features/Contexts	*District Context*	*School Context*
Decision-making	Mandated versus optional	Imposed versus chosen
Teacher selection	Seniority versus merit	Required versus volunteers
Program support	Individual versus broad-based	Individual vversus broad-based
Policy setting	Ad hoc versus specific comprehensive plan	Lone initiative versus linked to school improvement plans

the in-service course on the basis of their qualifications for the position. In other schools, issues of seniority may dictate the selection of teachers, or, limited flexibility with staff roles and responsibilities may mean all reading specialist teachers in a school are required to complete the in-service, whether they want to or not.

It is presumed that the complexity of the organizational contexts for Reading Recovery and the distinctive features of the in-service course play a role in an individual teacher's perceptions, positive or negative, of this particular professional development experience. The following sections will address the analysis and interpretation of the written observations of a particular group of Reading Recovery teachers, about their in-service course experiences.

Framework for analyzing teachers' written comments

Marton's (1981) distinction between a 'first-order' and 'second-order' perspective is used here as a methodological framework within which to consider the written comments of individual teachers, at the end of their year-long in-service course. Marton's argument is that a second-order perspective, which attends to 'the ways in which people experience, interpret, understand, apprehend, perceive or conceptualize various aspects of reality' (p. 178), is a valuable focus of inquiry in its own right. In particular, this second-order perspective is helpful in focusing attention on the process and content of learning in terms of the meanings attributed to a particular content by learners. Marton describes it in this way:

> In the teaching process, students have various conceptions which we try to change, modify or successively replace . . . if we accept the thesis that it is of interest to know about the possible alternative conceptions students may have of the phenomena or the aspects present in, related to or underlying the subject matter of their study, it is these questions specifically which we must investigate. (1981, p. 183)

In general, professional development, including the Reading Recovery course, is focused on changing, or modifying teachers' practice to fit new demands for school improvement and effectiveness. In the following sections of this chapter the focus is not on the influence of professional development on teachers' practice, but on their self-reported perceptions of the professional development learning process designed to influence their practice. In particular, attention is paid to individual teachers' written comments, which appear to reflect tensions between the demands of the in-service course, and their own perceptions of their learning needs.

At the end of each year of the operation of Reading Recovery within a school system, the teacher leader who manages the programme at the school system level, distributes and collects written responses to questionnaires targeted at different stakeholder groups. These stakeholders include principals, classroom teachers, parents and Reading Recovery teachers who have just finished the in-service course. These 'spring' questionnaires, which are completed anonymously, were initially designed as an evaluation instrument for in-district use and have been part of a larger data collection process, required for school districts participating in Reading Recovery. The eleven questions asked of the newly trained Reading Recovery teachers focus on changes in teachers' perceptions of the reading process, changes in their views of how children learn to read and write, future teaching goals, and their most valued, and least valued experiences during the year. Although not designed as a research instrument, and essentially biased toward presumptions of change, these written responses are nevertheless a source of insights into, and impressions about, teachers' perceptions of this particular professional development experience.

The teachers and their perceptions

Questionnaires were collected from all the 206 teachers who had just completed the Reading Recovery in-service course in June 1998 across fourteen different school systems. These school systems were evenly split between urban and suburban areas in the New York metropolitan region. In the end, 112 teacher questionnaire responses were used, the rest being either unreadable (poor xerox copy) or completed in response to local variations on the standard set of questions. Demographic data on participating teachers were not available for this particular cohort. However, from observation of many in-service classes, it would be fair to say that most teachers were Caucasian females, who had at least three years early childhood teaching and in many cases, considerably more years of experience.

As indicated earlier, newly trained Reading Recovery teachers typically respond positively to their in-service experience. Teachers in this 1997–8 cohort wrote: 'I feel that I have acquired so much more knowledge regarding how children learn to read.' 'I could never teach reading the old way again.' 'My view of the reading process has changed greatly this year because through the R.R. program I have been able to analyze, self-reflect and predict better what's going on while a child's reading.' 'I now understand more clearly the complexity of reading and the reading process. Never before had I thought all that we were asking students to do when we teach reading. I now understand that to teach a student to read we must first understand their understanding and sort out their confusions.'

These comments are the bright side of professional development. The Reading Recovery in-service course for these teachers appears to have been a positive 'interference' in their teaching lives, as one teacher rejected 'the old way' whilst another valued the addition of 'so much more knowledge.' These comments convey a sense of the value the teachers attached to the course and its impact on their thinking and practice as teachers of reading.

However, the purpose of this paper is to attend to alternative, and less positive, teacher perceptions of this particular professional development setting. A simple process of 'pattern coding' (Miles and Huberman, 1994) was used to identify themes which consistently emerged as responses to the question, 'In your work with Reading Recovery what have been the least valuable experiences? Why?' An initial sorting from the 112 questionnaires was undertaken through an analysis of the affective dimension of each response to this question. Responses were categorized as positive, neutral, negative, or some combination thereof. Responses were deemed positive if the teacher indicated 'none' or 'everything was valuable'. They were deemed neutral if the teacher made a suggestion for a change in some aspect of the course like 'Attending the north-east conference seemed premature', or a combined dimension as in 'I love the program but some urban issues need to be addressed.'

Of the 112 teacher responses drawn from this 1997–8 cohort, most (eighty-four), used the questionnaire to identify some negative experiences associated with the in-service course and the simultaneous teaching of children in their schools. (It should be noted that all these teachers also reported on positive experiences in response to other survey questions.) These teachers' alternative perceptions fell into four broad descriptive categories:

- Professional development is undermining
- Professional development is time-consuming
- Professional development is isolating
- Professional development is frustrating

Professional development is undermining

Teachers' perceptions of professional development as personally undermining focused exclusively on the course requirement of teaching in front of colleagues, behind a one-way viewing mirror, and afterwards of engaging in dialogue about their teaching. This experience was variously described as one of 'tension and anxiety' and 'uncomfortable'. One teacher wrote that it was 'uncomfortable, nerve-wracking and unpleasant'. Another teacher, in describing the difficulty of this teaching situation, likened it to being in a fishbowl. These teachers did not welcome the public scrutiny of teaching that is a standard feature of the Reading Recovery in-service. As indicated earlier, this practice may have conflicted with a prevailing belief embodied in the organization of their schools about the privacy of teaching, or conflicted with beliefs about the individualism associated with being a classroom teacher. Such tensions may also have arisen as, teachers, who have many years of teaching experience, are encouraged to try new methods, a process which temporarily renders an expert teacher something of a novice. Mevarech (1995) describes this as the U curve process of teachers' professional learning and growth, in contrast to the linear model of development which may more typically shape teachers' expectations of their own learning.

Professional development is time-consuming

Teachers were unanimously critical of the amount of paperwork they were required to complete, in most cases because it took too much time, or they could not see the purpose of it. One teacher put it this way:

> I [also] resent the extra paperwork I have been required to complete which it is quite apparent, will lead to some grant, study or doctorate for someone I will never meet and from which I will not benefit but in the most abstract way.

Much of the paperwork associated with Reading Recovery is completed for programme evaluation purposes, both for local use and as part of a national evaluation design. This is a good example of tension between school system leaders' demands for high levels of accountability, through evaluation of resources used in relation to student outcomes achieved, versus individual teachers, who experience completing data forms as an onerous activity. The time it takes to complete the data forms on each Reading Recovery child (and on two other student comparison groups) takes teachers away from other more desirable activities. It appears to interfere with teachers' wishes for more productive uses of this precious commodity – time. Their resentment of this requirement conflicts with the value the larger organization of the school system attaches to collecting data for accountability purposes.

Professional development is isolating

Teachers expressed considerable concern over the personal and professional isolation they felt as a result of participating in Reading Recovery and the in-service course. Missing the first day of the new school year and an opportunity to see colleagues because of starting the course, having course work to do during the year so that social networks with colleagues were disrupted, and not being appreciated by other school staff for the commitment they had made to this new experience, were all unwelcome negative 'side-effects' of participating in Reading Recovery. These feelings of isolation associated with professional development may be aggravated by the organizational context within which Reading Recovery is operating at the school level. A lone teacher selected for the course, rather than a team of two, will be more vulnerable to isolation. Alternatively, an individual teacher may be eager to advance his/her own learning by completing the course, but be ostracized by colleagues in a school context which has not typically valued the pursuit of further learning by teachers.

Professional development is frustrating

Teachers expressed many frustrations with their initial experiences of teaching Reading Recovery children in school, something that is undertaken simultaneously with the in-service course. Children's behavior problems, poor school attendance, apparent lack of parental support for reading at home, mobility of children who were just beginning to make progress, and the need to refer some children to special education services, all contributed to these feelings of frustration. One teacher wrote: 'To constantly be faced with failure each day that I saw him made me negative and put a damper on the rest of the lessons for the day.' Another teacher described it as 'a very upsetting experience' working with children regarded as 'extremely high risk'. Yet another teacher expressed discouragement at working with a child who exhibited 'classic signs of needing self-contained special ed'.

From a teacher's perspective professional development is likely to be viewed as an opportunity to increase knowledge and skills. When that does not appear to be happening and instead feelings of incompetence and failure surface, scapegoating and resisting may be one way to resolve that conflict. Britzman (1998) would describe these teachers' responses not as resistance, in a negative sense, but as an appropriate defence, as a way of consoling oneself in the face of the demands of new learning which challenge a teacher's sense of personal identity. Indeed, Britzman questions the value given to reflection and critical thinking in education (more characteristic of the positive teacher perceptions of professional development cited earlier) and sees both these modes of thought as a search for control and rationalization in the face of what otherwise might be more instinctual responses of loss and doubt (p. 32).

Within the organizational context of the school an individual teacher's perceptions of teaching 'high-risk' children will probably be shaped by the value system of the school. That value system may not be open to scrutiny and discussion, and tacitly, certain children may be regarded as unlikely to learn. Through participation in the Reading Recovery course a teacher is encouraged to question a system that has automatically referred a poor reader and writer to special education services, before giving a child a 'second chance' in terms of literacy learning. If even with this second chance, success is not achieved, however, the teacher may scapegoat the child, or the approach adopted in Reading Recovery, or the attitude of the child's parents. Agyris and Schon (1996) point out that: 'Uncertainty over the nature of troublesome situations, over what is to be done and by whom, or over criteria for performance, increase individual feelings of defensiveness and anxiety' (p. 91). The Reading Recovery teacher defends his/her lack of success by attributing it to a simple cause–effect relationship with a particular characteristic of the child. This reassures the teacher that if that aspect of the child were different then his/her own teaching would be more successful.

Conclusion

This is at best an impressionistic account of the tensions teachers reported experiencing through their participation in the Reading Recovery in-service course. In some cases they described feeling personally undermined by the scrutiny given to their teaching of children, a tension perhaps between perceptions of teaching as a private, versus a publicly accountable, activity. Others reported on the tension between their own values about the use of time, and their experience of time as a commodity available both for use for completing course work and for use by the school system. This was manifested, in particular, around the completion of paperwork and data collection. Tensions appear to have occurred around the demands of the course as it reduced access to established personal and professional networks. Finally, teachers reported negatively on the frustrations they felt at not being successful with some children as they probably experienced tensions between their expectations that professional development would improve their skills, in contrast with the reality of a U-shaped learning curve (Mevarech, 1995).

What can be generalized to other professional development settings beyond the specifics of the Reading Recovery in-service course? How do those responsible for professional development take account of these tensions? Accepting conflict and tension as the inevitable outgrowth of the change process is one thing, finding ways to generate productive inquiry so that the seemingly undiscussable gets discussed, and more desirable learning takes place, is another. This is the kind of organizational learning that Agyris and Schon (1996) argue must take account of tacit underlying belief and value systems. It could be said then, that the design of professional development needs to specifically (rather than implicitly) attend to teachers' value systems through discussion, role play, observations of teaching, and analysis of case examples, to ensure that teachers' growth and development is not only about specific skill and knowledge acquisition, but also about the process of recognizing and addressing the complexity of their value systems and the impact such systems have on their teaching.

Second, linked to this attention to teachers' value systems, the design of professional development has to take account of the multi-directional nature of education as interference and the implied ethical dimensions to professional development that this raises. Professional development occurs at the intersection of organizational and individual identities. It can interfere with the wishes and interests of teachers, leading to the kind of defensiveness described earlier which masks the teachers need for reassurance about the possibilities for success. Schools as organizations may exhibit very little capacity to acknowledge and attend to this, colluding with the teacher's version of failure. Bell (1991) explains it as follows:

> A teacher cannot improve his or her performance consistently if the organization is in poor health, and the total functioning of the school rests on the sum of the individual teachers' contributions. Therefore, if the organization can harmonize the individuals' interests and wishes for personal and career development with the requirements of the organization as derived from its educational aims, it will improve both individual and organizational performance. (p. 4)

It might be said, then, that an ethically sound approach to professional development which addresses the kind of tensions and resulting negative experiences described earlier, must involve a recognition of the interdependence of the individual teacher and the school system. This might be accomplished through the kind of school development planning that Stoll and Fink (1996) describe. Again professional development's effectiveness and contribution to change becomes not only about its substantive content, but about the extent to which school and individual teacher needs are addressed jointly, in a productive and purposeful manner.

References

Argyris, C. and Schon, D. (1996) *Organizational Learning II: Theory, Method and Practice,* Reading, MA: Addison-Wesley Publishing Company.

Barnes, B. L. (1997) 'But teacher you went right on: a perspective on Reading Recovery', *The Reading Teacher* 50(4): 284–92.

Bell, L. (1991) 'Approaches to the professional development of teachers', in L. Bell and C. Day (eds) *Managing the professional development of teachers*, Milton Keynes: Open University Press.

Britzman, D. (1998) *Lost Subjects, Contested Objects: Toward a Psychoanalytic Inquiry of Learning*, Albany, NY: State University of New York Press.

Browne, A., Fitts, M., McLaughlin, B., McNamara, M. and Williams, J. (1997) 'Teaching and learning in Reading Recovery: response to "But teacher you went right on"', *Reading Teacher* 50(4): 294–300.

Day, C. (1999) *Developing Teachers: The Challenges of Life-long Learning*. London: Falmer Press.

Darling-Hammond, L. and Sykes, G. (eds.) 1999. *Teaching as the Learning Profession*. San Francisco, CA: Josey-Bass.

Elmore, R. and Burney, D. (1999) 'Investing in teacher learning: staff development and instructional improvement', in, L. Darling-Hammond and G. Sykes (eds) *Teaching as the Learning Profession*. San Francisco, CA: Jossey-Bass.

Fullan, M. (1993). *Change Forces: Probing the Depth of Educational Reform*. London: Falmer Press.

Guskey, T. (1995) 'Professional development in education: in search of the optimal mix', in T. Guskey and M. Huberman (eds) *Professional Development in Education*. New York: Teachers College Press.

Hawley, W. and Valli, L. (1999) 'The essentials of effective professional development: a new consensus', in L. Darling-Hammond and G. Sykes (eds) *Teaching as the Learning Profession*, San Francisco, CA: Jossey-Bass.

Lyons, C. (1998) 'Reading Recovery in the United States: more than a decade of data', *Literacy, Teaching and Learning* 3(1): 77–92.

Marton, F. (1981) 'Phenomenography – describing conceptions of the world around us', *Instructional Science* 10: 177–200.

Mevarech, Z. (1995) 'Teachers' paths on the way to and from the professional development forum', in, T. Guskey and M. Huberman (eds) *Professional Development in Education: New Paradigms and Practices*. New York: Teachers College Press.

Miles, M. B. and Huberman, A. M. (1994) *Qualitative Data Analysis*. Thousand Oaks, CA: Sage Publications.

Pinnell, G. S., Lyons, C. A., DeFord, D. E., Bryk, A. S. and Seltzer, M. (1994) 'Comparing instructional models for the literacy education of high risk first graders', *Reading Research Quarterly* 29(1): 9–39.

Richardson, V. (1992) 'The agenda-setting dilemma in a constructivist staff development process', *Teaching and Teacher Education* 8(3): 287–300.

Shanahan, T. and Barr, R. (1995) 'Reading Recovery: an independent evaluation of the effects of an early instructional intervention for "at risk" learners', *Reading Research Quarterly* 30: 958–96.

Stoll, L. and Fink, D. (1996) *Changing our schools*, Buckingham: Open University Press.

Thompson, C. L. and Zeuli, J. S. (1999) 'The frame and the tapestry: standards-based reform and professional development', in L. Darling-Hammond and G. Sykes (eds) *Teaching as the Learning Profession*. San Francisco, CA: Jossey-Bass.

Chapter 8

School portfolio development

A way to access teacher knowledge

Cheryl J. Craig

Introduction

When faculties from five schools associated with a major national reform movement asked me to act as their planning and evaluation consultant, I wondered how I could balance the agendas of the five schools, and their individual and collective reform responsibilities, with my personal research interest in how context shapes teachers' knowledge developments over time. As it turned out, I had more in common with the desires of the schools and the reform movement than was initially apparent to me.

When I met individually and collectively with the school principals, for example, I learned that the reform movement had charged campuses with identifying someone who would engage their faculties in conversations about the changes they proposed and help them to build a rich reform record of their school activities and experiences. I also discovered that the principals were adamant that the building of in-school reform evidence be something in addition to the numbered accounts. Given that the state[1] and the school districts stridently focused on achievement test scores, attendance and dropout rate data – and also ranked schools, like hotels, on a star system – the principals were desirous of exploring a different approach. They favoured a planning and evaluation method that would capture the fine-grained detail of what their schools attempted to do, what actually happened, and how those changes influenced teachers' learning and, ultimately, student learning. To the principals' ways of thinking, participation as leading campuses in a national reform movement called for something other than, as one of them put it, 'the same old tired approach to evaluation'. The principals' narrative knowledge of their situations caused them to seek me out as someone who could work with their faculties and themselves to dialogue about productive school change, to enact ideas that appeared most fruitful, and to analyse reflectively and portray their school experiences of reform. Hence, the principals requested that school accounts be developed that would reflect people's understandings of educational situations and illuminate the reform experiences from an insider perspective. They particularly hoped this approach would counter such negative press as finding their campuses collectively written up in 'disparaging ways' in national newspapers. The principals intuitively knew that this latter possibility would neither serve their campuses nor the reform movement well.

The sense the principals were beginning to make of their school situations with respect to school reform and participation in a national movement was close to my personal reading of what I term 'the school reform paradox'. While the rhetoric of reform emphasizes schools as units of change, the reality is that such an approach is totally reliant on individual educators as personal and collective agents of change. To my way of thinking, the focus on schools is a somewhat misguided emphasis. It occurred to me that the principals tacitly understood the problem of the school as a unit of analysis when they favoured an approach that would enlist faculty participation and honour human contributions to reform as opposed to relying on external instruments that render human experience irrelevant. The trick for the reform movement, the principals, and me, was to bridge the abyss between schools as institutions of change and educators as personal and collective agents of change. In the numerous discussions that ensued, portfolio work emerged as the substance, method and form best suited to addressing the reform paradox in which all of our work was situated.

In this chapter, I show how school portfolio development connects teachers' knowledge with the experience of school reform. As I work through my approach, I build a theoretical base for the portfolio work and for the narrative view of teacher knowledge as expressed in context. I then introduce the schools where the teachers' work was nested, as well as the teachers, and myself. I next present examples of how teachers and administrators consciously analysed their school situations and progress with respect to school reform. Lastly, I reflectively turn (Schon, 1991) on school portfolios as the substance, method, and form that comes closest to bridging the gap between schools as inhuman units of change and educators as knowing and knowledgeable agents of change who can personally and collectively capture and make sense of reform experiences in ways that others cannot do. Furthermore, educators can, in turn, use these repositories of shared meaning to determine additional avenues of reflection that will lead to more informed decision-making and action in the future.

Introducing the schools

The five schools with which I work are all ethnically diverse, each having a unique composition. One middle school had more Caucasian students than other groups while one elementary school and one middle school were predominately African-American. Hispanic immigrant students mainly populated the second elementary school that I mentored while the fifth school, a 2,500 student, comprehensive high school had roughly the same number of African-American and Hispanic students followed by more Caucasian than Asian students. The first middle school and the second elementary campus are situated in the same school district while the remaining elementary, middle school, and high school are located in a second school district. Together, these schools form a rich microcosm of the diversity present in American public schools.

While all these campuses are physically situated in the same metropolitan area and are involved in the same reform movement, each has been shaped in particularistic ways by a number of forces that contribute to their current situations. All the campuses, for example, are affected by the economy, urbanization, bureaucratization, community degeneration/regeneration, and by desegregation policies. The specific ways these phenomena have shaped the milieus of the schools, along with the unique contributions of the humans who inhabit them, provide essential background, not only in deciding the appropriate next steps for the campuses, but in choosing the interpretive lenses with which to make sense of their socio-historical developments.

Introducing the teachers in the portfolio group

The lead teachers in the portfolio group were teams of individuals from each of the five schools who participated in a half-day meeting held at the university once a month. These teachers co-ordinated the portfolio effort on each of their campuses and integrated the portfolio entries developed by their colleagues into their school portfolio document. At the monthly meetings, the teams of teachers presented portfolio entries to the group for reflection, analysis, and feedback. Issues relating to school portfolio development and mentoring the portfolio development process at their school sites were frequent topics of discussion at these meetings.

Introducing myself

A former Social Sciences and Humanities Research Council of Canada doctoral and post-doctoral fellow, I had previously conducted many personal practical knowledge and professional knowledge landscapes studies in Canada. While I had previously contextualized teacher knowledge in a variety of school settings (i.e. Craig, 1995a, 1995b, 1998, 1999), I had no prior experience of working with organized reform movements nor first-hand knowledge of their effects on school contexts.

Having recently been employed in the American context, I was highly desirous of working collaboratively with school-based educators, but understandably hesitant about the reform movement and its agenda. At the same time as the school-based educators were intrigued by my different background and knowledge, I was drawn to the different forces shaping their knowing. This reciprocal attraction reinforced our shared desire to understand school reform from an insider perspective, and bound us together in the common portfolio work.

Introducing the reform movement

School reform is a local, regional and national phenomenon in the United States. While all school reform initiatives are generally lumped together under the same category, each operates from its own 'theory of action', its own particular assessment of systemic problems that need to be comprehensively addressed in the educational enterprise (Argyris and Schon, 1978; Schon and McDonald, 1998; Hatch, 1998; McDonald, 1996).

The reform movement involved in this study took one of the least intrusive approaches from a fiduciary and a philosophical standpoint. Philanthropic funds were awarded to local organizations which then distributed awards to worthy schools and networks of schools based on their reform plans. The local and national organizations did not interfere with a school plan unless the campus did not identify substantive changes it would undergo. The nature of those changes, however, were shaped by each individual campus, not by the reform movement.

The reform movement tended to view the history of schooling as part of the educational problem and hence, invested funds to promote teacher learning, to break down isolation between and among individuals, schools, and communities, and to address size issues so that all individuals in schools could become better known. Each of these imperatives was developed to support student learning, the foremost goal of the reform movement.

One key feature of the particular reform movement was its Critical Friends groups (Cushman, 1999) that were formed to develop teacher leadership and to look systematically at student work. As teachers become more involved in the Critical Friends work, they develop teacher portfolios. Schools may similarly include student portfolio development as part of their campus reform plans. The high school in this study, for example, initiated a 'capstone' project that was field-tested in 1999–2000. This version of a portfolio involves 'graduation by exhibition'.

Research framework: situating the work in the teacher knowledge literature

A particular view of teacher knowledge is integral to the portfolio work in which I engage with the school-based educators. Understanding the term, personal practical knowledge, is essential to making sense of how the teachers and I approach the portfolio work. Deweyan in nature (1916, 1934, 1938), personal practical knowledge is:

> a term designed to capture the idea of experience in a way that allows us to talk about teachers as knowledgeable and knowing persons. Personal practical knowledge is in the teacher's past experience, in the teacher's present mind and body, and in the future plans and actions. Personal practical knowledge is found in the teacher's practice. It is, for any teacher, a particular way of reconstructing the past and the intentions of the future to deal with the exigencies of a present situation.
>
> (Connelly and Clandinin, 1988, p. 25)

In this view of teacher knowledge, teachers filter their reform experience through their personal practical knowledge (Olson and Craig, 2001). Furthermore, the entries they choose to include in their school portfolios are expressions of their personal practical knowledge. Hence, teachers' personal practical knowledge is central to school portfolio development in first- and second-order ways.

A second conceptualization that forms a critical underpinning of school portfolio development is Clandinin and Connelly's professional knowledge landscape metaphor (1995, 1996, 1999) which connects teachers' personal knowledge with the contexts of teaching. The metaphor of teacher knowledge constituting a professional knowledge landscape offers a way to think and talk about schools as units of change. In Connelly and Clandinin's words:

> A landscape metaphor is particularly well suited to our purpose. It allows us to talk about space, place, and time. Furthermore, it has a sense of expansiveness and the possibility of being filled with diverse people, things, and events in different relationships. Understanding professional knowledge as comprising a landscape calls for a notion of professional knowledge as composed of a wide variety of components and influenced by a wide variety of people, places, and things. Because we see the professional knowledge landscape as composed of relationships among people, places, and things, we see it as both an intellectual and a moral landscape.
>
> (Clandinin and Connelly, 1995, pp. 4–5)

Teachers' professional knowledge landscapes are comprised of both in-classroom and out-of-classroom places. In previous research, I outlined my former work as a teacher with respect to these places:

> As a teacher, I live in two different professional places. One is the relational world inside the classroom where I co-construct meaning with my students. The other is the abstract world where I live with everyone outside my classroom, a world where I meet all the other aspects of the educational enterprise such as the philosophies, the techniques, the materials, and the expectations that I will enact certain educational practices. While each of these places is distinctive, neither is totally self-contained. Together these places form the professional knowledge landscape that frames my work as an educator.
>
> (Craig, 1995c, p. 16)

A key challenge in developing school portfolios is to cohesively link these multiple, often conflicting, sites of teacher inquiry in productive ways to illuminate the complexities of the situation.

A number of sets of stories help to define the contours of a school landscape. In the case of school portfolio development, stories of school – the stories that educators are expected to live and tell about schools – and school stories – the stories educators personally tell about schools – are vital (Clandinin and Connelly, 1996). Also important are stories of reform – the stories that teachers are expected to live and tell about school reform and reform stories – the stories teachers personally tell about their experiences of school reform (Craig, 2001). The dynamic interplay between and among these multiple narratives forming a story constellation (Craig, under review) on teachers' professional knowledge landscapes are essential to school portfolio development. In short, they sit at the heart of school portfolio construction and reconstruction because they offer perspectives of what works, why, and the meanings that are held by those who live in the tensions between and among the multiple constellations within school landscapes.

Two additional conceptualizations relating to teacher knowledge make important contributions to this study because they show how the portfolio development process unfolds. One, the narrative authority of teacher knowledge (Olson, 1993, 1995), explains how teachers develop their knowledge transactionally. The concept of narrative authority offers an alternative to the dominant authority of positivism (Tom and Valli, 1990) that separates the knower and the known (Dewey and Bentley, 1949). The narrative authority conceptualization provides justification for teachers telling stories of their reform experience, the narrative view of teacher knowledge, and school portfolios as chronicles of reform experiences.

The second conceptualization, the notion that teachers have knowledge communities where they negotiate the meaning of their experiences, shows how personal meaning becomes public and shared (Craig, 1995a, 1995b). The creation of school portfolios provides an additional commonplace of experience (Lane, 1988) that brings educators lodged in different places in the educational enterprise together around a shared purpose. In their knowledge communities, teachers express the narrative authority of their personal practical knowledge in the company of others. Knowledge is mediated through the narrative authority of those who participate in relational conversations that involve dialogue, analysis, and reflection. Such an approach is pivotal to the personal and collective creation of teacher knowledge and to school portfolio development because it counters retreats into solipsism from institutional, personal, and collective perspectives.

The aforementioned conceptualizations: personal practical knowledge, professional knowledge landscapes, story constellations, the narrative authority of teacher knowledge, and teachers' knowledge communities, are all narrative terms that set the stage for important connections to be made between teacher knowledge and school portfolio development. In the next section, I locate school portfolio development in the literature, then elucidate the particular portfolio development method I used with the teacher teams from the five schools.

Situating the work in the portfolio development literature

In my planning and evaluation work with teachers and schools, I subscribe to a portfolio definition outlined by Lyons who refers to portfolios as: 'the dynamic process of teachers documenting the evidence of their work and growth, gathered and authored by them through careful reflection, shared with colleagues and students, and presented for public discussion and debate about their conceptions in good teaching'. (1998, ix). To this definition, I add that in school portfolio development, administrators are also included in the dynamic process and that the portfolios present not only evidence of good teaching, but also offer conceptions of productive school contexts that support good teaching and good learning. Furthermore, as portfolio work expands, school district personnel, reform agency representatives, parents, and the public at large may be invited into the process of school portfolio-making since they, too, are shaping forces that impact the professional knowledge landscapes of schools.

Like Shulman (1998), I regard school portfolio construction as an act of theory-making. In Shulman's words, 'what is declared worth documenting, worth reflecting on, what is deemed to be portfolio-worthy, is a theoretical act' (p. 24). In school portfolio development, the process publicly involves teachers and administrators working together in a collaborative manner to determine evidential material reflecting their notions of good teaching and good schools. Embedded in this idea is the presentation of student work and student stories that portray how the school-based educators' theories become realized in their practical work with students. In short, the development of a school portfolio embodies not only the continuous life of a school, it demonstrates – in powerful and connected ways – the continuous growth of individuals – administrators, teachers, and students – within. Furthermore, because the portfolio as a document is in a constant state of construction and reconstruction, it demands that school life be examined both longitudinally and episodically to ascertain the degree to which beliefs about good teaching and good schools are reflected in individual and collective actions.

In addition to drawing on the work of Lyons and Shulman in the research framework, Freidus' notion of portfolio mentoring is also an essential component of my theoretical base. Referring to Shulman's account of a failed portfolio experiment, Freidus notes that the presence of mentors is a necessary prerequisite to portfolio success. Freidus describes the mentoring process in the following manner:

> Mentoring . . . becomes the nexus of trust building and accountability. Mentors . . . validate . . . experience on both professional and personal levels without being judgmental . . . they articulate not only the strength . . . of the work but also the way in which they see the work as professionally substantive. (1998, p. 58)

In the school portfolio development process outlined in this paper, the mentoring that took place was a layered process where I worked directly with the portfolio group of teachers, but also with the overall reform teams of the schools and with the principals in an evaluation group. I also met informally in the schools with other faculty members. The portfolio group of teachers directly worked with their teaching colleagues and administrators, and also with the portfolio lead teachers from the other schools. In the mentoring process, the notions of the narrative authority of teacher knowledge and the idea of teachers forming knowledge communities to negotiate meanings for experiences figured largely. At this critical juncture vital links between school portfolio development and teacher knowledge were forged.

The portfolio method

The method that guides the school portfolio development approach I take arises from many sources. First, Chatman's work (1990) reminds me that because the schools are foremostly associated with a reform movement, the narratives the teachers choose to support the school reform stories will always serve the purpose of argument: the argument that the campuses are good schools, the argument that the schools are worthy of future funding. This was a reality that neither the teachers nor I could forget in the portfolio-making process because it sat in the background even when the work took on a life of its own.

A second notion that deeply informs the portfolio method I use with school-based educators is White's idea (1981) of annals, chronicles, and narratives. In mapping out narrative ways of knowing, as opposed to logico-scientific ways of knowing, Bruner (1986) posited that annals represent the blow-by-blow accounts of what happened during a particular period of time while chronicles comprise descriptions of the particular events. Narratives, in the meantime, penetrate selected events to illuminate people's experiences of them. It seemed to me that White's conceptualization of multiple kinds of text and Bruner's anchoring of these texts in narrative ways of knowing addressed some of the manifold complexities present in school portfolio creation. First, the annals account for all the reform activities undertaken by the schools, a requirement of the reform movement. Second, the chronicles offer enough description to the annals to render them meaningful. Third, the narratives represent highly developed portfolio entries that connect teacher knowledge with student learning set within the backdrop of a reforming school context. The first type of text meets the reform movement's compliance requirements while the third type centres on learning. The middle one bridges the other two and rounds out the overall account of school growth.

Another source that greatly influences the portfolio work with the school-based educators is the series of stories that Clandinin and Connelly use to describe the professional knowledge landscape of schools. Introduced earlier in this work, these stories (to which I have added) address the school reform paradox by illuminating a complex maze of stories on school landscapes and intentionally revealing points of tension and conflict as well as points of convergence and shared energy to which the teachers and I must be alert.

The fourth source that guides my portfolio work with the teachers and the schools arises from Grant and Huebner's research (1998). My reading of Grant and Huebner reminds me that even though the portfolio is a document that can be used for compliance, learning and other purposes, portfolio construction above all involves the cultivation of two important habits of mind: one, the view that teaching is an ongoing inquiry, another, the notion that collaboration is a valuable way of coming to know teaching. The orientations remind me that growth will be evident in the created document but much more so embodied in the hearts and minds of the educators who participated in the process.

The method I employ, then, draws on several sources: Chatman's uses of different kinds of text, White's notion of annals, chronicles and narratives, and by Bruner's interpretation of it, Clandinin and Connelly's storied landscape of schools, and Grant and Huebner's habits of mind. These bodies of thought, together with my 'telling stories' (1997), 'parallel stories' (1999) and 'story constellations' (under review) research methods, form the methodological foundation from which I draw as I engage in the portfolio-making process with the educators on five campuses.

The school portfolio-making process begins: year 1

Crafting school narratives

The portfolio creation process began in the first year that the school participated in the reform movement. The groups of teachers from each school and I took up the task of researching and writing their school narratives. In this section, narrative exemplars from two of the participating campuses are shared.

School narrative: Heights Learning Center

Heights Learning Center, an elementary school serving a high risk, immigrant Hispanic, Spanish-speaking population, captured the particularities of their context in the following excerpt from a portfolio entry:

> Located in the Heights neighborhood, Heights Learning Center recently celebrated its eightieth year as a school. The Heights school building was beginning to take on the appearance of neglect. Peeling paint, missing floor tiles, and leaking ceilings were all too common features. Then, in 1997, the Heights community received a torrential downpour of rain. Eighty-five percent (85%) of the school received water damage and . . . had to be restored . . .
>
> Evolved from a middle class neighborhood of Anglo-English speakers to one in which ninety-five percent (95%) of the students are predominately Hispanic Spanish-speakers, Heights Community Learning Center has been deeply affected by societal shifts from urban to suburban living and from public to private schooling. However, since the reform effort [focusing on a dual language program] began, the school has increased its number of Hispanic children from ninety (90%) to its current ninety-five percent. . . . These students are of a very low socio-economic status with a high at risk school drop-out percentage (64%). Ninety percent (90%) of Heights' students are on the free and/or reduced lunch program.
>
> Heights Community Learning Center School Portfolio, Year 1, 1–2

School narrative: Eagle High School

The teachers in the portfolio group (Table 8.1) at the large, comprehensive high school, described the changing context of the Eagle campus in the following manner:

Eagle High School, located in northwest Houston, is one of five high schools in a large school district. Eagle serves a community that is suburban by geography and urban by demography. Built in 1977, the school began as a small suburban high school. The downturn in the Houston economy in the mid-1980's hit the golf course community around Eagle particularly hard. Many families, who had bought the new executive homes and whose incomes flourished during the boom in the 1970's and early 1980's, lost their jobs. Unable to make house payments, they simply walked away, abandoning homes to foreclosure sales. This change, coupled with a tremendous increase in the building of area apartments, including those subsidized by the government, caused a shift in the demographics of both the community and the school. During the last decade, the community around Eagle has undergone rapid economic changes which have resulted in Eagle's transformation to a large school with a culturally, ethnically and economically diverse population.

Table 8.1 Eagle High School portfolio, year 1, p. 1.

	1976–7	*1986–7*	*1996–7*	*1998–9*
Number of students	1,242	2,150	3,104	2,480
Percent of students in free or reduced lunch programmes	7%	21%	37%	40%
Ethnic composition of student body	17% Black 80% Anglo 3% Hispanic N/A Asian	31% Black 48% Anglo 12% Hispanic 9% Asian	55% Black 16% Anglo 22% Hispanic 8% Asian	55% Black 12% Anglo 26% Hispanic 8% Asian

Excavating a school's history of reform

In this second section, an example of how teachers from T. P. Yaeger Middle School documented the recent history of school reform on their campus is made public.

Origins of school reform: T. P. Yaeger Middle School

Yaeger's path to school reform began in 1989 when a model laboratory was established in the school. The lab presented science curriculum in a dynamic, integrated manner and made the educative experiences of students academically rich and relevant to their lives. Lessons in the laboratory seized the attention of the student population and neighborhood students began achieving at levels commonly associated with gifted and talented students. The lab offered the school a prototypical example of how the school might be restructured to meet the learning needs of a student population that had begun to skip, loiter, and act in sullen and 'worldly-beyond-their-years' ways. The lab provided the staff and administration with a way to improve the tone and academic performance of students at Yaeger. The stark contrast between what was happening in the lab and what was happening elsewhere in the school suggested that Yaeger had not been as effective as it might have been in addressing the challenges which the malaise of modernity were posing in students' lives. The creation of the science laboratory, with its child-centered, integrated approach to student learning and teacher development represented a key juncture in Yaeger's reform history. The lab's early success formed a foundation around which all other changes were built. Attention was then turned toward systemic changes that would reorganize space and people and break down teacher and student isolation in ways that would make initiatives like the Lab project possible.

T. P. Yaeger Middle School portfolio, year 1, p. 5–6

Approaching schools as sites of inquiry

In this third section, texts from two campuses: Hardy Academy and Eagle High School, are shared. These portfolio excerpts present the inquiry questions that the teachers framed of their own accord.

Hardy Academy: inquiry questions

A newly formed campus located in an old school that was closed, then used for alternative behaviour purposes during the early desegregation years, Hardy Academy, and its partner school, Cochrane Academy, are magnet campuses. These magnet schools were created due to challenges associated with desegregating. The teachers at Hardy Academy created the following inquiry questions to capture the short evolution of their campus:

1995–6	
Problem experienced:	Named a magnet school, but was more of a neighbourhood school.
Inquiry question:	How does a school become a magnet campus?
1996–7	
Problem experienced:	Students at Hardy had five or six different schedules trying to accommodate the fine arts strand, teacher certification, and block scheduling.
Inquiry question:	How does a magnet school become more flexible in its scheduling?
1997–8	
Problem experienced:	Involvement of full staff; school reform, technology, and curriculum grants pulling people in seemingly opposing directions; few people did much of the work.

Inquiry questions:	How does Hardy Academy get reform going? How can we strengthen the magnet theme? How can technology be used more effectively?
1998–9	
Problem experienced:	Scheduling for magnet strands and new leadership.
Inquiry questions:	How does Hardy Academy accommodate the strands of the magnet program? What can new leadership do to help increase the magnet theme, school reform efforts, the use of technology, and promote academic education?

Hardy Academy School portfolio, year 1, p. 5–6

Eagle High School: inquiry questions

While Hardy Academy's teachers focused on inquiry questions on a year-to-year basis, Eagle High School's portfolio group centred on perplexing, over-arching questions that underpinned their reform effort:

> Can a school serving an 'attendance zone' rather than a community be the 'glue' that creates and holds together a community where no natural community exists?
>
> Can a school maintain academic excellence through demographic and economic transition of its student body?
>
> Is it possible to institutionalize reform in a particular site so that school reform is not dependent upon a particular charismatic leader?
>
> Can a large faculty re-shape itself into a mutually supporting learning community?
>
> Eagle High School portfolio, year 1, p. 6

Reflections on the school portfolio-making process

In previous sections, readers were introduced to a sampling of entries excerpted from the year 1 school portfolios. In this next part of the work, the teachers' reflections on the school portfolio-creation process will be summarized.

The ongoing challenge of including more educators in the portfolio opinion development process was a shared concern arising from all campuses. While the number of teachers engaged in the work had increased in all schools, the desire to draw more educators into the process was commonly and longingly expressed. At the same time, the portfolio group of teachers recognized how important the invitational quality of the work was and the negative effect that acts of coercion would have on the overall reception of portfolios in the professional knowledge landscape of each school.

A second challenge identified by the teachers was the duplicity of purpose embedded in the origin and evolution of the particular portfolio endeavour. The tensions between balancing the learning focus and the everpresent accountability agenda continued to be recognized, although the teachers overwhelmingly favoured school portfolios being used to feature learning.

A third response the teachers had to the school portfolio work was that it awakened them to 'the hundred-fold complexities of human experiences'. Participation in the in-school and across-school conversations and activities brought to the surface perspectives individuals had not imagined. While this greatly enriched the teachers' learning, and broadened their horizons of knowing, it also made them increasingly mindful about how to capture the fullness of human experience in a portfolio document. They were especially desirous of helping others to see and value the multidimensional experiences they had come to know about their particular milieus.

If the teachers had their horizon stretched with respect to the complexities of human experiences, they also had their perspective enlarged with respect to the complexities of their schools contexts. As each teacher brought events of classroom life to the table, the professional knowledge landscapes of particular schools began to be constituted. Furthermore, teachers' understandings of their schools became increasingly refined through contact with educators who brought other contextual experiences to the meetings.

New issues such as whose voice represents the voice of the school, and who should decide what is portfolio worthy in a school context, also rose to the surface. Additional matters that were discussed had to do with the representation of conflicting theories of actions within buildings and the need to align school portfolio development with other student and teacher portfolio work taking place in the schools.

The aforementioned issues, challenges, questions, and wonders, articulated by the teachers are matters that will receive careful attention in the next round of school portfolio making. The teachers' reflections in and on the portfolio-making experiences will deeply enrich the development of further generations of portfolios in their schools and will serve as exemplars (Kuhn 1962; Mishler 1990) to which other campuses considering this work will turn.

Parting comments

In this chapter, I have featured school portfolios as a way to access teachers' knowledge of their professional knowledge landscapes, particularly with respect to stories of reform being introduced to stories of school (Connelly and Clandinin, 1996) within the context of teachers' professional lives. I began by introducing the schools, the teachers, the reform movement and myself. I then built a theoretical framework for teacher knowledge and portfolio development work that gave rise to the portfolio method I employ. This led me to share excerpts from year 1 school portfolios that included school narratives, histories of school reform, and questions relating to schools as sites of inquiry. I ended with a discussion of the issues, questions, and wonders that the portfolio group of teachers named at the conclusion of their first year immersed in the portfolio creation process.

It seems fitting that I conclude this longitudinal inquiry at the first year point with words from a framed statement given to me by one of the teachers in the portfolio group. The expression aptly portrays not only school and individual development, but also the portfolio creation process in which we collaboratively engaged: 'Changes . . . there are no endings just new beginnings . . .'

Such is the human experience of personal change, school change, and the portfolio-making process. In these experimental commonplaces, critical connections between teacher knowledge and school portfolio construction can be found.

Acknowledgements

I deeply appreciate the opportunity to work with the five campuses and acknowledge the centrality of the school-based educators' experiences in the living, telling and reporting of this work. This research was supported by the Brown Foundation, Inc. and the reform movement.

Note

1 In this paper, the word, state means one of the fifty states in the United States. It does not mean 'central' or 'national.'

References

Argyris, C. and Schon, D. (1978) *Organizational Learning: A Theory of Action Perspective*. Reading, MA: Addison-Wesley.

Cochrane Academy (1998) *Cochrane Academy School Portfolio*, Houston: Cochrane Academy.

—— (1999) *Cochrane Academy School Portfolio*, Houston: Cochrane Academy.

Bruner, J. (1986) *Actual Minds, Possible Worlds*, Cambridge, MA: Harvard University Press.

Chatman, S. (1990) *Coming to Terms: The Rhetoric of Narrative in Fiction and Film*, Ithaca, NY: Cornell University Press.

Clandinin, D. J. and Connelly, F. M. (1995) *Teachers' Professional Knowledge Landscapes*, New York: Teachers College Press.

—— (1996) 'Teachers' professional knowledge landscapes: teacher stories–stories of teachers–school stories–stories of school', *Educational Researcher* 19(5): 2–14.

Connelly, F. M. and Clandinin, D. J. (1988) *Teachers as Curriculum Planners: Narratives of Experience*, New York: Teachers College Press.

—— (1999) *Shaping a Professional Identity: Stories of Educational Practice*. New York: Teachers College Press.

Craig, C. J. (1995a) 'Knowledge communities: a way of making sense of how beginning teachers come to know', *Curriculum Inquiry* 25(2): 151–75.

—— (1995b) 'Safe places on the professional knowledge landscape: knowledge communities', in D. J. Clandinin and F. M. Connelly (eds) *Teachers' Professional Knowledge Landscapes*, New York: Teachers College Press.

—— (1995c) 'Dilemmas in crossing the boundaries on the professional knowledge landscape', in D. J. Clandinin and F. M. Connelly (eds) *Teachers' Professional Knowledge Landscapes*, New York: Teachers College Press.

—— (1998) 'The influence of context on one teacher's interpretive knowledge of team teaching', *Teaching and Teacher Education*, 14(4): 371–383.

—— (1999) 'Parallel stories: a way of contextualizing teacher stories', *Teaching and Teacher Education* 15(4): 397–412.
—— Under review. Story Constellations: A Way to Characterize School Contexts and Contextualize Teacher Knowledge.
—— (2001) 'The relationships between and among teacher's narrative knowledge, communities of knowing, and school reform: a case of "The Monkey's Paw"', *Curriculum Inquiry* 31(3).
Cushman, K. (1999) 'Educators making portfolios. First results from the National Reform Faculty', *Phi Delta Kappan* 80(10): 744–9.
Dewey, J. (1916) *Democracy and Education*, New York: Macmillan.
—— (1934) *Art and Education*, New York: Macmillan.
—— (1938) *Experience and Education*, New York: Macmillan.
Dewey, J. and Bentley, A. F. (1949) *Knowing and the Known*, Boston: The Beacon Press.
Eagle High School (1998) *Eagle High School Portfolio*, Houston: Eagle High School.
—— (1999) *Eagle High School Portfolio*, Houston: Eagle High School.
Freidus, H. (1998) 'Mentoring portfolio development', in N. Lyons (ed.) *With Portfolio in Hand: Validating the New Teacher Professionalism*, New York: Teachers College Press.
Grant, G. and Huebner, T. A. (1998) 'The portfolio question: the power of self-directed inquiry', in N. Lyons (ed.) *With Portfolio in Hand: Validating the New Teacher Professionalism*, New York: Teachers College Press.
Hardy Academy (1998) *Hardy Academy School Portfolio*, Houston: Hardy Academy.
—— (1999) *Hardy Academy School Portfolio*, Houston: Hardy Academy.
Hatch, T. (1998) 'The differences in theory that matter in the practice of school improvement', *American Educational Research Journal*. 35(1): 3–31.
Heights Community Learning Center (1998) *Heights Community Learning Center School Portfolio*, Houston: Heights Community Learning Center.
—— (1999) *Heights Community Learning Center School Portfolio*, Houston: Heights Community Learning Center.
Kuhn, T. (1962) *The Structure of Scientific Revolutions*, Chicago: University of Chicago Press.
Lane, B. (1988) *Landscapes of the Sacred: Geography and Narrative in American Spirituality*, New York: Paulist Press.
Lyons, N. (1998) 'Preface', *With Portfolio in Hand: Validating the New Teacher Professionalism*, New York: Teachers College Press.
McDonald, J. P. (1996) *Redesigning School: Lessons for the 21st Century*, San Francisco: Jossey-Bass.
Mishler, E. G. (1990) 'Validity in inquiry-guided research: the role of exemplars in narrative studies', *Harvard Educational Review*, 60: 415–42.
Olson, M. (1993) 'Conceptualizing narrative authority: Implications for teacher education', unpublished dissertation, Edmonton: University of Alberta.
—— (1995) 'Conceptualizing narrative authority: implications for teacher education', *Teaching and Teacher Education* 11(2): 119–25.
Olson, M. and Craig, C. J. (2001) 'Opportunities and challenges in the development of teachers knowledge: the development of narrative authority through knowledge communities', *Teaching and Teacher Education*, 17(6).
Schon, D. A. (1991) *The Reflective Turn: Case Studies in and on Educational Practice*, New York: Teachers College Press.
Schon, D. A. and McDonald, J. P. (1998) *Doing what you mean to do in school reform*, Providence, RI: Brown University.

Shulman, L. (1994) 'Portfolios in historical perspective', presentation at the Portfolios in Teaching and Teacher Education Conference, Cambridge, MA.

—— (1998) 'Teacher portfolios: a theoretical act', in N. Lyons (ed.) *With Portfolio in Hand: Validating the New Teacher Professionalism*, New York: Teachers College Press.

Tom, A. R. and Valli, L. (1990) 'Profesional knowledge for teachers', in W. R. Houston (ed.) *Handbook of Research on Teacher Education*, New York: Macmillan.

—— (1990) 'Professional knowledge for teachers', in W. R. Houston (ed.) *Handbook of Research on Teacher Education*, New York: Macmillan.

T. P. Yaeger Middle School (1998) T. P. Yaeger School Portfolio, Houston: T. P. Yaeger School.

T. P. Yaeger Middle School (1999) T. P. Yaeger School Portfolio, Houston: T. P. Yaeger School.

White, H. (1981) The Value of narrativity in representation of reality, in W. J. Mitchell (ed.) *On Narrative*, Chicago: University of Chicago Press.

Chapter 9

Understanding and articulating teacher knowledge

John Loughran

Introduction

In 1985 at Laverton Secondary College (Victoria, Australia) a small group of teachers met together on a regular basis to discuss their attempts to improve the quality of students' classroom learning. The structure that developed and became the basis of the Project for the Enhancement of Effective Learning (PEEL) approach (Baird and Northfield, 1992) involved collaboration, support, sharing of ideas and approaches to teaching, and importantly, the development of an articulation of how to share knowledge about teaching for understanding. This occurred through the regular meetings in which the discussion of teaching and learning was the central focus and was supported by a small group of academics.

Research into student learning (Baird and White, 1982a; 1982b) was a catalyst for the project as the teachers readily identified with assertions briefly summarized in Table 9.1 (Baird, 1986). These assertions 'ring true' with teachers who have adapted and interpreted them in a variety of ways to shape and inform their teaching practice. They have also served to encourage further research by PEEL teachers.

From the early days of PEEL, the use of language was important and teachers found the term metacognition (Flavell, 1976) to be both acceptable and usable. Metacognition had meaning for the participants as they saw their teaching as a way of pursuing the enhancement of students' metacogntive skills.

Table 9.1 Assertions about learning.

1	Learning outcome is determined by decisions made by the learner.
2	Inadequate learning is due to inadequate decision-making.
3	Learners often are unaware of their learning problems. This lack of awareness generates poor attitudes.
4	It takes energy to learn with understanding, or to unlearn a misconception.
5	Increasing awareness of the nature and process of learning leads to improved attitudes and procedures. (Baird, 1986)

The nature of PEEL necessitated a language for the sharing of ideas and practice as discussion associated with ways of recognizing and responding to the dilemmas of practice became windows of opportunity for better understanding the nature of teaching and learning. Through the ongoing collaboration between the academics and teacher-researchers, many of these windows of opportunity have been grasped and this led to the formation of the PAVOT project. PAVOT (The Perspective and Voice of the Teacher) has become an important bridge to accessing teachers' professional knowledge and has created opportunities to articulate and disseminate this knowledge to others.[1]

PAVOT has been an interesting project as it has built on the solid foundations of the PEEL project and specifically aimed to develop ways of introducing the voice of the teacher into the research literature by communicating the findings of their work through their writing about their research.

The form of research and documentation in PAVOT has been influenced by case methodology (Shulman, 1992) which allows teachers to 'unpack' the complexity of teaching and learning, and, through case discussions, to develop insights into their own practice. Case writing and the use of cases have been helpful for PEEL and PAVOT teachers (see Mitchell and Mitchell, 1997) and has been another impetus for the development of a language of learning through the need to articulate and communicate the knowledge underpinning the practice.

This chapter then is one attempt to illustrate how the professional knowledge of teachers has developed through involvement in PEEL and PAVOT. This development has been as a result of the recognition and response to the need to share and learn with one another as they have begun to understand better and value their practice, and therefore, the knowledge that is at the heart of these understandings.

PEEL groups

The participants in this study were drawn from three different groupings of PEEL teachers. The three groupings each comprised three teachers who volunteered to be interviewed (at times convenient to them) about their understanding of their teaching practice and the principles which underpinned their actions. Each of the three groupings is an attempt to establish general categories of involvement including beginning PEEL teachers, experienced PEEL teachers and PAVOT teachers (PAVOT teachers being experienced PEEL teachers who choose to pursue teacher-research in a systematic and organized manner).

The first group (beginning PEEL teachers) included David and John (all participants have pseudonyms) who were English and humanities teachers and were recent graduates with 2–3 years teaching experience, and Sophie who taught mathematics and humanities and had been teaching for 8 years.

The second group comprised experienced PEEL teachers with more than 5 years involvement in the PEEL project. All had at least 15 years teaching experience. The teachers interviewed in this grouping (Olivia, Andrea and Jack) taught a range of subjects including mathematics, science, social studies, and technology studies.

The final group was made up of experienced PEEL teachers who had also been involved in conducting their own PAVOT projects. Two of these teachers (Jen and Joan) were elementary teachers, the third (Callum) was a high school mathematics and science teacher. All three of these teachers had been involved in developing and delivering professional development programmes for schools and had also been involved in presenting nationally and internationally at conferences for both teachers and educational researchers.

These groupings offered one way of viewing the development of teachers' professional knowledge through the PEEL project across the continuum of experience from early PEEL to PAVOT. All interviews were conducted at a time and place convenient to the teachers. Interviews were audio-taped then later transcribed for analysis.

Findings

The three groupings of teachers are presented separately in attempt to illustrate the changes in their knowledge in concert with their experience in PEEL.

Beginning PEEL teachers

These teachers, like many beginning teachers, were enthusiastic about their work and their hopes for their students. They were also a little critical of some of their more experienced colleagues whom they characterized as teaching in 'routine' or 'non-thinking ways'. Each of these teachers illustrated a desire to teach in ways that they saw as extending themselves beyond the 'norm'. Obviously this is not necessarily a trait peculiar to beginning PEEL teachers, but in their particular case a defining characteristic of their views was that they had an underlying purpose that directed their approach to teaching.

This sense of purpose that directed their practice was based on a genuine commitment to student learning derived largely from an understanding, or at least a recognition, of the poor learning tendencies which were the basis of Baird's initial work.

In the case of these teachers, involvement in PEEL created a situation with which they could readily identify. They came to see the relationship between teaching and learning as something important for their practice and therefore actively pursued ways in which to better understand the links. Consequently, they began to focus as much on learning as on teaching and this is a considerable shift in the manner of conceptualizing one's own practice. I would argue that it is much more common for teachers to explore teaching in terms of new or interesting activities to use in the classroom rather than specifically apprehending the implications for learning. This focus on learning was important in both conceptualizing teaching and discussing their developing practice and subsequent knowledge.

Learning: a basis for pedagogical reasoning

Amongst all three participants was a sense that the development of learning as an organizing principle of practice was something they had come to understand through reflection on their early teaching experiences. David was perhaps the most forthright in his views on this development:

> Now I choose activities to meet the learning outcomes I'm hoping for, whereas earlier I think I saw PEEL as offering a smorgasbord [of procedures] and I'd just try them all out, you know, to break up the routine a bit. But the class makes a big difference to what you do. (*David*)

John (who worked for a time between his initial degree and his teacher education program) believed that his use of teaching procedures as activities, rather than as purposeful choices to enhance learning, had been much more limited due to his experiences in the workplace before becoming a teacher. In any case, all three recognized that they had experienced a progression in their practice from managing the dailyness of teaching (Loughran and Northfield, 1996), through to the use of teaching procedures in order to break up the normal routine, to their present approach of explicitly linking their teaching practice to the intended learning approaches and outcomes they were hoping for.

One way that this development had been enhanced was through the support structure of PEEL. The fact that they met on a regular basis to discuss their teaching and their students' learning was an impetus for reconceptualizing their classroom practice. These meetings helped them to access a range of teaching procedures (see for example Baird and Northfield, 1992), but more importantly, through discussion, encouraged an understanding of the use of these procedures as much more than simply being a smorgasbord of classroom activities.

> PEEL is a way of staying in tune with the profession. It keeps your enthusiasm. (*John*)

> It's a support base. The teacher talk and support matters. (*Sophie*)

> It's other teachers going through the same things as you. You find out what's important to your colleagues and it makes you ready to reflect. (*David*)

The individual recognition of this shift in thinking and associated practice was perhaps most apparent to David as he had vivid memories of trying to do something different each lesson (in his first year of teaching) simply to maintain students' interest. His current understanding of his teaching had shifted such that he believed – just because a particular teaching procedure was used in a class did not mean that a student's approach to learning necessarily changed. He felt there was a need to both understand the procedure and to use it appropriately so that it encouraged learning, not just to maintain (or create) student interest. John concurred with this view.

> Kids get sick of concept maps just as much as chalk and talk. At some PEEL meetings a good idea might come up and if we all rush in and do it

> the kids say, 'we've done that in the last three lessons!' So, we need to use a procedure for a particular purpose and not all do it because we are keen to try it out. You have to think about what you're doing and why. (*John)*

A langugage of learning

This shift from the use of teaching procedures as activities to reasoned selection of teaching approaches particular to the anticipated learning has also become a basis for a language of learning – not unlike that described by Macdonald (1996). As these teachers have come to align their teaching with their intentions for their students' learning, they have developed a language to communicate these ideas with their students. Hence, the names of teaching procedures (for example, concept maps, venn diagrams, semantic maps) and terms such as metacognition, chunking and processessing have become a part of their teaching vocabulary. This was necessary so that students could be conscious of, and responsible for, their learning behaviours and so that the learning intentions could be better understood, communicated and realized in practice.

> Negotiation with students is important. We discuss what we are going to do and why, and then how to do it best. (*David)*

> You have to let the students know what you think a particular teaching approach is designed to do, they have to know what you mean. (*Sophie)*

To enhance students' metacognitive skills it is important to be able to highlight examples of them as they occur in the classroom. Therefore, there is a need to label them so that a sense of recognition and meaning can be conveyed. For these early career PEEL teachers, this language of learning was clearly being developed and used in their teaching and was a feature of their growth and professional development through PEEL.

> You come to know what you know about teaching through experience and then there is a need to be able to express this. Normal teachers operate by instruction and organization as a focus for their teaching, we focus on learning and discuss this with our students. Perhaps we create and see things as a learning environment, it's not a threatening sort of thing – but I can see how some teachers would see it that way . . . talking with students about learning [is important] so that they know how to learn and when they are doing things that help that, that's the point of talking about metacognition. (*David)*

> We encourage student learning [so] metacognition is important because you need to recognize the type of learner you are and PEEL groups help us develop the language to articulate what's happening. It's trying to move them into more use of higher order thinking skills and that. (*Sophie*)

> Students suffer more from not knowing about their learning and so we need to help them to learn and to see and use a learning language too. (*John*)

At this stage in their development, these teaachers recognized the value of a learning language as a way of communicating ideas with other PEEL teachers at their school. They had not yet begun seriously to consider how this use of language might vary across PEEL groups in different locations, but through our discussions, there was little doubt (for me) that they believed that a language of learning was important and was helpful for professional dialogue and the development of understanding about teaching and learning.

Sophie in particular explicitly related her views of teaching for enhanced metacognition to her pre-service teacher preparation programme in which metacognition and higher-order thinking skills had been an explicit organizing principle. Therefore, metacognition, as an important signpost of PEEL, was a label that created recognition as it echoed the intentions for teaching which she had identified within her teacher preparation programme.

Both David and John had come from a teacher preparation programme in which PEEL was an explicit approach for teaching about teaching. However, they did not link their current views on teaching to their teacher preparation programme in quite the same 'matter of fact' way that Sophie did, but they did note that PEEL was something they were aware of as a result of their teacher preparation programme. Perhaps then it is reasonable to suggest that for these teachers, the PEEL seeds had been planted and that when they found themselves in a sufficiently conducive environment, germination had been initiated.

Experienced PEEL teachers

The three experienced PEEL teachers (Olivia, Jack and Andrea), described their approach to teaching as 'flexible' in that they believed their main motivation for the way they organized their lessons was influenced by their students' learning needs and, as such, came before the specifics of the curriculum. This was not meant to imply that the curriculum was not important but that – as a result of their experience – they were skilled at carefully scrutinizing that which was 'on offer' (content wise) and appropriately adjusting it to the learning needs of their students. This issue was particularly highlighted through their descriptions of their purpose for the way they thought about, organized, and structured their lessons.

> I'm not into busy work [time consuming work with little engagement in learning]. We have made science relevant and exciting by developing our own curriculum so that it is meaningful. My repertoire is [built around] quality practice which generally is designed to get the kids thinking at a higher level – so they put an effort into their learning. I have taken on the PEEL strategies . . . and I suppose I find [at times] that I can take for granted the way things like POEs and concept mapping [White and Gunstone, 1992] work, they've just become part of my practice. (*Olivia*)

The need for school work to be relevant and meaningful seemed to be an expectation of their practice so that, as a result, their students could link their learning experiences to their existing knowledge in ways that would make it, 'useful and relate to their lives'. This approach to teaching was considered to be important if their students were to, 'think and be independent learners' and they constantly encouraged this by drawing on their students' own experiences.

By being able to explain these issues in the way that they did, they clearly illustrated a use of language that carried an understanding of both their views of professional practice and of student learning.

Explicitly linking teaching and learning

Like the beginning PEEL teachers, these teachers used a number of terms (eg. seeing the big picture, linking, analysing learning, complexity of processing, synthesizing, students' need for a sense of progress and delayed judgement) that were accepted descriptors and a natural part of their vocabulary – they did it in an almost 'matter of fact' way. They were also aware that they did have a vocabulary that encompassed ideas about teaching and learning that were not so common amongst all of their colleagues.

These experienced PEEL teachers' range of language seemed more diverse and carried specific meaning and was more explicit and more extensive than the beginning PEEL teachers.

> In considering a particular concept, you are aware of the context of the situation, the Poor Learning Tendencies they [students] display, the Good Learning Behaviours you try to encourage to tackle these and the teaching procedures you use to address the situation . . . having an opportunity to discuss and share ideas helps to challenge the isolation of teaching. (*Jack*)

This response by Jack was indicative of the language and thinking about teaching and learning that was apparent amongst these three interviewees. In effect, what their language illustrated was how they had refined their understanding of their approach through PEEL and how they then conveyed their understanding to others. The essence of their message seemed different to 'normal' teacher talk because they spoke in specific rather than global terms about their knowledge.

> Kids have to be active, interested and involved in their learning, they can't just be expected to soak the learning up . . . they have to learn to challenge teachers' chalk and talk approaches. (*Andrea*)

> I've come to know that people learn in different ways . . . I now know what is happening when someone is a good 'swatter' for exams while others need connections between ideas, or relevance to their life . . . so increasing experiences for students really matters and you need a wide range and use of questioning techniques . . . there's a difference between knowing and understanding. (*Olivia*)

> You come to see that teaching and assessment can be at odds and causes a conflict that you need to respond to if you want your students to learn, and to value the learning. (*Jack*)

It was noted that in some instances their use of language caused problems when talking to non-PEEL teachers because, as Olivia stated, there was a big difference between talking about good ideas and classroom activities and talking about enhancing specific aspects of learning through carefully chosen and well-understood teaching procedures. This led to a selective use of language in some situations:

> I'm almost bi-lingual, so I'm a bit selective about what [language] to use to talk about teaching and learning and where to use it. There's a big difference between saying here's a good idea or activity as opposed to talking about concept mapping, linking, etc. – some people would just see it as a wank. (*Olivia*)

Olivia offered an example that illustrated the value and importance of language when she explained her 'backsides' communication strategy. On the back side of the school's daily memo she had initiated discussions to help develop and share the knowledge of practice. She had found that asking teachers to write up their thoughts for this task had not been easy as there was an inevitable struggle for many to find a language to explain their ideas in conveying their message. She had therefore developed some key questions to help teachers do this such as, 'What was the concern that caused you to reconsider your practice? What did you observe before and after the change? How would you describe the practice? How have you analysed the procedure? How have you come to see your practice now?' Clearly, these questions require a language and an understanding of teaching and learning that prompt a reflective and meaningful response rather than the simple transmission of a 'good teaching activity'. Hence, she highlights the important difference between teaching as a series of interesting activities and the use of particular teaching procedures for specific reasons.

> [Through the use of backsides'] you can see that you come to know teaching procedures and the way they underpin your teaching . . . also talking at conferences is a big boost to your confidence and ability to share knowledge . . . and because it is from your own practice and you examined and researched it, you begin to better understand what's happening. (*Olivia*)

An issue which emerged was how the PEEL group served different functions. The first function was as a general forum for issues of teaching and learning:

> PEEL offers a social dynamic to teaching and supports a development of learning about teaching, you get an energy from PEEL groups, especially here with the large number of PEEL teachers and groups that all support each other. (*Jack*)

The second function was in response to a need for teaching and learning issues to be particularly well understood in terms of specific content – perhaps alluding to something similar to Shulman's (1986) notion of pedagogical content knowledge.

> I sometimes want to take PEEL and have my own science group [of teachers], to take another step, to want to link back again into science so that we can feed on the specific things that are different for teaching procedures just in some special science content things. (*Olivia)*

This issue highlighted an aspect of the value of PEEL which all three saw as important, an understanding of teaching and learning in a way which supported the development of specific professional knowledge for individual teachers in their own way in their own content fields. As most PEEL groups are cross faculty, the range of creative responses to different situations offers teachers opportunities to consider their content base in new and challenging ways. However, within individual subjects, there is a need to recognize and understand the way particular teaching procedures impact on specific content learning issues. This interplay is an important element in the way PEEL meetings and discussions can help teachers to develop their professional knowledge see Figure 9.1).

This development of teaching procedures with a particular focus on (and relationship to) specific content was well illustrated by Andrea who related how she had come to develop a case in which her understanding of the content knowledge was enhanced. She recognized through this process that:

> cases cause you to stop and think and present knowledge in ways that also help others to get the idea and that sort of feedback helps you to see – and challenge – misconceptions and assumptions. Some other teachers read my case and said it helped them understand the topic in a way they hadn't understood it before. (*Andrea)*

What Andrea had created in her case was a way of drawing on her wisdom of practice within her content field and writing it up in a way that demonstrated an intimate understanding of both the specific content knowledge and issues of learning which when combined, clarified what was for many learners a difficult concept that (Andrea believed) was often taught but not understood.

The development of experienced PEEL teachers (like these three interviewees) to a point where their professional knowledge is able to be well articulated and communicated (in various forms) to others is, in some instances, a platform from which a decision to explicitly research practice emerges.

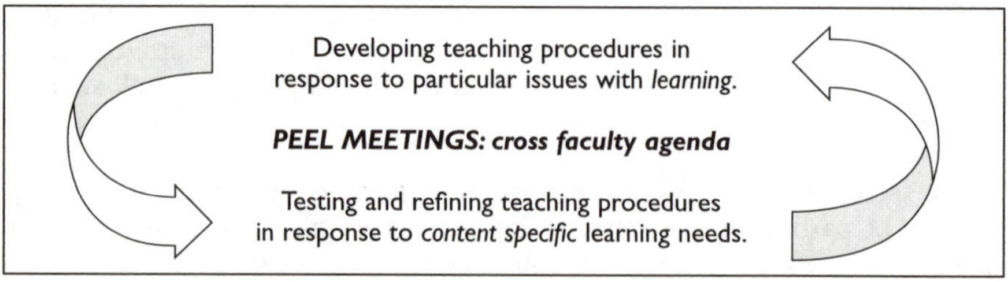

Figure 9.1 The dual agenda of shifting teaching needs addressed through PEEL meetings.

> Teachers can see the value to themselves and their students . . . I now know the difference between learning and understanding . . . you can teach kids to do a task but how they arrive at understanding is a different matter. (*Olivia*)

The knowledge that these teachers have of their practice is drawn from a recognition of, and response to, teaching and learning situations in which the need to understand practice better and the outcomes of learning demand (through interaction with colleagues in PEEL meetings) a language through which to share the knowledge being developed.

PAVOT: PEEL teacher researchers

The final grouping of PEEL teachers were members of PAVOT. These were experienced PEEL teachers who chose to further their professional growth and knowledge by purposefully researching their teaching and their students' learning. These teacher-researchers had been involved in a large range of professional development and leadership roles within PEEL, and the profession generally, and were also actively researching a range of issues within their classrooms.

For these experienced PEEL teachers, 'purpose' was a most important and unifying theme in their practice. This was most evident in the view that 'busy work' was not a common feature of their classes. Their emphasis on learning as the purpose for their work meant that a commitment to helping students learn necessarily ruled out teaching approaches which 'wasted students' learning opportunities'. Their image of busy work was that it was counter-productive as it did not encourage students to view school learning as engaging and meaningful.

Considering the fact that Jen and Joan were both experienced at teaching a range of elementary grades and that Callum had taught all high school grades, their expectations for student learning (and their expectations of teaching) obviously confront and challenge some of the 'taken for granted myths of teaching' eg. that students can not concentrate for extended periods of time, that working independently only happens in the (at best) latter years of schooling, and that students are dependent on teachers for decision-making and for directing (and/or controlling) the learning.

> . . . we've got so much to do and get through we can't waste time doing busy work. And that doesn't mean all that we do has to be intellectually challenging [all the time], but it has to have a purpose. . . . It's not [like in some classes where it's] let's take the kids so that they can do busy work, I mean that's what play times are for . . . [besides] the kids will tell us when they need to rest because they'll say my brain hurts, or we've had enough thinking or whatever. (*Jen*)

This sense of purpose has helped all three to reconceptualize their teaching in ways that have made their practice illuminative for others. However, what they see in their teaching is somewhat different to that which others might initially see. In many ways, the insights into practice and the ways of seeing the teaching and learning situations that these teachers illustrate, is as a result of their well developed understanding of their role. All three described their teaching practice using terms such as focused, motivated, idealistic, creative, reflective and strategic and their way of seeing their practice certainly appears to extend the possibilities for meaningful learning.

> our open day, in the beginning when people came and watched what we were doing [they came] because they wanted to see some of the things we did. We quickly saw that what they took away was ideas of activities that they could do and we were really entirely frustrated because they were not seeing what we saw was happening in the classroom in terms of the kids being more reflective . . . we're so intent on [students] making links and knowing what linking means and how to use their prior knowledge and how to use it to help their new learning . . . and because we were keen to make kids understand the value of questioning as a tool for learning and that they had a role in making decisions in the learning process, they became our important understandings about how kids learn. But the other teachers didn't see that, they, at that time, would see the activities by which the kids were displaying those behaviours to us, but they didn't see the [actual] behaviours, they just saw the activities and because the kids were performing on those quite well they thought it was the activities that led to the changed behaviour. They [the teachers] really often commented on how the kids didn't seem to interrupt and nag us over what we call irrelevant interactions and they just thought we'd trained the kids well. Whereas we believe that they're [students] deciding that they don't need to ask those questions because they can solve their own problems. So it's also about people looking at the same thing in a different way. . . . We had a forum for discussing things that came up, having a critical friend and a collaborative working relationship. And the outside discussions we had with other people through PEEL, I think you need the support, ongoing support and opportunities like mine. . . . I know that to make teaching better we need to have quality interactions with other people. (*Jen*)

Learning: a basis for practice

The teaching style illustrated by these teachers is based on knowing about teaching and learning in ways that draw the two together in a relationship such that their classroom 'manner' (Fenstermacher, 1999) is based on an understanding of learning that leads to teaching practice styled on expectations of learning. For example, terms often associated with learning such as linking, prior knowledge, reflection, purpose and independence (all used extensively by the interviewees), are translated into their teaching so that there is a direct correlation between these attributes of learning and the teaching used to foster their development.

My teaching practice has changed . . . I am constantly aware of what I'm doing, I've spent a lot of time out of the classroom thinking through what the kids have done, why it's happened that way, reflecting on what happened in the classroom. . . . I also describe myself as a learner in my own classroom . . . that's really important and it never ever bothers me if we're working on something and I am not the dispenser of knowledge . . . I want to see what happens in a classroom with this sharing between me and the kids and I write, I intentionally write assignments and things in terms of 'we' and not 'you' . . . it's [also] very reflective, I spend a lot of time thinking about what's happened . . . when I trained as a teacher they taught us how to plan lessons, so the notion that we were given was that the teacher directs it, it's like conducting an orchestra, you go in and you make it happen your way and you come out and the kids have learnt something. But there is nothing in that about looking at what the kids are doing, listen to what they're saying, sharing that learning with them. It was all teacher directed so I have no doubt I started off that way . . . and I know there's been a shift, but that shift didn't just come out of PEEL, that shift [also] came out of not being entirely happy with a classroom that didn't seem to meet the [learning] needs of all kids . . . [so] what PEEL gave me is this structure for thinking about what happens in my classes. (*Callum*)

This description by Callum is indicative of the development of understanding of classroom teaching and learning by all three of these interviewees. Their understanding of learning shapes their teaching and, for Jen and Joan in particular, also shapes the physical nature of their classrooms.

It is not uncommon in elementary classrooms for the walls to be decorated in a variety of ways to make an attractive and stimulating room. However, in many instances, although these decorations may comprise some student work, the students do not necessarily share ownership of the room, rather the teacher displays the products of particular activities. For Jen and Joan, they see the classroom as containing resources that will benefit students' learning so their intention is always to assist students' recollection of that learning, 'through linking'. Therefore, they see students' work as an opportunity for providing resources for the class. These resources are readily available because through their classwork students are continually constructing them. The resources come in the form of posters and materials that when displayed in the room provide a stimulus for remembering particular learning episodes and approaches. Further to this, these resources are only kept on display if they are being used by the students. If they are not being used then Jen and Joan believe they should no longer be taking up valuable wall (resource) space. In contrast to the image of a 'normal' elementary classroom, this is a clear change in understanding of what the physical environment of a school classroom has to offer.

This change in approach to the physical environment came about from looking more specifically at the way students linked (or did not link) their prior knowledge in order to enhance their learning. For Jen and Joan, they started examining their own practice and noticed that most of their 'best teaching', or the processes of 'building up a chart' or a 'sheet of information or teaching procedures', was erased from the chalkboard at the end of a lesson/day. Now they see the value in turning these learning experiences into resources that are useful in the classroom. Hence, the walls in their rooms have learning posters and student work which illustrate linking, venn diagrams, semantic maps, fact charts (and much more) and this has emerged in their practice from looking closely at how their students learn. The physical set-up of their rooms now explicitly fosters linking to both decrease the reliance on the teacher as the knower and to enhance student decision-making and independence.

A visit to these classrooms shows students (as young as 6 years of age; grade 1) working in ways that illustrate an independent approach to learning. Students can be seen discussing how they might embark on a task, they might then do a 'print walk' to review learning procedures illustrated on posters (that they have constructed) in order to decide how they might approach their work, they will also choose the individuals they decide to work with to complete their task – such decisions being made for a number of important reasons; who can they learn best with, what skills are needed to do the task, and so on.

Articulating the language of learning

To convey this understanding of teaching to others is not a simple task. Callum describes how he has developed in this regard:

> you just come to question your teaching from another direction. . . . I can see that through working with a PEEL group and the discussion that you have with them you start to take on a new language of learning and you're able to articulate what you're doing much better. So I think being able to articulate what happens in my classroom comes out of a couple of things, one is when you're in a PEEL group and you've got to put into words as clearly as you can what's happening in your classrooms, you find the language to describe it. And you [also] take on the language of the academics through the PAVOT groups, but I'm sure a lot of it also came out of just the need to articulate to the PEEL group what was happening. And I know I can remember looking for words and terms to express what was happening . . . now I have a way of doing it . . . you're trying to convey a very important message to people, and you've got to say it as clearly as you can. And you can't, you couldn't go and take any classroom teacher out of the classroom and have this conversation, I mean I'm not saying that what we're doing is exceptional but they couldn't have this conversation and articulate as easily what's happening in their classroom because, well 2 things, number one they haven't had the time, this is a teacher who perhaps hasn't been through the experience of you know discussion of everything else [that we have through PEEL and PAVOT] because they haven't had the time to frame the answers in their mind. They would be saying Oh I've never thought of it like that, or that's an interesting question I'll have to think about it. But when you've been through that discussion, you know the issues, you know how you feel about it, and then the second thing is you find the terminology to express it . . . so there's a knowledge base of teaching and there's evolving [for me] now this new language of teaching.

> And that language is of great importance when you do things, things like turn up for your annual review . . . [like] when I was interviewed for the job I have now, I'm sitting there talking teaching and learning and people's heads around the room are nodding because when you can articulate your professional knowledge well, people like to hear about it.

The way that these three teachers came to recognize, understand, and articulate their professional knowledge is important. It would seem that for each this development happened best when they had time to talk; with individuals and in discussion groups. In this way they were communicating their knowledge and that which they understood through their insights in their classrooms. Callum, for example, recognized his own development through the need to help a young teacher who wanted assistance. He noticed how he needed to use his knowledge to give some insight into what might be happening in the other teacher's classroom. He was easily able to recollect the way he spoke with the younger teacher and noted how different this was from the experience of many other teachers.

> And it gets back to what I said before, I don't think most teachers have had the experience of having to think through the issues to such a level that PEEL teachers have and therefore they are not in a position to say, oh well I think this might be what's happening. (*Callum*)

In essence, all three, through their involvement in PEEL and PAVOT, have been placed in situations where the need to be able to articulate and communicate their knowledge has been important. Their involvement gave them a need, and an opportunity, that almost demanded that they be able to articulate their practice, 'it can not be shared if there are no words to do that'. So there was a clear need to develop a language to share as what they had to say was significant.

Further to this, these teachers also needed to see that what made their practice different was a way of knowing what to look for in order to move to the depth of understanding (illustrated in Jen's open day experiences). Primarily, their growth had to do with helping their students come to understand their role in the learning process which led to a corresponding development in Jen and Joan's understanding of their role in the teaching and learning process.

> So yes, now I'm very confident in being able to say that I've got something to say about what's different about my practice. . . . There were times of personal growth, our points of consolidation, and they really are where we had to sit down and work out what it is that we wanted to say and where we'd come from and where we are at now. And it was because we had to share our practice with other people and it didn't really matter whether it was colleagues at school, or in a board of education, or community, or at the university, we had to have an explanation or reasons for why we were doing what we did. So each time we had to do something like that, we came a little bit further . . . we had to dig through what we thought was

> essentially different [in our teaching] from what we wanted to share with other people. . . . The first time we had to write, and that's another form of communication, and that was really hard and, as you know, the writing skill is not easy for us, but I suppose we're a bit better at it now than what we were.
>
> The other thing about communicating our practice and the reasons for having to articulate it was so that we could reproduce it for ourselves . . . we don't have to [continually] re-invent the wheel. And we now realise the benefits of organising our thoughts . . . so really to reproduce it so that next year in my teaching when something comes up I can base it [on my knowledge] so I'm maximising the thinking that I've done before. That's been really critical for ourselves as well as for others. (*Joan*)

Conclusion

There has been a growing recognition of the value of teacher research and of school-university collaboration as well as the need to include the voice of the teacher in the academic literature (Lytle and Cochran-Smith, 1992; Cooley *et al.*, 1997). PEEL and PAVOT are examples of such work starting from a desire by teachers to improve their students' learning. This chapter has illustrated some of the professional growth and development of knowledge of teachers through their involvement in such projects. In this case there are some clear similarities and difference in the three groups of PEEL teachers interviewed for this study. It seems reasonable to assert that they all conceptualize their teaching in terms of learning and it would appear that both the development of their practice and the manner in which they have learnt to articulate and communicate it to others are indicative of different points along a continuum.

For the beginning PEEL teachers there is a clear shift from seeing teaching procedures as activities to focusing on learning as an impetus for the appropriate use, and choice of, teaching procedures. Through this development they have also begun to develop a language to share their understanding, a language which is based on learning but is explicitly linked to teaching in order to lead to meaningful teaching and learning interactions. The experienced PEEL teachers illustrate an understanding of teaching and learning that is based on an extensive knowledge of learning and requires a well-developed language to enhance this understanding through practice. Their refined ability to articulate their approaches to teaching and learning go hand in hand with their confidence in, and growth of, their professional knowledge both in terms of learning generally and particular aspects of learning in relation to specific content. The PAVOT teacher-researchers illustrate how instructive the recognition and valuing of professional knowledge can be for practice and how choosing to extend and validate their knowledge is enhanced through researching their teaching and their students' learning.

> in the beginning because we were forced I think to learn a new language and that helped us make sense of what we were doing. Because Ian

> [Mitchell] saw a whole lot more happening in our classroom when he came to visit than we saw and when he started showing [that to] us, [it] made us look a bit broader, it forced us to see what we didn't see. And then the encouragement and the sharing of ideas and saying that I can't believe Grade 1s can really do that, he gave us confidence to keep going…that challenged me. (*Jen)*

Note

1 PAVOT was funded by the Australian Research Council through two large grants (Northfield and Mitchell 1995–7; Mitchell and Loughran 1998–2000) specifically designed to research the teacher learning through the application of PEEL teaching across a variety of school settings.

References

Baird, J. R. (1986) 'Learning and teaching: the need for change', in J. R. Baird and I. J. Mitchell (eds.) *Improving the Quality of Teaching and Learning: An Australian Case Study – the PEEL Project*, Melbourne: Monash University.

Baird, J. R. and Northfield, J. R. (1992) *Learning from the PEEL Experience*, Melbourne: Monash University.

Baird, J. R. and White, R. T. (1982a) 'A case study of learning styles in biology', *European Journal of Science Education,* 4: 325–37.

—— (1982b) 'Promoting self-control of learning', *Instructional Science* 11: 227–47.

Cooley, W. W., Gage, N. L. and Scriven, M. (1997) 'The vision thing: educational research and AERA in the 21st century. Part 1: competing visions of what educational researchers should do', *Educational Researcher,* 26(4): 18–21.

Fenstermarcher, G. (1999) On Making Manner Visible, a paper presented at the Annual Meeting of the American Educational Research Association, Montreal, April.

Flavell, J. H. (1976) 'Metacognitive aspects of problem solving', in L. B. Resnick (ed.) *The Nature of Intelligence*, Hillside, NJ: Erlbaum.

Loughran, J. J. and Northfield, J. R. (1996) *Opening the Classroom Door: Teacher, Researcher, Learner*, London: Falmer Press

Lytle, S. L. and Cochran-Smith, M. (1992) 'Teacher research as a way of knowing', *Harvard Educational Review*, 64(4): 447–74.

Macdonald, I. H. (1996) Enhancing learning by informed student decion making on learning strategy use, unpublished doctoral theses, Melbourne, Australia: Monash University.

Mitchell, I. J. and Mitchell, J. (1997) *Stories of Reflective Teaching: A Book of PEEL Cases*, Melbourne: PEEL Publishing.

Shulman, J. H. (1992) *Case Methods in Teacher Education*, New York: Teachers College Press.

Shulman, L. S. (1986) 'Those who understand: Knowledge growth in teaching', *Educational Researcher*, 15(2): 4–14.

White, R. T. and Gunstone, R. F. (1992) *Probing Understanding*, London: Falmer Press.

Chapter 10

Examining teachers' interactive cognitions using insights from research on teachers' practical knowledge

Paulien Meijer, Douwe Beijaard and Nico Verloop

Introduction

This chapter describes an investigation of the cognitions of twenty language teachers while teaching. After the teachers had given a lesson in reading comprehension to 16- to 18-year-old students, stimulated recall interviews were conducted to assess the content of teachers' interactive cognitions. It is argued that the stimulated recall interview calls upon a teacher's working memory while teaching. The content of teachers' interactive cognitions is described according to ten main categories, which are based on categories emerging from research on teachers' practical knowledge, in particular, teachers' pedagogical content knowledge. Patterns in teachers' interactive cognitions are identified, and similarities and differences are explained in terms of differences in teachers' approaches to students, and their approaches to the content of a lesson. On the basis of these results, it is concluded that studying teachers' interactive cognitions is of great additional importance in the examination of the cognitive aspects of teaching. We conclude with a critical discussion of the stimulated recall interview.

Teachers' interactive cognitions

More than two decades after the often cited 'cognitive change' in research on teaching (e.g. Clark and Peterson, 1986), teachers' knowledge or cognitions are still a topical issue. What teachers know and believe and what is on their minds when they are teaching has yet to be fully elucidated. In the 1996 *Handbook of Educational Psychology*, Calderhead reviewed and organized a range of studies that had been done on teachers' knowledge and beliefs (see also Fenstermacher, 1994) and wrote that it is now generally acknowledged that teachers hold various beliefs and knowledge in relation to their work. However, he also found that it is a contestable issue whether or not these beliefs and knowledge influence teachers' classroom practice and that some studies report large discrepancies between teachers' beliefs and their observed classroom behaviour (e.g. Galton *et al.*, 1980). Calderhead concluded that research on teachers' knowledge and beliefs has led to better insight into the nature and complexity of teaching, but that a clear understanding of the cognitions that are actually inherent in teachers' actions is still lacking (Morine-Dershimer, 1992).

Researchers have attempted to investigate the relationship between teachers' cognitions and their behaviour, but have had major difficulties in demonstrating this relationship (Calderhead, 1996; Richardson *et al.*, 1991). Kagan (1992) examined twenty-five studies on teachers' beliefs and although she found that teachers' beliefs usually reflected the actual nature of their practice, she was also aware of the problems researchers face in making teachers' beliefs explicit: 'Although the connection between teacher belief and teacher behavior may seem self-evident, it actually represents a highly significant finding, because of the difficulties inherent in capturing teacher belief'. (p. 66).

An important characteristic of most studies in which the relationship between teachers' cognitions and teachers' classroom action is investigated, however, is that cognitions and behaviour are studied separately, after which an attempt is made to establish relationships between them. A major criticism of this research pertains to the separation of cognitions and behaviour made in these studies, which cannot in fact be separated (Brown *et al.*, 1989; Richardson, 1996; Yinger, 1986).

Schön (1983, 1987) was one of the first to develop a new way of thinking about the relationship between a person's knowledge and his or her actions. He introduced the concepts knowing-in-action and reflection-in-action, indicating how teachers think while they teach:

> When we go about the spontaneous, intuitive performance of the actions of everyday life, we show ourselves to be knowledgeable in a special way. . . . Our knowing is ordinarily tacit, implicit in our patterns of action and in our feel for the stuff with which we are dealing. It seems right to say that our knowing is in our action. (1983, p. 49)

Schön argued that to understand the practice of professionals, we need to understand their knowing-in-action. This is comparable to Leinhardt's idea (1988) that teachers' knowledge should also be studied 'in use' in order to understand the complex process of teaching. Consequently, Leinhardt stated that teachers' cognitions and actions should be investigated while teachers are teaching because, at that moment, knowing and acting are inseparable. Brown *et al.* (1989) argued that all knowledge is produced in activities and situations. Knowledge is therefore situated in actions or, as Leinhardt defined it, it is 'embedded in the artifacts of a context' (Leinhardt, 1988, p.148). This implies, according to Brown *et al.*, that knowledge should be studied in the situation in which it is being used. They stated that the examination of knowledge can be inappropriate, or even invalid, if this knowledge is stripped from the way it is used.

Teachers' interactive cognitions is a term that is used in a genre of studies in which teachers' cognitions are examined in the context of the teaching situation and which focus on the cognitions teachers have while teaching. The studies on teachers' interactive cognitions were mainly based on the assumption that these cognitions could be seen as a link between teachers' beliefs and knowledge, on the one hand, and their behaviour, on the other (e.g. Gutiérrez Almarza, 1996; Morine-Dershimer, 1992; Verloop, 1989). Interactive cognitions are closely related to a teacher's actual behaviour, illustrated in the German concept *verhaltensnahe Kognitionen* (i.e. cognitions that are closely connected to one's behaviour and that are tied to classroom practice) and can be distinguished from *verhaltensferne Kognitionen* (i.e. cognitions that are more distant from one's behaviour, such as beliefs) (Wahl, 1981).

A number of studies on teachers' interactive cognitions focused on the process aspects of these cognitions. For example, in their chapter on the measurement of teaching, Shavelson *et al.* (1986) discussed methods used in research on teachers' interactive cognitions under the heading 'process tracing'. Other studies, on the other hand, specifically focused on the content of teachers' interactive cognitions and tried to describe how teachers' interactive cognitions related to specific educational theories (e.g. Verloop, 1989). Clark and Peterson (1986) reviewed six studies that tried to describe the content of teachers' interactive cognitions, but these studies were all limited to attempts to classify these cognitions in a predetermined set of categories. The results of these studies indicate how often teachers think about learners, management, and so forth, but the conclusions were merely general statements, for example, that 'the largest percentage of teachers' reports of their interactive thoughts were concerned with the learner' (Clark and Peterson, 1986, p. 269).

The interest in teachers' interactive cognitions decreased partly because of problems in investigating these kinds of cognitions, as well as doubts about the reliability and validity of the methods used to examine teachers' interactive cognitions (e.g., Yinger, 1986). Furthermore, many researchers started focusing on other newly developed concepts in research on teachers' cognitions, for example, on Schön's concept of reflection-on-action (Schön, 1983), which basically focused on cognitions that were not studied in the actual context of a teacher's actions in the classroom. The results of such studies, however, provide an incomplete picture of teachers' cognitions because it is not clear what goes on in teachers' minds while they are teaching. We think that the latter is of great additional importance to obtaining a comprehensive understanding of the cognitive aspects of teaching (see also Meijer, 1999). For this reason, we think it is necessary to reconsider the investigation of teachers' interactive cognitions, so that insight can be gained into all components of teachers' cognitions – the ones that are more distant from a person's behaviour, as well as the ones that are closely related with it.

The availability of new insights from recent research on teachers' pedagogical content knowledge provides interesting new opportunities to study teachers' interactive cognitions. In research on teachers' pedagogical content knowledge, teachers' knowledge and beliefs about various subjects were often investigated without a prior theory functioning as a standard or as a system of categories. Instead, by using mostly qualitative techniques, such as narrative techniques or open interviews, an open attitude is taken towards what teachers know and believe. Also, the stance is taken that teachers' knowledge and beliefs can only be studied in a useful way when it is investigated in the context of a specific teaching situation (Meijer *et al.*, 1999). In our view, teachers' interactive cognitions can be studied from the point of view of teachers' pedagogical content knowledge, instead of considering interactive cognitions only in relation to educational theories or only focusing on its process characteristics.

Teachers' pedagogical content knowledge

Many of the most recent studies of teachers' knowledge have focused on its content, generating insights into categories that teachers' knowledge and beliefs consist of (Calderhead, 1996). Shulman (1986, 1987) was one of the first to study the kinds of knowledge that teachers possess and that underlie their actions, and he developed a number of domains and categories of teacher knowledge, which other researchers have used, expanded, and refined (e.g. Cochran *et al.*, 1993; Grossman, 1989; Van Driel *et al.*, 1998). Studies in this area of research are usually conducted in a specific subject-matter context, such as English (Grossman, 1989), social studies (Gudmundsdottir, 1990; Wilson and Wineburg, 1993), mathematics (Marks, 1990) and science (Van Driel *et al.*, 1998). An important outcome of research into teachers' knowledge is the development of the concept 'pedagogical content knowledge.' Building on Shulman (1987), Van Driel *et al.* (1998) described pedagogical content knowledge as referring to 'teachers' interpretations and transformations of subject-matter knowledge in the context of facilitating student learning. . . . [It] encompasses understanding of common learning difficulties and preconceptions of students' (p. 673). Van Driel *et al.* interpreted pedagogical content knowledge as a specific type of teacher knowledge in the sense that it refers to, and is investigated in relation to, a particular (subject matter) content. In the studies they reviewed, pedagogical content knowledge is believed to be an essential domain because it focuses explicitly on the knowledge and skills that are 'unique to the teaching profession' (Borko and Putnam, 1996).

Following these developments, the purpose of the present study was to examine the content of teachers' interactive cognitions, using categories identified in research on teachers' pedagogical content knowledge. The outcomes of the study are relevant for two areas of research. First, more insight might be gained into the details of the content and characteristics of teachers' interactive cognitions. Second, results from this study might be used to expand and discuss the insights from research on teachers' cognitions in general, because they indicate whether the same categories can be used in the study of teachers' interactive cognitions and, furthermore, how the described categories of pedagogical content knowledge are used in teaching practice.

We confined our study to one specific group of teachers (twenty language teachers), the teaching of one specific subject (reading comprehension in foreign languages and the mother tongue), and to students of a specific age and level (high school students aged 16 to 18 in a university preparatory program). In The Netherlands, reading comprehension forms the core of the final exams in all languages because students are supposed to learn to understand texts and books in their native language as well as in foreign languages. This is considered particularly important for high school students in a university preparatory programme because they will have to deal with huge amounts of written information in various languages throughout their academic careers. Two questions were addressed in this study: (1) How can the content of teachers' interactive cognitions be described? (2) What patterns can be found in the content of teachers' interactive cognitions? In addition, we examined the usefulness of the stimulated recall interview as an instrument for capturing teachers' interactive cognitions. This study is part of a larger investigation (Meijer, 1999) into the practical knowledge of experienced teachers in which both teachers' knowledge and beliefs, on the one hand, and their interactive cognitions, on the other, were studied using several instruments.

Stimulated recall interview

Instrument

Shavelson *et al.* (1986) stated that to examine a person's interactive cognitions, a thinking-aloud method would be most appropriate. However, when a teacher is giving a lesson, it is not possible to use a thinking-aloud method as it would interfere with the lesson. For this reason, we chose the stimulated recall interview as a substitute for a thinking-aloud method. During a stimulated recall interview, teachers explicate their interactive thinking while watching a videotape of a lesson they have just given. The videotape is used to aid a teacher's recall of his or her interactive thoughts at the time of the lesson (Calderhead, 1981).

The pros and cons of the stimulated recall interview and related techniques have been described in detail by, among others, Yinger (1986; see also Calderhead, 1981; Ericsson and Simon, 1980; Verloop, 1989). Yinger's criticisms on the stimulated recall interview were basically centred around the use of the instrument and its theoretical assumptions. Although most of his critical comments have already been discussed by Verloop (1989), we will go into some detail regarding Yinger's most important criticism of the stimulated recall interview, which concerned the lack of a theoretical basis for the way teachers reconstruct their interactive cognitions. Yinger assumed that the stimulated recall technique calls upon teachers' long-term memory, when in fact interactive cognitions occur typically in teachers' short-term memory. Based on this assumption, Yinger had great doubts about the validity of the stimulated recall method as a means to depict teachers' interactive thinking.

We do not agree with Yinger's assumption that interactive cognitions are typically found in teachers' short-term memory. Following Ericsson and Simon (1980), Verloop (1989) argued that given how little time there is for reflection during a stimulated recall interview, and given that persons are provided with rich cues, such as a videotape of classroom events, they seem to recall long-term memory information. However, Verloop argued that it is not clear how people recall their long-term memory during the stimulated recall interview. Nonetheless, research on the human memory has provided a theoretical basis for the stimulated recall interview as a valid instrument to grasp teachers' interactive cognitions. Baddeley and Hitch (1974) introduced the concept 'working memory,' which they described as a distinct component of human memory. They considered this component as most important in complex (cognitive) activities, such as problem solving and reasoning (see also Baddeley, 1990; Cantor *et al.*, 1991; Taylor and Evans, 1985). Cantor *et al.* (1991) described working memory as 'the currently active portion of long-term memory knowledge. . . . Working memory is, in essence, whatever information is activated above resting state for current cognitive activity' (p. 232) . . . 'it is the arena in which sophisticated processing occurs, and where there is on-line storage of information currently being manipulated' (p. 244).

According to Baddeley and Hitch, incoming information (in our case: of classroom events) activates parts, or elements, of a person's long-term memory. This activation occurs by selecting from long-term memory the corresponding or appropriate knowledge of facts and procedures. When this selected knowledge is 'called up', it remains temporarily active and is used in a person's working memory.

It is not far-fetched to state that teaching involves cognitive activities that take place in teachers' working memory. Teaching involves dealing with complex situations that occur during classroom interaction. According to Baddeley and Hitch, complex situations are worked out by simplifying the situation, reducing the complexity by identifying elementary facts or procedures that have been experienced before, and can therefore be easily dealt with because these are stored in long-term memory and are directly available. This implies that teachers deal with classroom situations by reducing them to knowledge of facts and procedures that are stored in their long-term memories. When confronted with classroom events, teachers activate appropriate and familiar elements from their long-term memory into their working memory, and use these to establish a way to deal with the event (see Figure 10. 1).

By watching a videotape of a lesson they have just given, teachers most probably relive the classroom situation again, and we argue that this calls upon retrieving much of the same knowledge from their long-term memory into their working memory and that this process is comparable to the one during the actual lesson. This has already been illustrated by Verloop (1989). In his study of student teachers' interactive cognitions, Verloop asked the student teachers to 'relive' the lesson they were watching on videotape. He found that the student teachers actually recalled long-term memory information. He countered the critique that persons can come up with 'new' reflections about the lesson they are watching during the stimulated recall interview by arguing that it requires less cognitive energy to 'relive' the original lesson than to stand back from matters that are shown on videotape and to report impressions as if it concerned unfamiliar material. Following this argumentation, persons seem to retrieve many of the same elements from their long-term memory into their working memory during a stimulated recall interview. This means that, in contrast to Yinger's assumption, they do not need to recall the contents of their short-term memory.

A second issue concerning the stimulated recall technique which we would like to address here is the fact that a part of a teacher's interactive cognitions is not normally available and therefore difficult, or maybe impossible, to recall retrospectively (Verloop, 1989). Experienced teachers are often assumed to have 'compiled' their thinking (Anderson, 1987), resulting in routinized behaviour (Berliner, 1992). It might be the case, therefore, that these teachers have extra difficulty in explicating their interactive cognitions, possibly making the verbal protocol of their interactive thinking incomplete to some degree (Shavelson *et al.*, 1986). There was an extra reason not to take this matter lightly: the participants were all experienced teachers. During the try-out of the stimulated recall interview, teachers often said that they 'did not think anything' during the lesson, unless something unexpected happened. We dealt with the problem of routinization by paying extra attention to the way we probed respondents during the stimulated recall interviews (Ericsson and Simon, 1980), in which we focused teachers not only on their well-specified thinking, but also on more inarticulate thinking, for example, what they were paying attention to, and what they were noticing.

Design and procedure

We videotaped one lesson of each teacher. The teachers taught reading comprehension to 16- to 18-year-old students. Preliminary to the study, we had examined the most common ways teachers tend to work with texts they normally use in teaching reading comprehension. To make sure that the comparability of the results would not be impeded by a diversity of lesson contents, we sent the teachers a text in advance of the lesson to be taped. For every language, a text was selected that was comparable to the final exams – which focus on reading comprehension – because preparation for the final exams is a common element in lessons to students in the last years of secondary education. The teachers were asked to teach the lesson in their usual way. The text could be dealt with in one lesson (i.e. 50 minutes). The stimulated recall interview was to be conducted right after the lesson, preferably during one full

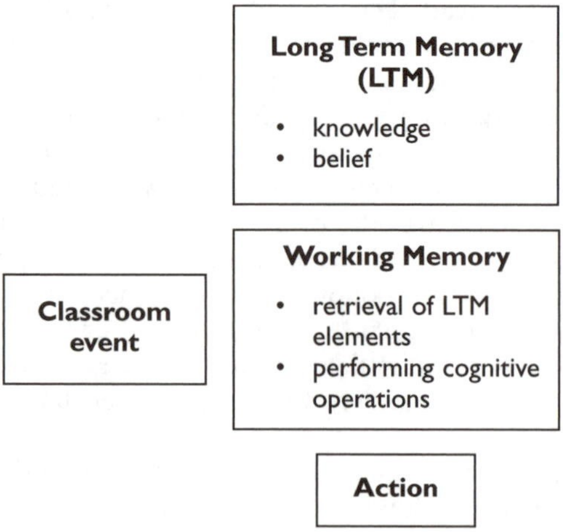

Figure 10.1 Simplified model of working memory in teaching.

session. The teacher was instructed on how to respond in the stimulated recall interview (for the exact instructions, see Table 10.1).

Analysis and results

The data consisted of twenty transcripts of stimulated recall interviews. In this section, the procedure we followed in analyzing these data is described and results are briefly reported (for a full description of the analysis procedure and results, see Meijer, 1999).

Developing a system of categories

As explained earlier, we argued that teachers' interactive cognitions are to be found in their working memory, and that in a teacher's working memory, elements are retrieved from his or her long-term memory (see Figure 10.1). This had a major implication for the process of analysis in this study because it implies that a teacher's working memory and his or her long-term memory are closely related in regard to their contents. Following this model, it was a natural procedure to analyse the content of teachers' interactive cognitions using the same categories that were used in analysing teachers' long-term memory (i.e., their knowledge and beliefs). Thus, we started the analysis procedure with a list of seven categories, which stemmed from Van Driel *et al.*'s review (1998) of studies that focused on teachers' knowledge and beliefs in general. These categories were used in this study as starting categories and are listed in the left column of Table 10.2.

However, we considered teachers' interactive cognitions to be of a different nature than teachers' knowledge and beliefs: Teachers' knowledge and beliefs are relatively stable, while teachers' interactive cognitions are dynamic in essence. This meant that the applicability of the starting categories for analyzing teachers' interactive cognitions had to be established. As a first step, we read through the transcripts and compared the starting categories to our data in order to assess their validity, reformulated them or generated new categories from the data, returned to the data to assess their validity, and went on doing so until the categories suited the data satisfactorily, which meant that no further categories could be formulated. Finally, changes on the starting categories were made, the results of which are listed in the middle column of Table 10.2. The right column contains sample quotations to illustrate the categories identified in teachers' interactive cognitions.

From Table 10.2 it can be inferred that the categories developed by Van Driel *et al.* (1998), although stemming from a review of studies done in different settings and focusing on teachers' pedagogical content knowledge, appeared to be very useful ones, and suited a part of our data quite well. Assessing their applicability for describing teachers' interactive cognitions indicated that it was necessary to omit the category 'knowledge of context'. The category student knowledge was divided into two categories, which concerned teachers' interactive cognitions about students in general and their cognitions about individual students. The new categories concerned thoughts about the particular class, about teacher–student interaction, and about process regulation. To complete this analysis stage, the data were coded with the ten categories identified in teachers' interactive cognitions (initial coding).

Describing and interpreting teachers' interactive cognitions

Further analysis commenced with an in-depth analysis of each of the ten main categories. To be able to describe the variety and range of the teachers' interactive cognitions in each of the ten main categories, each category was divided into subcategories, amounting to a total of thirty-eight subcategories with which the data were coded in more detail (second coding). Using these

Table 10.1 Verbal instructions to introduce the stimulated recall interview.

We are going to watch a video recording of the lesson you have just given. The purpose of this interview is to stimulate you to remember what you were thinking, or what was 'on your mind', during this lesson. Of course, in a 50–minute lesson, a lot of thoughts have gone through your head, and it would be impossible to remember them all without some help. I hope that the video-recording of the lesson will help you to recall what was on your mind during the lesson. Try to 'relive' the lesson when watching the videotape. Stop the videotape every time you recall what you were thinking during the lesson, or what was on your mind. Try to say everything you can remember thinking during the lesson, without asking yourself whether these thoughts are important, 'strange', etc. To illustrate what I expect you to do, I will first show you a short videotape with some examples of what teachers say while watching.

So, I want you to tell your thoughts while you were teaching this lesson. I want you to clearly distinguish these thoughts from the ones you will have while watching the videotape. These last thoughts are not the focus of this interview. Of course, sometimes it is hard to distinguish between these two kinds of thoughts. In case I have doubts about whether a thought you report concerns one you had during the lesson or one which arises now that you are watching the videotape, I will ask, 'Were these your thoughts during the lesson, or are you thinking this right now, while you are watching the videotape?'

Sometimes teachers become absorbed in watching the videotape of their own lesson and forget to report their thinking during the lesson. In case this happens, and you let the videotape run for more than 45 seconds without reporting your thoughts, I will stop the tape, and ask whether you can recall your thoughts at that moment in the lesson. In case you cannot recall your thoughts, you can say so, and start the tape again. In general, however, I will not interfere during the interview: You will be the only one talking. I will just listen and write something down every now and then. Perhaps I will ask some short questions.

It absolutely does not matter whether the lesson we are about to watch was a 'good' one or not, whether there was a marvelous atmosphere or not, etc. For this interview, which is focused on what you were thinking during the lesson, this is not of any interest. I do not intend to evaluate the lesson. This videotape and everything you say is confidential. Outside the context of my study, nobody will have access to this information.

Do you have any questions?

subcategories provided more insight into the details of teachers' interactive cognitions in each category.

Subsequently, we closely examined the relationship between the subcategories. We added a total of sixty-seven pattern codes, each of which indicated a relationship between two subcategories. The resulting code list was used for the final coding of the data. Consequently, the teachers' codes were compared, and the common features as well as the differences among the teachers' interactive cognitions were established. In doing so, we examined similarities and differences among teachers' interactive cognitions, which we described by distinguishing: (A) teachers' approaches to students, and (B) teachers' approaches to the content of a lesson. A teacher's approach to students was based on his or her thoughts about the particular class, about individual students, and about students in general. Three approaches could be identified, each focusing on one of these three categories respectively. The three approaches appeared to be related to teachers' interactive cognitions about student learning and understanding and about teacher–student interaction.

We also identified three approaches to the content of a lesson, based on teachers' interactive cognitions about subject matter and about curriculum. Two of these approaches were focused on one of these categories, while in a third approach these categories were clearly combined and could not be seen separately. These differences in focus appeared to be related to teachers' interactive cognitions about student learning and understanding and about goals. The identified approaches are summarized and illustrated with quotations in Table 10.3.

From the data it did not become clear if, and if so, how, teachers' approaches to students were related to their approaches to the content of a lesson. The fact that the category 'student learning and understanding' was related to both kinds of approaches, and that this category was more often coded in relation to another category (in a pattern code) than on its own (as a single code), indicates that this is an essential category. However, based on the small sample in this study, no sufficient evidence could be found that indicates how teachers' thoughts about this category would connect their approach to students with their approach to the content of a lesson.

Conclusions

Results from this study have implications for (1) insights into the characteristics of teachers' interactive cognitions, and (2) insights into teachers' pedagogical content knowledge. With respect to the implications for insights into teachers' interactive cognitions, the characteristics of teachers' interactive cognitions can be summarized as concerning:

- split-second thoughts;
- tied to the specific context (i.e. the lesson);
- closely connected to teachers' knowledge and beliefs on the one hand, and
- closely connected to teachers' classroom practice on the other;
- integrative in nature.

Table 10.2 Starting categories in PCK of van Driel *et al.* (1998), categories in teachers' interactive cognitions, and sample quotations.

Categories of van Driel et al.	*Categories in interactive cognitions (and number of thoughts and % of occurrences)*	*Sample quotations*
[a]	Thoughts about the particular class (93; 5.07%)	I have known this class for about a year, and I know that they just don't respond to such an open question. I was not surprised (T20, p. 4).[b]
	Thoughts about individual students (123; 6.71%)	Here I was thinking, well, it's her again. I'm not surprised, she's a notorious latecomer (T2, p. 2).
		That I thought was smart of her, of Patricia, and I thought, why didn't I think of that myself? . . . So I thought, what a smart girl this is (T9, pp. 19/20).
Knowledge of general pedagogy	Thoughts about students in general (127; 6.93%)	I was thinking, this text is about families in which there's no authority anymore, because both parents are working, and I'm thinking about the number of students for whom this is the case (T1, p. 4).
Knowledge of student learning and conceptions	Thoughts about student learning and understanding (277; 15.11 %)	I noticed from the way she read it that it was meaningless to her. There was no intonation. So I know she doesn't understand it (T14, p. 3).
		I hadn't expected them to know this word 'taugen' [i.e., 'be good'], they cannot recognize it from Dutch. . . . And it made it a lot easier to understand the title, so I thought: a lucky break (T14, p. 3).
		I thought of this on the spot, because I thought: How can I give them some more information, so they will be more able to place the text in a context (T14, p. 11).
Knowledge of subject matter knowledge of and media	Thoughts about subject matter (191; 10.42%)	I took a look at the curriculum scheme in the back of the book because I was wondering if I hadn't missed a step [in the procedure of text analysis] (T15, p. 12).
	Thoughts about curriculum (129; 7.04%)	I'm marking this spot in the text, because I thought: I have to study that matter further with them (T3, p. 7).

Table 10.2 (continued)

Categories of van Driel et al.	*Categories in interactive cognitions (and number of thoughts and % of occurrences)*	*Sample quotations*
Knowledge of purposes	Thoughts about goals (148; 8.08%)	I explicitly ask for attention. I thought: They need to listen to what I want to do in this lesson and why I want to do it (T12, p. 1). I didn't ask the question I originally had in mind, which was about the content. I thought, well, I'd better not ask it because the discussion had just flagged, so I thought, let's limit it to the vocabulary (T5, p. 9).
Knowledge of representations and strategies	Thoughts about instructional techniques (204; 11.13%)	He formulated a beautiful sentence with this term. I followed up on it immediately. . . . I thought it was a splendid example, one they came up with themselves, so that's even better than when I think of one myself (T16, p.11). I try to keep their discussion going, so I'm listening to what they're saying, and here I thought, I have to give them a suggestion so their discussion won't come to a standstill (T5, p. 20). Here I'm thinking of links that I can use which they can recognize (T18, p. 2).
[a]	Thoughts about teacher-student interaction (246; 13.42%)	She yelled the right answer again, but I was having this conversation with Arjen, so I only nodded to her. . . . At that moment, I was thinking: I must concentrate on Arjen, and not become distracted by her (T19, p. 11). Here I'm wondering, as I remember, do I have to prescribe this . . . I have some doubt. How shall I handle this? Do I have to let them make their own interpretation or do I have to prescribe it? (T4, p. 6).
[a]	Thoughts about process regulation (295; 16.09%)	I was thinking, doesn't this introduction to the text take too long, and hadn't we better start with the text itself? (T2, p. 6)

Notes: [a] absent.

[b] This abbreviation refers to a citation of Teacher number 20 (T20), that can be found on page 4 of the stimulated recall transcript concerned.

The final characteristic in particular is an interesting new insight as it describes that teachers combine and integrate their knowledge and beliefs of various categories while they are teaching.

An implication for insights into teachers' pedagogical content knowledge is that teachers' interactive cognitions display how teachers use elements of their practical knowledge in specific contexts and situations. Van Driel *et al.* (1998) described the purpose of research on teachers' pedagogical content knowledge as 'providing teachers with a knowledge base which enables them to teach specific topics effectively and flexibly in situations that are subjected to different contextual, situational, and personal influences' (p. 691). However, studies on teachers' pedagogical content knowledge are mostly restricted to their knowledge and beliefs. Focusing on teachers' interactive cognitions can be useful to investigate their integrated 'knowledge in use'.

We will now discuss the suitability of the stimulated recall interview as a method for capturing teachers' thoughts while teaching. Our assumption was that using the stimulated recall technique, which included watching a videotape of a lesson they had just given and specific probing, would enable teachers to reconstruct the content of their working memory while teaching. As explained earlier, we argued that teachers activate parts of their long-term memory knowledge in their working memory. Although, it is impossible to 'prove' this assumption, it can be made plausible that the teachers appeared to be able to reactivate their long-term memory knowledge. This is illustrated in the following examples:

> Here I was thinking about how they had been working on their own the last few weeks, and about how surprised I had been how well they worked. And when I saw them working like this, I thought, well, maybe they've learned this during the last few weeks, because normally this class is lazier (T1, p. 5).
>
> I was looking for what I call questioning techniques. Students can sometimes infer the right answer from the way I ask the question. . . . Here I thought, it's a pity I do not know how to ask questions with an open mind, without implying the right answer, but I was looking for it (T9, p. 7).
>
> This boy, I use him as a reference point. Here he was finished with the assignment, so I automatically thought, well, then most of them are finished (T14, p. 8).

In the first example, the teacher retrieved her long-term memory knowledge about the class' background and used this knowledge to 'explain' (in her mind) what was happening at that moment in the lesson. In the second example, a teacher tried to retrieve long-term memory knowledge about questioning techniques, but did not succeed, seemingly because the knowledge was not available. In the third example, the teacher retrieved his long-term memory knowledge of the pace of an individual student in relation to the rest of the students to use this to predict whether the whole class was finished.

However, we realize that a teacher's long-term memory during the stimulated

Table 10.3 Overview of teachers' approaches to (A) students and (B) the content of a lesson, illustrated by sample quotations.

Teachers' approaches	*Sample quotations*
A. Teachers' approaches to students	
A.1 An individual-student approach to students	A clever question from Mandy, that's what I thought to myself. Gee, Mandy usually doesn't contribute much, especially not when it comes to language matters, and here it turns out that she can formulate good questions. A typical one for her though, I remember thinking, because it contained a strong sense of humanity: 'Can such a man still be honest?' Beautiful question, and typical of her (T9, p. 20).
A.2 A general approach to students	Here I doubted whether it was clear to all of them. I felt this was one of those moments when you are busy talking and a class has developed a tremendous capacity for looking like they are interested and meanwhile they're busy doing something else. I felt this was such a moment (T3, p. 4).
A.3 A particular-class approach to students	Here I felt that it was getting boring, all this vocabulary; students were sitting there like burst balloons, and I thought we have to make it livelier. Let go of the boring translation thing, get away from the grammatical level and appeal to their empathy (T13, pp. 6/7).
B. Teachers' approaches to the content of a lesson	
B.1 A subject-matter approach to the content of a lesson	Here I found it necessary to emphasize these abbreviations. Although it's very much spoken language, if you are in France, you see these abbreviations everywhere on billboards and in magazines. And this one, I thought, was a very simple one to figure out from which word it stems, so I used it to point out to them that these abbreviations are quite common (T1, p. 10).
B.2 A curriculum approach to the content of a lesson	I thought I have some time left, and I wanted to challenge them to think of some examples that proved the opposite of what was claimed in the text . . . then they really understand what the text is about (T19, p. 12).
B.3 Combining subject matter and curriculum into the content of a lesson	Here it was, 'Hey, this text is simple!,' and I enjoyed the fact that she saw it herself. I agreed with her, but I hadn't said it in advance. And I considered the nice part, that they realized that this trick [a way to unravel the text structure] can make difficult texts easier (T16, p. 32).

recall interview is different from his or her long-term memory during the lesson. It can be inferred from Figure 10.1 that teachers' long-term memory changes because of events during the lesson (Baddeley, 1990). During the stimulated recall interview, teachers know how the lesson they are watching is going to proceed; a fact they of course did not know during the lesson. However, we found that teachers sometimes referred to the fact that they knew how the lesson proceeded, but they still appeared to be able to indicate their thoughts during the lesson. For example:

> . . . As we know by now, this gave rise to a lengthy debate, . . . but at this moment, that's not an issue yet, because now all I'm thinking is that if I give the right answer, we can continue the lesson (T9, p. 14).

We conclude that our results do not refute our theory that the stimulated recall interview calls upon teachers' working memory when teaching. Thus, we think it is justified to assert that this instrument can be considered a valid substitute for a thinking-aloud method, which Ericsson and Simon (1980) argued elicits data that are most valid for representing cognitive processes.

From the results of this study, it can be concluded that the insights from research on teachers' pedagogical content knowledge provided a useful starting-point to investigate teachers' interactive cognitions. However, we considered the categories that were added when we analysed teachers' interactive cognitions – thoughts about the particular class, about teacher-student interaction, and about process regulation – as specific to this kind of cognition, taking into account the fact that these categories concern aspects of teaching that are directly related to the actual teaching situation. Thus, although the categories about teachers' pedagogical content knowledge contributed to an understanding of what went on in the teachers' minds while they were teaching, studying teachers' interactive cognitions has a supplemental value when investigating teachers' cognitions in general because it retrieves information about additional categories.

Furthermore, the results of this study show that insight into teachers' interactive cognitions is valuable, and even of great additional importance, in studies on teachers' cognitions in general because it provides information that would otherwise not emerge and which is essential if one wants to obtain a complete picture of the cognitions that underlie teachers' actions.

References

Anderson, J. R. (1987) 'Skill acquisition: compilation of weak-method problem solutions', *Psychological Review,* 94(2): 192–210.

Baddeley, A. (1990) *Human memory. Theory and Practice*, Hillsdale, NJ: Lawrence Erlbaum.

Baddeley, A. D. and Hitch, G. (1974) 'Working memory', *The Psychology of Learning and Motivation* 8: 47–89.

Berliner, D. C. (1992) 'The nature of expertise in teaching', in F. K. Oser, A. Dick and J. Patry (eds) *Effective and Responsible Teaching: The New Synthesis*, San Francisco: Jossey-Bass.

Borko, H. and Putnam, R. T. (1996) 'Learning to teach', in D. C. Berliner and R. C. Calfee (eds) *Handbook of Educational Psychology*, New York: Macmillan.
Brown, J. S., Collins, A. and Duguid, P. (1989) 'Situated cognition and the culture of learning', *Educational Researcher,* 18(1): 32–42.
Calderhead, J. (1981) 'Stimulated recall: a method for research on teaching', *British Journal of Educational Psychology* 51: 211–7.
—— (1996) 'Teachers: beliefs and knowledge', in D. C. Berliner and R. C. Calfee (eds) *Handbook of Educational Psychology*, New York: Macmillan.
Cantor, J., Engle, R. W. and Hamilton, G. (1991) 'Short-term memory, working memory, and verbal abilities: How do they relate?', *Intelligence* 15: 229–46.
Clark, C. M. and Peterson, P. L. (1986) 'Teachers' thought processes', in M. C. Wittrock (ed.) *Handbook of Research on Teaching*, New York: Macmillan.
Cochran, K. F., De Ruiter, J. A. and King, R. A. (1993) 'Pedagogical content knowing: an integrative model for teacher preparation', *Journal of Teacher Education,* 44(4): 263–72.
Ericsson, K. A and Simon, H. A. (1980) 'Verbal reports as data', *Psychological Review* 87: 215–51.
Fenstermacher, G. D. (1994) 'The knower and the known: the nature of knowledge in research on teaching', *Review of Research on Teaching,* 20: 1–54.
Galton, M., Simon, B. and Croll, P. (1980) *Inside the Primary Classroom*. London: Routledge and Kegan Paul.
Grossman, P. (1989) 'A study in contrast: sources of pedagogical content knowledge for secondary English', *Journal of Teacher Education* 40(5): 24–31.
Gudmundsdottir, S. (1990) 'Curriculum stories: four case studies of social studies teaching', in C. Day, M. Pope and P. Denicolo (eds), *Insights into Teachers' Thinking and Practice*, London: Falmer Press.
Gutiérrez Almarza, G. (1996) 'Student foreign language teacher's knowledge growth', in D. Freeman and J. C. Richards (eds), *Teacher Learning in Language Teaching*, Cambridge: University Press.
Kagan, D. M. (1992) 'Implications of research on teacher belief', *Educational Psychologist* 27(1): 65–90.
Leinhardt, G. (1988) 'Situated knowledge and expertise in teaching', in J. Calderhead (ed.) *Teachers' Professional Learning*, London: Falmer Press.
Marks, R. (1990) 'Pedagogical content knowledge: from a mathematical case to a modified conception', *Journal of Teacher Education* 41(3): 3–11.
Meijer, P. (1999) Teachers' practical knowledge. Teaching reading comprehension in secondary education, doctoral dissertation., Leiden University.
Meijer, P. C., Verloop, N. and Beijaard, D. (1999) 'Exploring language teachers' practical knowledge about teaching reading comprehension', *Teaching and Teacher Education* 15(1): 59–84.
Morine-Dershimer, G. (1992) Patterns of interactive thinking associated with alternative perspectives on teacher planning, paper presented at the annual meeting of the American Educational Research Association, San Francisco.
Richardson, V. (1996) The role of attitude and beliefs in learning to teach, in J. Sikula (ed.) *Handbook of Research on Teacher Education*, New York: Macmillan, pp. 102–119.
Richardson, V., Anders, P., Tidwell, D. and Lloyd, C. (1991) 'The relationship between teachers' beliefs and practices in reading comprehension instruction', *American Educational Research Journal* 28(3): 559–86.
Schön, D. A. (1983) *The Reflective Practitioner: How Professionals Think in Action*, New York: Basic Books.
—— (1987) *Educating the Reflective Practitioner*, San Francisco: Jossey-Bass.

Shavelson, R. J., Webb, N. M. and Burstein, L. (1986) 'Measurement of teaching', in M. C. Wittrock (ed.) *Handbook of Research on Teaching*, New York: Macmillan.

Shulman, L. S. (1986) 'Those who understand: Knowledge growth in teaching', *Educational Researcher* 15(2): 4–14.

—— (1987) 'Knowledge and teaching: foundations of the new reform', *Harvard Educational Review* 57(1): 1–22.

Taylor, J. C. and Evans, G. (1985) 'The architecture of human information processing: Empirical evidence', *Instructional Science,* 13: 347–59.

Van Driel, J. H., Verloop, N. and De Vos, W. (1998) 'Developing science teachers' pedagogical content knowledge', *Journal of Research in Science Teaching* 35(6): 673–95.

Verloop, N. (1989) Interactive cognitions of student-teachers. An intervention study, doctoral dissertation, Arnhem, The Netherlands.

Wahl, D. (1981) 'Methoden zur Erfassung handlungssteuernder Kognitionen von Lehrern' [Methods to capture teachers' cognitions that steer action], in M. Hofer (ed.), *Informationsverarbeitung und Entscheidungsverhalten von Lehrern*, München, Germany: Urban and Schwarzenberg.

Wilson, S. M. and Wineburg, S. S. (1993) 'Wrinkles in time and place: using performance assessments to understand the knowledge of history teachers', *American Educational Research Journal* 30(4): 729–69.

Yinger, R. J. (1986) 'Examining thought in action: a theoretical and methodological critique of research on interactive teaching', *Teaching and Teacher Education* 2(3): 263–82.

Section 3

Reform and renewal

Chapter 11

How do we do it?

Global rhetoric and the realities of teaching and learning in the developing world

Beatrice Avalos

Introduction

This chapter examines the gap between optimistic declarations of educational reformers regarding the power of proposed changes to improve educational conditions and the reality they seek to change. It begins by placing the discussion in the context of world-wide themes of educational reforms, especially as they impinge on developing countries. The focus then switches to the relation between teachers and these reform efforts. Two perspectives are used for discussion: the perception of others regarding how teachers undertake or experience reform, and views of teachers themselves of their part in these reforms. The chapter finishes with considerations on how the gap can be bridged or at least what could be done to bring change policies closer to the realities of teachers' lives and work.

The Context

In the last decade of the twentieth century, around the world an important educational policy concern was quality in the context of equity. An influential factor in this respect was the recommendations stemming from the *Education for All* Meeting in Jomtien, Thailand, in March 1990 organized by the big lending and aid agencies. Recognizing that many developing countries were well on the way to achieving universal access to primary education but not able to retain children for the complete primary cycle nor to ensure relevant learning, the Meeting proposed a new crusade to meet the basic learning needs of all children and adults by the end of the century. Following the Jomtien conference, countries embarked on educational reforms. Various agencies such as UNICEF and UNESCO supported programmes in poorer country contexts to ensure access of vulnerable populations and to improve the quality of their learning. The same was true of non-government and government initiatives such as the Bangladesh Rural Advancement Committee (BRAC) in Bangladesh, the Compensatory Programme to Address Educational Lag (PARE) in Mexico or the Accelerated Learning Programme (in the North and Northeast of Brazil).

In relation to this crusade to meet basic educational needs and foster quality in education, teachers re-emerged as key players. While Jomtien mentions teachers more or less in passing, later international documents and country policy statements deal with teachers either as a subject of criticism for their role in the non-achievement of educational objectives or, paradoxically, as persons with whom educational systems and processes cannot dispense. The following activities exemplify this international positioning regarding teachers. The Commonwealth Ministers of Education dealt with teacher issues in their 1990 meeting in Barbados and so also did the Latin American and Caribbean Ministers at their 1996 meeting in Kingston, Jamaica. In 1996, UNESCO decided to centre its forty-fifth session of the International Conference on Education on the theme of teachers in a changing world. The 1998 World Education Report provided information and perspectives on the same theme (UNESCO, 1998).

Reforms of teacher education emerged in the latter part of the nineties in the policy formulations of developed and developing countries alike. Teachers recognized as 'necessary' companions in the road to improving education. The improvement of educational opportunities and learning results are seen as key to the various levels of country concerns: as a means for economic development and for positioning in competitive world markets, as a form of reducing poverty and social ills such as violence, crime, drugs or unwanted pregnancies; as a means to develop values and skills for participation in reconstructed democracies (for example, in Latin America and southern Africa), and also to achieve peace in war-torn contexts. A number of these countries, recognize great inequity in the distribution of wealth coupled, in turn, with inequity in the quality of education to which people have access, with most having very little chance of learning what is required to succeed in these societies. Thus, most reforms frame their policy statements around the two key terms of 'quality' and 'equity'[1].

The roles assigned to teachers in these reforms are often stated in highly moral terms as duties they have in relation to the education of children and young people. In their concrete forms these statements require teachers to ensure learning by: (1) embracing new curricula and teaching them in schools, (2) thrusting aside 'frontal' forms of teaching and using active learning methods instead, (3) responding to reform initiatives' requirements such as use of new textbooks, developing school improvement projects or working with parents and communities. Teacher education comes to the fore because teachers must 'learn' about these new behaviours they are to engage in. Teacher education means both the urgent quick strategies of 'informing' teachers about what they must do embellished by cliché sentences such as shifting from teaching to 'learning to learn', as well as longer term reviews of initial training provisions and opportunities for continued education.

Improvement of the quality of education and how teachers will be prepared for the kinds of teaching and learning tasks they are asked to engage in are embedded in processes which are complex. These processes reflect 'global' issues and are also a 'condition' that characterizes poor or less developed societies. In what follows, the demands for quality of teaching and learning are considered from three points of view. First, attention is directed to the influences that affect the framing of roles for teaching and schools in the context of the developing or poor world (although they are similar in the developed world). These influences are related to stated reform targets, the principles invoked to justify the selection of such targets, and finally, to the constraining factors that impede a neat achievement (or even mere implementation) of targets. Second, there is a discussion on teachers and their realities as seen by others (research and informed opinion). Third, we hear the voices of teachers about reform and their roles in it (research and informed opinion). Seen together, these three perspectives point to the complexities of implementing designs to improve teaching and learning and of securing teacher participation, and suggest the need to search for flexible approaches that recognize all these realities. Some of these approaches are presented as a conclusion to this chapter.

Improving teaching and learning: what – why – why not?

The Delors Report (1996) highlighted, as a sign of educational quality, the kind of learning to be achieved by children and young people. Its view of learning was a comprehensive one: learning to learn, learning to do, learning to live together and learning to be. While society as a whole is responsible for these kinds of learning, teachers and schools were viewed by the Report as being particularly responsible. However, how this responsibility will be exercised is shaped by a number of conditions. These conditions are partly embedded in the school culture, partly determined by the society, and partly affected by the political circumstances in which the school operates. To a large extent, however, today the policies that express the kind of school, teaching and learning that are desirable are framed by global influences. The interplay of all these influential conditions can be viewed in Figure 11.1.

Schools and teachers have their ways of organizing activities and of judging what it is they can and cannot do. Experience and history within a school form a solid ground that affects whatever new elements are introduced within its walls. Current reforms constitute at present such elements with their variety of inputs and demands for action. These reforms in turn are shaped by national concerns of which the principal ones today are to raise school attainment, prepare human resources, and develop social and ethical values and habits.

That reform actions around the world are so uniform can be seen as resulting from influence of the international context in the framing of policy. This international context influence is often mediated through the policies of lending banks (World Bank, Inter-American Development Bank; Asian and African Development Banks) and other funding agencies. In the Figure 11.1, examples of such influences are shown. There is a large flow of information stemming from research and theory especially in the fields of teaching and learning. To provide just one example, Howard Gardner's 'Multiple Intelligences' theory was introduced in Bangladesh by UNICEF consultants engaged in improving classroom practices. The theory was discussed with teacher educators and local teachers and its practical implications were tried out in schools. Teachers in the state of Guanajuato, Mexico, also experienced the practical implications of 'multiple intelligences' theory in their schools as a result of the work of an

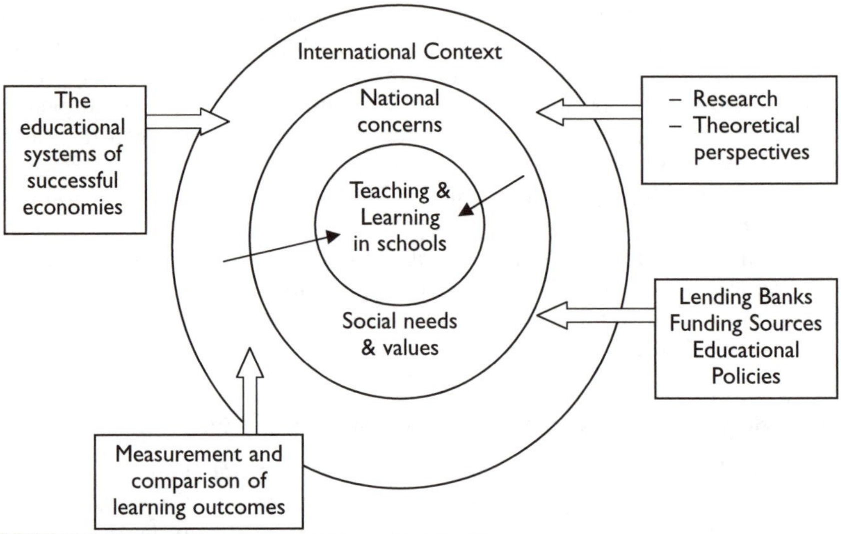

Figure 11.1 Local, national and international influencing policies on school teaching and learning.

outside researcher (see Uttech, 1999). Reflective teaching, action-research, constructivist learning, are all concepts written into policy documents that feed into reform efforts. This of course is not new. Progressive education ideas, at the turn of the twentieth century, moved around the world influencing teacher organizations in Chile in 1929, for example, and the educational system in Japan. The framing of curriculum through 'behavioural objectives' and the concepts of mastery learning as well as competency-based teacher education travelled the world in the sixties and seventies influencing reforms and practices in very definite ways. But today, ideas travel much faster and so too do consultants hired by lending banks and other organizations who act as powerful vehicles in this respect. In his very interesting account of policies and practices regarding teacher education in Malaysia, Ratnavadivel (1999) notes how international trends became especially important from the eighties onwards:

> It ushered in a series of innovations into the arena of teacher education in Malaysia, such as action research, collaborative and co-operative teaching, pair teaching, peer evaluation, clinical supervision, journal writing, and self-reflections. The introduction of these innovatory concepts was specifically a reflection of the internationalisation of thinking about teaching-learning. It was catalysed by increasing globalisation. (p. 195)

The example of Malaysia brings us to another important international influence bearing on educational policies: the influence of the so-called South East Asian economies. In the early nineties, the examples of Singapore, South

Korea and Malaysia were brandished around the world, especially through lending agencies, as models of successful economic development achieved through educational practices shown to be effective in international comparisons of achievement. The new democratic Chilean government sent a mission in 1993 to look at and to learn from these systems of education. The conclusions reached served to justify a number of policies proposed in the official report on modernising of Chilean education (*Comisión Nacional para la Modernización de la Educación*, 1995).[2]

At amost every international meeting on education we hear of the importance of measuring educational attainment, not just nationally but also through international comparisons. Such comparisons suggest implicitly that there is value in learning from the successful achievers. The most far reaching comparison of educational attainment is the Third International Mathematics and Science Study (TIMSS) in which the few participating developing countries did not fare well. Yet, these comparisons are important to policy makers particularly as a pressure for quality; and countries such as South Africa and Chile have chosen to take part in them. Results are not always as expected. A recent comparison of learning scores carried out in the Latin American region by the UNESCO office yielded a startling result that overturns the usual explanations for success. In mathematics and language learning Cuba, with the lowest per capita income of the region, is significantly ahead of all countries (see UNESCO-Santiago, 1998).

These international influences together with each nation's concerns blend in such a way that it is not too difficult to detect a commonality in reform targets and change principles, together with similar constraining factors. Table 11.1 sketches some of these commonalities.

The constraints sketched in Table 11.1 are not all of the same order. Some are related to principles that are part of the global ideology (such as competitiveness as a regulating factor for quality) and as such their targets are promoted by international organizations. These organizations, in turn, often disregard the constraints that are voiced by the social body (teachers and parents). Realities in countries show, for example, that in practice poorer families with theoretical freedom to choose schools have little possibility to do so. Other constraints that are closer to the way institutions work can be dealt with through changes in rules, procedures and support systems, although they also imply the need for changes in resource allocations. Table 11.1 as such is not further examined in the remainder of this chapter but some of its themes are evident as I review how teachers are regarded in relation to reform efforts and how teachers see themselves in this respect.

Teachers and reform efforts: how others perceive their possibilities

Different sources provide information on teachers' capability to undertake reforms as planned. Studies on schools and teachers provide insights into how teachers are handling reform implementation, as well as the reflections of those

Table 11.1 Common features of education reform programmes around the world.

Change principles	*Reform targets*	*Constraining factors*
Modernization (of systems, contents, management) as a determinant of quality improvement	Curriculum frameworks – teacher development of teaching programmes. Decentralization of school management (not necessarily financial).	Teachers' time and 'know-how'. High pupil–teacher ratios. Authoritarian school management and bureaucratic rules and procedures. Teacher salaries and working conditions.
Competitiveness as a determinant of Quality	Vouchers – school choice by parents. Incentives for schools and teachers. Public knowledge of achievement differences. National and international systems of measurement.	Parents in poor communities cannot choose. Non-winners get worse. Equitable national measurement systems are difficult to construct and implement. Unclear understanding of what kind of teacher incentives work.
Equity – education of quality for all	Targeted programmes for poor, fragile populations. Targeted financial support to favour girls' education or poorest populations.	Quality of teachers and administrators in these locations. Quality of support systems (supervisory assistance). Maintenance of funding levels.
Teacher education as a continuum through a variety of procedures	Initial teacher education reform (length, level, contents). Workshops, distance, school-based and courses as a means of professional development.	Poor co-ordination of teacher education policies. Quality of teacher educators and teacher education institutions. Quality of support for school based programmes.
Active teaching and learning processes (constructivism, action-research, reflective and co-operative teaching)	Public messages favouring active teaching style – anti 'frontal' teaching; developing 'critical learners'. School-based teacher and head-teacher workshops.	Quality of support. Time for teachers to work out strategies and implement them.

involved in reform and who work with teachers. Some of these perceptions are synthesized in the following statements about teachers.

Teachers have inadequate cultural background and subject knowledge to cope with new curricular demands and ensure student learning

Curricular reforms are undertaken following different models. One of these, influenced by international experience, consists of providing curricular frameworks for teachers to transform into classroom teaching programmes or syllabuses. This is the case in South Africa and Chile.[3] To translate such curriculum into classroom practice teachers must select from their own repertoire the appropriate teaching and evaluation strategies needed.[4] Studies carried out in South Africa, as the new Curriculum 2005 began its implementation, provide evidence that teachers (mostly those inadequately trained under the apartheid regime) are poorly equipped to handle the design of teaching programmes on the basis of a mere statement of learning outcomes. Teachers lack enough content and pedagogical knowledge to become curriculum designers (Taylor and Vinjevold, 1999). Classroom observation provides evidence of low levels of conceptual knowledge among teachers, poor grasp of their subjects and errors made in the content and concepts presented in lessons. Despite teachers voicing adherence to a learner-centred pedagogy, classroom observation shows that 'pupils were never given the opportunity to discover, there was no evidence of building on prior knowledge, and exclusive whole class teaching occurred' (Pile and Smyth cited in Taylor and Vinjevold, 1999, p. 142).

In another setting, Mexico, there is a new curriculum with a strong focus on conceptual knowledge and subject differentiation and a constructivist approach to teaching and learning. For teachers to work with this curriculum as planned, there was a need for appropriate professional development for practising teachers. Tatto's (1999) study of Mexican teachers involved in a constructivist oriented in-service programme provided evidence of a similar situation to that in South Africa. Teachers in this study, while articulating a belief in the philosophy of constructivism, could not teach as required by the approach in primary maths classrooms. Their mathematical knowledge, for example, was insufficient to deal with pupils' alternative ways of resolving problems. This led teachers to fall back into the usual teacher-centred authoritarian classroom style that does not leave room for exploration of how children understand concepts.

While the above cases belong to developing country contexts, the same can be true wherever curricula are designed without sufficient consideration of what teachers know and can handle. Jones study (1999) on the *Learning in Technology Education Research Project* in New Zealand highlighted the disjunction between the technology contents of the new curriculum framework and the knowledge and experience of the teachers studied. There were teachers who had a good concept of technology but lacked understanding of technological knowledge and of hands-on processes. These teachers appeared lost in the middle of the 'activity' portion of a lesson, but could handle the beginning and the end of the lesson where verbal explanations sufficed to explain the activity. Other teachers with a good technological base but a narrow concept of technology education were not able to link the activities to issues about technological knowledge and technology and society as required by the curriculum statement.

The Argentine curriculum for primary schools designed in the late eighties (the fourth one in 20 years) had a considerably different approach to former ones. Subjects were integrated into thematic areas and teachers were offered suggestions on how to interpret the curricular contents according to the classroom and student needs. Feldman (1994) studied the way in which teachers perceived this curriculum. His study provided insight on the criteria teachers used to process this new curriculum and decide on its worth. In fact, Feldman noticed that teachers were blasé about the importance of the new curriculum; they all could recall very clearly the extent to which previous curricula were altered. Some teachers saw few content changes (even though there were clear differences in relation to earlier ones); and in any case, they believed new curricula were never more that the 'adding or subtracting' of topics. Regardless of the degree of innovation the curriculum might have, for these teachers a curriculum is always a 'mosaic' constructed with bits of the old and the new:

Teacher: I mean this: maths – you always have to teach calculations.
Researcher: Is maths always the same?
Teacher: Yes, but adapted to changes. But there are things that don't change. To bring designs up-to-date, they must have made some adaptations.
Researcher: How do you add topics?
Teacher: In my own experience. Because what 's not in the current design was in the old one. I'm not sure if that means adding'. (p. 94)

Teachers have neither time nor opportunity to work out for themselves how they will cope with curricular and other reform demands

Insufficient time for teachers has been documented in relation to implementation of reforms (see for example, Murphy, 1993; Avalos, 1998 and 1999). Little time is devoted to teachers being able to understand and own a reform programme. In the case of curriculum changes this is particularly so. Teachers are often literally 'informed' about changes by means of a cascade type of in-service programme. In Bangladesh, for example, a four-tier, 3-day information course was used to prepare teachers for the secondary curriculum introduced in 1998. In South Africa, faced with a similar experience of cascade in-servicing, teachers commented: 'we attended the workshop – new terminology – but when we asked questions the person was unsure what to answer'.[5] If 'cascade training' were the beginning of a process of assisting teachers to understand and implement a new curriculum it could be acceptable as a quick form of alerting them about the changes. But that rarely is the case.

Feldman's (1994) study of Argentine primary teachers captured statements about the way in which curricular changes are thrust on the system, illustrating this problem of time.

> You can't just say that we have to finish with the former syllabus – cut it out. For us it is a mesh. They change it now and you feel disjointed. . . . In other words, continuous change does not lead to positive results. Change must be gradual. (p. 59)

Teachers' history, their experience of other changes, need processing in relation to what is being presented as new.

The multiplicity of reform initiatives that reach the school and require implementation or attention conflict with the scarcity of time. The Chilean reform, for example, requires teachers to design school improvement projects, prepare proposals on how the longer school day structure will be filled, develop teaching programmes on the basis of the new curriculum framework, take part in teacher workshops, assist with the secondary youth programme, input into the drug programme, and so on. Many teachers try hard to comply with all these demands but the scarcity of time causes tensions and complaints: 'There are problems of space and time to be creative – we cannot link research and teaching if there is no time. Only by overcoming a mountain of difficulties would a teacher, once a year, be able to develop a curriculum unit' (cited in Avalos, 1998). Overburdening of teachers and stress problems related to the number of reform demands have been documented in several studies around the world (see Whitty, 1997).

The time of politicians is not the time of teachers and teaching – yet reforms are governed by politicians' time.

Teachers 'don't bother' or 'don't want to bother'

Seen from the perspective of implementers, a frequent observation is that teachers, even though they may be articulate about a reform and its merits, in practice may not exert the effort necessary for successful adoption. While this observation is recognized as true in certain cases, others note these attitudes are an expression of frustration generally connected with the circumstances in which teachers work. Coping simultaneously with large classes and difficult students is often given as a reason for not collaborating. Pupil–teacher ratios in South Africa, for example, have been raised, and in the judgement of observers this is one reason why it will be difficult for teachers to implement Curriculum 2005 (Jansen, 1998; Jansen *et al.*, 1999). For these teachers, the curriculum represents a 'crisis': 'We have overcrowded classrooms, 51 children in the classroom – we have to teach in dual medium – the not so bright children suffer'. Arguments for raising pupil–teacher ratio are based on research results that teachers do not recognise as valid, because they are always lower that what the teacher experiences in their rooms. In this respect Duraismy *et al.* (1998) noted detrimental effects on student performance in a study relating high pupil–teacher ratios in Tamil Nadu, India. Inadvertently, he proved the argument of teachers: a ratio of fifty students to a teacher in a real school becomes seventy if the teacher teaches 70 per cent of the full day. Anybody who has visited schools in India, Bangladesh and many African countries will have seen classrooms with up to ninety children in one room and children with little more than a pencil, notebook and perhaps a dull text.

Who is responsible for results?

A condition for change is acknowledgement that one has the capacity to do it and also that if one does not act the losers will be the children. The issue of teacher responsibility is a contested one. Once entry was granted into classrooms to observe teacher behaviour and practices, there was evidence that teachers could have a positive or negative effect on pupil results. On the negative side, the quality of teacher practices could affect a child dropping out or repeating a class or simply failing to achieve desired standards and this was the case especially among the poor. An ethnographic study in four Latin American countries (Avalos, 1986) designed to address the question of 'why children fail' in the primary school, did in fact show that teaching processes, such as they were, made it difficult for children to learn even if they wanted to. However, often rather than analyse the situational complexities affecting the quality of teaching, teachers were and are blamed publicly for these results (see Tedesco, 1999; Ornelas, 1998). This 'culpability' of teachers made it possible to apply structural adjustment policies in the eighties and lower teacher salaries without improving their working conditions (see UNESCO, 1998; Reimers, 1994). This, of course, did not help improve teacher morale. It increased their anger and unwillingness to work in reform conditions. The effect of this situation carried over into the nineties and in part explains the lack of co-operation of teacher unions in some countries such as Chile and Bolivia regarding reform efforts.

While teachers were being held responsible for student results, they did not feel they had such responsibility. For example, the Latin American study referred to above found that poverty and parents were considered by teachers to be the main causes of pupil failure. 'What I understand by school failure, the main of what I understand is children malnutrition, because as soon as we dictate something . . . there are those who understand immediately . . . those who have been well fed.' 'When I look at the pedagogical panorama of parents, what I see is that those who have the highest level of education rarely have moved beyond 2nd or 3rd year of the primary school; they are potential illiterates.' 'His parents are illiterate and cannot help him' (Avalos, 1986, p. 147–8). I heard similar statements from teachers recently in Bangladesh.

Teachers and reform efforts? How teachers view themselves

Teachers have mixed opinions about reforms. They realize they are the subjects of policies that can make a difference to how public opinion views the government of the day, and this is a big burden for them to carry. Hence, their position may be defensive ('the victims') regarding change. On the other hand, many teachers value their profession and feel it is their duty to give it a chance. These teachers will consider the degree to which change is important and give it a try, especially if it affects the teaching and learning domain of their professional life, as a study of teachers in four countries shows (Churchill *et al.*, 1996).

It's too much for us! It's not worth our effort! It's really not a change from what we were doing

Some teachers regard mandated reforms as a burden. Experience in the implementation of reforms in Chile points to a number of teachers who declare their lack of faith in the innovation by arguing against its feasibility, or they may interpret the reform tasks in the light of other issues that have not been solved. Among teachers who work in the poorest schools of the country, there are those who feel conditions are too difficult for any change to really succeed. These teachers lose hope that anything can actually be improved. Other teachers qualify the merits of the innovation in relation to persistent grievances such as low salaries:

> Yea, I think the MECE programme is a good try to improve the quality of education as its acronym indicates, but in my view it is somewhat incomplete. Because it only touches some things, for example, the curriculum, physical infrastructure, text-books . . . but does not touch teacher salaries. When Mr Lagos [referring to Minister of Education at the time] negotiated the loan, not a cent was considered to improve teacher salaries (quoted in Milesi and Trucco, 1996).

Teachers who have experienced constant change may also develop a cynical view of reforms. Feldman's study of the reception by Argentine primary teachers of a new curriculum provides evidence of these views: 'It's a known fact: every time the government changes, our teaching programmes also change.' 'What I have seen is that every time a government or the authorities change, what was good before is no longer good.'

We care, we'll try – we are trying!

When asked about their work, some teachers describe it with enthusiasm or at least show that it is a job they do as best as they can and this brings them satisfaction. These teachers come close to seeing teaching as a mission. In the context of an educational reform that touched their school in many forms, Reyes and Mendizabal's (1999) case study of a teacher and head teacher in a Chilean primary school exemplifies this attitude. Both teachers believed and had strong views about the importance of their tasks. With pride they noted their school, although poor, had achieved good results and was moving along with the reform. It was a well led primary school, and the teachers studied felt highly committed to the children. Although dissatisfied with the salary reward structure, one of the teachers declared: 'one must operate professionally; it's not the children's fault that we get such low salaries'. She dealt with children in the classroom in line with this caring attitude. Jessop and Penny's study of teachers in Gambia and South Africa (1998) also found teachers who exemplified the caring role, which the authors conceptualized as a 'relational' one:

> For the relational teacher, education is a moral activity, which takes place in a complex and fluid environment, where the process is fundamentally a human activity rather than a technical enterprise. The means are more important than the ends. In this view, learning is seen as a process in which pupils actively engage while the teacher guides or facilitates this process. Teaching therefore involves moving beyond knowing what the curriculum requires, to knowing how best to teach it, and finally to knowing why it is being taught. (p. 394)

These teachers are generally open to change, willing to enter into it, but not necessarily successful in achieving it as planned. Nhi Vu's (1999) study of Vietnamese teachers' conceptions of teaching and learning in the context of educational policies bent on producing active learning and creative thinking simultaneously illustrates a willingness and an inability on the part of teachers to comply. The nineteen teachers in the study, when interviewed, could describe accurately their teaching practices in the words used by the reform, but when probed further it was clear that they had not really understood or made the approach a personal one. For example, they did not believe that a learner-centred approach was appropriate for moderate or slow learners. Asked to describe their teaching, they provided a picture of traditional methods of repeating information to make sure pupils had grasped the facts. They saw themselves as having a dual responsibility: to pass on knowledge and be responsible for moulding students into good people and citizens. The authors of the study felt these views were closer to a teacher-centred understanding of teaching rather than to the learner-centred approach espoused by the country's reform.

We believe in the reform . . . we perform despite difficulties . . . we have our objections

In all change processes there will be teachers who embrace change with enthusiasm either as an initial step, or as something they work on as they move along in the process. Evidence of teacher collaboration in the context of the 900 Schools' programme in Chile (see Filp, 1993) is rich in these examples. These teachers work in the poorest schools with children who perform substantially below what are considered reasonable standards. Yet, a good number of these teachers exert considerable energy to make their school work even though the process to accept this task may have involved a good amount of soul searching. In this respect, a supervisor in charge of facilitating the teacher workshop in one of the schools (a reform initiative) recounts how the teachers decided to 'go for it':

> It was a terribly defeated school . . . I went to the extent of telling them [the teachers] if you do not believe its worth doing something, if everything is so difficult, let's leave the school just how it is. There was silence. At that moment all I wanted was to leave. And then, they said: 'No, it's not all that bad!.' At that moment it was evident to me that they had decided, that what they most wanted to do was to change and they said it well.
>
> Larraín, n.d.

Teachers embrace a reform proposal either because it 'fits' with a personal position about what should be the case, with what they were doing before, or because some activity of the reform itself (often a teachers' workshop) assisted them to review held positions or beliefs. Below are examples, extracted also from testimonies of how reform is viewed by teachers:

> I would get to the school with only a photocopy of the topics I had to teach.. You were kind of given papers, but never a concrete reference point. They were loose contents, no theoretical explanations about what the kid was supposed to do. The new design provides a theoretical framework and occasionally, it even suggests how the contents should be taught. The old syllabus was just a set of contents and no reason about the why of things.
>
> Feldman, 1994, p. 33

> It was very difficult when I came to this school. . . . The class with which I started is now in 8th grade. What I heard teachers say about those 8th graders [unfavourable comments], it seemed to me was my legacy to them. The problems of these kids, which I left when they were in 6th grade, are of my doing. As I realised this, I decided to be totally different. As a teacher I had left my children little room for, I was apprehensive. I was always deciding for them, and they learnt the lesson. Children depend very much on what their teachers say. So I said to myself: I will change. In this 1st grade this year, the children work independently, they organise the handing out of teaching materials, they . . .
>
> statements of Chilean teachers during a focus group meeting, quoted by Larraín, N.D.

This self-criticism made by teachers who believe in the reform is a powerful building block for success. Such is the case also regarding responsible criticisms of situations or conditions that teachers do not see as being in line with reform principles. Chilean teachers, for example, have not hesitated to criticize the controversial System for Measuring Educational Achievement, known as SIMCE, because they perceive it as inimical to equity and fairness. This examination measures school results in Spanish Language and Mathematics every 2 years (and other subjects on a sample basis). Schools are ranked according to results and the rank order is published in newspapers. Teachers have different reasons for being against it. For example, it imposes pressure and causes tension among teachers in the schools that do not get good results: 'teachers who teach in lower classes are blamed for the results'. Teachers argue that it is not a fair instrument for comparison, because as is well known, teachers in the better schools coach children for the exam. A teacher working in both a private and public school points out that the private (subsidised) school:

> gets results of 80–85% in SIMCE tests, and yet results in this poorer public school are never higher than 60–65%. But if I compare what children here know, they know much more than the other ones, they have progressed much more, they are more humane and have more values
>
> Larraín, n.d.

Responsible criticism arising from the practical experience of teachers provides important evidence to gauge the soundness of that system.

What can be learned from the preceding discussion: what do we do?

These two questions can be posed for different audiences: the academic-research community and policy-makers. My response is directed primarily towards those engaged in policy research and implementation.

First, the realities of teachers as seen by others and the reality of educational change and teachers' role as seen by them are both valid while neither affords an adequate response. To know that a teacher lacks enough subject knowledge to transform a beautifully designed curriculum framework into appropriate teaching approaches and learning opportunities, does not invalidate the curriculum. It suggests only that more attention must be given to conditions of implementation, to time for change and to how the process will be supported. To know that teachers who work in appalling conditions may view change as impossible because of such conditions does not mean that they should be left aside or forced to change. It does mean, however, that these teachers need greater support than is provided in schools with more favourable working conditions. To know that teachers have to account for student learning does not transform them into culprits when failure occurs, nor should they become victims of the poor learning conditions of their children. There are well-documented examples of what teachers (and schools) in those conditions achieve with children.[6] There are many good examples of teachers who display great dignity in the way they advocate improved conditions to increase their pupils' chances of success.

Second, reform efforts throughout the world need to take more cognisance of what teaching and teacher situations are. In many situations, teachers become suspicious about the new programme – not necessarily because they want to reject it but because it is unfamiliar (they cannot see the ties with what they know) or because of the natural fear of change. Often teachers react negatively to lack of consultation about a curricular reform as happened in the United Kingdom in the eighties and nineties. But even when consulted, resulting policies may not reflect very much the views expressed by teachers. In this situation, a danger evident in the study of Gambian and South African teachers (Jessop and Penny, 1998), is that they use the 'new' processes instrumentally without conviction. Only a close fit between teacher education and teacher professional development opportunities at the time of implementing a new curriculum or other changes can overcome some of these difficulties.

Third, the uniformity of current reforms in terms of their targets, their principles as well as their constraining factors suggest the need to develop strategies. These strategies should provide teachers with the chance to become creative recipients of reforms, convinced of what merits action and therefore able to criticize knowingly what does not. Although imperfect, such strategies are already in place in many countries, although often only as small-scale projects. They consist in assisted, collaborative school-based professional development in all the guises available: teacher support groups, schools clustered around professional development centres (especially in rural, isolated conditions), and assistance from experienced teachers to those in fragile, vulnerable school situations. Previous reform efforts indicate that the expected pace of planned change frequently results in resistance by teachers. In the rush to implement reform, cascade systems may serve the purpose of informing teachers rapidly – but it is known that not even the purpose of providing accurate information can be assured. Greater effort, therefore, must be made to provide time, resources, leadership and materials for professional development. In the context of such support, additional incentives for teachers may have a role to play (See Kemmerer and Thiagarajan, 1993).

'This is a good reform but it's operating in an old structure' said a teacher in Santiago, and he was absolutely right. Reforms frequently take place without accompanying structural changes, especially the accompanying legislation. The fourth point therefore is to recommend that policy-makers and reform designers create a positive and supportive implementation framework prior to dissemination.

Finally, international messages indicating that change processes are to be regulated by principles of competition and incentives, are resisted by teachers. This resistance has many reasonable roots. One is the 'education for all' principle – the belief that quality belongs to all and that there is no reasonable justification for turning the educational scene into a battlefield with losers and winners. Another, is the traditional corporate sense of the teaching profession. In most countries teachers are still employed by the State and view themselves and see themselves as civil servants. When these patterns change, as for example with decentralization in Chile, teachers resist as a group. They do not wish to be 'up for grabs' in the open market. It conflicts with their view of the teaching profession. However, with growing pressure for teacher evaluation and changing patterns of employment, teachers inevitably have to reconsider their traditional views on the profession. There are positive ways of stimulating teacher improvement through performance evaluation schemes inserted in appropriate teacher career structures (Ingvarson, 1998). Few developing countries have this and teachers are not even given the opportunity to consider such schemes as desirable. In this advancing meritocratic society, as Ornelas (1998) suggests in relation to Mexico, it is reasonable to require from teachers more than moral conviction about their profession. Teachers can expect to be held accountable for 'punctuality, personal and collective initiative, willingness to give the best, expect the best but prepare for the worst' (p. 5).

There are certainly disjunctures between the global rhetoric of educational change and the way in which teachers interpret and act out such messages. As suggested above these disjunctures need to be faced and handled through a variety of approaches. Above all, I think that Voltaire's pragmatic dictum that the best is the enemy of the good, holds true in the context of educational change and of the situation of teachers.

Notes

1 Many of the reform programmes in Latin America that are assisted with World Bank and the Inter-american Development Bank funding are referred to as Programmes for Improving Quality and Equity in Education (e.g. Chile, Uruguay, Paraguay). UNESCO in Latin America states as one of its target policies: 'Education Quality with Equity for All throughout life' (UNESCO/OREALC, 1998).

2 For an interesting analysis of what can and cannot be learned from the South East Asian Educational systems see Delannoy's article (1997) in a PREAL publication (Program for the Promotion of Educational Reform in Latin America).

3 In relation to these curriculum models, which are similar only in that they provide frameworks international influence is noticeable. The Chilean curriculum draws inspiration for its format from similar projects in the United Kingdom, the United States, Australia and Canada. The South African curriculum has a United States source.

4 In the South African case the 'outcomes based curriculum' is organised in eight learning areas with each one specifying student outcomes (generic or cross-curricular and specific) rather than content inputs. Assessment criteria are provided for each specific outcome. Performance indicators provide the relevant steps for achievement of the outcome.

5 The inefficiency of the cascade system is well documented. For a recent study see McDevitt (1998) on a cascade method used to train teachers for mixed-ability teaching. While he notes the advantages of 'rapid communication' as well as forcing facilitators to check back on their knowledge when challenged by teachers, his study points to the same shortcomings found in other studies: a one-way transmission process where there is no guarantee that the listeners will have understood or changed views and attitudes.

6 Sra. Rosa, a teacher in the poverty stricken Alto La Paz area in Bolivia in fact, who without the experience of a wide variety of teaching methods, within the limits of her frontal teaching methods, had as her main concern that children understand - meaningful learning. See: Avalos (1986) for the description of her classroom. Also illustrative is Christie's study of 'resilient schools' in South Africa (1997).

References

Avalos, B. (ed.) (1986) *Teaching Children of the Poor. An Ethnographic Study in Latin America*, Ottawa: International Development Research Centre.

—— (1998) 'School-based teacher development. The experience of teacher professional groups in secondary schools in Chile', *Teaching and Teacher Education* 14(3): 257–71.

—— (1999) 'Desarrollo docente en el contexto de la institución escolar. Los Microcentros Rurales y los Grupos Profesionales de Trabajo en Chile', support paper for the Meeting on Teachers in Latin America, 'New Perspectives for their Development and Performance', San José, Costa Rica, 28–30 June.

Christie, P. (1997) 'Stability against the odds: resilient schools in South Africa', paper

presented at the Oxford International Conference on Education and Development, Education and Geopolitical Change. Oxford.
Churchill, R., Grady, N., Duncan, J. and McDougall, M. (1996) 'Teachers' work lives in four educational change contexts', paper presented at the 9th World Congress of Comparative Education Societies, Sydney, Australia.
Comisión Nacional para la Modernización de la Educación (1995). *Los Desafíos de la Educación Chilena Frente al Siglo XXI*, Santiago: Editorial Universitaria.
Delannoy, F. (1997) 'Tendencias mundiales y educación secundaria en Asia del Este y el Pacífico', *PREAL, Formas & Reformas de la Educación1* 4: 13–21.
Delors, J. (1996) *Education: The Treasure Within. Report of the International Commission on Education for the XXI Century*, Paris: UNESCO.
Duraismy, P., James, E., Lane, J. and Peng-Tan, J. (1998) 'Is there a quantity–quality trade-off as pupil–teacher ratios increase? Evidence from Tamil Nadu, India', *International Journal of Educational Development* 18(5): 367–83.
Feldman, D. (1994) *Curriculum, Maestros y Especialistas*, Buenos Aires: Libros del Quirquincho.
Filp, J. (1993) *The 900 Schools Programme. Improving the Quality of Primary Schools in Impoverished Areas of Chile*, Paris: IIEP.
Ingvarson, L. C. (1998) 'Professional development as pursuit of professional standards. The standards-based professional development system', *Teaching and Teacher Education* 14(1): 127–40.
Jansen, J. (1998) 'Essential alterations? A critical analysis of the State's syllabus', *Perspectives in Education*, 17(2): 1–11.
Jansen, J., Maqutu-Senior, I. and Sookrajh, R. (1999) 'A very noisy OBE: A report of the implementation of OBE inside Grade 1 classrooms', in N. Taylor and P. Vinjevold (eds) *Getting Learning Right*, Johannesburg: Joint Education Trust.
Jessop, T. and Penny, A. (1998) 'A study of teacher voice and vision in the narratives of rural South African and Gambian primary school teachers', *International Journal of Educational Development* 18(5): 393–403.
Jones, A. (1999) 'Teachers' subject subcultures and curriculum innovation: the example of technology education', in J. Loughran (ed.) *Researching Teaching. Methodologies and Practices for Understanding Pedagogy*, London: Falmer Press.
Kemmerer, F. and Thiagarajan, R. (1993) 'The role of local communities in teacher incentive systems', in J. B. Farrell and J. B. Oliveira (eds) *Teachers in Developing Countries. Improving Effectiveness and Managing Costs*, Washington, DC: The World Bank.
Larraín, T. (n.d.) 'La reflexión pedagógica como tensión entre la teoría y la práctica. El caso de la formación para profesores en servicio del Programa de las 900 Escuelas', draft Diploma thesis, Université Catholique de Louvain.
McDevitt, D. (1998) 'How effective is the cascade as a method for disseminating ideas? A case study in Botswana', *International Journal of Educational Development* 18(5): 425–8.
Milesi, C. and Trucco, D. (1996) 'Estudio sobre la implementación y receptividad de las instancias de trabajo colectivo del Programa MECE-Media', case study as partial fulfilment for the Licenciate Degree in Sociology, Catholic University of Chile.
Murphy, J. (1993) *Restructuring Schools*, London: Cassell.
Ornelas, C. (1998) 'El perfil del maestro del siglo veintiuno. Apuntes para una sociología del magisterio Mexicano', paper presented at the International Meeting Educación para la Vida, Educación más Allá de la Escuela, Tabasco, Mexico.
Ratnavadivel, N. (1999) 'Teacher education: interface between practices and policies – the Malaysian experience 1979–1997', *Teaching and Teacher Education* 15(2): 193–214.

Reimers, F. (1994) 'Education and structural adjustment in Latin America and sub-Saharan Africa', *International Journal of Educational Development* 14(2): 119–29.

Reyes, L. A. and Mendizabal, P. (1999) 'Creencias sobre práctica docente para la educación básica chilena', Master's thesis, Universidad Metropolitana de Ciencias de la Educación, Santiago, Chile.

Tatto, M. T. (1999) 'Improving teacher education in rural Mexico: the challenges and tensions of Constructivist reform', *Teaching and Teacher Education* 15(1): 15–35.

Taylor, N. and Vinjevold, P. (eds) (1999) 'Getting learning right', report of the President's Education Initiative Research Project, Johannesburg: The Joint Education Trust.

Tedesco, J. C. (1999) 'Fortalecimiento del rol de los docentes. Visión internacional', in B. Avalos and M. E. Nordenflycht (eds) *La Formación de Profesores. Perspectiva y Experiencias*, Santiago: Santillana.

UNESCO/OREALC (1998) *La UNESCO y la Educación en América Latina y el Caribe*, 1987–1997. Santiago: UNESCO/OREALC.

UNESCO-Santiago (1998) Laboratorio Latinoamericano de Evaluación de la Calidad de la Educación: Primer Estudio Internacional Comparativo: Santiago: UNESCO/ OREALC.

Uttech, Melanie (1999) *La Imaginación Social, la Diversidad y las Inteligencias Múltiples en el Salón Multigrado*, Guanajuato: Gobierno del Estado de Guanajuato.

Vu, N. (1999) 'Vietnamese teachers' conceptions about teaching and learning', paper presented at the Annual Meeting of the *American Educational Research Association*, Montreal, April.

Whitty, G. (1997) 'Marketization, the State and the re-formation of the teaching profession', in A. H. Halsey, H. Lauder, P. Brown and A. Stuart Wells (eds) *Education: Culture, Economy and Society*, Oxford: Oxford University Press.

Chapter 12

Between professional autonomy and bureaucratic accountability

The self-managing school within a Norwegian context

Jorunn Møller

Introduction

The self-managing school, or school-based management, has been defined as a megatrend in education. In one form or another it seems to appear as a global phenomenon (Caldwell and Spinks 1992, Caldwell, 1997). It involves the delegation of authority and responsibility from central authorities to the school site. Around the world the scope of decisions given to schools under decentralization varies from a small to a large amount of district resources. Schools within a district are allotted money to purchase supplies, equipment, personnel, utilities, maintenance, and perhaps other services to their own assessment of what is appropriate. This is in contrast to a practice which requires that such decisions are made at the central office.

The self-managing school is emphasized as an important means for school improvement and school effectiveness. This paper focuses on potential effects of changed decision-making structures on the relationships between principals and teachers, and how this may be connected to school improvement. Two upper secondary schools were selected as cases to investigate the questions. They are within the same county, yet possess different course structures; one school offers general subject courses and the other offers both general and technical vocational courses. Both schools are noted, by the county director, for their good organization and leadership. Interviews have been used as the main method of investigation. All those holding formal administrative position in addition to some teachers have been interviewed. In addition, policy documents have been examined.

The Self-Managing School

In developing the concept as well as offering a normative model of a self-managing school, Caldwell's work and research have played an important role. In *Leading the Self-Managing School* (1992) he and Spinks presented a model of school planning as a means of achieving school effectiveness that was used in an extensive programme of training for parents, principals and teachers in Victoria (Australia). Caldwell (1997) emphasizes that the concept of the self-managing school also implies a powerful role for central agencies in respect to formulating goals, setting priorities and building frameworks for accountability. He defines the self-managing school as the systematic decentralization to the school level of authority to make decisions on the allocation of resources, defined broadly, within a centrally determined framework of goals, policies, priorities, standards and accountabilities. The centre may remain concerned about the ends for education, but those at the school site are responsible for the means of education and for demonstrating their success at achieving goals set both locally and centrally. Based on his research, he concludes that the trend towards self-management has resulted in greater awareness of what resources schools receive and why. He argues that the findings reveal effects on capacity for self-management, on improved learning outcomes for students, and that these effects have important implications for the role of school leaders. The move towards decentralization of governance has also implied unfulfilled expectations and lots of problems for principals, for instance, frustration at 'bureaucratic interference', inadequate resources, and intensification of work. Nevertheless, his research reports that the overwhelming majority of principals would not wish their schools to return to previous arrangements.

Based on his research on decentralization and school-based management in Canada, Brown (1990) found that principals and teachers generally agreed on the strengths and weaknesses of decentralization. The strength was the flexibility, while the weakness was the time requirement. Often external constraints imposed on schools under decentralization limited their flexibility. Brown's research also showed that the participation of teachers and support staff in the budgetary process varied a lot. When the principles of decentralization are applied to schools, they match Mintzberg's (1989) divisional form quite well, but decentralization has tended to die at the principal's desk.

Current discourses of self-managing schools incorporate notions of democracy, participation, choice, community and society. Critics have emphasized that the self-managing school is not fundamentally about choice and grassroots democracy, but the reverse where the process is about tightening central controls through national curricula and frameworks, national and state-wide testing, teacher appraisal and curriculum audit. In reality there is no shift in central power. Particularly the frameworks of accountability have constrained decision making at school level instead of empowering schools. The notion of democracy seems to have been reduced to a simplistic concept of parental choice, and the move towards the self-managing school can be characterized as part of a discursive trick where schools control their own decline. What has occurred is that there has been a rhetoric of devolution in a context of centralism and managerialism (see Anderson and Dixon 1993; Angus, 1993; Ball, 1993).

Smyth (1996) refers to studies in Canada, USA and UK which support this argument. In Canada, for instance, school-based management seems to result in a reduction in the overall quality of educational provision, because there is no longer any provision for ensuring an equitable balance of services and facilities within the system. Resources are allocated to schools before educational needs are assessed. According to Smyth, power, control and resources are kept at the centre; while responsibility, blame and guilt are decentralized to the schools. In the USA where there is support for school-based management, the support tends to come from school administrators, not from teachers and the wider school communities. In the UK budget cutbacks have accompanied devolution, and heads say that self-managing has increased their administration, and schools are forced to supplement their funding from private sources. Herein lies the equity issue: schools have vastly different capacities to do this owing to their socio-economic make-up (Simkins, 1996).

Smyth (1996) argues that the discourse of self management has a different Bill of Sale depending upon who it has to be sold to. To the principals and teachers it is put as a form of empowerment, made possible by removing bureaucracy. In addition, it is a way for principals of reclaiming control over the day-to-day running of the school. To the parents it is said to be a way of making schools more accountable and giving them a greater say over what is happening to their children. At the same time, the devolution to self-management has been accompanied by centralizing tendencies, and the struggle between political and professional power over education has been sharpened. A crucial question is therefore who at the local level obtains more autonomy; the principal, the teachers, the parents or the students?

Lundgren (1990) has pointed out that a decentralization of the educational system, irrespective of motives, puts in focus the balance between political and professional power over education. It shows four main models for governing education: central, local, professional, political. In Lundgren's grid, the horizontal axis refers to the tension between political versus professional power over education, while the vertical axis refers to central versus local governing of schools. The first quadrant shows a system of central governing where the politicians are in command. The second quadrant shows a centralized system where the educational bureaucrats in the governing boards have the power. The third quadrant shows a model for local governing where the professionals set the agenda, and in the fourth quadrant the local politicians have obtained the power.

The movement towards decentralization has focused questions around the professional ability of teachers, and the diffuse borderline between political and professional responsibility seems to represent a major problem. Conservatives see opportunities for potential abuse in school-level control, particularly if teachers are able to capture the process of school governance. If school-based management is to be introduced, they suggest that lay control must be assured. From the left it is argued that deregulation, choice, local control will ultimately favour those with greater personal and family resources. Greater inequality will result, with the best getting better; the education gap between rich and poor will widen. At the same time, blame will be decentralized. Central agencies will no longer carry the political burden of confronting those who accuse them of ineffectiveness and inefficiency.

The model of decentralization chosen in Norway is one where the political authorities state the goals to be achieved, whereas local authorities or professionals have the freedom to pursue the practice that they find most suitable to achieve the objectives. Decentralized governing is praised, but schools work to fairly detailed curriculum guidelines in terms of timetable and syllabuses, and with central approval of textbooks. During the early 1970s these specifications were replaced by looser guidelines from the centre. However, in the 1990s curriculum guidelines have become more detailed again. A tight-loose management approach is used to set standards, while encouraging local initiative in fulfilling the objectives. So far it is uncertain who at the local level, obtains more autonomy – the principal, the teachers, the local school authorities, the parents, or the students. Different municipalities have chosen different approaches to school-based management from a small to a large amount of district resources. What is clear, is that evaluation has become an important method both of reconstructing the role of the centre and the role of local politicians.

Conceptions of accountability

The concept of accountability means having to 'answer for one's actions, particularly the results of those actions' (Brown 1990, p. 159). During the 1980s both politicians and top administrators have raised doubts about the extent to which teachers are making claims on behalf of their clients, or perhaps rather on behalf of their own interests as a group. The politicians use the notion of 'provider capture' in this connection. It implies that those who provide the service, capture the benefit (Lawton, 1992). This is probably the reason why external evaluation of education at various levels has come into focus in recent years. Education policy could no longer be based on widespread trust in the professional competence of educators, their performance should be controlled and judged according to criteria established outside the profession.

Thus, policies of decentralizing the governance of educational systems, seem to carry the seeds of their own contradictions. Weiler (1990) has analysed three arguments or models which one normally encounters where decentralization in educational governance is discussed. These arguments are: (1) the redistribution model, which has to do with the sharing of power; (2) the efficiency model, which is geared to enhancing the cost-effectiveness calculus of the educational system through a more efficient deployment and management of available resources; and (3) the cultures of learning model, which emphasizes the decentralization of educational content. He concludes that there is a need to go beyond these kinds of arguments in understanding the political dynamics of centralization and decentralization in educational policy. He says that decentralizing 'the implementation of educational policy affects in very important ways the nature and the interests of the state, particularly its ability to cope with the dual problems of policy conflict and the erosion of its own legitimacy' (p. 61). Against this background he examines the relationship between decentralization and external evaluation, and argues that evaluation tends to be used for its legitimating rather than its informative capacity. The linkage between external evaluation and control is obvious, and therefore evaluation enters into a competitive relationship with the basic premises of decentralization.

Accountability can be understood as an obligation for professionals in teaching. Sockett (1993, pp. 108–28) distinguishes between bureaucratic accountability and professional accountability. Bureaucratic accountability can be compared to a salesman model which has very limited applicability within schools. In this view, accountability refers to 'an agent's responsibility to a provider, the provider being the beneficiary as measured by the results produced through the agent's skill in handling resources' (p. 110). The salesman is only accountable to the owner of the shop. Teaching as a profession requires an alternative model of accountability because the exercise of teaching demands greater autonomy than the salesman model would allow, and there are many different constituencies of accountability for the teacher. Sockett has articulated an approach to the question of professional accountability that is consonant with teaching as a moral endeavour. He argues for four main positions: (1) accountability is akin to moral obligation; (2) trust is a primary condition for the development of professional accountability; (3) a professional code of practical guidance could provide a vehicle for accountability; and (4) a moral stance toward professional accountability is central. This accountability includes not only classroom conduct, but also relations with colleagues, parents, and the community. A professional teacher will try to find ways of explaining achievements and failings in recognition of the need to build trust in the practice and in the judgments made.

In Norway accountability issues related to the school sector were put on the public agenda after the OECD evaluation of our educational policies in 1988. The government still praised decentralization of education, but proposed that evaluation should become a key element in the improvement of Norwegian education (Granheim *et al.*, 1990). This led to a long debate about the potential and the dangers of a strong evaluative system. In December 1997 a committee on behalf of the Ministry of Education, Research and Church Affairs launched a proposal to a new national evaluation system (KUF, 1997). The White Paper based on the hearing of this proposal was postponed several times, but, eventually, in June 1999, it was presented to and discussed by Parliament (KUF, 1999).

The proposal was in line with a new management practice in Norwegian schools, which has been combined with greater concern for documenting results. It stated that all levels should show their efficiency by what results they have obtained, and the idea of a Norwegian inspectorate body with the Scottish system as a model, was carefully mentioned. The committee also underlined the importance of school-based evaluation, but clearly the tendency was towards greater emphasis on external accountability. The White Paper, on the other hand, focuses on the importance of giving the control of curriculum development and teaching back to teachers. It criticizes conceptions of accountability that appear to be couched in terms of a bureaucratic audit. The White Paper emphasizes school-based evaluation as the key element in improving schools. At least rhetorically this White Paper represents a shift in educational policy. It argues for professional accountability, and states that external evaluation should not be used as an instrument for direction and control. There is a risk in being so preoccupied with measurements and tests, that we forget to evaluate quality issues that cannot be measured so easily but are more often the object of sound judgment.

However, it remains to be seen what local politicians will decide to do in this connection. It will take time to implement a new practice. For more than 10 years there has been a focus on school self-evaluation in the educational debate and in in-service-training for teachers and principals in Norway. In an evaluation of the upper secondary school reform in Norway, Monsen (1997, 1998) found that schools which have succeeded in developing their own model for school-based evaluation, are still exceptions within the Norwegian school system. According to his research only 20 per cent of the schools are doing some kind of systematic school-based evaluation. So far Norwegian teachers, to a very little degree, have entered the public debate with their internally defined criteria of teacher professionalism. They are angry and tend to concentrate on pragmatic matters relating to their use of time (Møller, 1998).

Perspectives on professional identity

Teachers and administrators, at various levels within schools, have different functions and knowledge, but they have a joint responsibility for providing pupils with a quality education. The professional identity one develops, becomes apparent through interaction with others working at the same school, with other schools and other areas of the education system.

In his analysis of quality within the education system, Dale (1997) has focused on the relationship between the identity one develops at work, the reference frames one uses in defining each others' duties, and the joint effort made to develop quality in schools. He views this identity in relation to four dimensions which form the basis for a social system: collaboration, stability, homogeneity and communication. In contrast to these, Dale places individuality, mobility, heterogeneity and isolation; hence, creating a series of contentions. If a system consists solely of contentions, an imbalance arises, preventing a common professional identity. However, a certain amount of contention between collaboration and individuality, between stability and mobility, between homogeneity and heterogeneity is required for school development.

When examining different layers of school bureaucracy, it becomes apparent that teachers, principals, local, regional and central leadership constitute different sub-cultures with different jargons, problem definitions and loyalties. Professional identity is to a large degree defined locally by tradition, and separated groups define separate identities. Dale's main argument is that there must exist a common knowledge of technical language and concepts used for discussing quality within education. He claims that today there is a lack of common reference frames among those working at different layers within school bureaucracy, and he argues that communication between sub-cultures must be rooted in teaching-related criteria. This can only be acquired through an extensive formal socialization in the theory of education. Otherwise, there will continue to be low permeability between the different groups. This increases the possibility that collaboration between administrators and teachers may be dominated by administration, regulation and sanctions.

The schools in the study

Soltun Upper Secondary School was built as a combined, upper secondary school in Oslo. The modern buildings encompass comprehensive study facilities. The student population is 700, age 16–19, and 150 trainees are attached to the school. There are ninety teachers. The school offers foundation courses for general and business studies, building trades, health and social studies, mechanical trades and technical building trades. Advanced course 1 includes general studies, car mechanics, hair-dressing, carpentry, skin-care and general care. Advanced course 2 includes general studies and skin-care. In addition to this there is the trainee school for building trades and scaffold construction. There are also unemployment courses.

Soltun recruits students primarily from its local catchment area, although the vocational training course students do tend to come from further afield. Thirty per cent do not have Norwegian as their mother tongue. According to the staff, this creates tensions because different cultural groups have conflicting behavioural norms. The school is situated on the city's outskirts, which appears to influence the recruitment of general course students. At present, the city centre schools appear to be most attractive to students. There is competition for students among schools, and Soltun is struggling against a negative reputation established by the media. As a result, teachers are working extra hard to encourage students to be proud of their school.

Good inter-faculty relations have always been encouraged to avoid divisions and cliques occurring. However, an awkward conflict arose a couple of years ago when a quarrel within the administration team led to a rift among the staff. Discrimination and whispering behind closed doors resulted in the head's resignation and the appointment of a new head. The new principal, who was recruited internally, had worked at the school since its opening. Following this upheaval, it became vital for the school to regain administrative stability and order.

Borgen Upper Secondary School is an old, respected school which was built as an upper secondary school more than 80 years ago. It is located in Oslo's centre. The school's exterior is impressive, but refurbishment is required internally. Borgen offers mainly general subject courses and courses for music, drama and dance. It is very popular, and competition for entry is tough. The student population is 450, age 16–19. On average, the students have extremely good, lower secondary school grades, and they come from all over Oslo. The school has almost no foreign-language speaking students. Fifty teachers are working at Borgen.

Many of the school's past principals have been described as pioneers of school politics. The instruction of more traditional subjects is deeply rooted, and many believe much of the traditional Latin school remains. The school is built upon strong subject identities with a high academic emphasis. The present principal was appointed 2 years ago, after having been principal at a combined, upper secondary school, within the same county. The administration team consists of the principal and three deputy heads, and three persons hold positions as faculty heads.

Reorganizing the local administration at school level

Running an upper secondary school is a complex task. Therefore, it is usual to consider the management as a team effort, with numerous members of staff fulfilling different administrative roles, (KUF, 1990–1). The larger the organization, the more important it is to distribute administrative duties. A position of faculty head was established in the 1970s to help the teachers co-ordinate teaching activities within each faculty. Responsibilities included co-ordinating department meetings, promoting subject/pedagogical collaboration among teachers, supervising the preparation of internal examinations, initiating work placement contacts and co-ordinating budget plans and faculty purchases. The main purpose was to improve quality in teaching. In practice, the tasks have primarily been administrative. An award of 29 March 1996 led to a decentralization of internal organization. Schools were given greater freedom to appoint faculty heads. At some schools, this resulted in a reduction of faculty heads, whereas at other schools, it resulted in an increase in number. There has been a general tendency to introduce a system of middle managers instead of faculty heads (Paulsen, 1999). The principal appoints these middle managers, while the faculty heads were elected by their peers. There is a wish to abolish the 'tacit deal' where teachers and administrators generally respect each other's 'zones of influence' (Shedd and Bacharach, 1991). To a larger degree both teachers and leaders should collaborate in improving the quality of teaching.

Soltun school has reorganized its local administration, and the principal has appointed eight middle managers and has abolished the old system with faculty heads. Every second year contracts may be renegotiated. Positions are now regarded as part of the school's administration team. They are no longer solely the teachers' representative, as they have often been regarded before. The faculty head is in charge of pedagogical affairs and has the task of coordinating teaching and ensuring directives are followed. In addition, they prepare local curricula, internal examination papers and oversee budgets and teaching materials but, as yet, personnel responsibility is not part of the position.

The old administration team at Soltun consisted of the principal and four deputy heads. They have all been actively and strategically involved in setting up this project. They are convinced it will cause both pedagogical and administrative duties to be carried out effectively. The principal points out:

> The school has become autonomous. We have financial management and complete responsibility for personnel and property. Indeed, everything concerning the management of the school is part of our responsibility. Therefore, we have many more duties. The running of a large, combined upper secondary school, such as this, requires management similar to corporation management. The top management is removed from individual affairs, whether they concern teachers or students, due to the incorporation of intermediate level. This is what we are working on. It is impossible for the head of a large school to supervise, for example, 800 students and 120 members of staff.

Another administration team member argues:

> The reorganization of the administration is exciting. It will award greater responsibility to faculty heads. Previously, the faculty head functioned as an administrator dealing with course inquiries and taking necessary action, discussing the written exam and other mundane tasks with little definite responsibility.

The newly appointed middle managers at Soltun feel they should have educational leadership responsibilities connected to specific subjects, but so far, they have been acting in a purely administrative capacity. The principal wishes to see them as part of the formal administration team, whereas many teachers still want to go on with the old system where the faculty heads were their representatives.

One of the middle managers explains:

> For many teachers, the faculty head or the middle manager is the sorter and the fixer: 'Set things up for me, make sure I have books, find things for me, always know what is written in the circulars', and so forth. I prefer to be an educational leader. Today, there is often a lot of improvisation. People come and seek advice when they are unsure how to grade work, or about subject related matters. I like these kind of inquiries. It becomes an extension of my role as a teacher. At the moment, we are debating whether the middle manager should have personnel responsibilities. The concept of personnel responsibilities is complex, and there are some things I am glad we do not have responsibility for, for example, granting leave. It is quite all right that it is decided centrally; particularly when the middle managers' responsibilities comprise different subject areas; sometimes one teacher can actually be accountable to three different middle managers. In time, individual staff hours could be handed over to the middle managers. I think that would be wise, but not yet. None of us are ready for that yet. There is strong resistance among some of the teachers.

Thus, the support for these structural changes seems to come from those in formal leadership positions. The teachers are more divided in their feeling towards the reorganization. Some fear it will be difficult to adhere to the administrative links, the distance between them and the principal will be increased and contact reduced. Nevertheless, two teachers have positive expectations and other teachers regard the faculty head's possible personnel responsibility as both positive and negative. The following quote captures this sentiment:

> Now they are talking of the faculty head being given greater control over personnel. This has both positive and negative aspects. We will have a closer relationship with the faculty head in a teaching situation, but the distance to the rest of the administration will be increased. Sometimes, you want a little more distance between you and the person who has personnel

> responsibility above you. Yet, on other occasions, it can be advantageous to have them more closely involved in your teaching. They get to know the pupils so they can provide pupil-related advice, especially if it concerns a specific pupil. On the other hand, a middle manager does not have the same weight of authority as the others in the administration team.

The following quote summarizes the scepticism among the teachers:

> The faculty heads are now to function as intermediaries; . . . I am rather sceptical towards this because of the many steps between you and the person you really want to deal with. I find myself asking: Is it really necessary to have more administrative levels at our school? How many more are going to control us?

At Borgen school, so far, no steps have been taken formally to introduce a new local administration, and the traditional system of elected faculty heads remains. However, their framework has been enlarged, as have their responsibilities. Each faculty head has been given several pedagogical duties by the principal. She has meetings with the faculty heads approximately twice a month and they have been assigned the responsibility of setting up planning days, following up local curricula work and initiating collaboration. The administration team considers it necessary to make demands upon the faculty heads to realize the reform.

But the faculty heads do not think their allocated tasks are in keeping with the administrative resources available to them:

> The instructions we receive are so vague you can do almost anything and nothing. During the few years I have been faculty head, my tasks have grown in number. For example, budgeting was never my responsibility, but now I am forever called upon to draft budgets, sign requisitions and oversee orders. The faculty head is called upon in connection with numerous matters. We have heard that now there is to be an intermediate level. I feel we are about to become intermediaries without being given the time and economic resource required. As a result, I go around with a constant guilty conscience. I feel it is affecting my teaching. Neither am I able to do all the things I am supposed to as faculty head. I either don't get the work done on time, or I don't get it done at all. I go around with a bad conscience thinking of all the things I should have done or followed up. It is very frustrating.

The teachers consider the faculty head as their representative. This opinion is shared by the faculty heads, as exemplified by the following quote: 'I am a teacher, not a manager, so I will always be loyal to my teachers. That is where I belong. I am a kind of spokesperson for them, against the administration if need be.' The debate surrounding faculty heads is not an issue among the teachers at Borgen. But they will probably soon have to face it. The county administration is following carefully the experiences of other schools such as Soltun.

The above describes how the principals at both schools have opted for different strategies. The principal at Soltun has appointed middle managers, and they are regarded as part of the administration team. Borgen still has the old system where faculty heads are elected and look upon themselves as spokespersons for teachers. This may be due to a combined school being a complex organization and better suited to a divisional structure. Many of the vocational subject teachers have experienced an intermediate arrangement in the private sector before they applied for a job as a teacher. The altered administrative system will be nothing new to them. The crisis within Soltun's administration team, which occurred several years ago, may have quickened the process to establish a new administrative system. The principal at Borgen school was recruited externally and, therefore, must learn to handle an established culture before proposals for change may be promoted. In addition, the need for an intermediate structure may not seem so pressing when the school has mainly general subject studies. Both schools experience the pressure towards more administration, and the principal has to respond to external pressure. Both principals, interviewed in the study, are critical of what they call 'bureaucratic interference of local politicians', and both have experienced difficult relationships with these local politicians. Even though the main purpose of the structural changes was to improve quality in teaching, the effect, so far, is that more time is dedicated to administrative duties, and less time is left for pedagogical purposes.

Teachers' experience is that the quality of personal relations with the principal owing to his or her presence around school is reduced. To a larger degree, the principals feel they have to choose to define their role in relation to outside constituencies and audiences. The result is that they are seen as absentee heads.

Who at the local level obtains more autonomy?

The self-managing school within the Norwegian context has meant that principals have become targets as well as agents of change in a drive for improved standards in schools. They are responding to external imperatives while trying to create conditions for staff to participate in organic school development. It is quite obvious that the principal's role as employer, personnel manager and educational leader cannot be fulfilled effectively with the present organization structure in school. The administration team at Soltun views the intermediate administrative level as the key to solving problems surrounding regulation of staff collaboration and evaluation of individual teachers. However, established zones of influence are challenged, and the extra administrative level disrupts the school's flat organizational structure and traditional distribution of power and duties. Hierarchical structures and administrative duties seem to be intensified. When this is coupled with external regulatory demands from society, the teacher's traditional autonomy is threatened.

So far, principals seem to have strengthened their formal power, and the administrators in this study seem to support the move towards a self-managing school. However, all over the country increasing demands and intensification of work has led to a recruitment crisis. There are very few applicants for each vacancy, on average less than three, and often the applicants do not have the required competency. In 1998, because of high work loads, low salaries and high stress levels, one in four principals quit the job to go back to classroom teaching, because there was too much stress connected to the job as principal. Chief Education Officers, Teacher Unions and politicians see this as a great problem. Right now principals' salaries are the focus of debate. The Ministry has announced that a White Paper about recruitment to teaching and leadership jobs will be launched in September 1999.

At the same time a continuing struggle between political and professional power over education goes on. As Tiller (1990) has pointed out, trust should be a central term in a decentralized school system, but some uncertainty has been spreading lately. During the seventies it was correct to talk about bottom-up strategies in school development. Today it is seen to come from above, but the talk is about decentralization. Politicians and educational bureaucrats at municipal level seem to have a strong belief in top-down strategies in order to improve schools. They argue for more regulation of classroom activities, and reports are seen as a means to guarantee educational quality in schools. Tensions are heightened, and this explains the resentment felt by some teachers towards the revision of local administration at school site. It has come to symbolize the authorities' lack of confidence in teachers. Decentralization is perceived and experienced as rhetoric.

Lack of confidence coupled with putting the market alternative in education on the political agenda. Right-wing parties, which now hold power in Oslo, would like to see more private schools receiving state support at all levels, to give state-maintained schools more competition. They wish to give students freedom of choice among schools. Throughout the country it is, so far, more talk than action. But in the future Norwegian education will probably see more differentiation and more privatization. There may be a deterioration of some public schools, and an emerging market for private schools (see Tjeldvoll, 1997).

The politicians want to reduce the professionals' power over education. For instance, in Oslo they established local governing in January 1994, giving the principal a lot more power and autonomy, but in January 1999, the politicians introduced a board between the local school and the Chief Education Officer, restricting the principal's autonomy and with the intention of empowering parents. This board consists at primary and lower secondary level of three parent representatives, two teachers (or other employees) and one external representative. At upper secondary level there are three external representatives, three students, and two teachers (or other employees). Using Lundgren's (1990) models for governing of education, this can be understood as a move from central and professional governing to local and professional governing and now to local and political governing. It might result in less power for principals, but not necessarily. The competency of board members will probably be crucial. The school principal is the board's secretary and has to prepare all meetings, and the power may still be in the hands of the professional. So far, it seems that the board has turned out to be an important support group for the school against the local politicians. When external representatives experience how small a budget the local school receives, they are ready to fight together with teachers for their school. However, participating in this board is time consuming, and it results in more administrative work for principals and less time for educational matters.

Quality in teaching – who is setting the standards?

The struggle between political and professional power over education includes a power struggle in society for who should define qualitative teaching. From a political perspective, there are other social groups wishing to define educational quality, but, as yet, they have had little bearing upon practice in schools. Intensified administration, in the form of external regulation, might solve some problems, but new problems will undoubtedly appear. In the long term, there is the risk that teachers' enthusiasm and commitment will be lost – a far greater problem for schools. It has still to be proved that intensified administration produces better schools. Education cannot be developed mechanically with administrative decrees and regulations.

However, teachers continuing fight for their individual right to set their own standards for teaching does not correspond with the conditions of professionalism (Dale 1997, Handal 1989). It is not the individual who is awarded autonomy, but the profession. And as a profession teachers should enter the public debate with their critique and internally defined criteria of teacher professionalism. In addition to their efforts of voicing protests against more managerialism in schools, teachers should lead the drive to resolve the tension between public and professional control by promoting forms of accountability that are publicly acceptable.

A gap between administration and teaching?

Dale (1997) claims that a lack of reference frames for discussing quality in schools makes collaboration difficult. Is this the case if we analyse the educational background of those who work in schools? To hold an administrative position in Norwegian schools, one must have three years teaching experience and formal teacher training. Therefore, one would imagine that both administrators and teachers have the background Dale describes. However, an upper secondary school teacher's education is primarily in their specialized teaching subject(s) and not in pedagogy. The majority of upper secondary school teachers have only 6 months practical pedagogical education, in addition to 5 to 7 years of their specialized subject studies. It is true that most teachers identify closely with their subjects, and they have developed pedagogical identities that are congruent with their subject being communicated in strongly academic ways. At the same time, administration teams, to a larger degree, identify with new constructs of educational leaders as managing directors.

Communication is unproblematic within a group possessing homogeneous reference frames and interests, but difficulties arise when the administration team and the teachers develop different reference frames. There is a risk of discussions becoming centred around administration matters when management does not have an identity connected to educational theory. According to Dale (1997), the gap between administration and teaching increases when the administration team identifies itself with the co-ordination of school activities through administration and regulation, and the teachers identify themselves with teaching their specific subject areas.

This tendency has been emphasized lately. At county level, for instance, further education courses for school administrators are often based upon general management and administration strategies used in the private sector. And school administrators at county and municipal level do not have to have an educational background as a teacher anymore. People with education in economy and law are in particular demand. As Røvik (1998) points out, in his report about modernization within the public sector, the same solutions are applied in both public and private sectors, and in large and small companies. If an organization is to prove its worth, it must be seen to incorporate the latest administrative strategies. Organizations create meaning and belief through symbols, including myths. Such myths are thought to be objective, but, in reality, they result from specific social and political definitions and dominance. They are circulated to promote legitimacy in areas of inconsistency. For example, outwardly, a new administrative system is seen to indicate renovation and increased efficiency within schools. But modernization often runs the risk of discarding the old before fully understanding the new. The key management concepts for the 1990s were total quality management and quality assurance, and these stem from economic rather than educational theory. This would support Dale's claim that the education system lacks a common identity.

However, the Ministry of Education, Research and Church Affairs has outlined competence objectives for educational leadership within schools, as part of the administrative programme (KUF, 1996). These include educational politics, curricula theory, evaluation and advisory topics, and may counteract the general tendency towards managerialism when it comes to governing of education. This type of knowledge is equally important for all teachers as it is for administrators, but it will take more than a few, brief courses before it is firmly established. So far, that seems more like a vision for the future.

Conclusions

The trend toward the self-managing school is probably irreversible within the Norwegian context. However, it is less evident as to who is likely to obtain more autonomy at the local level. The introduction of a board between the local school and the Chief Education Officer in Oslo could be a step towards more managerialism and less power to professionals, but not necessarily. The competency of board members will be crucial. So far schools have experienced the board members as a support group against politicians.

The new arrangement with middle managers allows the principal to take a greater educational leadership position, but that may strengthen the hierarchical management structure in schools. It may lead to a sharper division between the administration team and teachers. Furthermore, school administrators will be more closely linked to the county administration that probably will expect school administrators to enforce their directives. The question is whether or not the education policy lays down a managerial rather than an educational agenda. Will it be an emphasis on 'school image' rather than 'educational vision'? School democracy and teacher professionalism are emphasized in national curriculum guidelines. However, other things like requirements of assessment reports from local schools, detailed descriptions of how to do things, new agreements on regulation of teachers' work time, which are happening simultaneously, may reduce the educational emphasis. Right now the political wind is shifting, at least rhetorically, from control to trust.

Attacks on teachers in the media and the political will to regulate classroom activities appear to have drained teachers of their enthusiasm. Unfortunately, energies are being concentrated upon the protection of established practice as opposed to educational improvements. Both parents and students wish to make their voices heard in the schools. Teachers voice their protest against managerialism, but without initiating school-based evaluation and promoting alternative forms of accountability. When this occurs, they loose the opportunity of coopting parents as their alliances. There is a tension between the teachers' demand for autonomy, for an independent right to draw up and discuss the ethics of professional practice, and the control of this practice by the democratic state. This should mobilize teachers in collaboration with principals to enter the public debate with their critique and internally defined criteria of teacher professionalism. A professional role entails professional responsibility, and this implies that teachers make their experience more visible. Within the Norwegian context there are still spaces and opportunities for teachers to promote alternative forms of accountability that are publicly acceptable.

References

Anderson, G. and Dixon, A. (1993) 'Paradigm shifts and site-based management in the United States: toward a paradigm of social empowerment', in J. Smyth (ed.) *A Socially Critically View of the Self-Managing School*, London: Falmer Press.

Angus, L. (1993) 'Democratic participation or efficient site management: the social and political location of the self-managing school', in J. Smyth (ed.) *A Socially Critically View of the Self-Managing School*, London: Falmer Press.

Ball. S. (1993) 'Culture, cost and control: self-management and entrepreneurial schooling in England and Wales', in J. Smyth (ed.) *A Socially Critically View of the Self-Managing School*, London: Falmer Press.

Brown, D. J. (1990) *Decentralization and School-Based Management*, London: Falmer Press.

Caldwell, B (1997) 'The impact of self-management and self-government on professional cultures of teaching: a strategic analysis for the twenty-first century', in A. Hargreaves and R. Evans (eds) *Beyond Educational Reform. Bringing Teachers Back In*. Buckingham: Open University Press.

Caldwell, B. and Spinks, J. M. (1992) *Leading the Self-Managing School*, London: Falmer Press.

Dale, E. L. (1997) *Etikk for Pedagogisk Profesjonalitet*, Cappelen: Akademisk Forlag.

Granheim, M., Kogan, M. and Lundgren, U. (eds) (1990) *Evaluation as Policymaking, Introducing Evaluation into a National Decentralised Educational System*, London: Jessica Kingsley Publishers.

Handal, G. (1989) 'Lærerne og den andre profesjonaliteten', in K.Ø. Jordell and P. O. Aamodt (eds) *Læreren – fra kall til lønnskamp*, Oslo: Tano.

KUF (1990–1) 'Parliamentary Report No. 37', *On Organization and Guidance in the Educational Sector*, The Royal Ministry of Education, Research and Church Affairs.

—— (1996) *Educational Leadership towards year 2000, Skuleleiing mot år 2000*, The Royal Ministry of Education, Research and Church Affairs.

—— (1997) *Nasjonalt vurderingssystem for grunnskolen. Forslag fra utvalget oppnevnt av Kirke-, utdannings- og forskningsdepartementet* (A proposal for a national evaluation system within compulsory school)

—— (1999) 'Mot rikare mål. Om einskapsskolen, det likeverdige opplæringstilbodet og ein nasjonal strategi for vurdering og kvalitetsutvikling i grunnskolen og den vidaregåande opplæringa', *Stortingsmelding nr. 28 (1998–99)* (The White Paper for a National Evaluation System within Compulsory School).

Lawton, S. (1992) 'Why restructure? An international survey of the roots of reform', *Journal of Educational Policy* 7(2): 139–55.

Lundgren, U. (1990) 'Educational policy-making, decentralisation and evaluation', in M. Granheim, M. Kogan and U. Lundgren (eds) *Evaluation as Policymaking. Introducing Evaluation into a National Decentralised Educational System*, London: Jessica Kingsley Publishers.

Mintzberg, H. (1989) *Mintzberg on Management. Inside our Strange World of Organizations*, New York: The Free Press.

Monsen, L. (1997) 'Evaluering av Reform -94. Delrapport nr. 4. Innholdsreformen: Skolenes arbeid med læringsmiljøet', Arbeidsnotat nr. 37/1997, Høgskolen i Lillehammer.

—— (1998) 'Do we have a Scandinavian model for evaluation of schools?', paper presented at the annual Nordic Conference of Educational Research (NCER), in Lahti, March.

Møller, J. (1998) 'Educational policy and school leadership in upper secondary schools: new relationships and new tensions', paper presented at AERA, San Diego, April 13–17.

Paulsen, J. M. (1999) *Mellomledelse i videregående skolen. Ledelsesorganisering i videregående skole. Arbeidsnotat 27*, Hønefoss: Høgskolen i Buskerud.

Røvik, K. A. (1998) *Moderne Organisasjoner. Trender i Organisasjonstenkningen ved Tusenårsskiftet.* Bergen: Fagbokforlaget.

Shedd, J. and Bacharach, S. (1991) *Tangled Hierarchies. Teachers as Professionals and the Management of Schools*, San Francisco: Jossey-Bass.

Simkins, T. (1996) 'Equity and efficiency: tensions in school-based management in England and Wales', in: S. Jacobson, E. Hickcox and R. Stevenson (eds) *School Administration. Persistent Dilemmas in Preparation and Practice*, London: Praeger.

Sockett, H. (1993) *The Moral Base for Teacher Professionalism*. New York: Teacher College Press.

Smyth, J. (1996) 'The socially just alternative to the 'self-managing school', in K. Leithwood, J. Chapman, D. Corson, P. Hallinger and A. Hart (eds) *International Handbook of Educational Leadership and Administration*, The Netherlands: Kluwer Academic Publishers.

Tiller, T. (1990) 'Evaluation in a decentralised school system: where do we stand? Where are we heading?', in M. Granheim, M. Kogan and U. Lundgren (eds) *Evaluation as Policymaking. Introducing Evaluation into a National Decentralised Educational System*, London: Jessica Kingsley Publishers.

Tjeldvoll, A. (ed.) (1997) 'Quality of Equality? Scandinavian Education Towards the Year 2000', *Education and the Welfare State in the Year 2000. Equality, Policy and Reform in Scandinavia*, New York: Garland Publishing.

Weiler, H. N. (1990) 'Decentralisation in educational governance: an exercise in contradiction?', in M. Granheim, M. Kogan and U. Lundgren (eds) *Evaluation as Policymaking. Introducing Evaluation into a National Decentralised Educational System*, London: Jessica Kingsley Publishers.

Chapter 13

A critical first step in learning to teach

Confronting the power and tenacity of student teachers' beliefs and preconceptions

Ruth Ethell and Marilyn McMeniman

Introduction

Concerns with respect to the tenacity and pervasive power of student teachers' initial beliefs and preconceptions about teachers and teaching are well documented. Students enter preservice teacher education with beliefs and preconceptions that, although misinformed and naive, typically play a critical role in the acquisition of new knowledge from both on-campus and practicum courses. Preservice teacher education institutions run the risk of having their courses dismissed as irrelevant unless practices are adopted that relate the programme of study explicitly to the beliefs and preconceptions of the student teachers.

The study reported in this chapter demonstrates the importance of providing early opportunities for student teachers to make explicit their personal beliefs and preconceptions and to examine these in light of what is known and understood as effective teaching.

Learning to teach: theoretical perspectives

Teaching is a complex, consciously performed, intellectual and social practice which must be guided by fundamental beliefs and theories (Carr and Kemmis, 1986). The underlying principle that 'beliefs are the best indicators of the decisions individuals make throughout their lives' is evident in the early philosophical writings of Dewey (1933) and more recently Bandura (1986). Following this principle it is commonly accepted that teachers' beliefs influence decision making and thus classroom teaching practice. However, there has been relatively little focused research on understanding the 'things and ways that teachers believe' (Pajares, 1992; Tillema, 1995) or on tracing the development of teachers' beliefs from preservice through to inservice (Kagan, 1992a).

In a review of the teacher belief literature Pajares (1992) suggests that the avoidance of explicit studies on teachers' theories and beliefs is due to the difficulty of defining teachers' beliefs clearly, coupled with the perception that teachers' beliefs are 'messy' and do not readily suit empirical investigation. This lack of clear definition is reflected in the range of terms used by researchers to describe teachers' beliefs: world images (Wubbels, 1992); pedagogical beliefs

(Kagan and Tippins, 1991); images (Calderhead and Robson, 1991); preconceptions (Clark, 1988; Corporaal, 1988; Weinstein, 1989, 1990; Wubbels, 1992); implicit theories (Clark, 1988; Weinstein, 1989, 1990); teacher perspectives (Goodman, 1988; Tabachnick and Zeichner, 1984); intuitive screens (Goodman, 1988); prior beliefs (Feiman-Nemser and Buchmann, 1986); and, latent culture (Tabachnick and Zeichner, 1984). Clandinin and Connelly (1987) suggest that the research on teacher beliefs reflects the use of a range of different terminology for essentially the same thing, that is, 'how the personal is being conceptualized' (1987, p. 487).

The distinctly personal nature of teachers' beliefs contributes to the influence they exert over teachers' conceptual change and subsequent teaching practice. Beliefs draw their power from previous personal episodes or experiences and have a strong affective and evaluative component (Nespor, 1987). The 'episodic' character of beliefs, noted also in the writings of Goodman (1988) and Calderhead and Robson (1991), supports Nespor's assertion that beliefs, although idiosyncratic, are far more influential in determining teachers' decisions and behaviours than knowledge. In line with the aforementioned researchers, Pajares concludes that it is the 'potent affective, evaluative and episodic nature of beliefs' that makes them a filter through which new information and situations are interpreted (1992, p. 325). Pintrich *et al.* (1993) cautioned against ignoring the powerful affective and emotional aspects of teachers' beliefs.

Studies by Cole (1989) demonstrate that student teachers have implicit thoughts, ideas and beliefs about education, teaching and learning which provide the personal foundations upon which novice teachers build their professional practice. Bolin (1988) claims that individuals, during the course of their pre-service teacher education, are exposed to personal and social meanings and experiences which are 'screened' through their private, often implicit, conceptions of teaching which he terms their 'latent philosophy of education'. Goodman (1988) refers to these preconceptions as 'intuitive screens', while Calderhead and Robson (1991) report students holding particular 'images'. While such studies contribute to an understanding of the nature and function of student teachers' implicit beliefs and theories, they provide limited insight into the genesis and development of these prior beliefs.

Student teachers enter pre-service teacher education with a body of values, commitments, orientations and practices about teachers, teaching, students and classrooms developed from their 'apprenticeship of observation' as school students (Lortie, 1975). Thus the socialization of prospective teachers has occurred before pre-service teacher education commences. Contributing to this early socialization there is often a critical schooling experience provided by the teaching practices of an influential teacher (Nespor, 1987). This experience provides a 'template' for the future teaching practice of the student (prospective teacher). That student teachers' beliefs and preconceptions are formed as a result of their socialization as students is not in itself unexpected or problematic. However, the enduring nature of student teachers' beliefs and preconceptions, formed predominantly without understanding of pedagogical principles and theories, raises significant concerns for teacher educators.

Common to the research on teachers' theories and beliefs is continued evidence of the robust nature of the preconceptions or beliefs of pre-service student teachers. Goodman (1988) reports that students, when exposed to new ideas or experiences tend to act first on an intuitive rather than intellectual level, rejecting those new ideas (no matter how soundly argued) that contradict the students' intuitive screens (preconceptions). Clark (1988) reports that students' implicit understandings and beliefs about teaching can be adhered to even in the face of considerable evidence that demonstrates they are in some way flawed, incomplete, erroneous or unsound. Wubbels (1992) attributes the tenacity of student teachers' beliefs to the students' long 'apprenticeship' as pupils, the implicit nature of the beliefs, and, the failure of teacher education to 'reach the world images' of their pre-service teacher education students. In a more recent study student teachers' implicit beliefs are shown typically to contradict what is commonly accepted as effective teaching and reflect an 'unrealistic optimism' of their future abilities as teachers (Richards and Killen, 1994).

Research demonstrates that pre-service teacher education students enter university with preconceptions of teachers, teaching, students and classrooms, and, further, that these preconceptions persist through the course of their pre-service teacher education and subsequent years of teaching. Preservice teacher education programmes fail to have the expected influence over beginning teachers' underlying attitudes or consequent behaviours (Zeichner, 1986) and thus do not appear to engage students in conceptual change (Kagan, 1992a; Richards and Killen, 1994; Tillema, 1995). The overwhelming message from the research is that teacher education programmes need to reconceptualize their programmes to ensure that educational beliefs are an explicit rather than implicit part of teacher education.

The conceptual change literature offers an insight into processes through which student teachers could explore the adequacy of their beliefs and preconceptions about teachers and teaching. Posner *et al.*, (1982) propose that students' preconceptions can be revised or replaced with more appropriate conceptions through a time-consuming procedure involving: (1) encouraging and enabling students to make explicit their typically implicit pre-existing beliefs and preconceptions; (2) exposing and challenging the students with the inadequacy of their beliefs and preconceptions (if appropriate); and (3) allowing extended time for students to explore, elaborate and finally integrate new conceptions into their existing belief systems. It is acknowledged that recently some teacher education institutions have undergone radical changes in the nature of preservice courses through introducing self and collaborative reflection as a means of confronting personal beliefs (Clark, 1988; Kagan, 1992a, 1992b). Tillema (1998), in a recent study, explores the viability of a model which he suggests can be used to interpret belief change in student teachers during the learning to teach process.

Drawing on the conceptual change literature and the work of Tillema (1998) this writer asserts that a necessary first step in the process of conceptual change is the articulation and exploration of beginning teachers' beliefs and preconceptions. This is to be supported by participation in collaborative activities designed to challenge their beliefs and preconceptions and time allowed for the investigation of alternative perspectives. This chapter reports on stage one of a longitudinal study that traced the changing conceptions of student teachers engaged in pre-service teacher education. The paper describes the different activities used to enable a small group of student teachers, in the initial stage of their pre-service teacher education, to make explicit and explore their personal beliefs and preconceptions about teachers and teaching. Data are collected during these activities to enable the identification and reporting of the nature of the student teachers preconceptions on entry to teacher education. At the end of their preservice teacher education, a reflective group discussion and individual interviews provide the opportunity for participants to reflect upon and report their perceptions of the importance of the workshops conducted in the first 4 weeks of their preservice course.

Participants

The participants were nine pre-service beginning teachers (seven women, two men) enrolled in the 1 year graduate diploma of education at a metropolitan university in Australia (Anna, Damien, James, Justine, Louise, Mary, Rachel, Sally and Tami). All but one of the participants (Anna) were graduates of a BA Modern Asian Studies and were preparing to be teachers of Languages Other Than English (LOTE) in their specialist language (Japanese, Chinese or Indonesian). Anna held a BA in English and was preparing to teach as a secondary English and History teacher. Participation was voluntary and involved attendance at weekly, 2 hour workshops with the researcher. This chapter is restricted to a report on the effects of group workshops conducted early in the participants' preservice course.

Research design

Workshops were held in weeks 1–4 of the academic year and were structured to provide opportunities to make explicit and explore the participants' beliefs and preconceptions of teachers and teaching on entry to pre-service teacher education. Participants were encouraged to articulate and examine their personal theories of teachers and teaching through a range of structured, reflective activities including reflective written tasks, repertory grid interviews, written personal histories, peer interviews and reflective group discussions. Repertory grids revealed how the participants construed teachers and effective teaching and their image of self as teacher; written tasks and reflective discussions made explicit the participants' beliefs about teachers and teaching; and, personal histories and peer interviews exposed the origins and development of participants' beliefs and preconceptions. Each of these activities was designed to support the student teachers in their explication and exploration of their personal beliefs and theories while simultaneously providing qualitative data for the study. Interviews and reflective group discussions at the end of the year provided data to evaluate the effectiveness of these initial workshops. The workshops were typically of 2 hours duration and were designed to be interactive and reflective.

In keeping with the researcher's commitment to be explicit with the participants about the purposes and intentions of this study and of the workshops, the biographical transformation model (Knowles, 1992, p. 137), (Figure 13.1) was presented to the students as a theoretical model. This model described the beginning teacher's schema or 'way of understanding or resolving present and future contexts, . . . a cognitive filter and a basis for future teacher-centred classroom practices' (Knowles, 1992, p. 138).

Data collection

Elucidating the participants' beliefs and conceptions of teachers and teaching and images of 'self as teacher' is both complex and abstract, since much of the data sought are personal and typically tacit in nature. A number of different data collection procedures contributed to the validity of the study. Following the process of triangulation demonstrated by Morine-Dershimer (1983, 1993), each data set served to test, corroborate and elaborate on the others, and each contributed to the emerging findings which were subject to revision and reassessment as subsequent data were collected and analysed.

Written tasks: beliefs about teachers and teaching

In preparation for the compilation of written personal histories, participants completed written responses to questions about the participants' conceptions of teaching. Responses to these statements were further explored through peer interviews that were audiotaped and transcribed for subsequent analysis. The schedule of questions was informed, in part, by the work of Kagan and Tippins

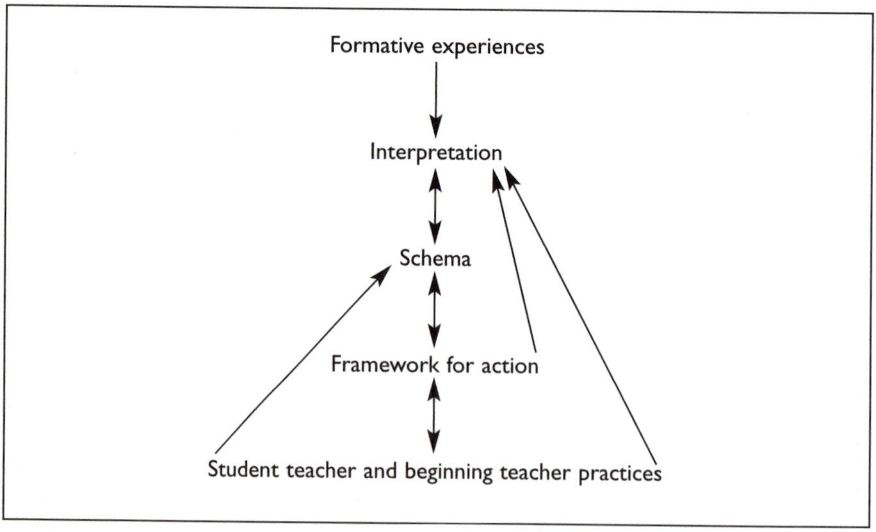

Figure 13.1 Biographical transformation model linking experience with beginning teachers' behaviours.

Source: Knowles, 1992, p. 137.

(1991), who investigated student teachers' pedagogical beliefs through consideration of their responses to interview questions.

Repertory grid interviews

The repertory grid technique was developed by Kelly (1955) to make explicit, and come to an understanding of personal constructs, that is, the ways in which persons interpret and experience particular aspects of their world. Repertory grids serve to access the implicit theories of the teachers through utilizing the teachers own conceptual apparatus (Corporaal, 1991) resulting in a two-dimensional numerical matrix capable of statistical analysis. Computer analysis of the participants ratings was conducted as part of the more extensive longitudinal study but is not reported in this chapter. This chapter restricts itself to reporting the content analysis of the constructs which provides insight into what aspects of the teaching and learning world contribute to the participants' constructions of effective teachers and effective teaching. Categories emerging empirically from the data were identified and frequencies of categories noted.

Personal histories

The writing of personal histories has emerged as one form of teachers' narratives, through which teachers' implicit beliefs and theories can be made explicit and subsequently explored. The use of personal histories is informed primarily by the work of Knowles and Holt-Reynolds who accept that student teachers' prior experiences are powerful instructors and that 'students cannot be *talked out* of what they know and believe about schools' (original emphasis) (1991, p. 103). Personal histories have been demonstrated to provide: a means to make explicit the hitherto tacit and unexamined beliefs and preconceptions of student teachers; a springboard from which student teachers can explore, experience and, if appropriate, adopt alternative conceptions; an opportunity for student teachers to gain an insight into their knowledge base of teaching and, evidence of the student teachers' image of self as teacher (Bullough 1991, 1992; Bullough and Gitlin, 1991; Cole and Knowles, 1993; Knowles and Holt-Reynolds, 1991).

Personal histories can take many forms but in general are accepted to be retrospective constructions by a person (in either written or spoken form), of a part of their life relevant to the particular inquiry. The thinking and writing processes involved in the compilation of a personal history were modelled by the researcher who 'walked the participants through' the processes undertaken in the writing of her own personal history. Utilizing stimulus questions that were to be used subsequently by the participants, the researcher related her confusion, frustration and sense of fulfilment in making explicit those formative experiences that shaped her journey towards becoming a teacher. The researcher's completed personal history was presented to the participants in different forms, diagrams, brief notes, narratives, and tabulations, in an effort to reinforce that personal histories can be completed in a number of ways. Participants were given a list of stimulus questions as an aid to writing their own personal histories. At this initial stage the researcher's support was provided as a scaffold to participants who were embarking on a task with which they were unfamiliar and which could also be considered to be both challenging and, for some, confronting.

Peer interviews

The participants formed small peer groups (two or three) to share relevant issues about the development and the outcomes of their personal histories. The purpose of the interviews was to allow the participants the opportunity to articulate and to explore their personal histories and those of their their peers. The articulation of personal histories enabled the participants to place the personal and idiosyncratic process of becoming a teacher within the context of their evolving life stories. According to Tyson (1991) participation in peer interviews compelled participants to make their own thinking and understandings more explicit in response to probing questions by their peers. In this way the dialogue emerging in the discussions reflected the hitherto private, personal dialogue of the participants (Holt-Reynolds, 1991) and as such provided a 'window' into participants' thinking (Cole and Knowles, 1993, p. 467). Peer interviews were audio-taped and transcribed subsequently for analysis together with the participants' written personal history documents.

Analysis of data

The raw data available for analysis comprised: responses to written tasks; repertory grid constructs; personal history documents; and, transcripts from audio tape recordings of guided group reflections, peer interviews, and group discussions. Data were first transferred to the text analysis computer programme 'Textbase Alpha' to assist with the organization, coding and sorting stages of analysis (Tesch, 1989). Textbase Alpha allowed the researcher to organize data for analysis, attach codes to segments of text (text can have multiple codes attached and segments can overlap), sort segments of text according to codes assigned, and quantify the frequency of occurrence of specific codes.

Analysis of the data from the different sources was an ongoing activity throughout the course of this study. At the outset, the transcripts were read by the researcher and significant segments of text were identified and assigned tentative, descriptive codes. After successive readings (total of three), codes were refined and final codes assigned. The empirically grounded approach of having codes emerge from the data enabled the researcher to be more 'open-minded and context-sensitive' (Miles and Huberman, 1984, p. 57) and to have some confidence that the analysis reflected more accurately the perceptions of the participants.

Findings

Findings are reported first under the key data sources: written beliefs about teachers and teaching, repertory grid constructs, and, personal histories and related peer interviews. These are followed by a summary that identifies key themes in the participants' beliefs and preconceptions of teachers and teaching evident during the first 4 weeks of their pre-service teacher education course. Finally, data are presented from reflective group discussions and individual interviews conducted with participants at the end of the year as an evaluation of the effectiveness of the early workshops.

Beliefs about teachers and teaching

Analysis of the participants' conceptions of teachers and teaching and their perceived strengths and weaknesses as teachers and subsequent peer interviews resulted in the identification of four main themes.

1. The relationships established between teachers and their students emerged as an important criterion of good teaching of all but two participants (Mary and Tami). The teacher/student relationship was described in terms of affective factors such as genuine care, interest and respect for the students as individual members of the class. A key feature of many of the participants' preconceptions of good teachers and teaching was that teachers should be approachable and available to students both within and outside the classroom.
2. Personal attributes of teachers with particular reference to teachers' affective attributes were portrayed as attributes of good teachers by all participants. Often these affective attributes were embedded in descriptions of teacher/student relationships, or in the ways good teachers established appropriate classroom management. The data revealed that the participants' preconceptions of good teachers included teachers who were caring, compassionate, friendly, positive and who possessed a sense of fun and good humour.
3. Teachers' content knowledge was referred to explicitly by some of the participants while teachers' procedural knowledge was only referred to explicitly by Mary and was implicit in the data of Tami and Louise. Tami viewed content knowledge as essential to good teaching and further suggested that good teachers were able to communicate that knowledge clearly to their students. Anna, James, Justine and Mary also acknowledged the importance of teachers' content knowledge to good teaching. Damien and Rachel made no references to any forms of teachers' knowledge in their written responses or associated peer interviews.

   There was agreement by some of the participants (James, Louise, Mary, Sally and Tami) that good teachers had the ability to 'impart information to their students' in interesting and creative ways. Only Mary, however, referred explicitly to teachers' pedagogical knowledge. Mary proposed that good teachers required expertise in their lesson planning and implementation in order that they could identify and subsequently meet the different needs of their students.
4. Classroom management skills were nominated as important attributes of

> good teachers by four of the participants (Anna, Damien, Mary and Rachel). A caveat was included, however, that effective classroom management should ideally be established through non-authoritarian, non-critical means such as support, encouragement and a focus on the positive achievements of students. Those participants who identified a lack of classroom management as a personal weakness (Justine, Sally) indicated that they expected to develop these abilities through classroom practice.

When considering their own strengths as teachers, participants focused predominantly on personal characteristics which they identified as attributes of good teachers and good teaching. In contrast, the participants' self-reported weaknesses reflected a number of quite distinct categories. Personal attributes presented as strengths included personal, predominantly affective attributes such as having caring, understanding, compassionate, genuine and humorous natures. In addition to these affective attributes, participants nominated specific skills that they perceived reflected their personal teaching strengths: 'Positive nature and good communication skills, particularly the ability to listen' (Justine).

Participants were not as forthcoming with their perceived weaknesses and often offered only very brief comments. Weaknesses included references to personal attributes, skills and the lack of both content and pedagogical knowledge. Participants' weaknesses included lack of confidence and fears of taking on too much, or becoming too involved with students. The demanding nature of teaching was acknowledged by Anna and Damien who expressed

Table 13.1 Repertory Grid No. 1. Categories of elicited constructs with verbatim examples from participants

Category	*Verbatim examples from participants*	*F*
Personal attributes of teachers	Sincere and understanding; kind; very caring. boring; funny; interesting; communicates well; ability to listen and respond positively; sexist.	53%
Elements of teachers' preparation and classroom practice	Totally organised for lessons; concise and coherent lessons; imparts information in a captivating way; questioning techniques need to be better.	28%
Relationship with students	Respects students as individuals; good rapport with students; students seen as human; desire to learn about students' ideas.	9%
Knowledge of content	Confident in subject matter; good subject matter knowledge.	7%
Classroom management	Good classroom management skills; well controlled classroom management.	7%
Knowledge of teaching and learning theory	Knowledge of theories of effective learning; teaches from students' prior knowledge.	2%

concerns regarding lack of time management and organizational skills. Lack of content knowledge was identified as a personal weakness by both Damien and James, in particular, their fluency in the Japanese language (Japanese language was their main teaching area).

To summarize, the participants' preconceptions of good teachers and good teaching were dominated by affective elements such as establishing caring, compassionate relationships between students and teachers. Teachers' personal qualities such as being fun, friendly, approachable and available to students both within and outside the classroom were viewed by the participants as essential attributes of good teachers. In addition, good teaching was perceived as being dependent upon the teachers' enthusiasm and interest in their subject and in the students within their classes. Participants' self-reported strengths and weaknesses as teachers were revealed also as predominantly affective attributes. Where personal weaknesses were acknowledged, participants expected these weaknesses to be addressed through teaching experience rather than on-campus teacher education courses. At this very early stage of their teacher education course it was apparent that participants, with the exception of Mary, failed to acknowledge explicitly that good teaching was informed by any theoretical knowledge.

Content analysis of repertory grid constructs

Six categories emerged from the composite content analysis of the elicited constructs of seven of the nine participants (two participants did not complete grids). The six categories with verbatim examples taken from participants' repertory grids are presented in Table 13.1 with the frequency distribution of participants' elicited constructs across categories expressed as a percentage of the participants' total constructs. Constructs were clustered predominantly within two categories: personal attributes of teachers and elements of teachers' preparation and classroom practice, which together accounted for 81 per cent of the total elicited constructs.

The constructs elicited from the participants in these initial repertory grids reflected the participants' perceptions of effective teaching at the beginning of their graduate diploma course. It was apparent that the majority of the participants construed effective teaching primarily in terms of teachers' personal characteristics, in particular, affective characteristics. The constructs revealed that participants referred to some aspects of teachers' preparation and classroom practice in their conceptions of effective teachers. With the exception of one participant (Mary), however, there was no acknowledgement of teachers' theoretical knowledge or of the thinking underlying teachers' classroom practice. The data showed that in addition to teachers' affective attributes and sound content knowledge, Mary construed effective teachers in terms of teacher' theoretical knowledge.

Personal histories and peer interviews

Following completion of the written activities reported above, participants were introduced to the writing of personal histories. The personal histories and related peer interviews exposed how the participants' previous experiences of schooling, childhood, youth, and interactions in families and society served to shape the ways the participants viewed teachers and teaching at the beginning of their pre-service teacher education course.

As was evident from other data sources (repertory grids and written workshop tasks), the participants recalled primarily those teachers, or experiences of teaching, that were represented by caring teachers who were interested in their students and able to give them individual attention. There was an emphasis on the affective attributes of teachers. Teacher role models were viewed as people who nurtured students, much like parents, and people who took the time and energy to care. These caring teachers were credited with having influenced the participants' preconceptions of teachers and teaching. The most positive of these teachers were credited as important role models for the participants: 'I was encouraged and nurtured, they just helped me so much . . . I had that close school environment that I just thrived on, I loved it' (*Sally*).

Many of the participants reported negative personal school experiences. The participants believed that as future teachers, they could 'do it [teach] better' than many teachers from their own schooling experiences. Participants related experiences of how they were unhappy or unsuccessful in school due to the actions of uncaring and insensitive teachers. The implication was that since 'bad teachers' were able to be identified as uncaring and insensitive, the participants recognized in themselves the characteristics of the other extreme – 'good teachers'. Anna, Rachel, Justine and Louise nominated their early schooling experiences as having influenced their preconceptions of teaching with regard to the importance of teachers fostering the self-confidence and self-esteem of students.

> I can now see the value of teachers giving personal attention, . . . the results were not only academic, but also [an improvement] in self confidence. In knowing that you can achieve something and that you have the support of the teacher to catch you again if you should fall (*Louise*).

Mary was unique among the participants in that, through her written personal history, she articulated her awareness of the complexity of learning to teach and awareness that teaching involved understanding of both propositional and procedural knowledge. Mary acknowledged that she still had much to learn in these areas. 'I am fully aware that teaching is a thinking, comprehensive and skilful activity demanding important personal qualities and professional knowledge. Indeed there is a great deal to be learned about teaching' (*Mary*).

Summary of the findings

Participants' beliefs and preconceptions of teachers and teaching at the beginning of their pre-service teacher education course

The participants at this early stage of their teacher education course portrayed preconceptions of teachers and teaching which were formed from their own experiences as students, and were concerned primarily with teachers' personal characteristics of a predominantly affective nature. Good teachers were considered to hold some degree of content or subject matter knowledge which they imparted to students in interesting ways. Teachers' knowledge and expertise was, for the most part, considered to be a product of teachers' personalities, personal experiences and teaching experience.

One of the data sources (reflective written tasks) provided evidence of Tami, Louise and Mary having understandings of teachers' knowledge that extended beyond subject matter knowledge. For Tami and Louise this was the only indication that their preconception of teaching included teachers' knowledge of pedagogy and principles of teaching and learning theory. However, Mary demonstrated consistently a conception of teaching that included understanding of relationships between teachers' knowledge of content, pedagogy and student learning. Mary recognized that teaching was represented by an interdependence of teachers' cognition and practice.

Participants viewed themselves as caring and compassionate with genuine interests in working with children and so identified strongly with their preconceptions of good teachers. Some participants acknowledged that they lacked knowledge of both content and classroom management, however, they expected such knowledge to be developed through practical experience as opposed to teacher education instruction at university. This indicated that they perceived teaching to be predominantly a skills-based activity requiring procedural knowledge developed through repeated practice.

Participants' reflections on and perceptions of the effectiveness of the weeks 1–4 workshops

At the end of the year participants engaged in both group reflective discussions and individual interviews with the researcher as part of the longitudinal study. During these occasions participants identified specific elements of the early workshops as contributing to the development of their beginning teachers' 'knowledge in action'. These are reported below with the support of salient quotes from the data.

Making explicit and exploring participants' personal beliefs and theories was the key principle underlying the workshops reported in this paper. Participants reported that the workshop activities involving personal and collaborative reflections challenged them to reflect critically on their personal beliefs about teaching that had formed predominantly through their own experiences as school students. Both Anna and Damien suggested that the critical aspect of these activities was the articulation and, in particular, the subsequent justification and defence of their personal beliefs among their peers.

> Sometimes the group meetings really challenged me to re-think my ideas. I didn't like it at first, I can tell you, I really resisted changing what I believed about teaching. . . . That was what was so powerful about our group, we had the chance to talk about our beliefs and ideas about teaching and were

> challenged, I suppose, to come up with plausible explanations of why we were thinking the way we were. (*Anna*)

> You got us reflecting on what we believed about teaching, on what we thought we knew about teaching. . . . And I think if we weren't able to talk about it we wouldn't be able to learn from our reflections. . . . [From] being able to express it, being able to talk about it, I began to make links and understand why I thought about teaching the way I did. (*Damien*)

Anna argued that only through making explicit her beliefs and exploring the genesis of such beliefs was she, as a beginning teacher, able to take on new conceptual knowledge and understandings of teaching.

> I think that is a realization that I wouldn't have come to without the group workshops. I don't think I would have even ever taken the energy to question why I believed what I did, or where I was coming from as a teacher. I think that unless the focus is placed on examining yourself, where you are coming from, your own beliefs, you can't move ahead, you can't take on new ideas. (*Anna*)

Participants agreed that although making explicit and exploring their beliefs and preconceptions was confronting, it gave them greater insight into themselves as beginning teachers and their conceptions of teaching. Through the experiences provided within the group workshops they were more willing and able to engage in self-reflection during their subsequent practicum experiences.

> Once you begin to evaluate yourself you have to be honest about what you are teaching and why, so you have to know how to reflect honestly on your own teaching. I think we have done a lot of that sort of thing in this group and it was very scary for me to look so closely at myself and talk about myself with you all. But it has allowed me to get used to looking at my own teaching and assessing it objectively and so that can only help me be a better teacher. (*Tami*)

Participants agreed that their exploration of personal beliefs and theories was ideally a collaborative activity that should be available from the beginning of the pre-service course. This was evident through repeated references to the benefits of collaboration within the workshops and references to the confusion portrayed by peers who were not members of the group. Anna suggested that the process encouraged self discovery of misconceptions and thereby provided a 'path' for personally driven conceptual change.

> I think there are some students who don't have the opportunity to do what we did in the workshops, they only take all the university knowledge in on an intellectual level, there is no conceptual change. They don't explore their own beliefs and say well 'why do I think like that?' and acknowledge that 'I think like that because that was my experience as a student, being a teacher is different, now lets have a look at what good teaching should be for both

> the student and the teacher.' I mean you had us looking at what we believed, what each other believed and why, and then tying in what we did in classes. (*Anna*)

> It is the process that is important, the way you [researcher] did it. The self reflection and group discussions in our group allowed me to discover where I was perhaps a bit misguided in my beliefs and thinking, rather than you or someone just telling me I was wrong. (*Anna*)

Some participants, at the end of their teacher preparation, acknowledged that without engaging in the articulation and examination of their own beliefs they would have been unlikely to have been receptive to new ideas encountered during their teacher preparation. Anna suggested that she was not 'ready to learn anything new at the beginning of the year because I thought I was right anyway'. The participants argued that making explicit and exploring their personal beliefs and theories about teachers and teaching was critical to their subsequent understandings of the roles of personal beliefs and theories and of propositional and procedural knowledge to learning to teach effectively.

Peer support and collaboration within the group workshops offered participants collegial support that was not available from other sources or to other student teachers in their graduate diploma course. Participants reported that the size and structure of the group, the regular meetings, the structured activities requiring group reflection, the guidance provided by the researcher and the opportunities for sharing ideas and concerns, countered their initial feelings of isolation and of having to 'tackle the journey to beginning teaching alone'. The group meetings provided a forum through which they were able to come to terms with conceptions of teaching that in many cases contradicted their own long-held beliefs. The structured reflection on their own beliefs and personal theories conducted within the group workshops provided for some participants a model for their own personal reflection outside of the group's activities:

> Being able to talk issues through and having Ruth to guide and question us in order to further our understanding. The group has enabled us to get a clearer understanding of the 'problems' we as student teachers experience, finding that these are common to us all, and then being able to talk through and think about how to resolve them. It's given me the opportunity to have a more guided way to reflect on my teaching. (*Justine*)

> Because of the support I got from the group. You know if you are alone out there you don't get an opportunity like you gave us. It wasn't just a group getting together though, we really worked quite hard on group reflection and resolving any issues that arose. (*Mary*)

The group workshops provided opportunities to make explicit and explore areas of their own beliefs and conceptions that they would not necessarily have subjected to examination under the standard course requirements. Anna reported that she would not have 'even taken the energy to question why I believed what I did or where I was coming from as a teacher' without the collegial support of the group. For many of the participants it was their regular participation in the group workshops that contributed most strongly to their changing conceptions of 'teachers as colleagues'. The peer support that was cultivated in the group, gave rise to participants viewing teaching as a collaborative, rather than an individual, endeavour.

> I mean it was pretty scary at first I didn't like being challenged by you [Ruth] or the other guys but it was worth going through it all because I learned so much and eventually I realized that I could take on new ideas and look at other approaches without being threatened. Yes it was in that group that I learnt about being a collaborative teacher. (*Anna*)

In support of the group workshops, participants all recommended the establishment of similar cohorts that would facilitate: making explicit and exploring personal preconceptions of teaching; reflecting on the thinking underlying effective teaching practice; and, integrating theoretical and practical components of the learning to teach process.

Conclusion

The participants began their graduate diploma of education with preconceptions of teachers and teaching which were formed as a consequence of their own experiences of schooling and their personal life experiences, including parenting. At this early stage of their teacher preparation, the participants portrayed conceptions of teaching which were predominantly founded on their 'apprenticeships of observation' as school students. As school students, the participants would have had limited, if any, access to the pedagogical purposes and principles underlying teaching and learning. The participants' preconceptions of teaching were, in the first 4 weeks, limited to a delivery or transmission model of teaching (Stones, 1992). Their perceptions of teachers' knowledge were restricted to content knowledge that was conveyed to students in 'interesting ways'. At this initial stage of pre-service teacher education participants (with the exception of Mary) failed to acknowledge any understanding of relationships between the propositional and procedural knowledge of teaching. Teaching was perceived as a practical endeavour to which particular people were suited due to their innate, essentially affective attributes.

A preoccupation with teachers' affective attributes allowed participants to align their images of 'self as teacher' close to their conceptions of good teachers and resulted in participants displaying 'unrealistic optimism' of their own, as yet untested, potential as teachers. Although acknowledging their own lack of knowledge in some areas (primarily with regard to what they refer to as the 'what' and the 'how' of teaching), the participants assumed, at the beginning of their teacher education course, that their positive personal attributes would ensure their own success as teachers when they too had the benefit of repeated opportunities for classroom practice.

The participants failed to recognize the importance of pedagogical knowledge. They perceived that teachers' strategies for the delivery of content were learned largely through trial and error as a result of years of teaching experience in the classroom. The literature reveals that such naive preconceptions are not atypical of beginning teachers entering preservice teacher education courses. Many studies have determined that the preconceptions of student teachers, although often naive and misinformed, are very robust in nature and evidence from the literature suggests that in many cases teacher education courses have little impact on addressing these misconceptions (Kagan, 1992a, 1992b; Rust, 1994; Tann, 1993; Weinstein, 1989).

The group workshops provided early opportunities for beginning teachers to make explicit and examine their personal beliefs and preconceptions through the writing of personal histories, repertory grid interviews, and written reflections on teachers and teaching. The collaborative nature of the group activities demanded that participants examine and justify their beliefs about teachers and teaching in light of the knowledge and experiences of themselves and their peers. Acknowledging the robust nature of beginning teachers' beliefs and preconceptions, often in the face of new and contradictory knowledge and experiences, the process adopted in the group workshops allowed beginning teachers to come to their own new conceptual understandings of teachers and teaching:

> I feel like I haven't just been told that what I believed and really held on to about teaching was wrong, but it is like I've been given the opportunity in this group to examine my own beliefs and test them against new ideas and knowledge and see that maybe they don't fit. I think it's a progressive thing. I think that you [researcher] deliberately set it up like that. You set out to make us examine our own beliefs and link what we thought we believed to what the others here at university were trying to teach us and to what we experienced at [practicum] and it worked. (*Anna)*

References

Bandura, A. (1986) *Social Foundations of Thought and Action: A Social Cognitive Theory*, Englewood Cliffs, NJ: Prentice-Hall.

Bolin, F. S.(1988) 'Helping student teachers think about teaching', *Journal of Teacher Education* 40(2): 10–19.

Bullough, R. V. (1991) 'Exploring personal teaching metaphors in preservice teacher education', *Journal of Teacher Education* 42(1): 43–51.

—— (1992) 'Beginning teacher curriculum decision making, personal teaching metaphors, and teacher education', *Teaching and Teacher Education* 8(3): 239–52.

Bullough, R. V. and Gitlin, A. D. (1991) 'Educative communities and the development of the reflective practitioner', in B. R. Tabachnich and K. Zeichner (eds) *Issues and Practices in Inquiry-Oriented Teacher Education*, London: Falmer Press.

Calderhead, J. and Robson, M. (1991) 'Images of teaching: student teachers' early conceptions of classroom practice', *Teaching and Teacher Education* 7(1): 1–8.

Carr, W. and Kemmis, S. (1986) *Becoming Critical: Educational Knowledge and Action Research*, Victoria: Deakin University Press.
Clandinin, D. J. and Connelly, F. M. (1987) 'Teachers' personal knowledge: what counts as "personal" in studies of the personal', *Journal of curriculum Studies* 19(6): 487–500.
Clark, C. M. (1988) 'Asking the right question about teacher preparation: contributions of research on teacher thinking', *Educational Researcher* 17(2): 5–12.
Cole, A. L. (1989) 'Making explicit implicit theories of teaching: starting points in preservice programmes', paper presented at the annual meeting of the American Educational Research Association, San Francisco, CA.
Cole, A. L. and Knowles, J. G. (1993) 'Shattered images: Understanding expectations and realities of field experience', *Teaching and Teacher Education* 9(5/6): 457–71.
Corporaal, A. H. (1988) 'Building blocks for a theory of teacher education', doctorate, De Lier: ABC.
— (1991) 'Repertory grid research into cognitions of prospective primary school teachers', *Teaching and Teacher Education* 7(4): 315–29.
Dewey, J. (1933/1974) 'How we think: a restatement of the relation of reflective thinking to the educative process', in R. Archambault (eds) *John Dewey on Education: Selected Writings*, Chicago: Chicago University Press.
Feiman-Nemser, S. and Buchmann, M. (1986) 'The first year of teacher preparation: transition to pedagogical thinking?', *Journal of Curriculum Studies* 18(3): 239–56.
Goodman, J. (1988) 'Constructing a practical philosophy of teaching: A study of preservice teachers' professional perspectives', *Teaching and Teacher Education* 4(2): 121–37.
Holt-Reynolds, D. (1991) 'The dialogues of teacher education: entering and influencing preservice teachers' internal conversations' (Research report No. 91–4), The National Center for Research on Teacher Learning.
Kagan, D. M. (1992a) 'Implications of research on teacher belief', *Educational Psychologist* 27(1): 65–90.
— (1992b) 'Professional growth among preservice and beginning teachers', *Review of Educational Research*, 62(2): 129–69.
Kagan, D. M. and Tippins, D. J. (1991) 'How teachers' classroom cases express their pedagogical beliefs', *Journal of Teacher Education* 42(4): 281–91.
Kelly, G. A. (1955) *The Psychology of Personal Constructs*, New York: Norton.
Knowles, J. G. (1992) 'Models for understanding pre-service and beginning teachers' biographies. Illustrations from case studies', in I. F. Goodson (eds) *Studying Teachers' Lives*, London: Routledge.
Knowles, J. G. and Holt-Reynolds, D. (1991) 'Shaping pedagogies through personal histories in preservice teacher education', *Teachers College Record* 93(1): 87–113.
Lortie, D. (1975) *Schoolteacher*, Chicago: University of Chicago Press.
Miles, M. B. and Huberman, A. M. (1984) *Qualitative Data Analysis: A Source Book of New Methods*, London: Sage Publications.
Morine-Dershimer, G. (1983) 'Tapping teacher thinking through triangulation of data sets' (Information Analyses No. ED 251 434), National Institute of Education, Washington, DC.
— (1993) 'Tracing conceptual change in preservice teachers', *Teaching and Teacher Education* 9(1): 15–26.
Nespor, J. K. (1987) 'The role of beliefs in the practice of teaching', *Journal of Curriculum Studies* 19(4): 317–28.
Pajares, M. F. (1992) 'Teachers' beliefs and educational research: cleaning up a messy construct', *Review of Educational Research* 62(3): 307–32.

Pintrich, P. R., Marx, R. W. and Boyle, R. A. (1993) 'Beyond the cold conceptual change: the role of motivational beliefs and classroom contextual factors in the process of conceptual change', *Review of Educational Research* 63(2): 167–99.
Posner, G. J., Strike, K. A., Hewson, P. W. and Gertzog, W. A. (1982) 'Accommodation of a scientific conception: toward a theory of conceptual change', *Scientific Education* 66: 211–28.
Richards, C. and Killen, R. (1994) 'Preservice teachers' perceptions of the problems of beginning teachers', paper presented at the annual conference of the Australian Association for Research in Education, Newcastle, Australia.
Rust, F. O. (1994) 'The first year of teaching: it's not what they expected', *Teaching and Teacher Education* 10(2): 205–17.
Stones, E. (1992) *Quality Teaching A Sample of Cases*, London: Routledge.
Tabachnick, B. and Zeichner, K. M. (1984) 'The impact of student teaching experience on the development of teacher perspectives', *Journal of Teacher Education* 35(6): 28–36.
Tann, S. (1993) 'Eliciting student teachers' personal theories', in J. Calderhead and P. Gates (eds) *Conceptualizing Reflection in Teacher Development*, London: Falmer Press.
Tesch, R. (1989) *Textbase alpha. Computer software package*. Desert Hot Springs, CA: Qualitative Research Management.
Tillema, H. H. (1995) 'Changing the professional knowledge and beliefs of teachers: a training study', *Learning and Instruction* 5: 291–318.
—— (1998) 'Stability and change in student teachers' beliefs about teaching', *Teachers and Teaching: theory and Practice* 4: 217–28.
Tyson, P. (1991) 'Talking about lesson planning: the use of semi-structured interviews in teacher education', *Teacher Education Quarterly*, 18: 87–96.
Weinstein, C. S. (1989) 'Teacher education students' preconceptions of teaching', *Journal of Teacher Education* 40(2): 53–60.
—— (1990) 'Prospective elementary teachers' beliefs about teaching: Implications for teacher education', *Teaching and Teacher Education* 6(3): 279–90.
Wubbels, T. (1992) 'Taking account of student teachers' preconceptions', *Teaching and Teacher Education* 8(2): 137–49.
Zeichner, K. (1986) 'The practicum as an occasion for learning to teach', *The South Pacific Journal of Teacher Education* 14(2): 11–27.

Chapter 14

Shared and subjective in curriculum making

Lessons from Finnish teachers

Tapio Kosunen and Jyrki Huusko

Introduction

It is difficult to find a universal definition for the concept of curriculum, because there are several alternatives. Jackson (1992, p. 12) comes to the conclusion that when we define the concept of curriculum, 'all we can do in the final analysis is to proffer reasoned arguments in support of one definition over the other.'

There are two main approaches to studying the curriculum. It can be examined in the traditional sense as a course of study or – as teachers prefer to do – as an educative experience. In their work, teachers revise and apply continuously the written curriculum to create unique educative experiences for their pupils. Ultimately, application of the curriculum is always a question of the quality of learning and teaching, and of what or how the pupils learn, how they advance, and how their learning can be supported most effectively (for a more comprehensive analysis of the concept of curriculum for teachers see Kosunen 1994a, 1994b; Kosunen and Huusko, 1998).

The curriculum, therefore, can be studied as a text or as a process where pupils and teacher(s) interact in order to implement the objectives of education. In Finland, the curriculum has often been defined as 'a dynamic *process* that is constantly reacting to the results of evaluation and changes in the environment. The aims that have been set show the direction in which to go, but they are not to place restrictions on the tuition' (Framework Curriculum for the Comprehensive School (FCCS) 1994, p. 10). Defining the curriculum as a process accentuates its significance as an instrument for developing school. This emphasis is also an important starting point in this chapter, where teachers are examined both on an individual and group level, as developers of the curriculum of their school and thus, also, as developers of their own work and the entire school community.

In Finland the curriculum is an important instrument for directing education policy and promoting educational equality: 'The curriculum is an expression of the local decision-makers' political will as part of the national education policy' (FCCS, 1994, p. 4).

Finnish schools draft their own curricula independently on the basis of national guidelines. The foundations of the national core curriculum determine the social and cultural changes central for the development of the education

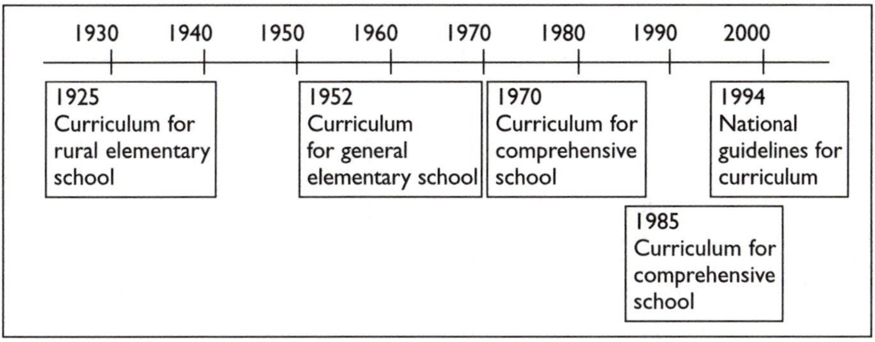

Figure 14.1 Curriculum reforms in the Finnish school system.

system, and the value basis of schoolwork. When the society as a whole is in a continuous state of change, curricula also need to be flexible. The significance of local decision-making and expertise and the needs of local actors have become strongly accentuated. The teachers have a high level of professionality and are experts on the possibilities and restrictions for successful schoolwork in their own working community and municipality. In this sense, they are the best possible experts for planning the curriculum for their own school.

Continuous Curriculum Reform

The interval between reforms of the national guidelines for curriculum has become shorter and shorter in Finland. This accelerating change is represented in Figure 14.1.

Since the mid-80s (1985 Curriculum for comprehensive school and 1994 National guidelines for curriculum) the responsibility for drawing up a curriculum increasingly has been transferred to the teachers. Since 1994, the national development work of curriculum has been informed by ongoing evaluation of the reform process.

The next national curriculum development projects are related to pre-school education. During the years 2000–1, every Finnish child under 6 years old gains the right to pre-school education. The curriculum work began in autumn 1999, and the new national guidelines for curriculum had a planned date for introduction of 1 August 2000 when legislation on pre-school education was to be enacted.

After the publication of the guidelines for curriculum, the providers of education have 1 year to prepare the local curricula. Renewal of the foundations of the curriculum for comprehensive school is to commence in 2002.

Teachers and the teacher community in the school-based curriculum process

The idea of the teacher as the maker of his or her own curriculum has been a consideration when drafting curriculum guidelines. It has been presumed that this might transform the teacher's work from practices dictated by habits and traditions into a more reflective direction. The process itself has been seen as a strategy for supporting the professional growth of teachers (Kosunen and Huusko, 1998).

The work and role of a teacher are not necessarily collegial and reflective. Teacher isolation, indviduality, presentism and conservatism have been identified as characteristic of teacher's work (Berg 1985; Lortie 1975). It is essential in developing school, as in developing the school's curriculum, to provide teachers with instruments for analysing their working community and individual work. An important dimension of this work is to expose embedded beliefs and routines to enable teachers to reflect critically on their practice. More traditional approaches to teacher learning and curriculum development are contrasted with this reflective turn in Table 14.1.

What characteristics are evident among Finnish teachers as they engage in the curriculum process?

In this chapter, on the basis of two extensive empirical studies, the status and significance of individual teachers, teacher community in the curriculum process and in developing the school are critically analysed. Data are selected from the following studies:

- A study (Kosunen, 1994) that combines quantitative and qualitative approaches while focusing on individual class teachers as planners of their teaching and users and developers of the written curriculum.
- An ethnographic case study (Huusko, 1999) that includes interviews, observations and document analysis of a primary school teacher and the teacher's school community as planners and developers of the curriculum.

Evidence from both of these studies is presented separately.

From individual to collaboration: teachers as curriculum planners

The essential factors in developing curriculum and schools are individual teachers, groups of teachers, and the teacher community. The aim of Kosunen's study (1994a; see also Kosunen 1994b) was to understand primary school teachers' interpretations of the intended curriculum and to ascertain how the intended curriculum and curriculum development are related to their instructional planning and teaching practices. Curriculum knowledge was examined as an integral part of teachers' practical knowledge.

The theoretical background of this study can be found in studies of teachers' thinking, studies of primary school teachers' work and studies of teachers' professional development. In addition, theoretical aspects applicable to the study are found in curriculum studies and studies of teachers' instructional planning. Accordingly, the most important theoretical aspects and main concepts in this study are found in three models: Calderhead's (1988) model of Knowledge Use in Teaching, Jaggar's (1989) model of Teachers' Sources of Knowledge and Ways of Learning and Cornett *et al.* (1992) model of Analysis of the Impact of Teacher Personal Practical Theories on their curricular and instructional decision making.

The methods used to determine the views of primary school teachers were both quantitative andqualitative: a questionnaire with attitude scales and open questions (n=85), in-depth theme interviews, journal writing, and thinking aloud techniques in authentic instructional planning situations.

The results indicate that teachers' sex, the amount of working experience they have as well as their participation in curriculum development projects were connected with attitudes the teachers have towards the use and development of the curriculum. In addition, the three background factors mentioned above were related to the willingness of the teachers to put the curriculum into practice.

Experienced teachers possess a broad and many-sided body of knowledge related to learning and instruction. They use this practical knowledge in constructing their teaching practice. Professional experience and broad knowledge of instructional and management routines seem to enable experienced teachers to understand essential ideas and principles written in the curriculum and to put them into practice. Accordingly, experienced teachers are able to process 'the spirit' and the goals of the curriculum in planning their instruction. Experienced teachers are more able than their less experienced colleagues to connect curricular goals with pupil learning and learning situations.

Of special interest was how the experienced teachers, as members of planning teams developing the curriculum, interpreted the written curriculum. These curriculum-makers had internalized the core idea of the curriculum innovation. They used student-oriented teaching methods more often than other teachers and were more often development-oriented. They tended also to individualize and differentiate their instruction more often than their less experienced colleagues. The curriculum-makers stressed the importance of using the written curriculum as a basis for their instructional planning. They also showed consideration for collegiality in their work and in developing the curriculum for school. In this study teachers were considered as potential

Table 14.1 Teacher community v teacher isolation.

Teacher community in the school's curriculum process	*Teacher isolation in the school's curriculum process*
The community has the ability to analyze itself and to conduct open, reflective discussions	Openness and reflectivity do not reach the entire community; there is little professional dialogue
The community is willing to develop its culture of practice in order to improve its basic task	Teachers create their own curriculum without input from others
The community is able to work interactively- all members actively participate in the planning process with a critical perspective	Interaction is limited

breakers of the isolation of teachers' work (see Lortie 1975). In addition they were seen as developers of the curriculum, their own professional practice and school.

The findings on the vital importance of collegiality and teacher groups inspired Huusko's study (1999), which concentrated on studying the teacher community's activity during the planning process of school-specific curriculum.

Community of teachers in the curriculum process

Huusko's (1999) study investigated the organizational characteristics of the teacher community and analyzed dominant characteristics of school culture. The teacher community was examined as a loosely coupled expert organization in which a shared and pervasive school culture is prevalent. In such a case, the improvement of the school – the enhancement of learning and educating the pupils – is understood primarily as the improvement of the school culture, a process in which the teacher community plays a central role in defining the characteristics of a desirable culture. Educational dialogues clarify the direction of development. In addition to specifying the tasks of the school, they define the views of 'up-to-date' teaching and learning, teachership, and the direction of the curriculum process.

Huusko's inquiry is a qualitative case study consisting of interviews of the teacher community, observations and analyses on documents mainly related to the preparations of a school-based curriculum. From the standpoint of the curriculum, the most interesting area of study was observing the teacher community planning the school-based curriculum. In addition to the teachers' own views of themselves (interviews), also their activity (observations) and products (document analyses) were examined.

The study indicates that the activity of teachers is guided by good practice norms – a culture shared within the teaching staff, directing its observations, interpretations and behaviour. This was summarized in a model of the interaction of the teaching staff. The model consists of three levels: (1) job satisfaction – liberalism: the positive experience of the community based on the markedly autonomous status of the individual teacher; (2) auto-censorship as a tool for maintaining and preserving the community spirit; (3) small groups, forming 'cliques,' which function as a realization method and a discharge channel for the need for development.

The basic assumption in this model is that the teachership maintains the feeling of satisfaction and community spirit by means of preventing and avoiding conflicts. The teacher avoids expressions of his or her own opinion, thus practising auto-censorship. In this situation, development work and dialogue are essential for transfer from the community level to small groups. In these groups, the teachers' efforts for development are supported by like-minded teachers. Pedagogic like-mindedness and common objects of interest are crucial criteria for the teachers' grouping, forming 'cliques'.

The character of the interactive culture in the teacher community leads to the question of whether school practices could become more reflective through curriculum reform. To evaluate this, the teacher community and its activity can be examined by means of a three-level model related to interaction between teachers.

First level: job satisfaction – liberalism

Teachers share an idea of the curriculum and its significance as the disposition of the teacher's work. At this point, the written curriculum is seen as the framework of activity, liberal and responsive to diversity. Within the framework of the curriculum, an individual teacher can work according to his or her own internal, idiosyncratic visions and values. It is regarded merely as a series of recommendations, from which an individual teacher can get ideas that influence his or her own work.

Second level: auto-censorship

At this level the teaching staff does not want to, or is unable to, comment on the activity of their individual members in the curriculum process. The eagerness of individual teachers to participate is considered a private matter, and the other teachers do not regard it as appropriate to comment. This indicates a lack of community-level discussion on the content of curriculum. Practical, everyday matters are discussed while teaching, learning and whole-school issues are avoided. Examination of the teacher community as a whole, therefore, does not reveal the activities of teachers or groups of teachers. It is, therefore, necessary to shift the focus from the level of the entire school to small groups – the 'cliques'.

Third level: commitment to the activity of small groups – forming 'cliques'

The school curriculum is drafted on several separate levels, even in individual schools. The 'official' curriculum groups are divided by subject and/or by class. In practice, the working intensity of curriculum groups fluctuates considerably. In Huusko's (1999) study, only some groups of teachers implemented the process to create 'a somewhat acceptable result'. Some groups of teachers tackled the task in a more active manner with the intention of bringing about real changes even in the pupil's work and methods.

In their own opinion, the target-oriented teachers gained more personal benefit and satisfaction from the curriculum process. These teachers compared the drafting of curriculum to professional guidance, or regarded the process as 'a valuable forum for professional discussion'. They found the effects of the curriculum work positive and productive as well giving direction to the overall development of the school. More passive teachers did not grasp this connection between the development of the school and the curriculum work. They did, though, mention that the school-specific curriculum work was 'one of those rare situations, where you can honestly talk about your job with your colleagues'.

For the development of school it is essential that all the members of the working community learn from the productive co-operation of the active teachers. At the community level, this means acknoledging members' heterogenic activity in the teacher community. The teacher community of Huusko's study (1999) took its first steps towards a more active and open development of school. The curriculum process enabled collegial, professional discussion between the teachers. On the basis of the study material, however, it seems as though the need for professional dialogue disappears as quickly as it comes into existence.

Community dimensions of curriculum development

Problems have been detected regarding teacher's participation in the drafting of the curriculum. Firstly, the teachers are poorly acquainted with the theory of curriculum. There are courses on curriculum, or at least on matters directly linked to it, in teacher education programmes. Unless in-service training on the drafting and use of curriculum can be provided for the teachers, the 'know how' in this area may remain deficient. Secondly, the lack of process thinking has proven problematic in the drafting of curriculum. The teachers do not appear to understand the drafting of curriculum as a continuous, dynamic process evolving through evaluation. Rather, the curriculum is too easily regarded as a one-off product, using the principle of 'over and done with'.

What, then, has been achieved through school-based curriculum work during the past five years? What are the effects of the curriculum reform on teachers' professional practice? Has the process of making school-based curricula been successful from the point of view of teachers and school organization? And, finally, has the process of making school-based curricula empowered the teachers to reflect on their practice and profession both individually and collectively and thus provided 'added value' to their professional growth?

In Huusko's study (1999), the level of commitment to the curriculum process of individual teachers was very inconsistent and fragmented. The collegial groups that were used for multilateral co-operation in their work concentrated on the process. The teachers in these groups felt that they acquired tools for their own pedagogic development and reflectivity. A majority of the teachers in the study did not, however, show an adequate communicative/reflective competence to advance into real development discussion during the process. For these latter groups the process did not meet anticipated outcomes. Curriculum work did not increase these teachers' capacity for curriculum and school development.

The teachers were quite unanimous in their opinions, stating that the process was an event where they were obliged to discuss work, the development of school and its future. This was perceived as a positive and useful experience that was expected to continue.

However, observation of these group meetings indicate that the hopes for continuing the curriculum process were not fulfilled. In this community, the school-based curriculum was seen as 'finished for good', and the process was not continued after the complementation of the written curriculum. This process automatically excludes new teachers in the community from the school-based curriculum process, thus leaving them without any possibilities to influence the commitments referred to in the school-based curriculum.

One of the objectives of the curriculum reform was to increase the collegial cooperation between the members of the teacher community. However, self-censorship within the school was a barrier to altering its culture.

We have identified a number of strategies that may be useful to teachers to continue their curriculum work.

Acknowledging dominant interaction patterns

Open communication is prevented by unconscious sets of actions. In order to alter these models it would be necessary to acknowledge the structures and their effects, after which they could be detected and worked on. The starting point for development must be the present state of the community with its specific features.

Methodological approach

The objectives and activities of schools can be documented. A school-based curriculum process provides an excellent framework for community-level professional discussion. A possibility to participate in the decisions made concerning making the activity more efficient, principles for activation and development areas must be worked on for all members of the community. The community should also cultivate shared ownership of the development process. Commitment to the development work of individual teachers must be commonly accepted. The input of active teachers and teacher groups as the gatherers of development experience becomes significant towards these ends.

Utilizing 'cliques'

The school development work becomes easily concentrated in the cliques created by active teachers. The existence of different teacher groups should, then, be acknowledged and accepted, thus increasing the openness and manageability of the teacher community. Even teachers outside the cliques should be communicated with on the work and observations of the various cliques.

Leadership

The principal of the school is a central person in the school's development. The central elements in the activity of the leader of the school are the creation of development opportunities, support for development work by the leader's own example, and the acquisition and allocation of the resources needed for development work.

The function of a school-based curriculum process as contributing to teachers' reflective approach to work is quite problematic. Current patterns of present a formidable challenge. To create a universal development model is particularly problematic in a situation where the capabilities of both individual teachers and teacher communities are different, and when the learning environments of schools differ significantly from each other.

The East Anglia Center for Applied Research in Education evaluated the success of the Finnish curriculum reform (see Norris *et al.*, 1996). The evaluators stated that when they first visited schools in early 1995, the curriculum process was only beginning. At that time, many of the schools lacked a strategy for curriculum work. There were no common strategies for negotiating curriculum targets, and no agreement on the measures for implementing the objective of change. Many of the teachers had not read the curriculum guidelines and did not understand their implications for their teaching. Norris *et al.* (1996) noted significant differences between schools and teachers in their ways of utilizing the possibilities inherent in the curriculum reform. They concluded that: 'Only in a minority of schools was there an explicit recognition that developing the curriculum might involve a continuing cyclical process of innovation, evaluation, and development' (Norris *et al.* 1996, p. 37).

Particularly interesting in the Norris *et al.* study (1996) was the division of schools into five different classes in relation to the development of the curriculum. These are summarized as follows.

1 Non-starters – schools that have little or no conception of the framework for the comprehensive school, have not started implementing the reform nor do they have the organizational capacity or staff to do so.
2 False starters – schools that have adopted some of the features of the reform (e.g. options or consulting parents) but are not in tune with its spirit and do not have the organizational capacity for school-based curriculum development.
3 Slow starters – schools that understand the main themes of the curriculum reform and have started to implement some of its features but appear to lack the organizational capacity or vision to take things much further.
4 Up-and-running – schools that have the organizational capacity for school-based curriculum change, have made progress in developing the main lines of the reform but have yet to engage the issue of classroom change.
5 There or thereabouts – schools that are engaged in school-based curriculum development, in changing classroom practice and appear to have organizational capacity to sustain such work.

Conclusions

It seems that basing one's hopes on school-based curricula as a conduit for improving teachers' reflective capacity development expertise is not entirely without foundation. However, there is need for further research on how teachers interpret curriculum frameworks and to support the development of strategies to promote ongoing professional development. However, improving the curriculum and the school in a way that provides effective education requires patience and time. As Olson suggests:

> new ideas are shifts in orientation, new sets of unclear meanings, whose implications take time to emerge. What these meanings are we must learn from teachers who can tell us what they understand the new ideas to be and what significance they attach to them. We need to see how the intentions of teachers are connected to problems they are trying to solve. (1992, p. 4)

In view of the continuous development of the curricula, information collected by means of continuous evaluation is essential. More external evaluation is needed both for national development and international comparison. Evaluation is vital also for internal feedback as a formative professional influence.

There are several opportunities inherent in the processing of school-based curricula. The 'slow starters', 'up-and-running' and 'there or thereabouts' schools, identified by Norris *et al.* (1996), are not a problem. However, the 'non-starters' and 'false starters' schools present a more obdurate challenge to a reform process that is premised on a school-based approach. However, the expertise of active teachers and groups of teachers should be better utilized and school principals need to be more aware of their pivotal role in the process.

References

Berg, G. (1985) *Skolans sociala arbetsmiljö – vad forskningen visar*, Lund: Studentlitteratur (in Swedish).

Calderhead, J. (1988) 'The development of knowledge structures in learning to teach', in J. Calderhead (ed.) *Teachers' Professional Learning*, Basingstoke: Falmer Press.

Cornett, J. W., Chase, K. S., Miller, P., Schrock, D., Bennett, B. J., Goins, A. and Hammond, C. (1992) 'Insights from the analysis of our own theorizing: the viewpoints of seven teachers', in E. W. Ross, J. W. Cornett and G. McCutcheon (eds) *Teacher Personal Theorizing. Connecting Curriculum Practice, Theory, and Research*, Albany: State University of New York Press, pp. 137–157.

'Framework Curriculum for the Comprehensive School 1994', *National Board of Education*, Helsinki: Painatuskeskus.

Huusko, J. (1999) 'The teacher community as the formulator, user and developer of the distinctive strengths of the school', University of Joensuu. Publications in Education No. 49 (in Finnish).

Jackson, P. W. (1992) 'Conceptions of curriculum and curriculum specialists', in P. W. Jackson (ed.) *Handbook of Research on Curriculum: A Project of the American Educational Research Association*, New York: MacMillan.

Jaggar, A. (1989) 'Teacher as learner: implications for staff development', in G. Pinnell and M. Mattlin (eds) *Teachers and Research. Language Learning in the Classroom*, Newark: International Reading Association.

Kosunen, T. (1994a) 'Primary school teachers as curriculum implementers and curriculum makers', University of Joensuu, Publications in Education No. 20 (in Finnish).

—— (1994b) 'Making sense of the curriculum: experienced teachers as curriculum makers and implementers', in I. Carlgren, G. Handal and S. Vaage (eds) *Teachers' Minds and Actions. Research on Teachers' Thinking and Practice*, London: Falmer Press.

Kosunen, T. and Huusko, J. (1998) Koulukohtaiset opetussuunnitelmat – väline reflektiivisyyteen opettajan työssä? (Schoolbased Curricula – a promotor of reflectivity in teacher profession), in M.-L. Julkunen (ed.) *Opetus, oppiminen, vuorovaikutus*, Helsinki: WSOY (in Finnish).

Lortie, D. C. (1975) *Schoolteacher. A Sociological Study*, Chicago: The University of Chicago Press.

Norris, N., Aspland, R., MacDonald, B., Shostak, J. and Zamorski, B. (1996) 'An independent evaluation of comprehensive curriculum reform in Finland', *National Board of Education*, Helsinki: Yliopistopaino.

Olson, J. (1992) 'Understanding teaching. Beyond Expertise', Milton Keynes: Open University Press.

Chapter 15

A case study on the relationship between the innovative process of a secondary school and the reform of the Spanish national curriculum

Juana Maria Sancho and Fernando Hernández

Introduction

This chapter explores the implementation of an educational innovation in a secondary school with a view to enhancing the students' learning process and how the participants in this innovation interpret it. It is not about assessing the work done by teachers and learners but about organizing the theoretical side as well as the practice of the innovation so that everybody involved in it may understand it better and create an alternative culture of innovation in education.

Background: a historical note

After 40 years of dictatorship, the Spanish Socialist Party won the 1982 general election by a landslide. Educational reform began 1 year later. Reforms were a response to teachers demands in the 1970s for raising the period of compulsory schooling to the age of sixteen, to provide comprehensive secondary schooling for all students, to unify the teaching force and to improve teachers' salaries. A reform process was initiated between 1983 and 1986 that advocated the kind of teacher empowerment promoted by Lawrence Stenhouse in England in the 1970s. At the same time a legislative framework was being created to favour public schooling, something that was strongly resisted by the Catholic Church (whose privileges could be threatened) and by private schools (whose 'customers' and benefits might also be jeopardized if public schooling was improved). These factors placed education in the eye of the political storm and, to an unprecedented extent in the history of Spain, large sums of money were invested in the creation of new schools, and the improvement of teachers' salaries and teacher training. Additionally, educational management was decentralized and often transferred to the newly autonomous regions.

In 1986 the Spanish Socialist Party won by a landslide again and, for several different reasons, the earlier educational policy changed completely resulting in the approval of a new national curriculum. One of its consequences was the adoption of a 'curricular frame', which was initially intended to create a common language for those who taught children with special educational needs in Catalonia (Coll, 1986). This document espoused a constructivist approach to teaching and learning (Reigeluth and Merril, 1980) as the frame to organize the contents of the national curriculum and the new compulsory education. This gave rise to a protracted debate on the new national curriculum, which in 1990, resulted in new legislation (LOGSE) to regulate that curriculum throughout Spain. This law was to become the icon of the defenders of the pedagogical transformation (the extension of compulsory education until the age of sixteen, the inclusion of Infant Education as another educational phase and a comprehensive curriculum and non-discriminatory orientation in education). Moreover this proposal also set a given conception of teaching and learning, a set of objectives based on competence, curriculum content and assessment criteria.

Some schools started experimenting in parallel with the previous process by organizing the curriculum in order to meet the needs of all students. Within the former system, students were segregated at 14 years old, and those who were thought to be 'more capable' studied for the Bachillerato (BOP) and those 'less capable' attended the Vocational Schools (FP) or simply started working, something that could not be done legally until the age of sixteen (see Hernandez and Sancho, 1993; Hernandez, 1995).

The chapter focuses on a case study that documents the history of one of those schools, while the case is part of a larger research project (Sancho *et al.*, 1998) carried out in three schools in Barcelona (two secondary and one primary school). All three schools were involved in several reforms processes and attempted innovations in the late 1980s.

Focus of the case

All of the innovations sought to promote change. In this case study a number of changes were envisaged, including some alteration to the manner in which curriculum was conceptualized, but more particularly the innovation was intended to transform teaching learning and evaluation or student assessment as well as the use of curricular materials and the nature of the teacher–student relationship. A generative principle of the innovation was that the educational system would enable all students to develop their potential. We have gathered the impressions of those participating in the innovation process (teachers, school headmasters, students and ex-students, families, city council) as a means of indicating (1) how all the different voices conceptualized the innovation; (2) its phases; (3) what can be learned from this innovation that may be useful to others who seek to innovate to enable their students to find 'their place'.

The school

The school (B7) is located in a large post-industrial town near Barcelona. It was opened in 1984 closely related to the educational reform, and is attended by students from the middle class, middle-lower class and the working class. When this case study was carried out it was one of the icons of the experimentation process of reform in Catalonia. This was strikingly evident since the administration was quite permissive with the innovative experience, the debates due to the innovation and the spreading of the experience carried out by the teachers in different media.

Case study: learning from the innovation

Innovation?

All the teachers from B7 thought the reform that began in 1983 was aimed at allowing school management to offer alternatives for the promotion of students. In this respect, the school headmaster pointed out the following at the beginning of the project:

> When we started we felt that above all the aspects involved in the reform we especially had to promote all the students and it had to be somehow different from our former experience . . . where there could be more segregational situations. Hence, one of the baselines of the school had to be that all the students could feel promoted

This initiative was non-specific and supported by other schools in the city. The city council and all the secondary schools requested a centre where the reform could be experimented in the very city. The representative of the city council in the School Board stated that 'the initial project was initiated by a group of four or five headmasters, an Education Supervisor and a representative of the Instituto Municipal de Educación (Local Institute of Education)'. This initiative was strongly supported by the General Director of Bachillerato (Post-compulsory Secondary Education) for a number of reasons:

> I think we asked for the creation of the centre quite in the right moment. At that time the Administration saw how the initial project [the Reform] was being strongly criticised and failing to succeed. The Administration supported our initiative straightaway both economically and in terms of infrastructure. But we had to work very hard and on our own and so we became very critical. . . . The Administration disliked it and started neglecting us

What did they intend to do once they had the formal support from the Administration? Creating an organization and management of the resources in the centre so that the students could be promoted by restructuring whatever had been done before? As the first co-ordinator of studies points out, 'We had a challenge: tackling and designing everything.'

Integrating education: the reasons for the innovation

There is a basic assumption that underpins the innovation, namely the creation of an organizational structure together with the practice of teaching-learning to facilitate an integrated (rather than segregated) education for all students throughout the period of compulsory schooling. This main idea is clearly expressed in the words of the first school headmaster:

> Our idea of comprehensive curriculum and integration intended to get rid of the feeling of disintegration in our former experience and hence we wanted all the students to be treated equally. . . . Our students are all equal and so we have to provide them with material, strategies and subjects which can be adapted and differentiated leaving all the negative experiences aside.

The city council representative endorsed this idea, 'All the teachers have regarded diversity as an essential aspect in the pedagogical project.'

The starting group of teachers saw the educational reform as the ideal frame to undertake the project since there was some concern about social compensation through education. The ex-school headmaster stated that 'The school started experimenting with the reform in an effort to create an educational project as well as some internal coherence . . .' to bring some stability to the innovation.

Diversity, integration, avoiding segregation, all involve educational intentions. When those intentions have to be implemented they allow a set of definitions and need a series of organizational strategies so that they become part of school routine.

The following sections deal with the different phases of the innovative process and and emergent 'lessons' are summarized in the concluding section.

Three phases in the evolution of the innovation

Phase I: Volunteering, intuition, leadership and the wish to change in the first three years

As indicated above, the Administration provided all the material resources to facilitate a group of teachers who wished to experiment with the reform proposal. The teachers themselves were being allowed to conceptualize and to put into practice this reform as they thought appropriate. Personal relationships played a very important role. 'The starting group of teachers . . . all came from Barcelona and we all knew each other and shared sociological, personal and academic references, which was sort of a guarantee . . .', the first headmaster pointed out.

Despite these pre-existing relationships, the process of experimentation generated some ambivalence amongst the students' parents.

> When we learnt that the students in this school would be affected by the Reform we were also given the option to register our children in a different school. We didn't do it because they were already halfway through their academic year; but many parents did. Later many people tried to register their children at the school but it was impossible.

There may be two reasons for this situation: there were those people who thought that a school accepting 'anyone' would endanger the smartest students. This idea is corroborated by the words of a student's mother: 'When I registered my daughter in this school I was told it was a shame, if she was really academic, because she didn't have many chances to improve here.' Yet this school was the right alternative for those children who had problems with their studies: 'My son had had many difficulties during his Primary School years . . . when we were offered the opportunity of the reform we thought it was the only way out for someone like my son, who intended to keep on studying'.

Volunteering was present throughout the initial phase of the innovation process. Everything was based on personal initiative since they did not have any external support and teachers had to work hard in order to redefine a reality to be faced in a holistic rather than a sequential or fragmented manner.

There is general agreement that the volunteerism of the teachers involved at this stage is the pivot of the process. 'I believe in the first year the common link was an enormous will to do many different things in the abstract. Concretion appeared along the way, as the group became more solid', states the ex-headmaster. Moreover, a student's father adds that:

> This system is based on the teachers' volunteering. It is a system which demands more from the teachers than the traditional system; I mean more training, more working hours, paying more attention to what they are doing. They can hardly forget the school and not everybody is able to do that.

This opinion is supported by the city council's representative when he says: 'I believe the teachers have a clear idea of the school's role and I am sure this was necessary in order to require so much volunteering.'

Volunteering has two dominant aspects. First, those who get involved feel the process to be something of their own, a commitment. Second, it can lead to disappointment due to the great effort involved and the need for compensation.

Phase 2: The crisis of the first Curso de Orientación Universitaria (COU)

All the disorder provoked by the innovation taking place in the school, together with the lack of guidelines and follow-up on the part of the Administration, reached its climax when the first group of students who had studied COU in a different way had to sit their University entrance examination. This experience emitted warning signals about the lack of understanding of the tasks being carried out and made everybody involved wonder whether they were going in the right direction. The first co-ordinator of studies recalls that moment as follows:

> Last year was terrible for me. When we saw the maths exam we realised it didn't have anything to do with what we had done in class. It was devastating. We were alone. We complained and the Administration said it had only happened to us because some students had even got an A. ..Of course there were students with an A! The rest of the schools had followed the traditional COU syllabus! Then you realise that all the teachers had made a tremendous effort, trying to deal with the math in a more referential, more significant and less abstract way, taking a step forward.

> And in the end you feel you are completely alone, with all the parents complaining. A disaster.

She also recalls that this experience 'made us question absolutely everything' and made the teachers at the school feel uncertain about their task and in particular when questioned by the students' parents.

> It was very hard. We jumped from a happy honeymoon into bitter criticism. The first year had created great expectations and the school was said to be very good. Everybody wanted to attend this school. It was not until that first University entrance examination that the students' parents started complaining. And so they all started accusing us of fooling them and playing games with their children. It was very hard!

Phase 3: 'the normalization of the school': tensions between different interpretations of the innovation

Until then the school, despite the crisis, had lived an exceptional situation. Just like the first headmaster says:

> All during the first three years one of the greatest contributions from the Administration was the absolute trust in whatever we did. They catered for our needs (. . .). There were no inspections. They also provided us with all the material and economical resources we needed, and we shouldn't forget the country's situation at that time. But on the other hand we lacked all the theoretical and methodological follow-up of the process, which is quite a negative thing.

However, once all the material needs were catered for, this exceptional situation began to normalize. There were no more selection processes for recruiting teachers and the Administration decided which teachers would work in the school. Hence, two educational cultures began living together at the school: those who started the innovation process and those who joined it later. The fact of volunteering was also important as the ex-school headmaster points out:

> working at the school voluntarily implied a certain level of availability, and both availability and will are key elements in the process since they imply working as a team, sharing a project, etc. As I said before, volunteering and availability have been the key elements.

In this respect, a maths teacher says that non-integration of teachers leads to confrontation since:

> on the one hand those teachers who are acquainted with the school and its problems would like everybody to get involved. However, it is often hard for senior teachers to understand the whole scope of the new approaches. Then there is always a time [when] one group becomes the leader and the

> rest feel manipulated, creating reasonable tension. This situation does not benefit anyone because those who have more responsibilities, namely the management group, may also feel somehow embarrassed if . . . planned change does not appear to benefit anyone. On the other hand, if the rest of the people start feeling that nobody informs them of the decisions made, you can't ask them to stick to them.

Despite all their efforts to adapt to the new reality, the first head of studies states:

> I have the feeling that despite the fact there are more new teachers this year and the objective conditions are worse, the debate last year led us to an extreme situation. Thus we already take many things for granted. But I don't really know if a system which keeps changing its teachers every year will be strong enough to absorb all this.

The whole situation prevents the school from entering the normalization phase and institutionalization of the innovation. Despite growing tensions between established and more recent teachers, the first head of studies reported that he thought it was time to press ahead. He says:

> The experimental programme is over and we should now focus on moving forward regarding the concrete aspects of the innovation. That is what we should do if there were some cohesion among the teachers, instead of starting from scratch every year. That is why the school's development is a key issue.

Review of the process

What is remarkable about all these phases is the continuous review and questioning effort carried out by the school, which has counterbalanced the lack of any advice or the explanation of certain obvious criteria on the part of the Administration. The first school headmaster says that they tried to deal with this lack of 'signposts' by 'writing about what was going on, trying to make discussion schemes in the groups, which quite often turned out to be the co-ordinators' reflections and worries rather than the teams'. The former head of studies points out that the mechanics of the first phase were essential in the process since

> We were a group of thirteen people and we held a staff meeting twice a week. The meetings lasted about two hours, namely four hours a week aimed at putting in common the whole of our experiences in quite a disorganized way. We should praise the first school headmaster, who was quite able to synthesize, reorganize, organize what we had said before. That is why the first year was so innovative; we lacked most theoretical foundations but the teachers were most willing to innovate. But I think that was also our mistake.

We should also consider, as the first headmaster says, the fact that 'you can't have all the previous training and the reflection along the way, which is what we tried to do, lacking all the theoretical and methodological stimuli. You do need all that in order to make the most of one's creative energy and proposals.' It is quite a discouraging situation, not because of the amount of hours devoted to it but because of 'the feeling of being lost'. Some expertise or outside support is vital in such circumstances if voluntary efforts are not to flounder.

However, this review activity does not end here since 'every year we survey our students about the purpose and use of the methods we used. Actually the results do differ from subject to subject, but you feel a nice working atmosphere'. But if we had to focus on one conclusion from the innovation process as a result of the different reviews undertaken by the teachers, we would take the first school headmaster's opinion: 'I often think that the innovation of all the different aspects of the school should have been carried out step by step . . . because it would have been less tiring and we would have consolidated far more aspects'.

Conclusions

The factors involved in the process of the innovation studied are summarized as follows:

1 The teachers' willingness, the initial cohesion of the proposal and the consolidation of a driving group who believed in the innovation appear to be the essential ingredients at the beginning of the project. The appearance of a crisis after the initial euphoria turned out to be a constant, which may allow some elements of analysis and alternatives to be predicted when such crises take place. The complete lack of acknowledgement and support from the Administration, and especially, the clash between pedagogical cultures amongst the teachers led to moments of crisis within the innovation process. Such situations usually imply a reopening process and the need for reviewing thus allowing the innovation to be sustained beyond its initial phase.

2 The history of the school influences the innovation. You go from an initial stage of euphoria and volunteering, which most of the teachers and the students' families agree with, to a stage of weariness, crisis and 'normalization'. New teachers join the school at the beginning of its development and they do not join the innovation process in a planned way. This situation gave way to two different cultures amongst the teachers: one represented by the starting group (who joined the project voluntarily as if it were their own) and the other represented by teachers appointed by the Administration. This situation created a conflict between all the different ideas about the educational approach. Four years later the initial group thought about leaving the experiment and starting it again somewhere else.

3 The clash of two pedagogical cultures becomes evident in the history and the process of the innovation. The lack of stability within the team is an additional factor accompanied by progressive and natural evolution

rhythms and sudden splits. There really exist different levels of assimilation on the part of the teachers indicating the orientation and evolution of the innovation.

4 The degree of innovation in the process of teaching and learning is higher in those schools where the curriculum is made from one's own experience and with an absolute professional autonomy than in those schools where the official curricular pattern reduces the pedagogical autonomy to the simplest curricular adaptations and concretions.

5 Participating in the decisions, which affect assessment on the part of both the teachers and the students, is still irrelevant and unequal, except for some exceptions, especially in the case of the students. Another difficulty lies in the confusion around the conceptualization of training for assessment, especially when it comes to assessing the process and attitudes.

6 An experience aimed at altering concepts so as to modify pedagogical practice may result in a change in rhetoric only. Proposed or intended changes may be adapted to existing practice so that for some teachers established routines remain unaltered. Throughout the innovation, tensions may generate conflicts that need to be dealt with in a considered and professional manner, avoiding dogmatism, narrow-mindedness and imposition.

7 Ensuring open channels of communication allowing the teachers and everybody else involved in the process to know the state of the innovation is vital. Documenting the multiple perspectives represented within the innovation is essential if a large number of people is to be involved in this innovative experience and its dynamic sustained. These communication channels may include the follow-up and systematizing of all the process and it may be done by those carrying out the innovation or by an external consultant.

8 All innovation processes are highly demanding but they do compensate for all the time and effort involved, initially at least. In this innovation process there are a few compensating factors which seem to eclipse the main one, namely improving the quality of teaching; these are an increase in professional self-esteem (due to the multiplicity of elements influencing better relationships amongst the teachers) and the disappearance of those aspects counteracting the monotony in school practice and opening new professional dimensions (from research, reflexive practice . . . or even facilitating professional promotion within the educational system.

9 Finally, all the innovations are idiosyncratic both to the schools and those undertaking them. However, despite idiosyncracy, the features we have summarized here may be taken into account by other teachers when attempting a similar innovation.

Epilogue

This story underwent a curious development. The lack of support from the Administration together with all the new teachers who did not share the initial experience of the process made those teachers who had actually started the innovation start working for the Administration. However, it was all in vain. Consequently, they moved to a a new school where they continue to work on the innovation, to maximize learning opportunities for students.

In 1996 the Partido Popular (i.e. the Conservative Party) won the General Election. This party has always been against the reform and even nowadays they try to stop the integration cycle at the age of fourteen. Hence, just like in the previous period, students were to be segregated again.

In 1998 reform of the secondary school became compulsory. Since the Administration had neglected all the projects of experimentation about the reform, teachers were not prepared to work with 'all the students' instead of working with 'the best ones'. This resulted in dissatisfaction and the reform was criticized. For instance, most families in Barcelona took their children to private schools subsided by the State (i.e. paid by all taxpayers but applying exclusion criteria). In response to this situation, such educational authorities as Catalonia's do allow 'difficult' students to be supported by external private services.

Meanwhile, several groups of teachers long for a past that never existed; others try to think schools out again while trying to survive more intensive demands for change.

References

Coll, C. (1986) *Marc Curricular per a l'Ensenyament Obligatori*, Barcelona: Generalitat de Catalunya.

Hernández, F. and Sancho, J. M. (1993) 'Suefian los innovadores con realidades galacticas?', *Cuadernos de Pedagogia* 214: 68– 71.

—— (1995) '20 alios de Cuademos de Pedagogia', *Cuademos de Pedagogia* 232: 16–29.

Reigeluth, Ch. M. and Merrill, M. D. (1980) 'The elaboration theory of instruction: a model for sequencing and synthesizing instruction', *Instructional Science* 9: 195–219.

Sancho, J. M., Hernández, F., Carbonell, J., Tort, A., Simó, N. and Sánchez-Cortés, E. (1998) *Aprendiendo de las innovaciones en los centros* (Learning from schools innovations), Barcelona: Octaedro.

Index